Faith, Family & Music

Published by Mission Point Press
2554 Chandler Rd.
Traverse City, MI 49696
(231) 421-9513
www.MissionPointPress.com

Design by Sarah Meiers

ISBN Softcover: 978-1-958363-90-4
ISBN Hardcover: 978-1-958363-99-7
ISBN Softcover b/w: 978-1-958363-91-1
Library of Congress Control Number: 2023907926

Printed in the United States of America

Faith, Family & Music

150 Years of History & Tales of the Ed and Irene (Lamie) Fleis Family in Leelanau County

Ruth Ann (Fleis) Smith

MISSION POINT PRESS

In memory of Mom and Dad,

and dedicated to my immediate family,

with special appreciation to my sister, Joan Gauthier.

Her assistance was more than I ever expected,

from start to finish!

Contents

Preface

I AM PART OF THE FOURTH GENERATION of the Fleis/Lamie descendants who live in Leelanau County, located in the "little finger" of northern Michigan, often referred to as the "Land of Delight."

Ruth Ann

When I began the writing process, I intended to only write about my parents, Ed and Irene, but then I started thinking about my Fleis and Lamie grandparents, whom I knew very well, and my Fleis and Lamie great-grandparents who emigrated to the USA. I decided to incorporate all three generations. After all, they belong with our family ancestry. I felt it was important. (There were many variations of the Fleis spelling. The last name changed from Flies to Flees to Flis to Fleas to Fliess to Fleis. I use the spelling "Fleis" so as not to confuse the reader. Maiden names and surnames of spouses are often in parentheses.)

This book is a composite of writings and remembrances from family members, friends, the community, and of course my own memories, along with pictures and documents. I also researched and added information to put pieces together of the history of both families. Many of the stories that were shared are written verbatim. Other times, I condensed and paraphrased what was shared with me. Most quoted stories have been edited slightly for clarity.

My personal life flooded my mind as I wrote, read, and researched for this book. Many of those recollections are interspersed throughout as well.

Introduction

Ed and Irene (Lamie) Fleis were both born in Leelanau County, Michigan; Ed in 1915, and Irene nearly ten months later, in 1916. They were married in 1937 and spent most of their married lives in Leelanau's Centerville and Solon Townships.

Their marriage brought together two nationalities: Polish and French, at a time when neither group was fully integrated into the local culture. Dad lived in a Polish settlement; Mom lived nearby, in a French-Canadian settlement. Both of my parents were raised in traditional Catholic, hardworking, farming families. Faith, family, a strong work ethic, and music defined their lives.

They survived the hard times of the Great Depression and World War II. Jobs were scarce. Dad did everything from building bridges to building bomb shelters. Eventually, he became a contractor well known in Leelanau County, building barns, silos, commercial projects, and family homes, plus more.

When he bought Cedar Hardware, he was the go-to person to get anything fixed at your home or the store. He also was dedicated to serving local civic organizations. Mom was resourceful. She preserved food and meat in abundance when we lived on the farm. She recycled fabric and sewed clothing for us. Her frugality contributed to the pocketbook. They parented twelve children, of which I am the oldest, born in 1939.

My parents would often say, "A little hard work never hurts anyone." My siblings and I learned to be responsible, whether on the farm or at the family's hardware store. We were entrusted to do the job and do it well.

It is true that life was difficult at times. Yet each day, Mom and Dad took time for personal prayer. We also prayed the Rosary as a family. My parents' motto was, "A family who prays together, stays together."[1]

* * *

"If you prepare the feast, they will come!" The Fleis household was always booming with company—especially on Sundays—except for the winter months. Some of our cousins stayed

---

1   Popularized phrase by Fr. Patrick Peyton, CSC (1909-92).

with us for several weeks at a time. Friends and relatives usually ended up playing cards and being entertained with a little music from me and my siblings.

We were toddlers when we first learned to sing and dance. Dad played the violin and Mom taught us to sing. Music created laughter in abundance. As we got older, family members sang and harmonized in public. Some of us learned to play musical instruments, and entertained professionally.

Praying, working, and playing together was what bound our family. Today, these same bonds hold us together. My parents expressed that bond near the end of their days ... when Dad wrapped his arm around Mom's shoulder and said to her, "Faith sustained us." They were thankful to God for the years He had given them, united as a couple and as parents of twelve children.

As you read on, I hope you feel the deep bonds of our family.

Love, and God bless!

Ruth Ann

Legacy of Great-Grandfather's Violin

MY GREAT-GRANDFATHER, TOMASZ FLEIS, carried his treasured violin—an Antonius Stradivarius Cremonensis Faciebat Anno 1640—on his back when he emigrated to the United States from West Prussia, Germany/Poland, settling in Isadore, Michigan, in 1875.

The old country-folk tunes Tomasz played on his violin were passed down to younger generations, beginning with his son, Thomas, my grandfather, then to his son, Edward (Ed), my father.

As a young boy, Ed loved occasions whenever his grandfather or father played violin. He was ten years old when allowed to borrow the cherished instrument for one full year at Holy Rosary School, where a nun gave him lessons in fifth grade. He considered it an honor to play violin for mass at church and school functions.

Ed advanced on his own. He had the gift of learning old tunes by ear instead of notes. As a young man, he joined other musicians in the Polish community. They entertained at special events held at homes with attached dance halls or a granary for dancing.

Ed met his sweetheart, my mother, Irene, when she was dancing and he was playing violin with his fellow musicians at Centerville Township Hall. (At some point, Thomas had decided to part with his treasured violin and gave it to his son.)

At approximately thirty years of age, Ed established a band called "Isadore Sodbusters" with his uncle, Steve Pleva, and Stanley Mikowski. His band entertained at various dance halls throughout Leelanau County until the early 1960s.

Meanwhile, my siblings and I learned the dancing steps of old country-folk tunes while my father played violin at home.

On occasion, Ed would pick up the violin and play along with one of four family bands. At Cedar's Polka Fest during various years, he played a few tunes with one of the bands, delighting family, friends, and the Cedar community.

After Ed's death in 2001, the treasured violin was up for grabs for all twelve of his children. My name was on the second golf ball drawn from a hat. I reached for the violin. I am humbled as a fourth-generation descendant to have the treasured violin that originally belonged to my great-grandfather Tomasz—mostly because my father loved it dearly, and enjoyed playing the violin until the age of eighty-six.

1

Tomasz and Jozefina (Kelinski) Fleis

MY GREAT-GRANDFATHER, TOMASZ, SON OF THOMAS AND MARIANNA (ANA BRUEGER) FLEIS, was born on April 8, 1854, in West Prussia, Germany. He was the sixth of seven children. "The area in north-central Poland where they lived, now known as the village of Minikowo, was ruled by Prussia," stated Paul Brzezinski, a cousin of my father's, in a *Leelanau Enterprise* article (2000). "The Prussian authorities were heavy-handed. Polish citizens were forbidden to teach their native language or practice their religion, which made life intolerable."[2] The article continues, "Therefore, many older Polish citizens convinced their adult children to leave the homeland to seek the freedom to practice their faith and culture in the United States of America."

During the 1860s and '70s, Tomasz, all of his brothers, and his oldest sister immigrated to America. (They did not all leave at the same time.) It must have been heartbreaking for my great-great-grandparents to bid farewell to their children, knowing they might never see one another again.

The final destination for some was Wisconsin, where there was a substantial

Left: Tomasz Fleis is sitting on the right; Marianna is sitting in the middle. Young Balbina, Marianna's daughter, represents Anna, who stayed back in Poland. Right: List of Fleis family and birth years.

---

2   Dad's cousin, Paul S. Brzezinski, Traverse City, traveled to Poland. Paul's story was posted in the *Leelanau Enterprise*, "Love and War in the Homeland," February 24, 2000.

Polish population, particularly in Milwaukee. Tomasz's oldest brother, Ignatz, had married Dora Kugacz in Poland in 1863. When they came to America is unknown, but the 1880 federal census shows they registered their residency as Milwaukee. The youngest brother, Jozef, came to America in 1875 and married Eva Goetzler in Lake St. Francis, Wisconsin, in 1879, where they made their home.

Many came to Michigan. So many, in fact, that the Fleis family was the largest single family to homestead in Leelanau County's Centerville Township. Tomasz's brother Frank arrived in America in 1865; he married Florence Kugacz in 1870 in Milwaukee and then settled in the small village of Isadore, Michigan. His brother John came to America in 1868 and married Kathryn Zinny in 1876 in Isadore. His oldest sister, Marianna, married Adam Cerkowski in Poland in 1868, sailed to America in 1873, and settled near Isadore the next year.

My cousin, Don Pleva of Traverse City, Michigan, learned from his father, Adam, the background of the Polish relatives. In his family notes, Uncle Adam told his son, "The Brzezinski,

Poland map

Fleis, and Pleva families were just a few of many to emigrate from the Poznan area of Poland to northern Michigan. The town of Lobzenica, in Poland, was their nearest mailing address. To the southwest of Lobzenica was a small lake with two small villages, Bugovo and Kunovo. The Plevas came from Bugavo and the Brzezinskis came from Kunovo. The Fleis family was in between, in Minikowo. All three families were united in their homeland where they came from. It was the same in Milwaukee, where, one by one, they either stayed there or came to Isadore. My Great Aunt Michaeline (Brzezinski) Pleva said that the three families settled in the same proximity to each other in Leelanau County as they had when living in Poland."

At the age of nineteen, Tomasz sailed across the Atlantic aboard the *Bristol,* a thirty-seven-foot-wide by 304-foot-long vessel. It had three masts and one funnel, as ships at that time were transitioning from wind power to steam. Among the few belongings Tomasz carried on this journey in 1873 was his treasured violin.[3] According to the ship's passenger list, he departed from Hamburg on March 1, then sailed to Liverpool and on to Ireland. On April 8, the *Bristol* docked in New York City.

Tomasz traveled alone. He was the only Fleis family member listed on the manifest. From there, he might have traveled through the Erie Canal as most immigrants to Wisconsin did at the time, and then by steamship across the Great Lakes to Milwaukee on Lake Michigan.

Tomasz was to be met by family members. I can vividly imagine as soon as the steamship was sighted that news would have quickly spread to those awaiting the new immigrants. They would have dropped whatever they were doing and rushed to the shore to welcome those on board, with hands waving high and prayers on their lips. As the passengers slowly disembarked, Tomasz scanned the faces below, while they in turn looked up at those walking down the plank, studying the faces, one by one.

I expect everyone from his family was there to greet him: Ignatz and Dora, Marianna and her husband, Adam, Frank and his wife, Florence, John, and some of the Pleva and Brzezinski boys. "Those boys would have been looking for him, too," Don Pleva explained. Imagine the scene when they recognized Tomasz carrying his treasured violin. "Tomasz! Tomasz!" they would have cried out, and when he reached them, they would have embraced like never before. It was heartwarming to be united again in America! A Polish priest was also at the dock in Milwaukee to greet the new immigrants and help them with the process of assimilation.

---

3   Dad wrote a letter to me in 2000. He said, "My grandfather brought the violin from Germany when he came to the USA."

OUR ANCESTORS

Henry (Joseph) Fliss, Homestead in Kenosha

Francis Fliss, married my aunt Florentine Kugacz-----15 children

Ignatz Fliss, married my cousin, Dorotha Kugacz......5 sons

Thomas Fliss, your Father, 8 girls - 3 boys

John Fliss, married Kasia Zimna.

Your Spinster Aunt, came on the same ship to Milwaukee, Wis.

All 5 brothers came to Francis Kugacz home, he had the first Baker Shop on
Grove St. across St. Stanislaus Church. From there they all Homestead.

Ignatz Fliss, New Colen, W"is. Francis, Thomas, Cedar, Michigan.

You know your spinster Aunt had her Homestead Land. My uncle and your
Father helped work the land. All the Flisses were prosperous. So they
all signed off from the Large Estate in Pomarania and your brother John,
18 years of age was sent to Pomarania and married Irma;. She was sixteen.

The same thing with the Kugacz. My Grandfather was a tailor had 2 sons
and 2 daughters. My uncle was the first one to come to Milwaukee, Wis.
Michael stayed with his Father so Francis Kugacz, the Baker, my mother,
and Florentina Fliss signed off from my Father's Estate to their brother
Michael Kugacz. I was trying to locate my Grandfather's Estate but Jan
could give me any report. Finally, I read in the Posłaniec Serca Jezusa
about Sw. Lipka, where my mother and sister Florentina and your Aunt
Anna Fliss were making the Pilgrimage and they brought large pictures
where the Blessed Mother appeared to several maidens but Bismark had
everything destroyed, cut the tree down. My mother used to have the leaves
in her prayerbooks. I recall everything my beloved Mother told me. I
was visiting my Aunt Fliss after my mother passed away to eternity. I
gave large memorials at St. Stanislaus Church. Each Memorial is $100.00
for my wife, son, Family are at the American Shrine of Our Lady of
Czestochowa.

Julius Senski informatory letter   *Julius Senski (deceased)*
                                           from
                                           Milwaukee

Ancestor Letter

One more brother, Jozef, would follow in 1875. Tomasz's youngest sister, Anna, would be the last of the Fleis family to emigrate. Although she wanted to come at the same time as the others, she was kept from doing so because the family did not want to leave their aged parents alone on the farm.[4] Anna finally settled in Isadore in 1901.

Tomasz was pleased to hear that his brothers had a place for him to stay. The Francis Kugacz boarding house on Grove Street had been their temporary home since arrival. There was a family connection through the marriages of his older brothers, Ignatz and Frank.[5]

The Fleis boys were fortunate that Mr. Kugacz (their landlord) was a carpenter and a baker. He established the first "baker shop" on the same street as his boarding house.[6,7] Jobs were scarce with the influx of Polish immigrants. Mr. Kugacz was good to the Fleis boys and gave them jobs. They all saved money to realize a dream common to many Poles: to become landowners.

My great-grandmother, Jozefina Kelinski, daughter of John and Susanna (Wojdanowski) Kelinski, was born on December 31, 1855, also in West Prussia, Germany/Poland. She and her twin brother, John Jr., born January 1, 1856, were the sixth and seventh of eight in the family. Their other siblings were Anna, Anthony, Felix, and Constantine. Laurentius and Ludwig died as infants. Jozefina's parents were elderly when they boarded the ship *Donau* with her.[8] John was sixty-five and Susanna was sixty-two. Jozefina was nineteen years old. It is unclear when Jozefina's older brothers and sister emigrated to America, except for Constantine. A family record shows that "Anna married Aloise Petrowski, Anthony married Rose Gersch, Felix married Gertrude, and later her sister, Mary Kawa, and Constantine married Frances Koplin.[9] They all lived in Leelanau or Grand Traverse County." John Jr. wasn't listed, but his residence was Centerville, Leelanau County.[10]

John, Susanna, and Jozefina departed from Bremen and sailed via Southampton to New ork City, where they arrived on June 5, 1875. Soon, they too docked in Milwaukee and met up with her brother Constantine, who had emigrated earlier. They settled briefly in a boarding house with him.

---

4   The article in the *Leelanau Enterprise,* February 24, 2000, made no mention of the mother; only an "aged father and maid daughter."

5   "Our Ancestors" by Julius Senski, Milwaukee (undated).

6   "My Heritage" revealed Frank Kugacz–rents, homeowner, carpenter, laborer.

7   "Our Ancestors" by Julius Senski, Milwaukee (undated).

8   The *Donau* was 347 feet long and forty feet wide, with double masts and one funnel, as the ship was steam powered with a provision for wind.

9   A purple booklet with handwritten information was in my parents' collection of photos.

10   *My Heritage* website.

When Tomasz left his homeland, he left behind Jozefina, whom he dearly loved. Now that they were reunited after a long absence, he hoped to marry her soon, but after hearing good news of homesteading in northern Michigan, the couple decided to wait.

Many Poles who had initially settled in Milwaukee had already traveled to northern Michigan after hearing of land available there for farming. A small booklet published in 1998 upon the centennial of Holy Rosary School in Isadore says of the earliest settlers, "After a couple of years in the area, some returned to Milwaukee and praised the wonders of northern Michigan and explained how land could be gotten for the asking. They soon succeeded in bringing more families to Isadore."

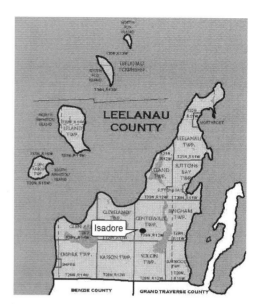

Leelanau County Map shows location of Isadore

The Fleis and Kelinski families heard such talk and decided it was time to make the bold move to leave Milwaukee and plan a journey to Leelanau.

First to arrive was Tomasz's sister, Marianna, and her husband, Adam Cerkowski, in 1874. Then, Tomasz and Jozefina, two of his brothers, and his sister-in-law, her parents, and a large group of Polish immigrants steamed across Lake Michigan to Manistee, then to Centerville Township, Leelanau County, in the late fall of 1875.

A Holy Rosary School's 1898–1998 booklet indicated, "When the ship docked at Good Harbor, there were no state roads—only one-lane trails dotted with tree stumps which were muddy in the spring and nearly impassable in winter." They would have carried their belongings as they walked the three miles to a little community that had sprung up by the railroad tracks. The same booklet also stated, "Later, when a post office was established, this area was named Isadore, after the patron saint of farmers." It was one of three local areas Poles would settle, the other two being nearby: Schomberg and Bodus.

Another parish booklet, *Holy Rosary Catholic Church, 1883–1983,* stated, "Treaties with the Indians, and the Homestead Act, which had taken effect just a dozen years earlier, on January 1, 1863, opened America's heartland to emigrating families."

The Homestead Law was signed on May 20, 1862, by President Abraham Lincoln. A settler could acquire 160 acres, free of all charges except a minor fee when filing a claim, and must live on the land five years before getting title. Improvements needed to be made; a house built, a well dug, ten acres plowed, and a specified amount of land fenced. For $1.25 an acre, a settler could even obtain the land after only six months of residence.[11]

Jozefina's parents, John and Susanna Kelinski, and Tomasz's sister and brother-in-law, Marianna and Adam Cerkowski, aligned their sixty- and eighty-acre claims near the site where Tomasz staked his 160-acre claim, described in Centerville Township's 1900 plat book.

The Polish settlers came with deep religious and community values. Foremost, they wanted their own church and school so they could worship and educate their children in their native language. An August 28, 1948, *Leelanau Enterprise* article, "History of Holy Rosary Church, Isadore," reprinted on March 2, 2017, provided the following: "In the beginning, missionaries like Father Frederic Baraga (later elevated to bishop), Father Mrak, and Father Zorn helped the families carry on their faith and culture. They traveled alone by pony, or on foot from Petoskey and even the Upper Peninsula, and in the winter on snowshoes or by dogsled. As soon as a missionary arrived, people would gather in a private home, where he would offer the Holy Sacrifice of the Mass, and the people would receive the sacraments."

On January 10, 1876, Tomasz and Jozefina were married by a missionary. Reverend Phillip L. Zorn officiated; Constantine Kelinski (Jozefina's brother), and Mary Zin were witnesses. The ceremony might have taken place in her parents' makeshift

Left: Narrow strip of wedding document. Right: Tomasz and Jozefina in elegant attire (circa 1900s).

---

11   Summarized from various sources on the internet.

home, one of the private homes the community eventually used for worship, or the Gatzke home, across from what is now Holy Rosary Church.

When Tomasz applied for a 160-acre parcel on Schomberg Road, little more than a mile north of Isadore, close to Marianna and Adam,[12] and Jozefina's parents, he would have had to go physically into the Land Office in Traverse City on at least two occasions to make the initial entry, and then to initiate the paperwork to obtain the final grant once the requirements for residency and improvements had been satisfied. Small payments were required on both occasions. The Land Office in Traverse City was run by the same folks who ran the *Grand Traverse Herald* newspaper. The paperwork was then sent by the Land Office to Washington, DC, and there it was reviewed by folks in the Land Office, and if satisfactory, a Homestead Act certificate (not actually signed by the president himself, as local folks often believed, but by an agent in the Land Office for him) was mailed back to the Land Office in Traverse City, where the person picked it up. (There wasn't an inspection process or a site visit; instead, the person submitted several affidavits from neighbors with regards to his actual residence there and the improvements that he made.)[13]

My great-grandparents were resourceful, living on land that had rolling hills and valleys, mostly thick with hardwood trees. "The first home Tomasz built was a log cabin near a spring with clean water. They had to have water to survive," my father wrote in a letter.

"Cut wood was their only fuel source. Their lives were further sustained by hunting game and catching fish in a nearby lake, and harvesting rye, potatoes, oats, beans (scarlet runners), sweet corn, and peas. Raising cattle was not profitable because pasturage was poor and there were no meadows," said author Jakub Rosinski Sr., in an Isadore book of early history.[14]

They observed Sundays as the Lord's Day, a day of rest from their laborious week. They would have attended church services held in a private home or spent time praying and singing hymns at home. A meal might have been shared with relatives, as the day brought great joy to everyone. My great-grandfather would have picked up his violin and played a few tunes from the old country to entertain the family. He had the music in him for sure. He didn't bring his treasured instrument all the way from West Prussia for it to sit idle in its case. Besides, my father's late memories revealed that he heard his grandfather "play the violin a little."

---

12   A 1931 newspaper clipping of Marianne (Mary) Cerkowski's obituary stated: "Marianne and Adam moved to Cedar when they were aged. Their daughter, Balbina, married Frank Fabiszak and they farmed the land."

13   Leelanau Historical Society Staff: info@leelanauhistory.org.

14   From the Leelanau Historical Society.

Tomasz and Jozefina received a written document, dated November 20, 1880, from President Rutherford B. Hayes, that a land grant of 160 acres was issued to "Thomas Fleas." They had fulfilled all the requirements. Tomasz's brothers, Frank and John, also earned homestead properties, which are recorded in the 1881 plat book of Centerville Township, Leelanau County.

National Archive seal (Leelanau Historical Museum)

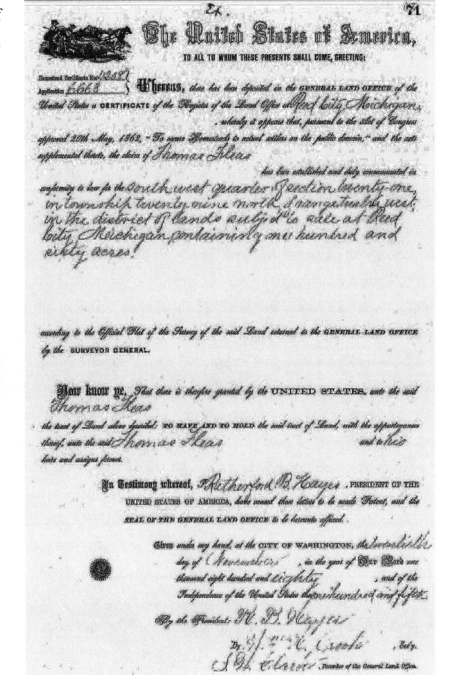

Fleis homestead document

2

The Fleis Families Settling in Leelanau

THERE IS NO LIMIT OF FAITH AND SACRIFICE shown to us by our ancestors. The Polish settlers in Isadore were determined to build their own church and school. As it happened, "When a larger number had flocked there, they decided to build their own little church in order to have some place to worship God," stated Jakup Rosinski Sr. in his book. "The biggest farmers got in on the consultations; those being Tomasz and his brothers, Frank and John, among A. Dziengielski, G. Czichacki, S. Niemczynski, J. Stefaniak, S. Zientek, S. Nowak, A. Skiba, F. Bodus, J. Rosinski Sr., and a few others. After talking the matter over they gathered the necessary funds to buy five acres of land, and to build in Isadore; first, a house of God, and later when there were more of them, a rectory and a school."

Another parish booklet, *Diamond Jubilee Memoirs*, published in 1983, provided additional information: "Word got out to the Polish community that the five acres of land was donated by John Szudowski," who then owned what now is the John Miller farm.

"In 1883, the first church was built in Isadore: a wooden structure in the shape of a cross, referred to as a 'mission church' built by Aloysius Piotrowski and many volunteers. Upon its completion, Reverend Father Ignatius Mrak (a former missionary and later a bishop) was the first to celebrate mass and bless the new, little church on August 16, 1883."

The Holy Rosary School centennial booklet also stated that, "A large stove in the rear of the church, beneath the choir loft, heated both the worshippers and the bricks or water crocks which the faithful used to keep their feet warm on their sleigh rides back home on

An engraved memorial of First Mission Church is embedded on the front exterior wall of Holy Rosary Church.

frosty days. On the south side of the church was a row of posts for hitching horses which pulled the buggies, wagons, or sleighs.

"For the next ten years, priests from Manistee, Petoskey, Traverse City, or Provemont brought the sacraments and celebrated the Holy Eucharist at least once a month. When no priest was available, the parishioners gathered weekly to hear the word of God, as Michael Gatzke would read the Gospel and the Epistle. Leo Peplinski directed the singing, and Adam Cerkowski (Tomasz's brother-in-law) with his booming voice, would often lead the rosary.

"The first presiding pastor, newly ordained Reverend Father Stephen Nowakowski, didn't arrive until 1892. That same year, a new school was constructed. The dream of having their own school had finally come true, nine years after the church was built. Unfortunately, the school burned down two years later. The Poles didn't give up, and another school was constructed in 1896.

"The school became part convent in 1898, when the first Felician Sisters arrived to teach the mostly Polish students, who ranged in ages from five to twenty. The earliest years of schooling only provided three grades, gradually increasing to more grades.

"Five years later, disaster struck again when the second school burned to the ground after a lamp exploded. The community rallied again and built a third school in 1905. This time, it was a two-story building with a chapel, constructed of brick, tin, cement, and lumber."

Holy Rosary Parish, early 1900s

Tomasz and his brothers, Frank and John, were among fifty pioneering families who contributed the first gifts, time, and talents to build the first church and school. Some of the other families were: F. Bodus, M. Brzezinski, A. Cerkowski, F. Galla, J. Gersh, M. Gatzke, C. Kelinski, J. Mazurek, J. Mikowski, M. Narlock, L. Peplinski, V. Pleva, A. Popa, M. Rice, J. Rosinski, A. Skeba, J. Szarnowski, among others.[15]

According to my dad, his grandfather, Tomasz, was an ambitious and generous man. When his family outgrew the log cabin, he built a second house in the middle of the farm, near the road. In 1888, when Jozefina was pregnant with their seventh child, Tomasz built a third home—a sturdy, two-story wooden structure.

Tomasz and Jozefina's second home was used later as a granary (2021 photo).

Third home of Tomasz and Jozefina's, built in 1888 (painting by Sue Lockwood, 2019)

On November 10, 1888, my grandfather Thomas was born, the seventh of eleven children. His brothers and sisters were: Lillian, John, Mary, Anna, Martin, Josephine, Agnes, Elizabeth, Suzanne, and Rose. With that many children to raise, Jozefina had to have been disciplined in her duties from dawn to dusk.

When the children were old enough, they were educated until the fifth or sixth grade at the mission school. Polish was the dominant language.

For a long time after the rest of her siblings had emigrated, Tomasz's youngest sister, Anna, had stayed in Poland to care for her parents. Their father had suffered a tragic affliction in his

---

15   Holy Rosary Catholic Church, 1883–1993.

aging years and became blind. For years, she pleaded in letters to her brothers for someone to return to Poland and take over the farm. "Whoever would take my place," she wrote, "could take title to the land in Poland and stay until our father and mother, Thomas and Ana Fleis, died, then sell the farm and return to America."[16]

* * *

In approximately 1898, John, the first-born son of Tomasz and Jozefina, decided to claim his grandfather's farm in Minikowo. Just eighteen, he obtained passage money by working as a fireman on a train from Chicago to the East Coast, then by ship to Prussia/Poland.

When John arrived at his grandparents' home, Thomas was unable to see who came back to help them, and reached out and touched his grandson's head. "I know you are a Fleis," he stated, "because you are tall."[17]

Shortly afterward, Anna, now fifty-five, came to America. The last of the seven Fleis children to emigrate to the United States, she would live in a small house across from the mission school.

The year, 1908, is listed for the deaths of our ancestors (my great-great grandparents) Thomas and Ana, in Minikowo, Poland.[18] That same year, Tomasz and Jozefina made one last trip to Poland to visit their son, John, who had been back in the old country for ten years.

In his application for a passport, Tomasz described himself as a fifty-four-year-old male, five feet, six-and-a-half inches tall, with a high forehead, medium nose, medium mouth, gray hair, and fair complexion. Tomasz also stated he was born in Stockholm, Germany.

On the trip, they did meet John's wife, Emma (Rybczinski), whom he had married three years earlier, in 1905. It's unknown whether Tomasz and Jozefina ever saw his parents before their deaths.[19]

Presumed to be great-great grandparents, Thomas and Ana Fleis, in Poland (photo from Linda Himmelmann)

---

16   *Leelanau Enterprise*, "Love and war in the homeland," Paul Brzezinski, author, Feb. 24, 2000.
17   A remark that cousin Butch Brzezinski heard from Paul when he traveled with him to the homeland in 2000.
18   Ancestry.com.
19   Tomasz and Jozefina's passports were clearly dated May 8,1908. I have not been able to collect the record of the exact dates of his parents' deaths, only that they occurred in 1908.

John's returning to Poland so that his Aunt Anna could come to the United States is an example of the kind of service Tomasz and Jozefina's children gave to others. John never did return to America, and died at the age of ninety-four.[20]

Left to right, in back: Sr. Faber Rose, Sr. Augustine, Suzanne, Sr. Damascene, and Sr. Leontine. Sitting: Thomas, Mary, Lillian, and Martin (circa 1956). Missing: John, who lived in Poland, and sister, Anna, who died in 1918.

Four of Tomasz and Jozefina's daughters became Felician Sisters in Livonia, Michigan: Josephine, 1886–1973 (Sister Mary Leontine); Agnes, 1891–1981 (Sister Mary Damascene); Elizabeth, 1893–1984 (Sister Mary Augustine); and Rose, 1898–1978 (Sister Mary Faber Rose).

Tomasz and Jozefina's married children were: Lillian, 1876–1964 (Theophil Czerniak); John, 1878–1971 (Emma Rybczinski); Mary, 1880-1971 (Martin Brzezinski); Anna, 1882–1918 (Frank Popa); Martin, 1884–1956 (Anna Popa and his second wife, Victoria Kruz); My grandparents, Thomas, 1888–1965 (Agnes Pleva), and Suzanne, 1895–1978 (Roman Pleva, followed by her second husband, John Schopieray).

* * *

20   *Leelanau Enterprise*, "Love and war in the homeland," Feb 24,2000. Paul Brzezinski wrote about John Flies (Fleis), son of my great-grandparents, Tomasz and Jozefina. More information about his family is provided by John's granddaughter, Krystyna Dobbek. See epilogue.

Grandma Agnes (Pleva) Fleis Family

Vincent and Apolonia Pleva immigrated to Isadore in the 1880s.
(photo from Ruth Bolton)

The family's lineage on our paternal grandmother's side begins with my great-grandfather Vincent Pleva (1855–1931), who immigrated to America around 1880. His parents, Michael and Mary (Brzezinski) Pleva, stayed behind in Bugavo, Poland. Vincent married Apolonia Grzybek-Galla (1859–1946) in Wisconsin on May 3, 1881. She had emigrated in 1880 or 1881. Her parents, Jakob and Marie (Krzesinska) Grzybek, remained in Poznan, Poland.[21]

---

21   Pleva lineage provided by Don Pleva.

Sometime later, Vincent and Apolonia Pleva came to Leelanau County and settled on a farm near Isadore. Agnes, my grandmother, was born on January 4, 1895, the sixth of nine children. Her siblings and spouses were: Gertrude, 1882–1960 (Frank Mazurek); Frank, 1884– n.d. (Gertrude Mazurek); John, 1885–1960; Roman, 1887–1956 (Suzanne Fleis); Joseph, 1890–1982 (Michaeline Brzezinski); Mary, 1892–1979 (Stephen Petrowski); Vincent, died at birth; twins Stephen, 1897–1984 (Josephine Witkowski) and Adam, 1897–1991 (Bernice Galla).

My dad wrote that his grandparents, Vincent and Apolonia Pleva, "were kind people. They were farmers, just like my parents, and hardworking people. I picked potatoes for them.

"My parents," he continued, referring to Thomas and Agnes Fleis, "were close friends [with the Plevas] and visited them regularly, usually twice a month. In the summertime, I went swimming with a group of friends almost every Sunday at a lake over a hill in the back of their home. They were good church people."

Thomas and Agnes's wedding day, November 7, 1911. Wedding party: Steve and Mary (Pleva) Petrowski on left, and Suzanne Fleis and Roman Pleva on right.

Don Pleva added, "As a young girl, Agnes loved to tag along sometimes with her brother Adam whenever he helped out at the Fleis farm. Adam was good friends with the Fleis boys, especially Thomas. It was quite a distance to walk across the fields from one farm to another, but they didn't mind."

Some years later, love blossomed and, on November 7, 1911, the Fleis and Pleva families united as Thomas, twenty-two, and Agnes, sixteen, exchanged wedding vows in Isadore at the wooden "mission church."

In their wedding photo, Agnes was clothed in a Roman-style, long-sleeved, white gown. A garland of fresh flowers encircled the top of her full-length veil, framing the innocence of youth so apparent in her delicate face. The bouquet of fresh flowers she carried complemented the boutonniere Thomas wore in the lapel of his dark suit. He wore a Roman-style white shirt with a white bow tie.

Following the marriage, the young couple stayed with Thomas's parents, Tomasz and Jozefina. One month after the wedding, Tomasz and Jozefina, having raised eleven children and established their homestead, decided they no longer wished to farm. The toil of the years had taken the best of their strength. And so, on December 5, 1911, Tomasz and Jozefina Fleis transferred their homestead of 160 acres on Schomberg Road in Centerville Township to my grandparents, Thomas and Agnes, by mortgage contract.[22]

It is hard to think of Tomasz and Jozefina without respecting their accomplishment. By hard work and perseverance, their farm was established with productive crops, livestock, farm buildings, and a spacious home. They lived in a community with other deeply loyal Polish families and were thankful for the years God had given them and the family with which He blessed them.

The Fleis elders purchased a home in Traverse City. But at the time of the transfer, it was winter. Part of their agreement was that the newlyweds take in Thomas's parents until they decided to move. They then delivered meat and vegetables from the farm weekly until the elderly settlers died. The mortgage note satisfied Tomasz and Jozefina's needs for the rest of their years, including all home repairs in Traverse City, "a horse and buggy or sleigh," a garden plot maintained for vegetables, plus firewood, provisions, water from the well and cistern, and the expense for their daughter (Thomas's sister) Suzanne's wedding, should she get married. They were also to furnish Suzanne, who would care for her parents until then, with a good milking cow on the occasion of her marriage.

Sometime later, Tomasz and Jozefina did move to 446 Elmwood Avenue in Traverse City. Suzanne accompanied them. However, two years later, on November 4, 1913, Thomas and Agnes paid for his sister's wedding, as she married Agnes's brother, Roman Pleva, making Thomas and Agnes brothers- and sisters-in-law to Roman and Suzanne Pleva. The newlyweds bought a home at 801 Randolph Street, not far from her parents.

---

22   Mortgage contract in epilogue.

3

Mother's (Lamie) Ancestors

THE SPELLING OF THE LAMIE NAME VARIED. Some of the variations are LaMie, L'amie, L'ami, and Lamieux, with the original name being Lamy, and changed to Lamie in the United States. French-Canadian children usually were given three names at their birth, as you will see.

Alfred and Regina (Belanger) Lamy

(Ancestral information was provided by my cousin, Edward Lamie.)

Maternal great-grandfather, Alfred Lamy (1866)

My maternal great-grandfather, Alfred, son of Celestin and Marie Ann (Carbonneau) Lamy, was born on August 11, 1834, in Yamachiche, Quebec, Canada, the fifth of eight children. His siblings were: Jean-Baptiste, Marie Oliva-Elisa, Louise-Agnes, Aime, Marie-Louise, Zoe, and Clement. Yamachiche was home for many Lamy families, located on the north shore of the Saint Lawrence River, fifteen miles south of Trois-Rivières.

In 1837–38, Lower Canada (now Quebec) was faced with severe economic hardships that led to the Lower Canada Rebellion. The rebellion was crushed, and the British executed or imprisoned many French Canadians. Alfred's father (Celestin) did not participate in the rebellion, but his family would be greatly impacted by one of the leaders of the insurrection. Colonel Edouard Elisee Malhoit was that rebel leader. He escaped to the USA when the rebellion collapsed. He was wealthy, and purchased a plantation in Assumption, Louisiana.[23]

In 1855, the entire Lamy family moved to Princeville, Quebec. Coincidentally, Colonel Malhoit grew up in a town about fifteen miles from Princeville. It is possible that Alfred knew him, or at least knew of him.

In 1856, Colonel Malhoit purchased fifty-two thousand acres of fertile land in central Illinois, intending to settle it with relatives and friends from Quebec.[24] He formed a town and named it Assumption, after his plantation in Louisiana. In 1857, he recruited about 150 French-Canadian men, women, and children to settle on his land in Illinois. Alfred, at age twenty-two, declined to make the move, and remained in Princeville, where he probably made a living as a farmer.

(Alfred's best friend, Onesime Lavanture's nephew, Joseph Lavanture, joined this group and moved to Assumption, Illinois, when he was fourteen years old. He joined the American Army to fight on the Union side in the Civil War in 1861, when he was eighteen years old. After he completed his enlistment in 1864, he returned to Assumption, where he was married in 1866 and had a child in 1868. Most likely, Joseph and his family traveled with the Alfred Lamy family and Onesime Lavanture's family to Michigan in 1870.)

My maternal great-grandmother, Regina (Reine Helene Domithile), daughter of John (Jean Baptiste Prosper, 1813–1878) and Marie Genevieve (Caron) Belanger (1811–1854), was born on May 22, 1839, in L'Islet, Quebec. She was the fourth of seven children. Her siblings were: Genevieve, Marie, Denise, Alfred, Josephine, and Thomas. L'Islet was a small town on the south shore of the Saint Lawrence River, which is within sight of the island farm of Pierre Lamy (1644–1725).

(Pierre was the first Lamy to migrate from a region in Normandy, France, to Canada in the 1600s. He is the earliest descendant of most Lamy families in Canada and the United States).[25]

We don't know when the Belanger family moved from L'Islet to Princeville, but it was before 1860, because this was the year Alfred and Regina were married. He was twenty-six, and she was twenty-one, when they exchanged wedding vows on April 24, 1860, at St. Eusebe Church in

23   Roby Y., Malhoit, Edouard Elisee. *Dictionary of Canadian Biography*, Laval, Quebec, Canada: University of Toronto/ Universite Laval, 1972, p. 10. Retrieved from http://www.biographi.ca/en/bio/malhoitedouard_elisee_10E.htm1.

24   Goudy, *History of Christian County, Illinois*. Philadelphia: Brink, McDonough and Company, 1880, p. 184. Retrieved from archive.org/stream/historyofchristi00goud.

25   Laforest, 1992, p. 142.

Princeville, Quebec.[26] Alfred had little or no formal education and could neither read nor write, but Regina could. Their wedding document contains his wife's signature and the signatures of Alfred's father, Celestin; Regina's uncle, Louis Caron; and Onesime Lavanture. Onesime was Alfred's best man, his best friend, and his brother-in-law, as Regina and Onesime's wife, Marie, were sisters. Alfred and Regina's first child, Josephine, was born in 1862, in Princeville.

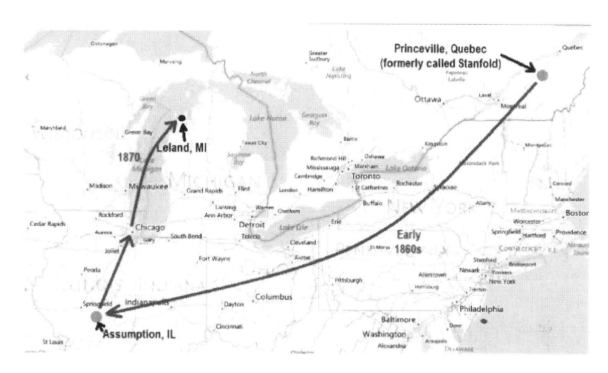

**Journey of the Alfred Lamie/Regina Belanger Family
from Quebec to the USA (early 1860s to 1870)**

As the economic situation continued to worsen, Colonel Malhoit continued to recruit more French-Canadian families for his settlement in Illinois. Around 1863, Alfred and Regina heeded the call and packed their belongings for the journey to Assumption when their daughter was one. They were joined by several other families, including Alfred's younger brother, Clement, and Onesime and Marie. Much of this journey was probably made on the railroad because the Illinois Central Railroad Company completed a rail line to the town of Assumption in 1855.[27]

---

26   Drouin, 1860. *Genealogie Quebec.* Retrieved from https://www.genealogiequebec.com/en/.
27   Goudy, 1880, p. 185 (see #2).

After they came to the United States, the spelling of their surname was changed from the original "Lamy" to "Lamie." In French, both names are pronounced identically.

We know little about our ancestors' lives in Assumption, Illinois. Most likely, Alfred was a farmer, as this area was well known for its abundant corn and wheat crops.

According to the church archives of the Assumption of the Blessed Virgin Mary Church in Assumption, Alfred and Regina had four children baptized. (Only two lived to adulthood.) Joseph was born in 1864 and died about 1867; an unnamed infant was born and died in 1866. Julia was born in 1867 and John in 1869. Alfred's brother, Clement, moved to Assumption, Illinois, and was married there in 1866.

Alfred and Regina with daughters, Josephine and Julia (1866)

The numbers of French-Canadian immigrants in Illinois were relatively small compared to the mass migration to the New England states.[28] We can only hope that our ancestors were treated well in Illinois because they were in the majority of that part of the state. Our ancestors were fortunate not to have migrated to New England, where churches and homes were burned and many people beaten because they were French-Canadian immigrants.[29] Perhaps life wasn't pleasant for Alfred and Regina, as they chose to leave Illinois after living there only seven years.

As early as 1870, there was a mass exodus from Assumption. Clement (Alfred's brother) moved his family back to Princeville, Quebec. The families of Alfred and Regina, Onesime and Marie Lavanture, and others moved to join the growing French-Canadian immigrant community in Leelanau County, Michigan, where they could stake a 160-acre plot of land for virtually no cost provided they made improvements to their homestead.

According to family legend, these families traveled to Chicago by railroad,[30] and then took a ship to Leland, Michigan, because there were few roads in Michigan at that time. We don't know

---

28   As late as 1892, *The New York Times* published an editorial ("The French Canadians in New England, 1892")about the dangers of French-Canadian migration.

29   Vermette, *A Distinct Alien Race: The Untold Story of Franco-Americans: Industrialization, Immigration, Religious Strife,* 2018.

30   Library of Congress, Map of the Chicago, Burlington and Quincy Railroad, 1870. https://www.loc.gov/resource/ g3701p.rr003730/?r=0.776,0.334,0.081,0.032,0.

which ship carried them to Leland, but it could have been one such as the SS *Roosevelt*, which was a passenger ship on the Great Lakes in 1870.

Upon arriving in Leelanau County, Alfred and his brother-in-law, Onesime, homesteaded across the road from each other in Centerville Township in August of 1872. Soon after, Alfred obtained a job as a laborer at the Leland Lake Superior Iron Company, earning about fifty cents a day. He frequently walked the eight miles of Indian trails between Leland and his homestead in Centerville with supplies on his back for his family. He was a small man at five feet, six inches, but had remarkable strength. The Leland Lake Superior Iron Company provided employment opportunities for many people from 1870 to 1884.[31]

Ultimately, Alfred made a living as a farmer. He became a citizen of the USA on April 2, 1878. (The circuit judge was R. Hatch Jr.) The "Final Proof required under Homestead Act May 20, 1862"[32] indicated improvements Alfred made. He had "built a house with board floors, one door and windows, shingled the roof, and built a barn. He had plowed, fenced and cultivated about 12 acres of land and planted 10 fruit trees" (certified by Alex Belanger and Thomas Pero on August 7, 1878). He paid fourteen dollars down in 1872 and the balance of four dollars in 1878. Alfred received clear title to his homestead on November 5, 1878.

Alfred Lamie's homestead document

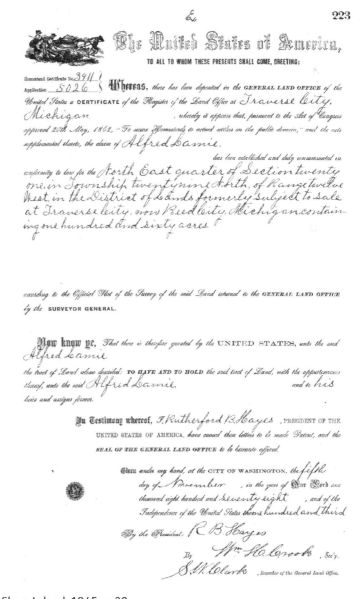

---

31   Littell, E., *100 Years in Leelanau*, The Print Shop, Leland, 1965, p. 39.

32   Documents provided by cousin Edward Lamie.

Meanwhile, the Onesime and Marie Lavanture family decided not to stay in Centerville Township and returned to Princeville, Quebec. This move would have caused great anguish. Alfred and Onesime had been best friends. Regina and Marie were sisters. They all were saddened at the thought of not seeing each other again. Onesime's homestead was occupied by his nephew, Joseph Lavanture and family. (Joseph had fought on the Union side of the Civil War from 1861 to 1864.)

St. Mary Parish in Lake Leelanau was the religious center for the French-Canadian immigrant community in Leelanau County. When Alfred arrived, it was a mission church built as a small log cabin.[33] The parish grew and a larger church was needed. Everyone in the community was expected to contribute money, materials, and labor to the building of the new church, and Alfred contributed his share. Alfred was a generous and caring man and did his utmost to support the parish and to build the new church, even though his homestead was five-and-a-half miles from the parish center. The new wooden-frame church was completed in 1881.[34]

St. Mary of the Assumption, Provemont, early 1900s

---

33   Littell, E.
34   Littell, E., p. 64.

Altogether, Alfred and Regina had eleven children, nine of whom lived to adulthood. My grandfather, Eugene (Lugie), was their seventh child, born on May 5, 1879. His other siblings were: Josephine, Julia, John, Onezim (Zim), Helen, Valare, Marie, and Jennie. (Lugie's oldest sibling, Josephine, married Dominic Couturier the same year he was born.)

Tragically, my great-grandmother, Regina, died on April 29, 1884, at the age of forty-four, less than a year after the birth of their last child. The circumstances of her death are unknown, although her death certificate indicates she died of cramps.[35]

(Thanks to John Elchert, publisher of the *Leelanau Enterprise*, for digging through the archived copies of the May 8, 1884, edition to find the death notice for Regina Lamie.)

Provemont Locals

Last Thursday, Mrs. Alfred Lamie
was buried. She was a good mother
and a good Christian. She leaves a
husband and nine children and a
host of friends to mourn her loss.

Mourning his wife, Alfred worked the farm while raising his eight children, ages one to seventeen. The older children helped care for the younger children; besides taking over the household chores, they also did farm chores.

Almost two years later, on January 7, 1886, Alfred's second-oldest daughter, Julia, married August Denoyer. Three days later, he married Elmira (Perrault) LaBelle at St. Mary of the Assumption Church in Provemont. He was fifty-two and she was thirty-one. Elmira, a widow, had four young children: Roselda, Mathilda, Adele, and Melinda. Elmira's first husband, Eugene LaBelle, had passed away in 1884.

---

35   Retrieved from *Leelanau.com*. https://leelanau.com/lake-leelanau-michigan/LeelanauEnterprise. (1884, May 8).

Alfred and Elmira had seven children during their marriage. Five lived to adulthood: Clara, Regina, Emma, and twins Clarabelle and Isabel. Their losses were an unnamed infant boy and Mary, during the year of her birth. Throughout the years of raising their five children, plus Alfred's six children and Elmira's four, respectively, they managed to live in the same wooden home Alfred built. Their French Road homestead sat across from

Alfred and Elmira (Perrault) Lamie.

Centerville Township Hall, separated by a two-track dirt road.

I presume all of the children attended O'Brien School, located next to the township hall, on French Road, named for the many French-Canadian families that settled along the eight-and-a-half-mile road extending from the corner across Holy Rosary Church to the northwest end of Provemont.

Alfred and Elmira endured much hardship. Their son, Zim, lived with them after he married his stepsister, Mathilda, who was ailing from tuberculosis, in 1895. It was good they were all living under the same roof, as Elmira took loving care of her daughter as she declined and died

Left: Lugie with brothers, Zim and John (circa 1925)
Above: Zim's brick home he built in 1910 (2022 photo)

at age twenty-one in 1899. She dealt with another tragedy four years later when her daughter, Melinda, engaged to marry Alfred's son, Lugie (my grandfather), died of tuberculosis, also at age twenty-one, in 1903.

Alfred, a man of deep faith, died at his homestead on June 25, 1909. That same year, his son, Zim, remarried (ten years after the death of his first wife, Mathilda). His new wife, Mary (Plamondon) Lamie, was the widow of his brother, Valere, who had four young children.

In 1910, after taking over his father Alfred's homestead, Zim built a stately, three-story, seven-bedroom brick home in front of Elmira's smaller wooden home. He and Mary raised seven children of their own besides her four children.

Elmira died on December 15, 1923. Zim and Mary's oldest daughter, Rosabelle, married Vincent Witkowski from Isadore in 1928. Zim sold the homestead to the couple in 1937.[36]

After raising large families and bearing the loss of many loved ones, my maternal great-grandparents and their combined families proved that life does go on. ...

Alfred and Regina Lamy (Lamie) Family and Spouses
Josephine, 1862–1933 (Dominic Couturier); Julia, 1867–1894 (August Denoyer); John, 1869–1931 (1. Mary St. John, 2. Hattie Lemay); Onezim (Zim), 1873–1939 (1. Mathilda LaBelle, 2. Mary Plamondon-Lamie); Helen, 1876–1935 (Joseph St. Jean/John); Valare, 1877–1908 (Mary Plamondon); Eugene, 1879–1948 (Jennie Plamondon); Marie, 1881–1960 (Alphonse Richard); and Jennie, 1883–1961 (Antoine St. John).

Alfred and Elmira Lamy (Lamie) Family and Spouses
Clara, 1887–1968 (Paul Plamondon); Regina, 1888–1966 (Ferdinand Plamondon); Emma, 1891–1967 (Alfred Richard); Clarabelle, 1892–1929 (John Plamondon); and Isabel, 1892–1965 (Amedee Plamondon).

---

36   The Witkowski family members were neighbors when my parents lived on the O'Brien farm from 1945-1949.

Eugene and Jennie (Plamondon) Lamie[37]

My grandfather, Eugene, was best known to his family and friends as "Lugie." He was Alfred and Regina Lamie's seventh child, born on May 5, 1879, in Leelanau County's Centerville Township.

In my mother Irene's words, "When Lugie was old enough, he helped his father [Alfred] clear the land and make logs, which were then hauled to Leland and sold for a small price. He saved his money. Lugie, at age twenty-three, purchased a lot for $175, on Hewitt Street in the village of Cedar, Solon Township, on November 24, 1902, from Mr. and Mrs. H. M. Gilman.

"In 1903, Lugie planned to marry Melinda LaBelle. His heart was broken when she died of tuberculosis that year.

"On April 24, 1905, Lugie sold the Hewitt Street lot and purchased a 120-acre farm from Evangelist Duperron."

"The farm had a new two-story farmhouse built by Mr. Duperron.[38] Lugie paid two hundred dollars down, and two hundred dollars a year until the death of Mr. Duperron. His farm was about a mile north of his father's homestead on French Road."

Lugie Lamie's farmhouse (1994 photo)

---

37   My mother, Irene (Lamie) Fleis wrote a story about her parents, Eugene and Jennie Lamie, in the book, *Lamy-Lami-Lemay-Lamie Families*, pp. 491–493. Material was edited or added to fit the narrative.

38   Lamie/Lamy family book, p. 7.

Mom continued, "Lugie's younger half-sister, Emma, came to live with him and helped with housekeeping while he tended the farming. Sometime later, Lugie met Jennie Plamondon and found happiness again. He decided to marry her."

Jennie (Plamondon) Lamie's family

My grandmother, Jennie, was the daughter of Benoit and Philomena (Minnie Couturier) Plamondon, born on June 8, 1885, in Elk Rapids, Michigan. She was the second of six children. Her siblings were: Vitaline, who lived a year, Helen, Genevieve, Zim, and Reuben.

When Jennie was almost ten, she was overcome with sorrow when her father (Benoit) died on May 6, 1895, at the age of thirty-five, in Leland. Her mother, Minnie, was now a widow with five young children.

On April 8, 1896, Minnie married August Denoyer, a widower from Isadore with two children, Julius and Josephine. One daughter, Margaretha, died in infancy. His first wife, Julia (Lamie) was Alfred and Regina's second oldest daughter, who died at twenty-seven years of age in 1894.

Maiden Jennie Plamondon

Minnie and August raised three children of their own: Julie, Emma, and Louis, besides her five children and his two children.

* * *

On July 9, 1906, Lugie was twenty-seven, and Jennie, twenty-one, when they were married at the Mission Church in Isadore. Lugie and Jennie were my maternal grandparents.

Maternal grandparents, Lugie and Jennie Lamie, on left. Others not identified in front of the old coupe.

My great-grandparents, August and Minnie, lived long lives and died within a few months of one another, he at age seventy-six in November 1940, and she in February 1941 at age seventy-five in Leland.[39]

---

39   Lamie/Lamy book, p. 139–140.

4

Ed's Boyhood

Left: Young Ed Fleis. Right: Fleis family (left to right): Leo, Roman, Susan, Ed, Agnes, Thomas holding baby Agnes, Theresa, Irene, Albion, Joe, Tom, Clem (circa 1935) before Anthony was born.

My paternal grandparents, Thomas and Agnes Fleis, worked the family farm as a team. Grandma Agnes milked the cows in the barn, and Grandpa Thomas did the farm work until their twelve children—eight boys and four girls—were old enough to help.

My father, Edward (Ed) Vincent, born on April 26, 1915, was their second child. His middle name, "Vincent," honored his maternal grandfather, Vincent Pleva. His brothers and sisters were: Leo, Susan, Roman, Albion, Thomas, Clemence, Irene, Joseph, Theresa, Agnes, and Anthony.

Beginning at a young age, Dad and his siblings learned the importance of family working together. They participated with their parents in gathering food and supplies that were hauled by horse and wagon until snow hit the ground, then by a horse-driven sleigh to the commercial district of Bodus, less than two miles down the road, and helped load the supplies on the MN & E train, to be delivered to Traverse City for their grandparents, Tomasz and Jozefina.

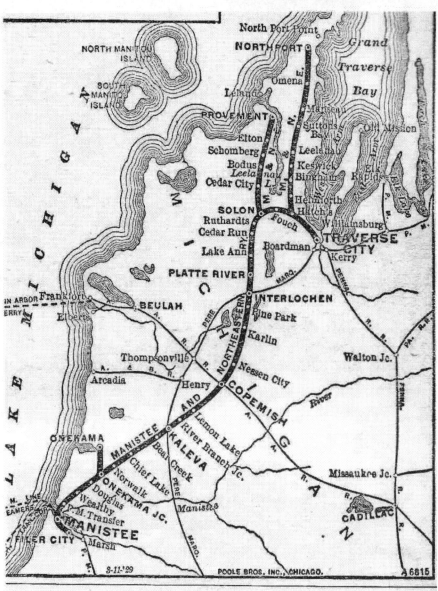

Top left: Railroad depot in Cedar, early 1900s (photo from Rick Brett). Top Right: View of Bodus, Michigan, in the early 1900s (Leelanau Historical Museum). Bottom: Railroad route, early 1900s (Leelanau Historical Museum).

On fair-weather days, Thomas and Agnes would take their children along with them to visit the grandparents, traveling a rugged road twenty miles each way.

Dad's younger sister, Theresa, was eighty-two when she shared this memory:[40] "My parents had an affectionate relationship. He wanted her to be with him whenever he traveled—to Traverse City or elsewhere." In accordance with the terms of their mortgage agreement with Tomasz and Jozefina, Thomas and Agnes furnished firewood, flour, coffee, sugar, potatoes, cabbage, and many other staples.

The three generations interacted frequently, which created responsible, loving relationships, and became an important aspect of my dad's younger life on the farm.

When the United States entered the Great War in 1917, it became compulsory for men ages twenty-one to thirty-one to register for the draft.[41] As Grandpa Thomas, having turned twenty-eight, filled out his draft registration card, he listed his dependents as "father, mother, wife and three children."

U.S., World War I Draft Re Thomas Flies
Michigan

Form 1 1 REGISTRATION CARD No. 69

A 21-6-14

1 Name in full: 378 Thomas Flies (Given name) (Family name) — Age, in yrs. 28
2 Home address: R.F.D. #1 Cedar Mich (No.) (Street) (City) (State)
3 Date of birth: November 10 1888 (Month) (Day) (Year)
4 Are you (1) a natural-born citizen, (2) a naturalized citizen, (3) an alien, (4) or have you declared your intention (specify which)? Natural Born
5 Where were you born? Centerville Michigan (Town) (State) (Nation)
6 If not a citizen, of what country are you a citizen or subject?
7 What is your present trade, occupation, or office? Farmer
8 By whom employed? Myself
Where employed: Centerville town Leelanau Co. Mich
9 Have you a father, mother, wife, child under 12, or a sister or brother under 12, solely dependent on you for support (specify which)? Father Mother Wife 3 children
10 Married or single (which)? Married Race (specify which)? Caucasian
11 What military service have you had? Rank None; branch None; years None; Nation or State
12 Do you claim exemption from draft (specify grounds)?

I affirm that I have verified above answers and that they are true.

Thomas Fleis (Signature or mark)

REGISTRAR'S REPORT

1 Tall, medium, or short (specify which)? Medium Slender, medium, or stout (which)? Medium
2 Color of eyes? Dark Blue Color of hair? Dark Brown Bald? No
3 Has person lost arm, leg, hand, foot, or both eyes, or is he otherwise disabled (specify)? No

I certify that my answers are true, that the person registered has read his own answers, that I have witnessed his signature, and that all of his answers of which I have knowledge are true, except as follows:

Frank Blonwick (Signature of registrar)

Precinct: Centerville
City or County: Leelanau
State: Michigan

June 5 (Date of registration)

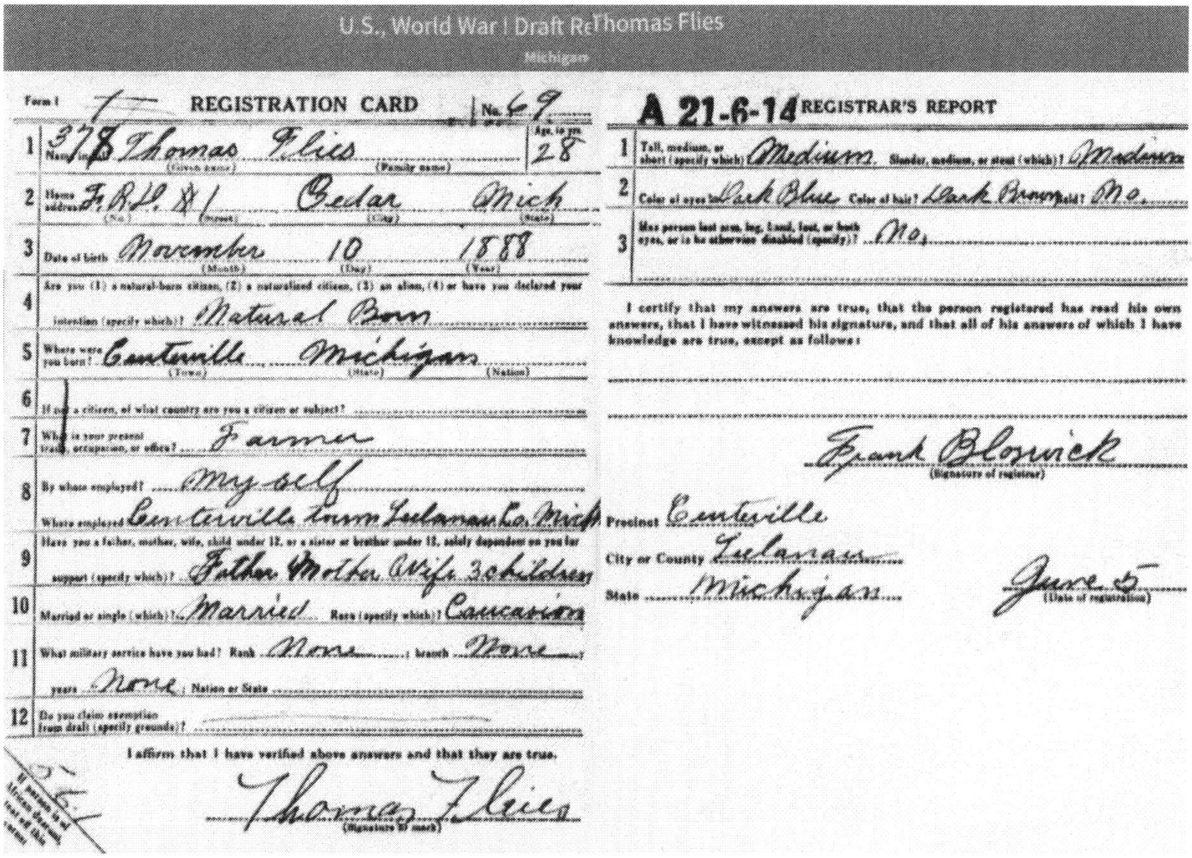

Thomas Fleis's draft card

---

40 At the 2012 Fleis reunion.

41 The Selective Service Act, which was passed by Congress under President Wilson, in 1917.

Although he was never drafted, the war raging overseas took an untold number of lives. Yet servicemen were also stricken and died on this side of the ocean from the mysterious Spanish flu. It was so contagious, army officials warned soldiers and citizens, "Don't sneeze, cough, or spit!"

Civilians fell to the disease as well. In our family, Grandma Agnes came down with it. A doctor came to the house, examined her, and advised the family on how to care for her.

Agnes Fleis with her brother, Adam Pleva

Don Pleva retells another story of his father, Adam: "The doctor was about to leave when someone said, 'There's another one upstairs.' That someone was [Agnes's] brother, Adam," a helping hand for Grandpa Thomas, who boarded at their home when he was on the farm.

"When the doctor saw [Adam], he said, 'This fellow is in much worse shape and needs to be taken down near the heat.'"

Miraculously, both Grandma Agnes and Adam pulled through. Sadly, that was not the case for millions of others worldwide. In Leelanau County, two hundred to three hundred cases of Spanish flu developed in one week, and the charge was made that they all originated in Grand Traverse County. As a result, sheriff deputies were stationed at all roads leading into the county to stop the entry of Traverse City residents.[42] My grandparents, Thomas and Agnes, were not able to visit my great-grandparents, Tomasz and Jozefina, during the pandemic.

---

42   "Remembering Solon," compiled by Carol Drzewiecki, *Leelanau Enterprise (no date)*. "Spanish Flu Hit Cedar with Force," submitted by Phyllis Sbonek.

One day, Don's father told him, "Adam was working in the fields with a team of horses, helping Grandpa Thomas. In the distance, he could hear church bells, school bells, and train and boat whistles ringing and whistling from every direction. It was eleven o'clock in the morning of the eleventh day of the eleventh month in 1918." World War I had ended.

This day became known as Armistice Day, the day when the long and bloody "Great War" finally ended. This was extremely significant for my family. After 124 years of partitions (refers to a country with separate areas of government) and oppression by Austria-Hungary, Germany (Prussia), and Russia, Poland had regained independence as part of the agreement signed that day by Germany.

* * *

Thirty-nine years after Tomasz and Jozefina first donated to have the first church and school built, their children, Thomas and Agnes Fleis, were among a large congregation to display the same generosity. According to the church's centennial booklet (1883–1983), "Father Stephen Narlock, the son of farmers living at Isadore, was the new pastor. He persuaded the people to erect a new church in 1920.

"He aroused them in such a way that parishioners hauled fieldstones all summer. Stonemasons John Wirt, John Mikowski, and Al Piotrowski worked all summer and fall in 1921–22, while many parishioners pitched in mixing the mortar and doing the carpentry."

The new Roman-architectural brick-faced church was beautified with thirteen stained glass windows fired in Munich, Germany. On December 12, 1923, Bishop Kelly blessed the new Holy Rosary Church and the school was renamed "Holy Rosary School," because of their loyalty to God and His Mother, our Patroness and Queen. "*Królowo Różańca SW. Módl Się Za Nami,*" is inscribed in the church sanctuary. It means, "Queen of the Most Holy Rosary, pray for us."[43]

"My parents were very religious," my dad wrote. "We always attended church services and devotions together. We prayed the rosary and litany every night with them, kneeling at the table."

Aunt Theresa wrote, "My mother sang in the choir. My father was always involved with the church. He was on the committee to get the bell."

The church bells rang three times a day—at 6:00 a.m., noon, and 6:00 p.m., when the Angelus, a Catholic devotion commemorating the Incarnation (the belief that Jesus Christ was made flesh by being conceived in the womb of a woman, the Virgin Mary) was prayed.[44] "I saw my father

---

43 Holy Rosary School, 1898–1998, pp. 5, 7.
44 Wikipedia.org.

Holy Rosary Church, Isadore (2010 photo)

[Thomas] drop down to his knees in the field and pray [the Angelus] when the church bells rang at noon," Dad said. They also had masses in the school chapel.

Dad became an altar boy and served mass at the "new" Holy Rosary Church. He said, "I was honored to serve both ordination masses of Reverend Boniface G. Winowiecki [later elevated to Monsignor] and the Reverend Adalbert Narlock, who were ordained on the same day," on February 2, 1925.

* * *

The musical tradition carried on as well for Thomas and Agnes's family. Thomas played violin, which he learned from his father, Tomasz, and played the same folk tunes from the old country. "Agnes sang beautifully and played organ and piano. Once she filled in for the whole mass when the organist didn't show up," Don Pleva stated.

Thomas and Agnes had the perfect setup with their own dance hall attached to the backside of their home, where they celebrated many occasions with music and dancing. All the girls—Susan, Irene, Theresa, and Agnes—sang beautifully and played piano. The boys all sang their hearts out when they heard music playing, and some, like Dad, even played a little piano. The youngest,

Anthony (Tony), was never shy about singing his favorite, a sad song about a dog called "Old Shep." I couldn't help but shed a tear whenever I heard Uncle Tony sing this song.

* * *

I consider my dad, Ed, as a natural-born violin or fiddle player. At the age of ten, he was allowed to borrow his grandfather's treasured violin. The one year of classical lessons he took from a nun at school in 1925 was his start. Sometimes, he played music at church for masses and school programs. Then, he taught himself how to play by heart the old tunes he loved hearing his grandfather or father play.

Tomasz's dream had come true. It must have been so satisfying to hear his young grandson playing the same violin he had carried on the ship when he immigrated to this country and to see a new generation taking interest in traditional music. Later, another grandson, Roman, also learned to play the instrument, and was "quite the entertainer," remarked Agnes, Dad's youngest sister.

As a young man, Ed shared his talents with other musicians, providing entertainment for the Polish community, and would one day form a band and play professionally. The same for his sister, Agnes.

Besides music for entertainment, Grandpa Thomas was a serious card player. "My father loved to play cards with his neighbors and family," Dad wrote. "They played pepper, penny-ante poker, and Pedro."

On a more serious note, many childhood illnesses plagued families in those days. Medicine wasn't what it is today. Thomas and Agnes's oldest daughter, Susan, was afflicted with asthma as a young child. The farm with its feather pillows and quilts was no place for her. In addition, she endured bouts of wheezing and coughing during certain times of the year.

Their son, Albion (Al), was afflicted with polio at the age of three. Dad explained, "The doctor operated on the wrong leg the first time in 1923, and [Al] was never able to walk decently. He had crutches and also learned to walk on his hands and later walked with a cane."

All of Thomas and Agnes's children attended Holy Rosary, the same place where they received an education. Dad started school in 1921, when the new church was being built. He awoke at 5:00 a.m. and hurriedly did farm chores helping his dad and brother, Leo, then the boys walked a mile to school. During the winter, roads were covered with snow and no plows. My sister, Noreen, shared a story she heard about Dad's school days. "One morning, when Dad and his brother were walking to school on top of eight-foot snow banks, Leo suddenly disappeared into the snow. Dad somehow was able to dig him out, saving him from sure suffocation."

Before classes, Dad attended 8:00 a.m. mass at the church, and nearly every day, especially during the winter months, he checked on his Aunt Anna Fleis before and after school. She lived alone across from the school. During the winter months, he would shovel a path to her outside door, carry in wood, and stoke the fire in her woodstove. Depending on the season, there were numerous chores he would do for her.

Those students who lived a distance of three or more miles from school boarded for two to three months during the winter. Everybody brought their own beds from home. The girls slept on the first floor. The boys slept in the basement.[45] On Monday mornings, parents brought their children to school by horse and sleigh, and enough food supplies to last until Friday when they returned to pick them up to go home for the weekend. Nuns supervised the childrens' activities, which included doing chores. Separate privies were outdoors. Fortunately, electricity was installed the year before, and the school was heated by coal and wood.

During class, three Felician nuns taught about one hundred students in three classrooms on the second floor. Only eight grades were taught at that time. Grades one and two in one room; grades three, four, and five in another; and grades six, seven, and eight in a third room. A fourth Felician nun served as cook. Subjects included the Polish and English languages, and besides academic subjects, there was religious education, art, and music.

Holy Rosary School photo of Clem Mikowski, Ed Fleis, Leo Mazurek, and Leo Fleis

The nuns made thirty dollars per month and lived in housing on the premises, with a plum and pear orchard and "lots of clotheslines," Dad recalled. There was a stable with forty stalls for the horses and buggies of churchgoers. The janitor, whose home was provided as well, rang the school bell at eight in the morning.

Dad says he "made First Communion in third grade because the church was under construction when he was in second grade," and he had to wait a year. It was quite an accomplishment when he

---

45   Holy Rosary School, 1898–1998, p. 147.

received the award for five years of perfect attendance; and in seventh grade, he won the Leelanau County spelling bee.

Dad was glad when warmer weather arrived each year, allowing him to wear short pants with long socks and garters above his knees, and buttonhole shoes six-to-ten inches high. When recess time came, there was no place to play except the dirt road, because of the many large fieldstones dumped on the playground by parishioners for building a foundation for the new church. Dad made some good friends at school. He and classmate Clem Mikowski would get into boxing and wrestling matches at school for fun. They were never disciplined for it. However, one time while playing tag in the barn, they were late for the bell, and both got a good scolding from a nun and were spanked. Dad didn't say how old he was, but it was the only time he ever got in trouble at school.

Golden wedding anniversary. Back row (left to right): Thomas, Lillian, Suzanne, Mary, and Martin. Front row: Susan Fleis, Clara Pleva, Jozefina, Tomasz, and two little ones not identified (circa 1926).

In Dad's memoir writing, he recalled celebrating his grandparents' (Tomasz and Jozefina's) fiftieth wedding anniversary in 1926, when he was eleven years old. It was a big celebration that began with church services and was followed by a reception at the farm with Polish food, peva (beer), and music played by three generations of family. Great Grandpa Tomasz, Grandpa Thomas, and my dad took turns playing the violin, with Grandma Agnes chording on the piano.

* * *

Grandma Agnes usually wore a plain, colored dress with a white cobbler apron. Her long, dark hair, graying slightly, was wrapped in a bun at the back of her head. Her face revealed worn lines. She was mild mannered and soft spoken. A wonderful cook, she served generous meals to her big family and all their company. She would stand near the table, refill bowls, pour coffee, and add fresh slices of homemade bread.

Agnes Fleis wearing her Sunday best

Dad wrote, "My mother became ill after Joe's birth in 1927. After that, three more siblings were born: Theresa in 1930, Agnes in 1934, and Tony in 1936."

Meanwhile, in February of 1929, Dad grieved two losses. The first was the death of his grandfather, Tomasz, on February 9. The death certificate stated that he died of apoplexy (sudden death). He was buried at Holy Rosary Cemetery. Then, five days later, Dad went to check on his Aunt Anna in the morning and found her dead and the house cold. He immediately went and told the priest. Her funeral was two days later. They put her in a seventy-five-dollar coffin on a sleigh. She, too, was buried at Holy Rosary Cemetery. The shock of this event lived in his memory forever, as Dad was eighty-five when he retold the story.

During Dad's eight years of schooling, Leo wasn't his only sibling in school. Susie, Roman, Al, and Tommy Jr. would have all been age appropriate for younger grades. Young Tommy was seven when Ed was in the eighth grade. Grandpa Thomas would have transported some or all of the children by horse and buggy or sleigh after Al started first grade, since Al could only walk with crutches, or perhaps earlier, when Susie started school.

After passing an official exam at the Leelanau County Courthouse, Dad proudly earned his eighth-grade diploma. His diploma clearly states the year as "1927," but Dad wrote, "I graduated in 1929." He was fourteen when he went to work full-time on the farm.

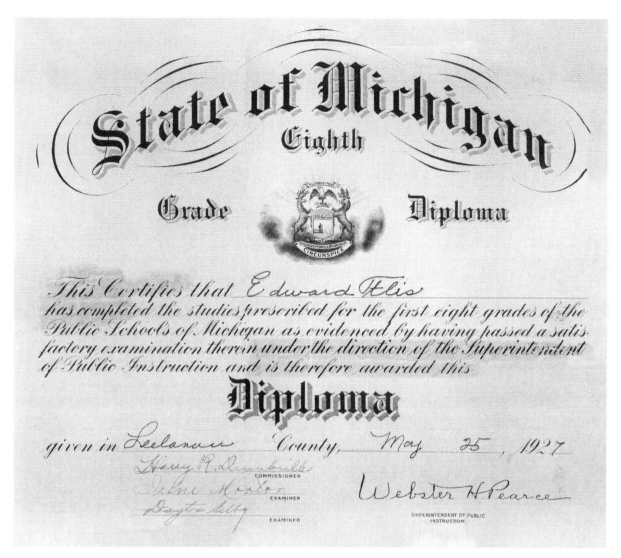

Ed's eighth-grade diploma

* * *

Great-grandfather Tomasz lived to be seventy-five years old. After his death, Roman and Susie Pleva sold their place on Randolph Street and moved in with Great-Grandma Jozefina. According to Dad, "They cared for her and furnished most of the groceries," until she passed on July 23, 1938, at eighty-one years of age.

5

Irene's Girlhood

Left: Young Irene in field behind Lamie farm. Right: Lamie family portrait. Standing, from left: Lucille, Ben, Mabel, Louis, and Irene. Sitting: Lugie, Meda, Cliff, and Jennie.

My Mother, Irene Lamie, was born on February 2, 1916, in Centerville Township, the sixth of eight children. Her siblings were: Mabel, Dominic (who died in infancy), Clifford, Benedict, Louis, Meda, and Lucille. French was the dominant language spoken at home, at least until the children attended school and learned English. Her parents, Lugie and Jennie, spoke only French until they learned English from their children; after that their children were no longer required to speak French at home.

Lugie raised a little of everything—wheat, oats, corn, string beans, potatoes, and lima beans. They raised cattle for milk and meat, besides having workhorses and chickens.

The family never made much money off farming, but they sold vegetables and fruits from a large, productive garden. The produce, along with fresh cream, eggs, and homemade butter, was hauled to Leland and sold to regular customers. Those sales paid the bills, and farming sustained the family.

The family's hard work in growing produce also allowed Lugie to purchase a car—his "Briscoe." Briscoe was an American vehicle that was manufactured in Jackson, Michigan, between 1914 and 1921 by a group headed by a man named Benjamin Briscoe.[46] After he purchased his "new" Briscoe car, Lugie kept his eyes on the garage doors, because he did not want his boys touching his prized possession.

One time, when my mother and her brother Louis were about seven and eight, they were talking about picking raspberries while they were in the garage with their pails in hand. Louis went up to his dad's new car, pretending to be like his father, and stood next to it, close to the gas tank. "I have to put gas in the car first!" he said to Irene.

"This was always a favorite saying of his," Irene said.

Lugie, who had noticed the open garage door and was standing beside it, listening, stuck his head inside the door and asked, "Who is going to pick the berries?"

They were caught!

He gave each of them a little spanking for touching his car and sent them back to the garden.

My cousin, Gene Lamie, told me a story about Grandpa Lugie (he heard from his father, Clifford) revealing what a trickster he was.

"Grandpa Lugie had a large gasoline tank for storing fuel to use on his farm. Once a week, he'd fill a five-gallon gasoline can to supply fuel for his car and tractor. He kept that gas can in a shed. He had the habit of filling the tank of his car on Sundays after coming home from church. For several weeks when he went to pick up the gasoline can, it was empty. He figured someone was stealing his gasoline while he was at church with his family.

"One Saturday, in trying to solve the problem, he added sugar to the gasoline can, a day before he would normally add gas to his car. The following week, he heard about the neighbor's engine (carburetor) freezing up. He never had a problem with someone stealing gasoline again!" Gene concluded.

Another story came from my cousin, Lucille, about her mother, Aunt Mabel, Mom's oldest sister. "Mabel graduated early from eighth grade at Martin School, a tiny one-room classroom

---

46   Wikipedia.org.

located on Amore Road in Centerville Township, because she had skipped a grade. Her seventh and eighth grades had been combined into one school year. She waited a couple years before attending ninth grade at St. Francis High School in Traverse City, where she stayed at an aunt's home.

"Mabel had been a student there for only a couple months when, while attending mass one morning, she distinctly heard a voice say to her, 'Go home. Your mother needs you.' She did, probably taking the train to Provemont. (The M&N railway (1908–1944) operated daily from Traverse City to Provemont.)[47] When she arrived home, her mother, Jennie, was glad to see her and thankful to have help as she was six months pregnant with Mabel's youngest sister, Lucille."

My mother also attended Martin School. I ran into one of her classmates, Celia "Sally" LaBonte, from Lake Leelanau one morning after a weekday mass in 2006. Ninety-two at the time, she was pushing the wheelchair of Mom's cousin, Rev. Father Albert Couturier, whom I knew very well. I was talking with him when Mrs. LaBonte recognized me. She poked me and said, "I knew your mom; she was a classmate of mine."

Mrs. LaBonte, it turned out, was two years older than Mom. We agreed to get together. A short while later, I interviewed her at her home on French Road. Then we took a ride to Amore Road, where Martin School once stood. We surveyed the area, which was overgrown with brush. She pointed to where a flowing creek used to be but now appeared to be dry. "When

Left: Celia LaBonte (2006). Right: Fr. Albert Couturier (2006).

children were thirsty in warmer months," she said, "they raised their hands for permission to go outdoors for a drink of water from an extended pipe that carried constant flowing water from that creek."

---

47   "Lake Leelanau Once Provemont" taken from *100 Years in Leelanau*, produced by the Leelanau County Prospectors Club. *Leelanau Enterprise*, May 20, 2021.

During our talks, and not long before she died, Mrs. LaBonte shared with me the following information, which I feel blessed to have learned:

"The one-room school had wonderful big windows and nice hardwood floors, a boy's cloakroom and a girl's cloakroom, and no electricity or inside plumbing. Kerosene lamps mounted to the ceiling provided essential light. A potbelly stove warmed the room. During the cold months, neighbors helped by stoking the wood stove every morning before school.

"About fifty students attended primer through eighth grade at one time. One teacher, Angeline Hominga, taught all the grades. Ms. Hominga's sister helped. Ms. Hominga rang a small bell whenever it was time for the next grade to begin instruction, while the rest worked on their assignments. A recitation bench sat in front of the class; so, when you were promoted to the next grade the following year, you knew what to expect after observing other grades being taught. Besides English language, other subjects included geography, physics, agriculture, spelling, reading, arithmetic, history, and penmanship."

School was special to Mom because it was exciting to learn. On fair-weather days, Mom walked about a mile and a half to school, through a pathway over the hills, with her siblings. On bad-weather days, parents from one family or another took turns picking up the children and taking them to and from school by horse and buggy or sleigh. During winter months, they frequently bobsledded to school.

Another student who attended Martin School had my Uncle Cliff, Mom's brother, for a teacher for two years. Theresa Walter of Suttons Bay was nearly ninety years old when we talked.

She said Uncle Cliff would take the whole class on walking field trips. On one of those walks, she saw a house being moved by a team of horses. On other walks, she saw barn raisings and tractor demonstrations. She said, "Those were real learning experiences."

My mother made her First Holy Communion at St. Mary's Church in Lake Leelanau on May 17, 1925, at the age of nine. "St. Mary's" was short for St. Mary of the Assumption, built in 1864, in the village of Provemont.

MARTIN SCHOOL — Back Row: Benny Lamie, Emil St. John, Harvey Schlueter, Elizabeth Plamondon, Genevieve Brow, Ottillia Schlueter, Alice Harpe, Florence Harpe, Teacher Henry Buckstahler. Third and Fourth Rows: Cornelia Brow, Helen Brow, ?, Marcella Plamondon, Celia BElanger, Lucille Brow, Therese Plamondon, Saraphine LaCross, Elizabeth Brow, Francis Plamondon, Louis Harpe, Elizabeth Harpe, Walter Harpe, Andrew Plamondon, Albert ?, Joseph St. John, ? Gauthier, Pearl St. John, Metalda Schlueter, Louis Lamie, Norman St. John. Second Row: Wilbert Gauthier, Sonny Brow, Meda Lamie, Elizabeth Boutain, Edith Brow, Genevieve Belanger, Wilmer Harpe, Elmer Amore. Front Row: Willard Brow, Elmer Boutain, Bernice Amore, Bernice Brow, Wilma Brow, Sylvia Boutain, Agnes Belanger, Lucille Plamondon.

Irene's brothers, Ben, Louis, and Meda Lamie are in this photo.

(Courtesy of Leelanau Historical Museum)

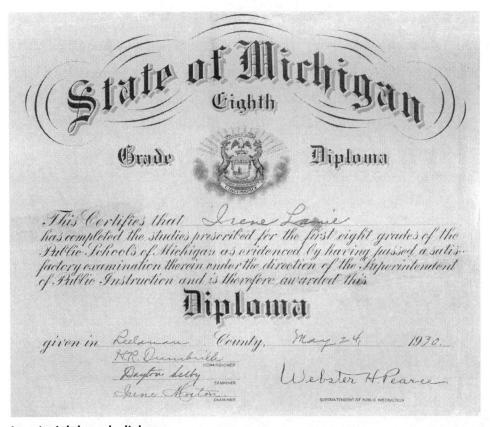

Irene's eighth-grade diploma

In 1930, when she was fourteen, Mom received her eighth-grade diploma from the Martin School. Proud of her accomplishment, she looked forward to high school at St. Mary's in Lake Leelanau.

She did begin her freshman year that fall, but when winter arrived, there was no transportation. Mom's parents were already paying room and board in Lake Leelanau for three of their older sons. For her to continue, they would have to do the same for her. These were the tough economic times of the Great Depression. Her parents felt it was more important for the boys to get a good education, because they would someday have to support a family. It was a sad time for Mom when she had to give up her schooling. Learning was important to Mother, and she never stopped educating herself.

Three of Mom's four brothers—Ben, Clifford, and Meda—received high-school diplomas. Louis made it to twelfth grade but did not graduate. Her sisters, Mabel and Lucille, both graduated from the eighth grade, just as Mom had.

Irene stayed home for another two years to assist her mother. During the summer, Irene helped weed the family's large garden and picked berries and cherries. She enjoyed helping in the house, while the rest of the family worked the fields with her father.

Mom learned cooking, cleaning, gardening, and canning fruit and meat. She inherited her mother's love of sewing on a treadle sewing machine. It ran on the rocking motion of both feet placed on the decorative metal base, called a "treadle." She learned resourcefulness by salvaging material from discarded clothing and creating home-sketched paper patterns. There was always mending to do and socks to darn. It was all about simplicity and thriftiness, traits that would impact her livelihood.

The Lamie home was known for having lots of company, especially relatives. Music played a big part in these gatherings. When Mom's Grandpa August and Grandma Minnie Denoyer would come visit, he and Frank Yankee would get together and play the violin, with her mother, Jennie, playing the organ. Everyone would join in and sing. Even Evangelist Duperron, a family friend and the previous owner of the farm, was known to come for a lengthy stay of a week or two.

Her father often served his visitors either his homemade wine, which he had a liking for, or his homemade root beer. When the guests were leaving, Jennie would give them fresh vegetables to take home.

Every New Year's Day, Lugie's custom was to give each of his children a blessing. The children would line up, youngest to oldest, and, one at a time, kneel in front of him while he prayed over them and gave each a kiss. After the blessing, Jennie also hugged and kissed them as she wished each one "Happy New Year, and good health and happiness."

Left-to-right: Lugie (Eugene) Lamie, Zim Plamondon, Louis Denoyer, Max Yankee, Frank Yankee

Lamie farmhouse (c. 1930)
Back row (left-to-right): Max Yankee, Frank Yankee, Zim Plamondon, Lugie (Eugene) Lamie, August Denoyer
Front row (left-to-right): Julia Denoyer Yankee, Emma Denoyer Yankee, Florence Brow Plamondon, Jennie Plamondon Lamie, Minnie

6

The Fleis Family in the 1930s

IN HIS WRITINGS, DAD DESCRIBED HIS FATHER, my Grandpa Thomas, as a "good manager." He was a strong voice in the Isadore community. He served as a representative of the Leelanau County Board of Agriculture and the Isadore Farm Bureau, and for many years as the Centerville Township treasurer.[48] "The first time he is mentioned in the minutes of the Centerville Township board is April 2, 1951. It doesn't state what his role was. Some of the minutes only stated 'all are present,' said Trina Pleva, Centerville Township treasurer (2020). Minutes back then were short and sweet, with no good records kept back then."

Thomas Fleis

Grandpa Thomas was an advocate for change and modernization. "When electricity became available to farmers," Dad wrote, "he went door to door, talking to them, and made it happen. At first, they didn't think it was such a good idea, but [they] finally gave in and pitched in some money."

After Aunt Theresa's birth in 1930, Grandpa Thomas donated "a statue of St. Therese to Holy Rosary Church," Dad also stated.

Saint Therese statue at Holy Rosary Church (circa 1930)

---

48   Thomas Fleis obituary, *Leelanau Enterprise*, May 20, 1965.

Although my aunt was given the name Mary Margaret at birth, at her baptism she was named Theresa Marie, after Saint Therese of Lisieux, and remembers seeing the statue in church when she attended school. I think the statue represented a thanks-giving from Grandpa Thomas for the healthy baby girl; for the health of Grandma Agnes, who had kidney problems three years earlier after Joseph's birth; and for all of his family. (The statue still remains in the church.)

These were hard times. The Great Depression had struck the year before and would last for a decade. My dad wrote, "In 1929, the big Depression hit. Herbert Hoover was President. Locals lost money in the bank, and prices went down." Cedar State Bank, which opened in 1905, survived the Great Depression, but closed in the late 1930s.[49]

Even so, Grandpa Thomas was full of ambition as he worked the fields alongside his oldest sons: my dad, Ed, and Uncle Leo. The farm produced forty acres of potatoes for a cash crop, wheat, oats, corn, and hay.

Grandpa Thomas was a mighty force until one day in 1930, when he suffered a sunstroke while out in the fields. At forty-one, his life was altered forever. "He worked very little on the

Top left: Fleis brothers: Clem, Ed, Leo, Roman and Tom taking a break working the field. Top right: Ed with the wheat binder (circa 1936). Bottom from left: Ed, Roman and Leo.

49   Village of Cedar History (http://cedarmichigan.biz/history.htm).

farm after that and depended on Leo and me to do the work," Dad wrote. As it weakened Grandpa Thomas, his demands became stronger. "He was bossier," Dad stated.

Ed was fifteen and his brother Leo sixteen when they took over farming the 160-acre parcel, working the fields with two teams of horses, and later, three teams. The boys pitched all the hay and grain. They did all the cultivating and chores, brushed the horses, put the harnesses away, milked the cows, turned the cream separator, and fed the pigs and cattle.

Potato digging in the fall was one job Grandpa Thomas could help with. He would walk behind the one-horse potato digger, pulling Maggie or Danny's reins, row after row. Each horse was so well-trained, it would move on to the next row before a command.

Grandma Agnes would treat her family with fresh potato pancakes on their days of picking potatoes in the fields, and they would work till dark!

Dad remembers "hauling potatoes to Suttons Bay," where his father earned nine cents for a single bushel, which averaged out to be $4.50 per load (fifty crates). The boys also helped haul potatoes to the commercial district of Bodus, where three buyers would have the boys load the heavy 150-pound bags of potatoes on the platform of the train cars. They could hear the train crossing behind the farm before stopping at Bodus, less than two miles away. (Years later, an abandoned caboose was found behind the woods.)

The district of Bodus also had a grocery store, and a mercantile store where Dad remembered getting a pair of shoes. There was a saloon and a "big draw" for dancing in the upstairs dance hall.

When the barn roof had to be replaced, Grandpa Thomas decided to make it of twenty-six-gauge steel. Dad accompanied his father to pick up the material at the O. J. Plamondon Store in Provemont. Then he helped lay the first steel roof on the barn. Dad said, "They put a rope over the roof and I was tied to it, so I wouldn't fall. It was a beautiful job!"

Dad credited his father for giving him many lessons. "When something broke down, my father told me exactly what to do, and I would fix it. There was always something breaking down with the farm equipment ... always something. I never knew why ... but for some reason, my father relied on me to do the fixing, instead of Leo."

Dad's youngest sister, Aunt Agnes, was seventy-eight at a family reunion in 2012, when she described the way the barn was as a child.

Side Note:

Every barn I've seen was square, but ours was long. The first section had the horses in their stalls, Nellie and Dolly, and Maggie and Danny. There was a little space left over if a calf was born. Then next, a space where the horses could pull in a wagon load of hay or whatever was in season.

At the very end of the barn was a space for the pigs. Next was a larger space for the milking cows. There were openings with doors, so the boys could feed the horses and cows with the hay and bed them with the straw. There also was an outdoor space fenced in for the cows in warmer weather. I remember one time when I had to go and get the cows, way out across the road into the woods, we had a bull who looked real mad, and I was scared, so I went into the teepee-shaped wood pile. What if he had come in and got after me? But all the cows and the bull went by—they knew how to get home—so then I went out and followed them.

Another time, on a windy day, clothes were on the line and I saw that mad bull go after the flopping sheets.

There were nine cows which had to be milked, and the milk would be placed in the big bowl on top of the cream separator, which had to be hand cranked (later we did have a motor on it). There were two spouts—one for the cream to come out that raised to the top, the other for the skim milk, which was fed to the animals—I think especially the young ones. And the cream was made into butter. We had to wash all parts of the separator, and we sure were glad when detergent was invented, instead of having plain hot water and no soap suds for washing dishes.

Aunt Agnes describes more about farming:

In the wintertime, the guys cut up wood from trees in the woods, as we had a wood furnace down the basement and a wood stove in the kitchen for cooking. When they cut up the wood in the woods, they piled it up into the shape of a teepee. A good part of the basement was filled with wood beside a huge woodshed, which they brought home with horses pulling the wagon.

In those days, everybody had outhouses, so besides the original one that was outside, we had one attached on the back end of the woodshed. So, it was the only indoor/outdoor outhouse I ever saw. When I was very young, the roads weren't plowed often like they are now, so I remember going to church in a Buda (which was sleigh-driven, and open to the air–perhaps with a covered top and no windows) that was pulled by the horses. It had benches on the side, and there were two holes for the lines to drive the horses so the driver could be inside, and even a fire inside for warmth.

Grandpa introduced his sons to a Farmall tractor (manufactured in 1939 by International Harvester, an American company). The tractor was handy when hauling heavy loads of potatoes or bulky loads of grain. However, the boys mostly drove horses with the old farming equipment.

Dad remained on the farm until he was nearly twenty-two. By then, his younger brothers were old enough to help and his older brother, Leo, was still living at home.

Left: The one and only time Agnes Fleis sat on the tractor. Right, from left: Theresa, Joe, Albion, Irene, and baby Agnes (circa 1935).

Albion (Al), who was afflicted with polio, was five years younger than Dad. He attended Holy Rosary School through the tenth grade. Grandpa Thomas saw to it that Al continued with his education at St. Mary's High School. On Sundays, Uncle Al was dropped off at the home of Raymond and Kathryn (Kolarik) Plamondon, across from Dick's Pour House in downtown Lake Leelanau. He stayed there during the week, and his father (Grandpa Thomas) picked him up on Fridays after school.

Raymond and Kathryn's daughter, Dorothy (Plamondon) Chimoski from Suttons Bay, told me in conversation, "I pulled Al on a sleigh during the winter months to school each day. His mother [Grandma Agnes] would send homemade bread or other baked goodies when he was picked up on Friday. Her bread was delicious!"

Uncle Al graduated from twelfth grade in 1939, the first of his siblings to do so. Following graduation, Al attended business school in Traverse City. Grandpa Thomas provided the transportation.

During the week Al stayed with relatives in town. Grandpa did everything possible to help his son become independent in spite of an affliction. Uncle Al earned a business degree.

Leo, Roman, Thomas Jr., and Clemence took over the farming. Joe took over later. Tony, the youngest, nine years younger than Joe, was under the wings of Grandpa Thomas, who liked having his youngest son near his side.

Aunt Agnes remembers an incident when playing with her brother, Tony, as he pretended to be a farmer.

> We had nice green grass around the house; by the icehouse, there was a little patch that Tony used to work up as if on the farm. He used a hoe on an angle for a plow and made the noises as if a tractor was going. Then he used a shovel sideways for a disc, then a rake for a drag, and he'd go back and forth on that patch which he had well worked up. Then we had a two-wheel cart, which Tony used to pull around.
>
> So, one day we were going to haul hay (along the side of the road), so since Tony was [pretending to be] the horse, I found some binder twine in the garage and fixed up a halter long enough to be used as lines to drive the horse (Tony). I put a couple of staples to draw the binder twine through, and out of wood slats made the "forks" to pick up the hay and let it go to the side to be dropped off in a crate. So then, we went out to the side of the road. Tony (the horse) pulled the cart, while I drove the horse (had binder twine for lines), picked up some hay on the side of the road and, of course, unloaded the hay with the binder twine and wooden forks, and it dropped into a crate.

According to Dad, between the spring of 1938 and 1944, Grandpa Thomas purchased the Harpe and O'Brien Farms, both located on French Road in Centerville Township. For some reason, Grandpa kept the original family names of those homestead properties for as long as he owned them.

After he bought those farms, he was growing up to one hundred acres or more of potatoes. Uncle Joe, who worked those two farms in addition to the family farm, told me: "That was a lot of potatoes to pick and sell!"

At the O'Brien farm, Uncle Joe walked two miles almost every day, year-round, to feed the cows. He drove the Farmall tractor one time. There was a jack pump, and he pumped water for

Joe Fleis on tractor with threshing machine behind. Tony (age five) on the wheel of the tractor, and Thomas. Other two unidentified.

twenty heads of cattle and left enough feed for three days. One time, he used the tractor on the pulley to pump five hundred gallons of water.

Uncle Joe continued, "I was fourteen years old in 1941, and driving five horses, pulling a two-double section drag. When I got to the woods, I had to open a gate. The gate was too narrow for five horses to go through, so I unhitched two or three. After I got through the woods, I started dragging again.

"At noon-time though, I gave the horses a break and went brook trout fishing in a creek behind the railroad track. I got about half a dozen!"

The farms sometimes shared the horses. Aunt Agnes recalls,

My sister, Theresa, and I rode the horses sometimes from one farm to the other. The horses' names were Danny and Maggie, and Maggie was a little friskier: you could shake a branch a little bit, and she would go faster.

I remember seeing Maggie one time kicking her back feet way up in the air … when we were crossing the creek. There were large cement culverts which weren't put under the road yet, so frisky Maggie must have gotten a little scared and pushed Danny (who I was on, and Theresa was on Maggie) way on the other side of the road, but we got them back on the road and away we went.

Side Note: Price of Potatoes

One time when I visited Uncle Joe in his late years, he said, "My dad owned three grain farms, which I helped, as early as I can remember, tending three teams of horses and picking bushels of potatoes.

He opened his refrigerator door and pulled out a nice sized potato. "Do you know how much this potato cost me?" he asked. Then he exclaimed, "One dollar! Back in the days when I was on the farm, potatoes were worth ten cents a bushel. This one potato is worth ten bushels! Can you believe that?

"Our potato fields produced six thousand bushels of potatoes … Some went into the pit for winter storage. One time, potatoes were sold to a potato chip factory. So, Tony Darga and I went to Detroit with a load of potatoes. We got stopped in the street by a cop who said, 'You can't drive that truck through here.' Cop gave me a ticket."

Near the farmhouse was a plain wooden building called an "ice house."

Uncle Joe told me, "After Pleva's Pond was frozen, big cakes of ice were cut and hauled to the ice house, with a horse and sleigh. The ice was layered with spaces between and along the sides, then all the spaces were covered with sawdust and the bottom and top of each layer. A pulley with huge ice tongs was used to lift out a block of ice."

Aunt Agnes said, "We had a screened-in front porch. There was a brown icebox at one end. The upper compartment stored the ice. The lower compartment stored the food. I do remember when we got our first refrigerator, and when mother [Grandma Agnes] made ice cream for home and the church festival, which was delicious. We even had cones!"

Uncle Joe told me a story about when he was fourteen years old and he and his father (Grandpa Thomas) were driving horses around Pleva's frozen pond to make a track. They thought the shoreline was frozen, but it was not, and the horse, Maggie, fell in. Uncle Joe was so scared! He hitched Maggie and pulled her by the collar, but the collar broke! It took a chain to get her out. Once they did, he rode Maggie for two straight hours to get her warm. The next day, they were back there again!

Another time, he said, "My brother Leo fell in when he stepped on a cake of ice." Neighbors helped save him. Luckily, he was okay.

7

Ed and Irene's Courtship and Marriage

IN THE ABSENCE OF A HIGH SCHOOL EDUCATION, my mother, Irene Lamie, educated herself by surrounding herself with books of a religious nature and with others about natural science and healing. She learned lifelong skills from her mother, Jennie. Two of her many qualities were common sense and perseverance.

When she was seventeen, Irene yearned for independence and found a way to venture from her parents' home. Wanting to earn a paycheck and save some money, she took a job in Traverse City, where she worked as a maid and babysat for $3.50 per week. She would return home for the summer to help her parents with a busy harvest and would take a different job in the fall.

In 1935, when he was twenty, Ed Fleis was a handsome, eligible man of Polish descent who had become popular as a fiddle player. He often played for dances alongside his Uncle Steve Pleva, Stanley Mikowski, John Stachnik, and Leo Sharnowski. Some farmers used their granaries for dance floors; others had a separate building attached to their home for the purpose of having their own dance hall, just as my grandparents did.

Beginning in the 1800s, settlements of many nationalities had popped up all over Leelanau County. The residents celebrated their own cultural events and built their own schools and churches—and this was true of the Polish and French-Canadian settlers in Centerville Township. Although both communities were Catholic, their heritage was different and language was a barrier for many.

It was common at that time for children to learn English in school and then teach their parents the language. After learning English from their children, Dad's parents carried on the tradition of speaking Polish at home. Mom's parents, on the other hand, refrained from speaking much French at home after learning English from their children. However, they switched to speaking in French whenever relatives visited.

In the 1930s, resistance to intermingling between the Polish and French-Canadians remained for the older folks, but music and dancing made a difference for Ed and Irene's generation, drawing both cultures together. It was something to do on a weekend afternoon for Irene and her group of friends, who all loved to dance. They attended some of the Polish dances where Ed played violin.

One early spring afternoon in 1935, he was playing his grandfather's violin at the Centerville Township Hall near Isadore for a Maslowski anniversary party, when he suddenly noticed an attractive, petite, French maiden dancing with her friends in the midst of a very crowded dance floor. He knew that he had seen her before at other dances where he had played. He was curious about getting to know who she was.

Irene might not have even gone to the afternoon dance at all if her friends hadn't coaxed her. Once she decided to go, however, she dressed especially nicely, choosing a lovely, tailored suit she had purchased by setting aside a dollar each week from her paycheck as a housekeeper in Traverse City.

Ed wanted to meet her. When his band took a break, he stepped off the stage, walked over, and surprised Irene by introducing himself. She was shy, yet cordial, and well aware that, except for her friends, she, who was of French-Canadian heritage, was surrounded by young women of Polish descent. Feeling somewhat insecure, she wondered, "Why would he be interested in me, when it's obvious that other gals have their eyes on him?"

Ed was smitten by Irene's wit, charm, and looks as they talked. Before the dance was over, he asked permission to court her. Politely, she agreed.

Irene's French-Canadian roots were no issue for Ed, although he was a third-generation Pole descendant. His Polish community was close-knit in their ethnicity, yet it was she who he wished to court. Ed knew full well his father would disapprove, and the disagreement at home was fierce. His father, Grandpa Thomas, would have much preferred his son find himself a "nice Polish girl."

Ed saw otherwise and remained steadfast in pursuing Irene. He would be the first in his nuclear family to marry at all, much less to cross nationalities in a community where it was not accepted. It was no secret how Grandpa Thomas felt about the relationship, and there was nothing the son could say or do to make a difference.

During the courtship, Ed usually had to walk three miles each way to court Irene because every time he asked permission to drive his father's car, Thomas wouldn't allow it. There were times, though, when Ed tricked his dad and would say that he and Leo wanted to go out and see a couple Polish gals. It was a half-truth, because they did pick up a couple of girls, but then Ed would drive over to see Irene, too, and asked if she'd go for a ride. She went along with him, but years later, would recall how awkward it felt to be sitting alongside the other girls. And why wouldn't she feel that way, understanding as she did why Ed took that risk and where his heart was?

Irene's situation with her parents was different. Even before she met Ed, she had her dad's approval to date outside their nationality. Lugie had told her, "It's okay if you marry someone outside the French line, but he must be of the Catholic faith."

Left: Ed and Irene before their wedding. Right: Irene's delightful birthday card Ed gave her on her twenty-first birthday.

After courting Irene for about a year, Ed asked Lugie for his daughter's hand, and the young couple received her father's blessing to marry. Irene was twenty-one when she accepted Ed's proposal.

Nearly twenty-two, Ed was a man of deep faith and with dreams of his own. He knew it was time to look out for himself and make plans for his future. When his friend, Bill Rosinski from Cedar, suggested that Ed come along with him to Detroit to look for jobs, he considered himself lucky to have that opportunity. The Depression was still going strong, and the offer was easy for Ed to accept. When he told his parents about his plans to leave the farm with Bill, I expect his mother showed her approval, hugged him, and regarded him as a strong, decisive son, while his father might have studied his son's face, grasped hold of his shoulder and said, "*Jestes teraz sam.*" (Translation: "You're on your own now.")

It was bittersweet for Ed to say goodbye to his sweetheart and his mother, father, brothers, and sisters. He was leaving home in pursuit of learning new job skills, to earn a real paycheck, and to prepare for his future with Irene.

The two farm boys headed for the big city of Detroit in the early spring of 1937. Ed didn't own a car, but Bill did, and offered to drive. Off they went! They found a boarding house in Detroit that cost five dollars a week for room and board. Streetcar fare was a "mere" six cents plus a one-cent transfer. Ed soon found work roofing new houses and wallpapering the interiors. Excited to learn a trade outside farming, he saw this as his chance to become his own man and experience independence, a goal which would shape his life.

While Ed was in Detroit, he wrote letters to Irene.

In the meantime, Irene delighted in preparing for her wedding, especially the selection of her gown. To help with wedding expenses, she worked the summer before the wedding doing housework in Leland instead of returning home.

Saturday, September 4, 1937, was a glorious day for a wedding. Irene was dressed beautifully in her white-satin, floor-length wedding gown with its brocade neckline and Juliet sleeves. Her brocade headpiece secured the lengthy nylon tulle veil edged with lace. She carried a beautiful bouquet of white lilies as her parents escorted her to the church.

Ed was decked out in a dark suit, white shirt, and white tie. He and brother Leo walked towards church (a stretch of eight and a half miles) down the road from his parents' home, hoping to hitchhike a ride. Fortunately for them, Frank Mazurek came by and gave them a ride. Ed couldn't borrow his father's car because his father, mother, and other family members needed it ... to go to Ed's wedding!

> Mr. and Mrs. Eugene Lanie
> request the honor of your presence
> at the marriage of their daughter
> Irene Dorothy
> to
> Mr. Edward V. Fleis
> on Saturday morning, the fourth day of September,
> nineteen hundred and thirty-seven
> at eight-thirty o'clock
> Saint Mary Church, Lake Leelanau, Michigan.

Ed and Irene's bridal party. Left to right: Lucille Lamie and Leo Fleis; Agnes Fleis, flower girl; Susan Fleis and Louis Lamie.

Provemont Bridge with St. Mary of the Assumption in the background, circa early 1900s

Ed and Irene exchanged vows as the sacrament of holy matrimony was bestowed on them during a nuptial mass at St. Mary's of the Assumption Church in Lake Leelanau. Reverend Albert A. Kohren, St. Mary's pastor, and Reverend Leo Piaskowski, parish priest from Holy Rosary, co-celebrated the mass, satisfying each cultural community.

Following the ceremony, the newlyweds cherished a horse-driven buggy ride over the old Provemont Bridge at the Lake Leelanau Narrows. Apparently, the ride was so special for my parents that in Dad's letter of reminiscences written late in his life, he mentioned it. Both of my parents talked about that ride and the bridge over the years. That old iron bridge was replaced two years later, in 1939.

A reception and dance followed at the Centerville Township Hall, the same dance hall where Ed and Irene met. Ed remarked in his writing that there was "no electricity, no bathrooms, and no loud music."

After the wedding, Ed still had no car, so the newlyweds hitched a ride back to Detroit with Bill Rosinski for their honeymoon. That trip was exciting for Irene as she had never been to Detroit. After arrival, the newlyweds took several days off for themselves. (A recent photo—of poor quality—revealed that they made the long trip to Niagara Falls, Canada.) Mother said, "We honeymooned first, then looked for jobs."

Ed and Irene honeymooning in Detroit

Jobs were still scarce, so Ed finally found himself two part-time jobs: a sales position and a roofing job, while Irene did housework.

Bill lived with them and lent his car to Ed whenever he and Irene needed to go somewhere. For their part, they treated him as their guest and gave him the one bedroom in the very small house they rented.

Although Bill lived there and helped with expenses, it presented problems. As a newly married woman, Irene wanted her privacy and preferred not to sleep on a sofa bed in the living room. Her only consolation was that Ed assured her it would be for only a short time, and it was. The three left Detroit in the spring of 1938, after living there only six months.

Ed and Irene returned to his parents' home, where his father surprised him with a 1924 Ford Model T coupe. Thomas was proud of the deal he had struck when he got the car. "A lady in Traverse City had this coupe stored in her garage," he told him, "And it was taking up room, so she sold it to me for ten dollars!" Ed was grateful. At the age of twenty-three, he finally had his own wheels.

Left: Ed's first vehicle, a 1924 Ford Model-T coupe. Right: Ed and Irene reuniting with his parents, Thomas and Agnes Fleis.

In addition to the car, Thomas had a place for Ed and Irene to stay. That spring, he had purchased the Harpe Farm, next to Irene's parents on French Road. "[T]he house was empty when we came back from Detroit," Dad wrote decades later.

Though Ed's marriage to Irene may have been a disappointment to his father, he and his father had a bond that was inseparable. It was a year since Ed had left home the first time, and his father missed him. He had depended heavily on his son after suffering a stroke nearly ten years earlier. Ed was the fixer-upper on the farm. Undoubtedly, his father appreciated him, and my dad was grateful for all the things he learned from his father. They had a strong relationship.

Although Ed had gone against his father's will when he married Irene, that is not what defined him as a son. He had the courage and strength to stand up for what he believed was right in his heart and mind. For the first time since their courtship and marriage, Thomas showed kindness to his son and new daughter-in-law, Irene. Although she may have noticed, it would take time for her to accept her father-in-law's ways.

Ed and Irene lived in the Harpe farmhouse briefly, and over the years, would return there, time and again, for temporary housing.

The couple wasted no time looking for jobs. They learned about a job opening in Elk Rapids, and after being interviewed by the Shippeys, they were hired as caretakers of the Shippeys' cottage and property on Elk Lake.

It worked out well. Ed and Irene worked as a team, with Irene on the inside and Ed on the outside. Irene was cook and housekeeper, and Ed did all the janitor work, gardening, and cared for the fruit trees. He also drove the Shippeys' 1926 Dodge pickup truck whenever his duties took him to Traverse City to pick up groceries, supplies, and liquor, which Mr. Shippey especially enjoyed.

Irene considered the time spent with the Shippeys as a second honeymoon. The pair stayed in a small guesthouse on the premises and relished the privacy of having their own place to come home to. They viewed this position as the perfect job for a young couple getting a fresh start in life.

The one sad event during this time was the passing of Ed's Grandma Jozefina (Fleis) on July 23, 1938. Even in the midst of the busy summer, the Shippeys gave Ed and Irene time off to be with his parents and family to attend his grandma's funeral. While they were gone, the newlyweds even managed to stay at the Lamie home for a couple of days, giving them time to visit Irene's parents too.

The job at the Shippeys' lasted from late spring until December, when the Shippey family returned to Chicago. So, Ed and Irene packed their car for the next adventure and bid the little guesthouse farewell. By the time they left, Mom was pregnant. Their first child was due in just a few short months.

My parents often expressed their utmost respect for the Shippeys.

A reunion at the Shippey cottage. It was great meeting Mr. and Mrs. Shippey. (Larry is the baby, circa 1952.)

8

My Early Childhood

I REFER TO MY MOTHER AS "MAMA," AND FATHER AS "DADDY," just as I did when I was a child.

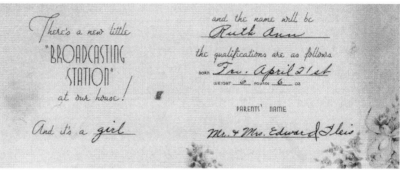

Top: Ruth Ann's birth announcement.
Bottom left: Ed and Irene holding Ruth Ann. Bottom right: Agnes Fleis holding her granddaughter, Ruth Ann, and Jennie Lamie.

After arriving in Traverse City from Elk Rapids, Dad and Mom found a small upstairs apartment to rent located at 530 E. Eighth Street. This became my first home.

My parents would have looked forward to starting their family. I think one of Mama's deepest desires was to become a mother and to nurture and care for her children. Her natural instinct was to sing sweet lullabies and to teach us and help us learn.

On April 21, 1939, when I came into the world, Mama was twenty-three and Daddy was five days short of turning twenty-four. Mama gave birth to me at Munson Hospital in Traverse City. I was their firstborn, a bouncing baby girl they named Ruth Ann.

From the time I was little, Mama spoke of the love she had for her own mother, who had taught her many things about life and whom I called *Memmier (*Grandma Jennie*)*, and her father, *Peppier* (Grandpa Lugie),[50] as they were my French grandparents. I was their fourth grandchild.

I was very little when Daddy taught me to call my Polish grandparents *Busia* (Grandma Agnes) and *Dziadzia* (pronounced "JaJa") (Grandpa Thomas). I was their first grandchild. They became my godparents at my baptism that took place nine days after my birth, on April 30, at St. Francis Church in Traverse City.

Daddy never shied away from his responsibilities as head of the household and provider for his family. In Traverse City, he held multiple jobs in succession, working as a construction laborer at the site of a bowling alley and a huge warehouse. Then he held a temporary position for United Parcel Service (UPS) as a warehouse attendant.

In the fall of 1939, several months after I was born, my parents moved us from Traverse City back to the Harpe farm, next to her parents.

"That winter of 1939 through 1940," Dad wrote, "I worked for the Leelanau County Road Commission, building roads in Northport and Schomberg Road north of Isadore, and Highway M-72, when the bridge passing Morgan Hill was built. I also helped build a root cellar for my dad on his farm," he continued. "The ground dirt was all hand dug. Supporting walls and a ceiling reinforced the inside. This was a large underground storage unit for potatoes and other vegetables."

At the Harpe farm, the only stove Mama had for cooking was a small two-burner kerosene countertop model. Aunt Agnes remembered seeing Mama cook on that stove and wondered how she did it. She had never seen such a small stove. The house had no modern conveniences. I don't know if it even had electricity.

In July of 1940, Mama went into labor for my sister Julie. She signaled Grandma Jennie next door by hanging a single piece of clothing on the outdoor clothesline.

Julie was born at home at the stroke of midnight, with the assistance of a doctor from Suttons Bay. Years

Ruth Ann and Julie (circa 1941)

---

50   *Grand mere, Grand et pere* (correct spelling).

later, Mama told Julie, "Your dad and I had a choice of June 30 or July 1 for your birth date and decided on July 1, because we knew from the start that you would be a firecracker." Ironically, Mama gave her a unique French name, Juliette. She now prefers to be called "Julie."

When the doctor brought baby Julie to Mama, all cleaned and wrapped up, Mama unwrapped the blanket and saw that one of her tiny hands was bandaged. The doctor asked, "Mrs. Fleis, do you notice anything different about your baby daughter?"

Mama answered, "I don't know about the hand that's bandaged, but look at this!" She lifted her baby's other tiny hand. An extra thumb perched out from the knuckle of her normal thumb.

The doctor, who had already surgically removed a double thumb on the bandaged hand, was shocked to see the other one, as he hadn't noticed it before. He decided it was best to leave it alone and wait until after Julie's other thumb healed. There was no rush.

Aunt Theresa, at age nine, helped Mama care for me for about three months that summer. She would chop wood and bring it in, as Daddy was away working quite a bit.

When the United States instituted the Selective Training and Service Act of 1940 in September of that year, it required all men between the ages of twenty-one and forty-five to register for the draft. Those selected from the draft lottery were required to serve at least one year in the armed forces. Dad was drafted but wrote to the Selective Service, requesting that he be deferred due to having a young family. He was relieved to be deferred and never had to serve, although he would soon serve his country in another way.

My brother, Edward, was born at home with the assistance of a local doctor on October 13, 1941. It was quite the blessing for my parents to have a son, and they named him Edward, after Dad, but also because he was born on the feast day of St. Edward!

Ruth Ann next to baby Edward, with Theresa, Agnes, and Tony in front of home on the farm

Shortly after Edward's birth, and facing a cold wintry season ahead, Daddy was out of a job. He needed to find work. He drove his 1924 Model-T Ford and headed back to Detroit with his friend, Bill Rosinski, in search of a job.

On the way downstate, they stopped for lunch and a drink of beer at a noisy bar/restaurant in Cadillac. A bunch of guys were talking loudly amongst themselves. Dad went over and talked to one of them, found out they were carpenters, and asked if they needed more carpenters.

The guy answered, "Yes!"

They were hired on the spot!

Dad and Bill found a room to stay and started working in construction the next day. That same week, Daddy came home early on Friday evening and told Mama about his job and finding a place for us to live, and that he had to be back to work by Monday morning. Mama was happy with the good news. The next day, they packed what little possessions they had. We were on our way to Cadillac on Sunday morning.

Mama held onto baby Edward, all bundled up in his blanket, in the front seat; Julie and I, at ages one and two and a half, were dressed warmly in the backseat as Dad drove the two hours to our new home.

Left: Irene holding baby Edward, and Julie, Ruth Ann, and Ed upon arrival in Cadillac
Right: Bill Rosinski and Ed Fleis

A month later, Dad was asked to be foreman on the job. He was surprised to receive the promotion instead of Bill, who was older than him. He then realized the valuable experience he had just gained working with a crew, particularly in the construction of a round-roofed barn and an airport office in Wexford County. Obviously, Dad's natural abilities in the construction field stood out. Chances were, Bill might have been promoted later while working on another assignment.

With the promotion came a transfer to Boyne City, eighty miles north of Cadillac, so we moved again to be closer to Dad's job. There, he and his crew built a huge office for Cherryland Electric Company. After he finished that job, we moved again for his next assignment.

9

The War Years

ON DECEMBER 7, 1941, Japanese forces attacked Pearl Harbor. The following day, President Franklin Roosevelt declared war. Three of Thomas and Agnes Fleis's sons—Leo, Roman, and Thomas, Jr.—would serve in the military during World War II.

Uncle Leo, the oldest, born in 1913, served in the Army Air Force beginning on March 12, 1942. He was stationed at Morrison Field, Florida; then in Jackson, Mississippi; and finally in Japan.[51]

Uncle Roman, born in 1918, was in the Army Air Corps from 1941–46. He served primarily in New Guinea and Japan, working on airplane instruments. He became a doctor of horology—clocks and watches—and was promoted to sergeant.

Uncle Tom (Thomas Jr.) was born in 1922. He reported to Fort Custer, Michigan, on January 8, 1943, for basic training and became an army cook in Europe and Africa.

"As a family, we prayed daily for the war to end and a safe return for everyone's sons and brothers," Aunt Theresa commented. "My mother [Grandma Agnes] sat down and wrote a letter to each of her boys every Sunday."

Meanwhile, Dad was notified by the government to build something completely different in Alpena and Oscoda, on the east side of Michigan. My brother Jim recalls Dad's story.

> During World War II, while many of Dad's brothers were off to war, what was he doing? He was a foreman and traveled between two air bases, Oscoda and Alpena. The work he was doing was building bomb shelters. He had about fifteen men at each base, and it was his job to float between the two bases and oversee the projects.
>
> At one of his inspections in Alpena, a stranger pulled up to the site [and] asked to find out who was in charge. Dad said he was and wanted to know what he was up to. The man informed

---

51   Uncle Leo Fleis Obituary. Fleis descendants, compiled by Linda (Fleis) Schulte.

him that he was [a] salesman, and that he had this new "electric saw" (now known as a Skil saw) and wondered if Dad was interested in checking it out.

Dad said, "Okay."

So, the man asked Dad to set up a couple of sawhorses and put some two-by-fours on them for the demonstration. Back then, these electric saws weighed in at about forty pounds.

So, all was set. The man gets up there, makes his mark on the two-by-four, and proceed[s] to start the saw and begin his cut.

He only made one mistake. He forgot to pull his hand away and proceeded to cut off four of his fingers.

Dad looked at what happened, and, while the guy was bleeding [and in] pain, said, "I don't want one of those damn things."

* * *

Holy Rosary High School offered twelve grades by the school year 1941–42. Clemence (Clem), three years younger than Al, received a high school diploma in 1942, the first of his family to graduate from there. The younger siblings followed. Irene graduated in 1943, and later, Theresa in 1947, Agnes in 1950, and Anthony in 1954. Joseph, who was older than Theresa, never attended high school. When his older brothers left home, he was held back by his father to help his brother, Clem, on the farm. It was a huge disappointment for Joseph.

Also, a few months after Aunt Irene's graduation, she enrolled at Madonna Academy, Livonia, in her pursuit to become a Felician nun, just as her four aunts from the previous generation did.

Like so many organizations, Holy Rosary School was deeply involved in the war effort, as the booklet of the school's centennial—1898–1998, stated:

During the war years (1942–45), the students at Holy Rosary School had sold $5,500 worth of bonds, $800 worth in stamps, collected 24,000 pounds of scrap iron, 10,000 pounds of scrap paper, and sent almost 400 articles to the Red Cross. This work rated them highest in the war effort in Leelanau County and merited two certificates for distinguished service. In order to buy meat or gas or any other necessity, families applied for stamps. This was known as rationing. Anything made of nylon or rubber was very rare because these materials were used for the war.

When Dad's job in Alpena ended in the spring of 1943, he and Mom decided to move back to Traverse City. We lived in a rental home on Second Street, several blocks from where he was working on the construction of the (former) Traverse City Osteopathic Hospital along Grand Traverse Bay, currently the Elks Lodge. Our home was across and down the street from Busia's brother, Great Uncle Adam, and his wife, Great Aunt Bernice Pleva. Their daughter, Lorraine, a first cousin once removed, became my best childhood friend.

Lorraine and I would spend hours together playing outdoors at her home or mine when the weather was nice. In a recent conversation, Lorraine recalled, "One time, you and I got in real trouble after we sneaked a few matches from the house and started striking them on the sidewalk. A good scolding cured us from ever doing that again!"

* * *

A couple telegrams from Ed's military brother, Roman, were received in 1943.

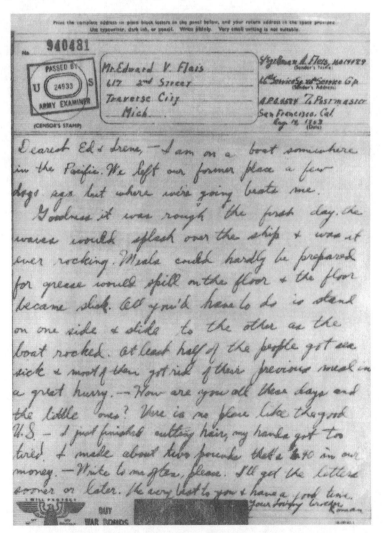

No58897

PASSED BY

24933

ARMY EXAMINER

[CENSOR STAMP]

To

Mr. Edward V. Fleis

617 2nd Street

Traverse City, Mich.

From

S. Sg. 7 Roman A. Fleis 16014489

66th Service Sq, 80th Service G.P.

A.P.O. 4584 c/o Postmaster

San Francisco, Cal.

July 15, 1943

Hello Ed and Irene,

Well, how are you? I'm fine. In fact, where I am stationed in Australia it's a pretty good place. We live in floorless tents and goodness is it ever cold in the mornings being that it's practically in the middle of winter here. We eat out in the open. Today at supper time it rained and ate a little faster than usual. There certainly are few cars around here and gas is very hard to get. People speak a lot different and sometimes I have a hard time to understand them. Autos drive on the left-hand side and sit on the right. I have a heck of a time watching the cars crossing the street. People also eat with their left and have some different costumes. Are you all in tip top shape including the children? How is little Junior getting along? The best to you Edward and Irene…till we meet again – Bye. Your loving brother, Roman

The next rental home we lived in was on Webster Street, near where Dad worked construction at the Traverse City Airport office building and for the Traverse City State Hospital. Jim recalls another story from Dad:

Dad was called to inspect the roof of the State Hospital building. Made out of slate tiles, it was suspected that some of the tiles were loose or missing.

Dad cobbled up ladders to make the three-story ascent. As he walked back and forth on the roof, one of the tiles broke away, and he went down and started to slide with his head facing the top of the roof. Though his full body on the roof slowed down the slide, he couldn't stop and felt sure he was a goner, with no chance to survive such a fall.

He said by some miracle, as he slid to the edge of the roof, expecting to fall to his death, the hard soles of his shoes landed firmly on the first rung of the ladder and saved him from a fall to the ground.

Mama had her own treadle sewing machine and loved to sew and make clothing for us. One time, Busia gave Mama a long, dark-navy-blue woolen coat that she no longer wore. Delighted with the gift, she decided to make matching coats for Julie and me. It was a long process to disassemble the coat and remove all the stitching. Mama washed the individual pieces by hand and laid them flat on a covered surface to dry. Next, she draped a wet cloth over each piece of fabric and pressed it dry with a hot iron. Then she cut new pieces. If the outside of the fabric was visibly worn, she flipped it over and used the opposite side to cut out the pattern. The inside of the fabric would become the outside for a new garment. Finally, she stitched the pieces together.

When we wore our matching navy coats, Dziadzia took notice of the quality of Mama's work. He would show off the beautiful coats to others. Mama appreciated his kindness and felt somewhat relieved that her father-in-law had finally warmed up to her.

Left: Julie and Ruth Ann wearing matching coats Irene sewed, next to baby brother, Edward (circa 1942). Right: Irene dressed in her wedding gown, with Ruth Ann and Julie as flower girls.

Sometimes, Julie and I would play dress-up with Mama's old dressy clothes and high-heeled shoes. One time, Mama decided to play dress-up, too! She dressed as a bride again and had us dress up as flower girls, wearing our Sunday-best clothes. Mama was beautiful in her long, white-satin wedding gown, with her dainty white veil crowning her long, brunette hair. She even made a fresh bouquet of flowers for herself, picked from the yard, and gave us each a single flower to carry. When I think of it, the only time Mama ever did this was captured in a photo by Daddy, as we were still all dressed up when he came home.

My parents considered making Traverse City a permanent place to live when they purchased their first home on Grant Street shortly after the birth of my baby sister, Mary Jane, on November 2, 1943. She was the first blue-eyed blonde in the family, and relatives on the Fleis side fussed over her, as she seemed to bear a strong resemblance to some Polish relatives.

After Mary Jane's birth, Mama was glad to receive help from her seventeen-year-old cousin, Betty Lamie, who helped to care for the four of us young children and helped with daily work duties.

Even though Mama or Betty would come with us when we played in the backyard, there was much concern for our safety, especially for little Edward, who was quick to walk and run, because a railroad train traveled less than two blocks from home.

Edward, Irene, Ruth Ann, and young Mary Jane

Mama wouldn't take any chances and made a special harness for him to wear. Every time he was allowed to play with us, Mama draped it over his shoulders, down to his waist, and anchored it by a rope to a tree, giving him room to move around and play.

Julie was three when she had surgery on the hand that still had a double thumb. After she got it caught in the oven door as it shut one day, tears were enough to convince Mama to arrange the surgery.

* * *

In 1944, Memmier and Peppier sold their farm to their son, Louis, and his wife, Pauline (Harrand). They stayed with their son and daughter-in-law for a couple months until they moved to the Detroit area to live with another son, Ben, and his wife, Agnes (Novak). Agnes was in need of care, so my grandparents stayed with them a while to help.

On April 26, 1944, Mama was planning a party to celebrate Daddy's twenty-ninth birthday. Busia and Dziadzia "would be

Jennie and Lugie Lamie in the mid-'40s

there, but only after Busia insisted that she finish painting the dining room baseboard trim white," Aunt Theresa said. "Their kitchen and dining room had recently been painted, and we finally had running water in the house.

"Upon returning home from the party, Busia suddenly started crying and said, 'I can't see!' She was blind. Dziadzia was in a panic and rushed to get the local doctor, who came and examined her. Her blood pressure had skyrocketed. She was diagnosed as having uremic poisoning (possibly caused from the lead paint). She was now bedridden but still alert."

As children, we got to go visit Busia. We were her only grandchildren. Upon our arrival, she would say, "Give me the baby," and hold baby Mary Jane close to her as she lay in bed.

Two weeks later, Busia was hospitalized at Munson Hospital. Dad wrote in his memoir, "I was working at the hospital doing repairs and requested to work near my mother so I could watch over her. I was glad they honored my request. My brother Leo came home on emergency leave from the military, so we took turns being near her bedside."

The youngest in the family, Tony, made his First Holy Communion while his mother was in the hospital. He was still wearing his dark suit when the family visited, and was lifted up from an outside window so he could see his mother. Busia died on May 24, 1944, at forty-nine years of age.

From left: Joe, Thomas, Agnes, Susan, Theresa, Tony, and young Agnes Fleis

Besides Leo, Thomas was also granted military leave for his mother's funeral. Roman, on the other hand, was denied bereavement leave. Aunt Theresa said, "Roman was grief stricken. He dreamt about our mother; she was coming toward him, and then faded away."

I was five years old and at my first funeral. It was sad for me, but I wasn't afraid to be near her. She was my Busia and godmother, and I loved her so much. The house was full to overflowing at Busia's wake. I saw neighbors and relatives kneeling on the grass in the front yard, praying the rosary while the rosary was being said inside the house.

Aunt Agnes continues with memories... She was only ten when her mother died.

Our house was big, with a large living room. We had a piano, and large pictures on the wall of the Blessed Mother and Sacred Heart of Jesus. A large dining room table could seat about ten. The kitchen was narrow. Our wood stove had to be fired up even in summertime to cook meals on and for canning.

Our mother must have baked bread several times a week. Beneath the upper cupboards … was a long, table-high "breadboard" on which we put several loaves of fresh bread to cool.

We had a tall tank by the stove that would get heated, and then we had hot water. I remember a square box of little chicks that actually came in the mail and was placed beneath the open space by the stove for them to keep warm, before they were transferred to the big chicken coop. The first time I picked some eggs, I learned a lesson: not to put them in my pocket, because at least one busted in there.

We had piezynas (feather quilts) to keep warm. We didn't have storm windows, and there was snow on the windowsill. I remember once there was a feather bee at our house; the ladies were at the big dining room table, and feathers were flying.

I recall the last gift I received from Busia—my first pair of brown knee socks that came up just below the knees. Wearing long, brown stockings held up by garters was popular then! When I told Aunt Agnes about my special gift, she said, "I remember getting a pair of knee socks, too!"

It was a sad time for everyone. Her death was a hardship on the family. A kind and merciful woman, she was a devoted wife and mother. One of the things Busia always did was write weekly letters to her sons in the military. According to Aunt Theresa, "It was now up to her daughters to take up the task."

Aunt Theresa noted the effect her mother's death had on the family:

> Her death at age forty-nine left us in shock and that year our country was still at war. Leo, Roman, and Thomas were in the service. Albion had a position as an accountant in Detroit, where he met the love of his life, Phyllis Richard. Sister Therese was in the convent. Susie, the eldest of the girls, was in poor health since her childhood; she had asthma and numerous allergies, so could not stay on the farm. She stayed in Florida for a while when Roman was stationed there. Ed was married to [our] wonderful sister-in-law Irene, busy raising a family.

After the funeral, the older siblings began to trickle away. The two boys, Leo and Tom, went back to their posts in the service. Others returned to the lives they had built in new places. That left Dziadzia with five of his children still in the house: Clem (twenty), Joe (seventeen), Theresa (fourteen), Agnes (ten), and Tony (eight). Clem stayed another seven months before entering the service.

Left: Susan, Agnes, Thomas, and Theresa Fleis.
Right: Joe, Albion, Clem, and Tony Fleis.

It didn't take long for it to dawn on Theresa that she was now the oldest female in the household, and what that meant. She recalls:

> A few days passed. Soon, I found myself almost alone. Realizing most of the responsibility fell on my shoulders, there was no one to prepare me for the days to come, to prepare meals, laundry, housekeeping, learning how to milk a cow, chores, and helping out in the fields.

Here I was, fourteen, just starting my teenage years, starting high school in the fall ... I studied on the bus or late into the night. I learned to make bread from Aunt Mary Brzezinski. She came over one day and showed me how.

There were days I prayed and cried a bucket of tears, wondering if it ever would become easier, though I always felt Mom's spirit beside me, holding my hand, giving me courage and stamina to carry on.

Aunt Theresa's father, Thomas, wanted her to quit school. One day she said to him, "If Mama were alive, she would want me to finish school." Four years later, she graduated "and life somehow became a little easier. I was thinking, 'I have accomplished much.'"

In the meantime, though, life was hard for everyone left on the farm.

Thomas had all he could do to stay alive after his wife's death. That fall, he, too, became sickly. "Dad was truly lost without Mom [and] lived with a broken heart," Theresa wrote. "He acted as if life was not worth living."

"Dad, you gotta get well," she told him. "We just lost Mama." He never stopped caring for them. In fact, thinking he might die, Theresa wrote, "He even had a will drawn up so that your parents, Ed and Irene, would take care of us."

Fourth Son Joined Military

Thomas couldn't handle the farming. That left Clem and Joe to work the farm, but Clem reported for duty in the military service on January 18, 1945, two and a half years after graduating from high school. He became the fourth son serving the military during World War II, and was stationed for a time at Ft. Sheridan, Illinois.

The only one left to farm was Uncle Joe, and he couldn't do it alone. Dziadzia needed help. And so, eight months after the death of Busia, a grieving Dziadzia reached out to my dad with a plea for help. He asked Dad to supervise farming the 120-acre O'Brien farm on French Road next to Centerville Township Hall.

Wanting my parents to live closer to him, he said, "I have a place for you to stay."

10

Making Do at the O'Brien Farm

IT WAS A MISERABLE, STORMY DAY in late January of 1945 when we left Traverse City. I remember looking out the backseat window, watching heavy snowflakes coming down as Dad drove the country roads, heading north to Cedar, all the comforts of a modern, city home left behind. My parents were about to settle us into a two-story farmhouse that my dad had wired for electricity only days before.

I was feeling sad, thinking about having to give up kindergarten at Oak Park Elementary School, when I was only halfway through. I was five years old, just three months from turning six.

Coming up the long driveway, I saw the farmhouse with its worn, blackened siding that had never seen a coat of paint. It was the same with the barn, the silo, the shed, and the two-hole outhouse. Clotheslines sagged from old posts and everywhere layers of snow covered the open fields.

It was dreary walking inside. The first room was a utility room with a water pump installed on the floor to the right of the entrance door that we soon discovered could make a racket at times. We opened the next door and stepped into the kitchen. Light filtered from two tall windows covered with worn, sheer curtains hung on rods. Freestanding cupboards for storing dishes, kettles, and the like lined one wall. There was no kitchen sink. The interior walls were plain, with no color to speak of,

Old shed on the O'Brien farm that Thomas Fleis owned back in the 1940s.

80

the woodwork dark. But it was a clean house, and it was warm. A floor fuel heater in the corner of the dining room put out plenty of heat.

Mama had no extra help and depended on Julie and me to do small jobs like sweeping the floor or "keeping an eye on the little ones," referring to young Edward and Mary Jane at the time.

"We'll make do," became her favorite saying. Everything there seemed normal, even if it wasn't. We had warm blankets for sleeping and Mama's home cooking on a wood-burning iron stove.

Mama washed dishes in a round, white-enameled pan set on the kitchen table, then rinsed them in another pan with clean, warm water. My chore, along with my sister, was to wipe the dishes. We took turns standing on a chair to reach the dishes in the rinse pan.

There was no running water or flushing toilet. We obtained water from a small room adjacent to the kitchen. First, you set your bucket on a basin and placed it under a large iron spout on the side of an iron water pump, which had a side pumping-handle. You steadily pumped the handle to draw enough water from the well to fill the bucket.

When we needed hot water for doing dishes and cleaning up, we would dip into a reservoir we kept filled with water located on the side of the wood stove. The heat from the stove heated the water.

Julie was four when we moved to the O'Brien farm on French Road. She still remembers our lack of plumbing. "We had to go to an outside john, summer or winter. For nighttime, we had a covered pot. … Our Saturday baths were taken in a large, galvanized tub in the middle of the kitchen floor. All the water had to be heated on the stove. We took our baths by age; the youngest children bathed first."

After Mama washed our hair, she would rinse it with plain water, then give another rinse with rainwater. Whenever it rained, she set a bucket outdoors under the roof to collect it.

Usually on Mondays, Mama washed clothes. Starting the day early, Daddy may have helped pump all the water, a bucket at a time, and then dumped it into the two large boiler kettles on the stove. When the water was hot enough, Mama used a large metal dipper to transfer it to a bucket, then dumped the hot water into the wringer washing machine. Then she filled two round galvanized-steel tubs that sat on a wooden contraption alongside the washing machine with buckets of cold water: one tub for the first rinse, with a faint amount of bleach; the other for a second rinse, with a few drops of bluing, which helped make white clothes whiter. By the time the dark clothes were added, the bleach and bluing had no effect.

The washing machine had an agitator that washed the clothes. The wringer was adjustable and had two rubber rollers that moved constantly, wringing out excess water from washed clothing she placed carefully between the moving rollers. A twist of a knob turned the wringer on or off.

Then she dropped the wrung-out clothing into the first rinsing tub, and so on. The process was repeated over and over. Mama was always careful and would not allow me to help her, afraid my hand would get caught in the wringer. She never wanted the young children near her when she washed clothes.

Clothes were hung outdoors on clotheslines to dry. During the winter months, they came off the lines stiff as a board. Sometimes, lines were strung in the unheated utility room where Mama washed clothes.

We didn't have many clothes. There were two small dressers in the whole house for storing folded clothing. My upstairs bedroom had metal hooks on the wall where I hung my clothes. When I needed fresh clothes to wear, I asked Mama for them.

In the warmer months, when clothes dried well on the lines, bed sheets were changed weekly. There was no linen closet for towels and washcloths. I don't know where Mama kept them, but we had one big closet off the kitchen that held a lot of stuff, including coats and boots.

Initially, Dziadzia expected Daddy's supervision and help on the farm. There was no farming during the winter months; only cattle to take care of. As far as I know, his brother, Uncle Joe, handled that job. Daddy was busy every day. He would go see and help Dziadzia or be working a side job. He was used to skilled labor and earning a paycheck to support his family. There was no money in farming. Dziadzia understood. I think more than anything, his father needed us living closer to him for support, following Busia's death.

When spring arrived, Dad had a job working for Cherryland Electric. Among other things, he installed a lot of electrical wiring for many farmers. He didn't need to be licensed and had learned the trade from his father as a young man.

Dad did help out on the farm too, but it was Uncle Joe, age seventeen, who did the bulk of it.

Whenever Uncle Joe stopped by our house before going to the fields, he would ask for my brother, Edward Jr., who was sometimes taking a nap. "Where is Eddie?" he would say. He took a liking to his young nephew, and Edward became his little buddy.

When Edward was between the ages of four and five and was allowed by Mama to go to the fields with Uncle Joe, he sat on his lap while Uncle Joe drove the tractor, cultivating the fields. Little did my brother realize he would be taking over Uncle Joe's job in a few years.

One great thing about moving back to Leelanau County was that Dad was able to get together with his former band members. Most recently, the cherished violin his father, Thomas, played that originally belonged to his great-grandfather, Tomasz, was passed down to him. He was now thirty and had missed playing violin with fellow musicians Uncle Steve Pleva and Stanley Mikowski. The trio reminisced, and the makeshift band reunited without missing a beat. They called themselves The Isadore Sodbusters.

Ed Fleis on violin and Steve Pleva playing concertina at Centerville Township Hall. (photo from Eunice Novak)

"We played for lots of weddings and parties nearly every week," Dad wrote.

How appreciated were the sounds as Dad bowed the strings of his grandfather's violin, along with the ancient sound of Uncle Steve's boisterous concertina. When Stanley played the concertina, multitalented Uncle Steve banged out rhythm chords on an old, out-of-tune, upright piano whenever one was available. Though the band had no microphone, they still sang many memorable tunes.

Whenever Dziadzia had a party at his built-in dance hall at the Fleis homestead, Dad and his band played the music. They sat on old wooden chairs on the built-in corner stage on which stood an old upright piano that Busia had played years before. The large, unvarnished dance floor and long, narrow, built-in wooden benches that lined both sides of plain wood walls would fill with guests.

Parties were held only on fair-weather days, as no heat source was available. Those occasions were special, a welcome break from the harshness of farm life, and everyone wore their Sunday best—the women in dresses, nylon hose, and heels, while the men wore suits, usually with white shirts and ties.

Whenever I was allowed to attend as a child, I wore my fancy best too! I recall some of the music The Isadore Sodbusters played—a nice variety of waltzes, polkas, *shadishes* ("one-two-three, hop, one-two-three, hop, hop-hop-hop"), square dances (four couples to a square, the moves called out loudly by Uncle Steve or Dad), and Polish folk dances.

On one of the latter, the couples faced one another, bowing frontwards, then backwards; then they shook their index fingers at each other (like scolding) and twirled round and round. In another popular folk dance, a couple faced one another, stomped their feet, clapped their hands, and danced together—repeated again and again until the music stopped. A few of us older children danced in the old dance hall and later taught our younger siblings some of these old-time Polish dances. Many a good time was had in Dziadzia's dance hall.

Another welcome break for all of us was the celebration of Uncle Leo's marriage to Elizabeth (Betty) Lamie when he was home on leave. The wedding took place on March 6, 1945, at St. Mary's Church in Lake Leelanau. Afterward, he returned to the service for another year.

Meanwhile, Grandpa Thomas was concerned. A letter had arrived at home notifying his youngest son, Joe, of his classification for military service. So, Grandpa wrote a letter to the Selective Service.

June 6, 1945
Selective Service
Local Board 401
Suttons Bay, Michigan

My son, Joseph S. Fleis received his classification on the 6th of June. I would like to have him deferred.

I kindly ask the board to give my appeal consideration.
I would like to present my case personally before the board,
and would like to have you notify me when this would be
convenient to the members of the board.

Yours Truly,
Thomas Fleis

This letter was found buried in a box of Uncle Joe's papers in 2019. His daughter Donna was surprised to find it and didn't know the details. Uncle Joe never explained the situation. He was deferred, so there must have been a hearing. Whether Grandpa consulted with him, we do not know. Eventually, Uncle Joe did enlist on his own.

On September 2, 1945, Aunt Agnes remembered, "We were all sitting at the supper table when our floor-model radio was turned on in the dining room. We heard the news about the end of World War II, and we all cheered!"

Soon afterwards, I was excited to start first grade at Holy Rosary School. Approximately thirty students were in the classroom, in grades one through three. Some students were from a public-school area that closed for lack of students. No cross hung on the wall, but the shadow of it was visible. Students studying religion were taught one half hour before the public-school children arrived. Regular classes began after a bell rang in the hallway. Everyone stood up and recited the Pledge of Allegiance, led by our teacher, Sister Mary Adolphine, who taught all three grades. Combined grades in the entire school, from one through twelve, were at least a hundred students. Every month, a county school inspector, Mr. Dumbrille, stopped by and did an inspection.

I loved everything about school, from learning about my faith, to reading, cursive writing, and some Polish and music. In a musical skit presented to our parents, I played the part of Sally Sue, and a cute boy, Roger, was Billy Joe. We sang the duet, "I'm Goin' to Tell My Ma on You" with motions ... of me scolding him for pickin' on me, and him accusing me of pokin' fun at him. It was hilarious!

The following year, the parish resumed being a regular parochial school.

Side Note:

A Holy Rosary booklet stated: "As early as 1933, after a public school, 'north of the parish' closed, due to having only eight children, the parish and public school consolidated with approval. Both sectors benefited until the public sector placed newer restrictions on removal of crucifixes and the study of religion in school."

In second grade, on May 11, 1947, I received my First Holy Communion from Reverend John Klonowski. Our prayers were recited in Polish, in keeping with the custom at church, besides learning them in English.

Sister Mary Adolphine was my teacher for all three grades.

Holy Rosary's red-and-white school bus took me to and brought me home from school. After walking the long driveway, I was so glad to be home with Mama and my younger siblings.

Mama was my first teacher. She organized simple activities for playing and learning. She depended on Julie and me to sit on chairs by a small table and help our younger siblings, Edward and Mary Jane, draw and color numbers or letters of the alphabet on plain-paper tablets. Mama would say, "It was easy for my younger children to learn from my older children." She never took credit for her own creative ways of teaching us and helping us learn.

11

Tidbits of Life on the O'Brien Farm

Edward, Ruth Ann, Julie, Mary
Jane, and Ted on Ruth Ann's First
Communion day (circa 1947).
Notice the rag curls in Julie's hair.

WITH EVERY NEW BIRTH, my parents counted their blessings. My brother Theodore (Ted) was born on November 27, 1945. When my parents brought him home from the hospital, each one of us were eager to hold him. I was the first who had permission; then the younger ones took their turns. From time to time, when Mama was busy, I was able to help by holding my baby brother for a while on the sofa in the dining room. My younger siblings would crawl up and sit close by us. I was six-and-a-half years old and felt grown up, being the oldest and given this privilege.

The following year, on February 2, the day of Mama's thirtieth birthday, Julie and I came up with the idea to make her a birthday cake while she was napping with the younger children. We looked inside her recipe book and decided to make an angel food cake after looking inside the refrigerator and seeing there were enough eggs for the number of egg whites the recipe called for. When we came upon the ingredient cream of tartar, we thought it simply meant plain cream, so that is what we used. The cake went inside the wood-stove oven, and we hoped it would be baked by the time Mama woke up from her nap.

When Mama woke up, she could smell something cooking and opened the oven door. Was she ever surprised when she pulled out the angel food cake! It was flat and hard as a rock. Surprisingly, we were not scolded. Julie and I learned a lesson that day in baking and understanding ingredients.

There was a special room in our home called the parlor. Just off the dining room, it was seldom used and never heated during the cold months. Enclosed by a French glass-encased door, it was the prettiest room of the house. A nice, big front window, embellished with tiny squares of colored glass, overlooked the front yard and driveway. The Victorian furniture, though pretty to look at, was impractical for young children.

One time, we had very special guests in this room. Dziadzia surprised us when he brought over his four sisters for a visit (our great-aunts): Sisters Augustine, Damascene, Leontine, and Faber Rose. All were Felician nuns. It was the only time all four visited us at the same time. Oh, the excitement and joy of the day! We were blessed by their presence, during a season when fields were ripened with golden grain.

Music began for Julie and me when I received a colorful, metal xylophone from my parents when I turned seven. Once I got that toy, we were inseparable. When I learned a new song to play, I taught it to Julie. Some of the songs were "Row, Row, Row Your Boat," "Mary Had a Little Lamb," "Twinkle, Twinkle, Little Star," and "Home Sweet Home."

Dad showed up one day with a pump organ, and he and another man moved it into the parlor for a place to store it. Julie and I would sneak inside this cold room, and I would perch up on the bench and pull out a few buttons above the keyboard. She worked the two-foot pedals with both of her hands at first, and later with her feet, because mine couldn't reach the pedals.

It took a while for us to figure out this instrument. If Julie pumped both pedals and held open one of the side wings for the air to go through, I could play the keyboard with my right hand and push out the other wing. That worked, and we made music as I played one note at a time on the keyboard. "Home, Sweet Home" was the first song I learned to play on it, and I could not have done it without Julie's help.

Mama would hear us making quite the racket and never complained. I think our music entertained the younger children as well. My brother Edward later said, "I remember hearing you and Julie playing music in that room."

Then, there was the old record player, called a Victrola. It sat on a ledge at the top of the stairs out of sight, keeping us kids from messing with it. Whenever my parents announced they wanted to play records, some of us kids tagged along to watch and listen.

The Victrola required no electricity. Instead, after a needle arm was placed at the edge of the record, a handle along the side of the mahogany cabinet was cranked continuously, creating movement for the record to spin around and around a spindle in the center of the turntable, and play the music. Daddy and Mama loved the music of Strauss waltzes. Their sparkling eyes and how they looked at each other revealed that they surely wanted to dance.

Daddy usually didn't go off on his own, unless it was work related or to see Dziadzia. But, this one time, Mama was a bit mischievous when he wasn't home at the time she thought he would be. It was still light outside when some of his guy friends had stopped in, and they all left together to go to the tavern for a drink. As far as Mama was concerned, he had been gone long enough, so she decided to make it fun. She had all of us hide inside the parlor, dressed in our pajamas, with blankets to warm us.

"Be real quiet so Daddy doesn't hear you when he gets home," she told us. Then she went outside and moved Dad's car behind the barn so he couldn't see it. When she came back inside, she turned off all the lights. We were awake the whole time.

When Daddy finally got home, he turned the dining room light on and walked straight to the bedrooms. There was no Mama in her bed and no children in their beds. And I'm sure he wondered why his car wasn't parked in the yard.

"Where is everybody?" he called from the dining room. I think he was one worried dad.

We opened the parlor door and rushed out yelling, "Surprise!" and wrapped our arms around him.

Mama called it a prank. Did it teach Daddy a lesson? For a while. ...

Daddy enjoyed his drinks. We had a tall cupboard in the dining room, and every now and then, I would see Daddy take a swig from a bottle. One day I was curious, and when no one was looking, I went up to that cupboard, reached on my tippy toes, took the bottle down, and took a little swig. It was awful. It cured me from ever trying that again.

One night when a thunder and lightning storm came crashing down, I became frightened all alone in my upstairs bedroom. I made my way down the stairs, planning to awake my parents but didn't have to, as Mama was standing alone in the kitchen. She was as scared as I was. She wrapped her arms around me tenderly. Daddy and my younger siblings were asleep the whole time.

She went to look for a candle and some matches; then she remembered the blessed palm she had received on Palm Sunday at church. She lit the candle and placed the palm on a shallow metal dish and lit one end of it.

"Let's say a little prayer," she said, and we did.

We stayed a while until the palm was all burnt and blew out the candle. I wasn't scared anymore. We then returned quietly back to our beds.

When we were old enough to learn how to pray, we knelt down in front of Mama's knees as she sat on a chair. She taught us how to make the sign of the cross and pray a simple prayer, "God bless Mama, Daddy, brothers, sisters, Busia, Dziadzia, Memmier, and Peppier," and so on. Then we'd pray for a person in need.

One time, when Aunt Agnes was babysitting us, we told her that we needed to say our night prayers. We were in our pajamas and knelt down in front of her and said our usual prayer, adding the name Aunt Kedsie, who had recently died. We had difficulty pronouncing her name, and not hearing us correctly, Aunt Agnes exclaimed, "AUNT CABBAGE?!?"

It was hysterical!

* * *

When my uncles returned home after the war, they didn't stick around for long. Uncle Tommy, honorably discharged on December 5, 1945,[52] moved to Wisconsin and got a job in Milwaukee, where he fell in love. Fourteen months later, on February 15, 1947, at St. Stanislaus Church in Milwaukee, he married Elizabeth (Betty) Equitz.

Uncle Leo received his honorable discharge at Fort Sheridan, Illinois, on February 18, 1946.[53] He and his newlywed wife, Aunt Betty (Lamie), made their home in Traverse City, where he found a job working for the Grand Traverse Metal Casket Company.

Uncle Roman, upon his discharge, married Virginia Radomski on July 3, 1946, at St. Josaphat Basilica, also in Milwaukee. Having earned his degree in horology in the service, he opened a business that same year, called Roman's Watch Hospital, and later renamed it Roman's Jewelers.

Uncle Clem met the love of his life at his brother Roman's wedding—the bride's sister! He married Roman's sister-in-law, RoseMarie Radomski, sixteen months later, on November 27,

---

52   Uncle Tom earned the Victory Medal, the American Theater Ribbon, the European African Middle Eastern Theater Ribbon with three bronze battle stars, one overseas ice stripe, and a Good Conduct Medal (per his military discharge document).

53   Uncle Leo received the Victory Medal, the American Theater Ribbon, an overseas service bar, a service stripe, a Good Conduct Medal, and an Asiatic Pacific Theater Ribbon. Fleis descendants compiled by Linda (Fleis) Schulte.

1947, at St. Josaphat Basilica in Milwaukee. He was honorably discharged from the US Army on October 24, 1953, then joined the Army Reserves, where he earned a watchmaker's license and worked for his brother at Roman's Jewelers.

In 1947, two years after we moved to the O'Brien farm, Dad began working for himself. In Mom's writings, she said, "Starting with little jobs, like building cupboards, Ed gradually worked his way to larger construction projects, until he eventually had people working for him." Dad became a general contractor that same year. From the start, he was fair, square, trusted, reliable, and known for minimal waste of materials. He had a mathematical mind and was sharp with numbers. He saved costs for his customers.

In his letter, Dad wrote: "My first building job was a garage for Uncle Steve Pleva. Then I did upgrades at Holy Rosary School—a new basement entrance, the first inside bathrooms, new stairways, and a front entrance."

Jim retells another story from Dad:

One time when Holy Rosary Church was hit by lightning, the pastor, Rev. John Klonowski, asked Dad to check it out. They didn't have the equipment then that they do today, so he had to put ladders together and slowly guided himself to the top, inspecting everything as he went.

Dad finally reached the belfry tower, and everything looked good. He couldn't see any damage. Then he got to the top, where the cross lies in the center. Again, everything looked good. Dad hugged the cross for balance and caught his breath.

For some unknown reason, he decided to see how solidly the cross was fixed to the roof. Sitting up as straight as he could, Dad grabbed the cross. When he pulled it upward, it came right out of its socket. Caught off guard, the fraction of a second he held onto it seemed like an eternity before he thrust it downward and luckily got it back into its hole. Otherwise, Dad knew he would have carried it to the ground.

* * *

When my brother Jim was born on June 21, 1947, our parents evened up the score with three girls and three boys. Jim and his brother, Ted, grew up together like twins, and Mama often dressed them alike. Ironically, one set of matching, patriotic outfits she made for them were sailor uniforms.

Mama held down the home front while Daddy provided for the family. We children were comfortable with what we had and with what we didn't have. Sunday clothes were special. They were always waiting and ready for us to put on for church and for visiting relatives. When Mama decided I needed a new dress, she sewed one and did the same for all her children when they needed new clothes. As for shoes, they were passed on if they were in good condition.

* * *

Living close to Memmier, Peppier, and Dziadzia made it easy for Mama and Daddy to take us along and visit them, especially on a Sunday afternoon. They were a very important part of our lives.

Ed and Irene Fleis family photo, from left: Ruth Ann, Mary Jane, Jim, Bernadette, Julie, Ted, and Edward

However, we didn't visit my mother's parents as often as Mama would have loved to. When we did, we always heard Peppier's jolly voice welcome us as we entered. He would be in a small room off the back of the house where he stored his home brew. This is where the men would gather for a drink and enjoy Peppier's wit and wisdom while their wives were in the dining room, where Memmier was sitting in her rocking chair, usually working with a small needle project.

Memmier was delighted to see us. She greeted Mom with a French saying: "*Comme ça va?*" (meaning, "How are you?"). Mom answered, "*Oui,*" (yes). Memmier fussed over her grandchildren. She made it a point to reach out her hand and touch each one of us. Whatever any of us had to say had her full attention. I saw how endearing it was for Mama and her mother to be together, and the strong love they had for each other.

We children would then go outside, weather permitting, and play games as well as enjoy some fun with their nice, friendly dog. It was customary then that Memmier would serve a simple, tasty meal in the afternoon.

At Dziadzia's home, it took a while for everyone to get past the sadness of Busia's death. It seemed like my Aunt Theresa had way too much to do. She would go from washing the cream separator parts to another task in the kitchen. Aunt Agnes gave her some help. Uncle Joe was usually busy with chores. Uncle Tony spent a good amount of time outdoors. I recall going there to visit with my parents and thinking, "We shouldn't be here."

Yet, Dziadzia wanted us there and Daddy knew life had to go on for his father and the family. Dad's younger siblings were three to twelve years older than me; I felt very close to them.

Joy slowly filled Dziadzia's home after Busia's death. My aunts played music on the piano. Dziadzia played cards with Dad and his other sons whenever their families were gathered there. He enjoyed a drink of peva (beer) with his boys and smoked cigars with my dad.

I always knew Dziadzia loved me even though he was more strict than friendly. He had rules and stuck by them. A leather strap hanging from a nail on a side cupboard was a bit frightening to see, even though I never saw him use it.

Sometimes, Dziadzia wanted us to stay for a meal that Aunt Theresa prepared so well. He would speak Polish with his family, but in English to Mama and us kids.

One time, while sitting at the table ready to eat, I was startled when Dziadzia told me to "leave the table." He mumbled something about having red polish on my fingernails. I left the table and sat in a corner of a stairwell, feeling sad. I found out later that he didn't like anything red; even food, and, neither did Dad, until he married Mama.

Another time, I was older when Dziadzia twisted my ear for no reason, and it hurt! I wanted to say something, but I didn't.

My parents taught us to respect our grandparents and the elderly, and it wasn't only about respecting them when they were nice to us. I wasn't raised in Dziadzia's time or my parents' time, but I can only imagine the disciplinarian tactics used then. I believe that the three generations preceding me did their best with what they knew.

The convenience of attending church and school within the Holy Rosary community at Isadore brought me face to face with my Fleis family heritage. The high school hallway displayed pictures of my aunts' and uncles' graduations. The fact that four of my great-aunts had become nuns, and Dad's sister became the fifth nun, left a legacy. Even so, I didn't realize the significance of the buildings at Isadore, where I worshiped and attended school, until I was much older.

In the fall of 1947, Edward started first grade at Holy Rosary School, Julie was in second grade, and I was in third grade. The three of us were in the same classroom. A school play presented that year featured Julie and Edward singing a duet to the song "When You and I Were Young, Maggie." It was too comical for words. Sister Mary Adolphine had taught them the full routine of singing the words and interacting with each other as if they were elderly and had rheumatism. They were dressed as old folks and used their canes as though they had to rely on them when they sang, "Oh, oh, ouch, there goes my rheumatiz." Our teacher recognized the blessings of musical talent in our family.

I received a most unusual gift in third grade. Everyone in class drew a name from a basket to buy a dollar gift to exchange with another classmate for Christmas. Sister Mary Adolphine included herself in the drawing. The gifts were distributed the day before Christmas vacation. I was shocked when I opened my present. Sister Adolphine had drawn my name and gave me a dress! It was red plaid with a wide-brimmed, white collar. It was "my first store-bought dress!" And that's exactly how I said it—when I opened the box, and then when I showed it to Mama after I came home from school. "LOOK, MAMA, I GOT MY FIRST STORE-BOUGHT DRESS!"

Christmas celebrations at the O'Brien farmhouse were memorable. The trimmings that Mama attached to the outer branches of a fir tree Dad cut fresh from the woods were a variety of ornate ornaments and metal clip-ons that held short, two-inch white candles.[54] A shiny star hung at the top of the decorated tree that stood tall by a side window near a corner of the dining room that we used for a living room. A small crèche displayed on a table honored the birth of Christ.

Santa would come early on Christmas Eve to give each of us a present. The younger siblings were sleeping in bed by the time Daddy lit the short, white candles that were deeply spaced between the tree branches. It was quiet, with only the lights flickering above the candles for a half hour or so, while we older children huddled next to Mama and Daddy on the sofa. The candles were lit only once. Christmas Eve was the exception for us staying up later.

One time before Christmas, Julie recalls finding all the Christmas presents wrapped and stuffed in an old washing machine. "I don't remember how I found them," she says, "but there was one wrapped for me. I unwrapped the present, then wrapped it back up. It was a toy telephone."

When Christmas Eve came, and Santa handed out all the gifts, there were none for Julie. "Everybody got a present except me," Julie said. "I knew I was supposed to get a present and looked at Mama with a sad face. Mama said, 'I better check ... Santa may have dropped one.'" (Most likely, Mama held back Julie's present because she could tell it had been opened and rewrapped.) So sure enough, Mama went outside and there was a present for Julie ... a toy telephone.

One year, when I opened my present from Santa, it was a doll that looked familiar ... except for her clothes. I was eight and a half, and had gotten a doll every year that I knew of. Mama must have seen the disappointment in my face and explained later, "When you girls were no longer

---

54   In 1949, tiny, colorful glass bulbs on an electric cord replaced the clip-ons.

playing with your dolls, I would take them away, hide them in a closet, and then, sometime before Christmas, I would clean up the doll real good, wash and set her hair, and make new clothes for her."

Mama had put a lot of love into my present. She created something new with her own hands, but at the time I didn't feel thankful.

The following year, Julie and I each received a small manicure set. We were both thrilled! Immediately, I thought to myself, "Mama must be thinking of us as more grown up."

Dad would inject humor when we least expected it. One year, on January 6th, the Feast Day of the Three Kings, he told us kids in the morning, while we were still in our pajamas, "I just got back from the airport and picked up the Three Kings today."

We responded, "Really? Really?"

It was his way of telling us that this day was special, and to remember the Three Kings. You know—the wise men who followed the star to Bethlehem and honored the newborn baby Jesus over two thousand years ago.

* * *

On my father's side of the family, Uncle Al married Phyllis Richard on June 12, 1948, at Holy Rosary Church. They made their home in Westland, a suburb of Detroit. Julie was a junior bridesmaid. She was eight. Their wedding reception was held at Dziadzia's (Grandpa Thomas's) homestead. Dad played violin for their wedding dance with his band, The Isadore Sodbusters, in the old upstairs dance hall. It was fun dancing up there.

Aunt Theresa explains, "Somehow at eighteen, I felt grown up. Dad (Grandpa Thomas) permitted me to go to the dances that were held above the Cedar Tavern."

Here's her happy story:

On November 23, 1948, my brother, Joe, and I went to the dance. As my girlfriend and I danced, out of nowhere a handsome young man approached and asked me to dance. Of course, I accepted. To this day, I believe my mom (Busia) had something to do with this encounter. We danced the night away. He revealed a few tidbits about himself–lived in Detroit, was in Cedar for the hunting season, and was staying at my cousin John Pleva's.

After that evening, I never would have dreamed I would see him again. He didn't know my last name or address, and we had no phone.

Fortunately, he was determined to get in touch with me. He wrote me a letter and sent it to my cousin, John Pleva. John delivered the unexpected letter.

For a moment, I was convinced. "This is the beginning of a fairy tale." I answered his letter, and for two years, we communicated through letters, and on most of the holidays he would visit.

* * *

Changes took place on Mother's side of the family; Memmier (now called Grandma Jennie) learned she had to have a hysterectomy in July of 1948. It was a matter of life or death. An osteopathic doctor in Traverse City performed the surgery. When she awoke after the surgery, Peppier (now called Grandpa Lugie) couldn't understand why she wasn't able to talk. All she could do was blow air through her mouth. Grandma Jennie had suffered a stroke due to her high blood pressure. She was paralyzed and couldn't walk or talk.

It was daytime, and Daddy wasn't home when Mama found out about her mother. Her brother Louis, who lived down the road from us on the Lamie farm, came to her as the bearer of the sad news. Mama, nearly seven months pregnant, was standing in the kitchen when he told her of their mother's stroke. It was a shock, more than she could bear, and Mama cried trying to console herself.

Grandpa Lugie stayed by Grandma Jennie's side for two weeks. At night he slept in a hospital bed next to her, worried that she wouldn't pull through.

Mama couldn't sit around and dwell on her sorrow. She had us children to care for and Daddy's love and support. He understood grief, having gone through the unforgotten loss of his own mother.

Jennie was left paralyzed on one side, and still couldn't walk or talk. After the hospital stay, Jennie and Lugie moved in with their daughter Mabel and her husband, Jacob, who lived in Kingsley, Michigan, southeast of Traverse City. Lugie was helpful, lifting Jennie from the bed and setting her in a wheelchair, then back to bed again. He did other things around the house to help out whenever he could.

Eventually, Jennie was able to walk with a cane and speak a little. She would say, "Oh, dear me," and "There, there."

On September 15, 1948, my sister Bernadette Agnes was born, her middle name honoring Busia. My sister was such a blessing. Two and a half months after her own mother's stroke, Mama held Bernadette close in her arms, healing over the sadness of her mother's stroke and reliving memories of her beloved mother-in-law, Agnes.

With Bernadette's birth, we were a household of nine—our parents and seven children, ages nine on down.

Bernadette, nearly a year old

* * *

My brother Edward became quite attached to Uncle Joe as his "little buddy" on the farm. "When he was working the fields with the tractor," Edward wrote, "He would set me on his lap, and we would talk and sing. He would let me steer the tractor, show me how to hold a straight line, and how to stop the tractor.

"He eventually would have me drive the tractor alone when he was loading hay. Having taught me how to push in the clutch and to take it out of gear, he would climb down from the hay wagon, get on the tractor and turn the tractor around and align it for the next row of hay to be loaded. He then would stop the tractor, get off, climb the wagon, and I would put it in gear and move forward.

"I helped Uncle Joe from the time I was probably seven or eight years old with the farm work, including the feeding of animals."

Uncle Joe drove the tractor or rode one of the horses from the Fleis homestead to the O'Brien farm when pulling farm equipment to work the crops. Otherwise, he walked the two miles. He was quite independent and a hard worker. He was relieved from working the third (Harpe) farm after Dziadzia sold it years earlier.

Edward continues, "I recall Uncle Joe working all the elements of the farm, from field preparation through harvesting. The farm had eighty acres or more of good tillable land.

"In addition to the tractor, he used a team of horses for planting and cultivating grain and potato crops. He would often help me to get up on the horse and I would ride it while he was working the cultivator."

Edward also recalled another occasion. "The team of horses were used to take a drill used for sowing grain from farm to farm. After the horses were harnessed and connected to the drill,

Uncle Joe put ... Julie on one horse, and me on the other, holding onto the straps of the harnesses, with us fully in charge of riding and driving the horses two miles. We were ages eight and seven.

"The horses started out fine on the road, with Uncle Joe following us in his truck. We had not gone a quarter of a mile, when the horses got spooked by someone tooting the horn of their car. They went into a gallop at a frightening speed, with Julie and I holding on for dear life, yelling, crying, and praying.

"The horses raced down the road, and then over another quarter of a mile or so to the neighbor's field, with us bouncing and slipping on the horses until they finally came to a halt at the neighbor's barn.

"Somehow, we managed to hang on. We both thought we would be killed. When Uncle Joe reached us within minutes, he was so terrified and thankful ... Neither Julie nor I fell off our horses.

"I have never had much interest in riding a horse since that experience," Edward concluded.

Grandpa Thomas's Fifth Son Joins the Military

In 1949, Uncle Joe enlisted in the Army when he was twenty-two years old. "He was in the states for nearly two years, and went on to fight in the Korean War for eleven months. He was a member of the 7th Infantry Division," stated his daughter Donna.

"It was a rough stint!" Uncle Joe exclaimed when it was all over. "One time, when I was in a foxhole, a grenade fell in the hole, but it was a dud. I was at Pork Chop Hill and lucky to come home alive," he continued, "as I was inches away from a comrade who was shot. God told me to get out of that foxhole, and a grenade fell in the foxhole, just as I got out." Seeing his comrades wounded and killed, lying on the ground, stayed with Uncle Joe.

Another time, Uncle Joe told his son, Dennis: "One of my jobs in Korea was driving the general around, and one time it was near the time of my furlough. The general told me to "speed up!" So, I sped up and got pulled over for going too fast and then got in trouble. My privilege to return to the US was taken away. I was mad and couldn't say a word." Uncle Joe's rank was private second class when he was honorably discharged on October 9, 1952. He was awarded the Combat Infantry Badge.[55]

Back to my mother's side. ...

From the time Grandma Jennie had a stroke in July of 1948, Grandpa Lugie rarely left her

---

[55]   Stated in Uncle Joe's obituary in the *Leelanau Enterprise*, February 27, 2020.

side as she needed full care. They were staying at Aunt Mabel and Uncle Jake's. Their assistance was indeed helpful.

December 1, 1948, brought yet another sudden tragedy for Mama, when Lugie collapsed of a heart attack and died suddenly while setting the table. Once again, Mama received the news from her brother Louis.

"No, no, no," she kept saying. "Not my father." She was heartbroken. Lugie was only sixty-nine years old.

One could tell that Jennie sensed instinctively that something happened, but the family waited until the following day to tell her the news so the rest of the family could be present.

Mama suggested they say a rosary with her mother and pray, "Eternal rest, grant unto him, O Lord."

Immediately after they prayed, Jennie dropped her hands and said, "There, there, there." Through those words, the family knew that she was aware her husband had died. It was sad for her family to see their mother unable to express her feelings.

I was nine and a half years old when Grandpa Lugie died. His sudden death was also a shock to me. He was a kind, jovial person. I very much respected his love and care for Grandma Jennie.

Following Lugie's death, Jennie stayed several more months at Mabel and Jake's home, then the rest of the family took turns caring for her in their homes. My aunts and uncles showed amazing love and care for their mother for the next nine years.

Besides Mabel (Jake Rahe), Ben (Agnes Novak), and Louie (Pauline Harrand), my mother's other siblings/spouses were: Cliff (Theresa Gatzke), Med (Gertrude Popa), and Lucille (Joe Harpe).

12

We Move to the Homestead

**Ed and Irene with Thomas Fleis in front of the
homestead farmhouse after the brick porch was built**

IN 1948, GRANDPA THOMAS decided to sell both the homestead and the O'Brien farms.
With Uncle Joe joining the military, Uncle Tony was at a good age to take over farming, but
Grandpa saw otherwise and wanted to retire.

I overheard Daddy and Mama talking about it. Dad later wrote: "I had my choice of buying
the O'Brien farm or the homestead. I chose the homestead, as it had a garage and was closer to
school and church."

Uncle Tom (Dad's brother) and Aunt Betty had moved back home from Wisconsin in 1948
and were staying with Grandpa Thomas on the homestead while all this happened. They purchased
the O'Brien farm, and moved there after things were settled.

On December 8, 1948, my parents signed the mortgage contract for the homestead. After they signed, Grandpa asked Dad to build him a house, to which Dad agreed. We couldn't move until the job was done.

Construction began immediately on Grandpa's new home. It was the winter season, and the basement was soon dug and concrete blocks laid for basement walls. The framing went up, and soon, the roof was shingled and windows installed. I recall going there when Dad was working inside, and it was dark outdoors. The electric work was done and lights strung on a cord lit the inside. Dad's crew was Uncle Tommy and a neighbor, Walter Novak. It was the first home built by Dad's new construction company.

Grandpa Thomas was sixty years old in the spring of 1949, when he left his beloved homestead with his children, Theresa (nineteen), Agnes (sixteen), and Anthony (thirteen). They moved into their small, white, wood-sided, three-bedroom home on a large corner parcel of the O'Brien farm on French Road, north of Centerville Township Hall. Grandpa was pleased with his new home.

* * *

Here's a review of the homestead farm to this point. Tomasz and Jozefina Fleis, my great grandparents, were granted 160 acres of land through the Homestead Act in 1880 after requirements were met. After building one rugged home on the land, and then another, the existing large farmhouse was built in 1888, the same year Grandpa Thomas was born—the seventh of eleven children. Within a month of Thomas's marriage to Agnes in 1911, my grandparents purchased the farm from Tomasz and Jozefina by a mortgage contract listing food, wood, supplies, etc. which were provided to them for the rest of their lives.

My father, Ed, born in 1915, was the second of Thomas and Agnes's twelve children. My parents, Ed and Irene, were the third generation to buy the farm through a mortgage contract. Their children, my siblings and I, were the fourth generation to live on the historic farm where Tomasz and Jozefina staked a claim shortly after arriving in what became known as Isadore in 1876.

* * *

I was very happy when we moved to the homestead in the spring of 1949, because back on the O'Brien farm when I overheard my parents talking about buying Grandpa's place, saying, "It'll be nice to live closer to church and school," I was thinking how much our living conditions would improve.

"Grandpa's place has a really nice home with indoor plumbing, and a large bathtub and a toilet that flushes. Besides, Mama will have a real kitchen sink for washing dishes. How convenient that will be!"

I never told my parents what I was thinking, but I just knew we would be better off moving to Grandpa's farm in more ways than just living closer to church and school.

I was ten years old; Julie was nearly nine, and Edward was seven and a half. The youngest children—Mary Jane, Ted, Jim, and Bernadette—were ages five and a half down to six months.

The next twenty years we lived on the homestead, my parents had five more children: Larry (1951), Shirley (1953), Joan (1956), Noreen (1957), and Rita (1959). Each birth was significant, as were the births of their seven older children, and shall be retold with small stories throughout these pages. (Some stories of my younger siblings will precede their births, as they did in previous chapters.)

After we moved in, the modern conveniences were nice, but my parents were right; the greatest convenience was living closer to church and school. Both were only a little over a mile away. We were the third and fourth generations attending Holy Rosary Church, and the third generation at Holy Rosary School.

The strong faith of our ancestors united us. When we were infants, at two weeks or younger, we were baptized into the Catholic faith. My parents didn't delay, and the original sin of Adam and Eve was washed away. Our godparents pledged to support our faith in the event our parents failed us, which they didn't. We made our First Confessions and First Holy Communions in second grade, after studies for preparation in school.

Holy Rosary was a traditional Polish parish, with Polish priests. Reverend Father John Klonowski served until 1953, and Father John Grzybowski until 1955. Mass was in Latin, with Polish and Latin hymns, and an occasional English hymn. Mary Narlock, a long-time organist, was excellent at teaching those of us in the choir the correct Polish and Latin pronunciation, as were the nuns at school.

When we attended church as a family on Sundays and holy days of the year, it was common to hear two sermons: one in Polish, the other in English. Dad understood Polish well. Mom didn't understand a single word, yet never complained about Sunday's Polish sermons, *Gorzkie Zale* devotions on Sunday afternoons, and Polish Stations of the Cross during the Lenten season.

At some point, the Polish sermons and devotions ceased. The Polish hymn *"Serdeczna Matko"* remained traditional and was sung on special occasions. The same with *"Witaj Królowo Nieba"* at Polish funerals. The traditional hymns of Polish and Latin, *"Panis Angelicus"* and *"Ave Maria,"* inspired me. To me, words had a special meaning when I didn't understand the language. It was sort of mystical, just as faith is a mystery.

Between the ages of ten and fourteen, we received the gift of the Holy Spirit in Confirmation. The preparation required a personal and deeper study of our faith. We were also given the opportunity to select a special saint's name and our own sponsor. On the day of Confirmation, our sponsors stood behind us and witnessed as we repeated the same vows that had been spoken by our godparents on the days of our baptisms as infants.

The whole family was involved at Holy Rosary Church and School, especially during church festivals and school functions. My mother became a member of the Ladies' Rosary Society and pledged to pray a daily rosary. My father joined the Holy Name Society for men, was an usher, and a member of the choir with Julie and me. Edward was an altar boy. My younger sisters became choir members when they were older, and the same for my younger brothers, who would serve as altar boys.

Mama set a powerful example for us. As a French-Canadian descendant, she might have lacked confidence sometimes, living as a minority within the Polish Catholic community, but she never complained about Polish sermons, devotions, or hymns. In spite of a cultural difference, she remained true to the Catholic faith.

We were also unified in faith at home. Mama would say, "A family that prays together, stays together." When Dad or Mom announced, "It's time to say a rosary," usually following an evening meal, we knelt down at our places and prayed.

My mother loved the convenience of her modern, white, cast-iron kitchen sink and the view she had looking out the double-pane windows above it. She could see her children playing baseball and taking a tumble sometimes, when running from base to base. The older ones would help the younger ones. Dad was the umpire until we fended for ourselves.

Also in view were farm buildings and the two-stall garage. A tall, red-iron gas pump with a red-and-white glass globe on top was next to it. Later, Dad built himself a concrete-block addition to the garage for his business.

The kitchen windows faced a well-established flower garden that produced wild-growing fragrant roses in summertime that partly climbed a wire fence bordering one side of a wood-slatted granary. A grassy, worn pathway alongside a mulberry tree led you to the entry door of the milk shed, where most everyone entered our home.

The mulberry tree produced tasty berries that didn't all ripen at once. We picked away at the darkish purple berries and waited for the green berries to ripen, then picked those, too! You can't imagine how messy we got, eating those berries out of the palms of our hands, getting our mouths and hands stained a bluish purple.

Mom's small kitchen was long and narrow, and very bright! Morning sunlight streamed through another double-pane window facing east. Her kitchen had white-painted cupboards, a hot water tank, and a Home Comfort combination range that had a two-burner wood stove and a four-burner gas stove. She could cook on either side at the same time. Mother's convenient kitchen motivated her to start making homemade bread each week.

Sometimes, she opened a window above her sink to cool the hot kitchen, especially when she baked bread. There was no better smell than when we stood outside near the open kitchen window and caught a whiff of freshly baked bread.

"Mom had a sense of humor," my brother Jim said. "I remember on more than one occasion, when Ted and I were outside doing whatever, we always knew when Mom was baking bread. It was obvious by the aroma in the air whether or not the bread was done. We would run in the house and beg Mom for a slice.

"She would always respond, 'It's too hot,' or 'It's not ready yet.'

"Invariably, we would go sit under the mulberry tree and wait. Sure enough, within minutes, a loaf of bread would appear on the windowsill with some home-churned butter. Never another word, just a Mommy smile when Ted and I came back in."

My mother loved those times when the children teased her, and there were times when she was quite the tease!

Grandpa Thomas was also a tease and doted on his grandchildren. He always came prepared with plenty of Black Jack gum, his favorite treat, tucked away in his front pocket!

"There are some moments when time stands still. One of those moments, for me," my sister Noreen said, "is remembering my grandpa. I remember, as a small child, the 'four little girls,' as we were called—Shirley, Joan, Rita, and I—all circling Grandpa. We had a small mulberry tree, and it was there where he pulled his hand out of his pocket, and in his hand was Black Jack gum, one for each of us. Oh, how I loved that gum, and I learned something about Grandpa. I could count on him. That picture of him in my mind is as fresh today as it was all those years ago."

Grandpa Thomas was a frequent visitor. He seemed to have no worry in the world when he stopped over to check that we were doing okay. He never failed to say, "*Niech Będzie Pochwalony*

Jezus Chrystus," when he entered our home, which means, "Praise be to Jesus Christ." We learned to respond, *"Na wieki, wiekow, amen,"* which means, "Forever and ever, amen."

I remember my mother still struggling with uncertainty as to whether Grandpa had fully accepted her as a French woman. Her doubts vanished when he started visiting regularly during the daytime, while Dad was away at work and the older children were in school.

No doubt Grandpa felt at home. After all, it had been his home before we moved there, where his own twelve children had been raised. He clearly enjoyed spending time with his playful, young grandchildren as they ran around and entertained him. Sometimes, he was still at our house when we returned from school. Quite often, he stayed for supper. By that time, Dad was home, too.

Four of us children were attending school after Mary Jane started first grade in September of 1949. Julie, Edward, and myself were in grades three through five. The neighbor's children boarded the bus with us every day. They had to walk a long pathway through the back hills behind our farm. Their parents, Myron and Irene (Bodus) Fabiszak, and their children were the third and fourth generation of Marianna (Fleis) and Adam Cerkowski (great-grandfather Tomasz Fleis's sister and brother-in-law). Myron's parents, Frank and Balbina (Cerkowski) Fabiszak, were the second generation. They lived north of us.

Mom would never sit down and enjoy a second cup of coffee after we left for school. She would wash the breakfast dishes before tackling anything else, besides looking after her three youngest children, Ted, Jim, and Bernadette. One time working in the kitchen, she never noticed when one of the three decided to be adventurous! I expect Mom was in a panic when she discovered Jim was missing, or maybe Ted told her where his younger brother had gone. Either way, Mom couldn't do a thing about it. We had no telephone. She had to wait until Dad came home for lunch.

Jim had sneaked out the back door and climbed off the concrete porch to skip home to go to school. "The best I can figure, I had to be three years old, and my brother Ted, four years old," Jim said. "The older siblings often came home from school, telling their tales of the day. I watched them board the bus in the morning and wouldn't see them until they got home from school.

"One day, I remember talking to Ted and feeling jealous that the older brother and sisters were at school having all the fun, while we stayed home. 'It's not fair,' I told him. It was close to noon that day, and I knew that after we ate, we would be taking a daily nap. 'I don't want to take a nap,' I said. 'I want to go to school.'

"'You can't,' Ted said. 'Dad is coming home for lunch and he will be really mad if you go.'

"I was relentless and told him I was going. I headed out from the porch to the ditch behind, and was walking next to the road when I recalled Mama warning me to never cross the road. I kept on walking and came across a tunnel. Found out it was a large culvert, and walked through the culvert to get to the other side of the road.

"Then, in the distance, I could see Holy Rosary School, and, just like Ted and I thought, everyone was outside having fun. Some were laughing, some playing baseball, some on the swings. As I neared the school, I started feeling scared. There was this building by the cemetery (the old bus garage) and I hid behind it and kept peering at all of them kids having fun.

"Then I heard this car ... oh, boy ... It was Dad. I could see Ted, the brother who was supposed to be taking care of me, standing in the front seat, pointing at me ... I could read his lips saying, 'There he is. There he is.'

"You big tattletale," I thought.

"On our way home, Ted sat with a sucker in his mouth and a big 'I told you so' smile on his face! 'Thanks, brother. I'll remember this,' I thought.

"Ted explained later that he had gotten in trouble for not watching me."

Dad would always come home for lunch whenever he had a job close by. I recall him and his crew building a two-story family home for Barney Schopieray on Lake Shore Road in Centerville Township, five or six miles from home, about this time.

Shortly afterwards, Dad's construction company was building the Leelanau County Road Commission building, in Maple City. Dad had designed the eighty-foot clear span with no posts, as stated in the contract.

My brother Edward remembers the job well. He said, "Dad was an engineer without a degree. He not only built the concrete block building, he designed and built the roof trusses eighty feet long, outside wall to outside wall, that ultimately handled dead loads of heavy snow and high

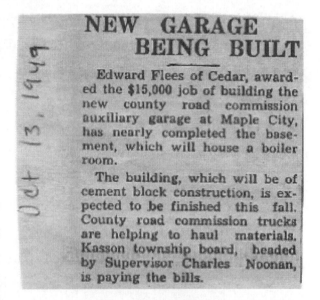

NEW GARAGE BEING BUILT

Edward Flees of Cedar, awarded the $15,000 job of building the new county road commission auxiliary garage at Maple City, has nearly completed the basement, which will house a boiler room.

The building, which will be of cement block construction, is expected to be finished this fall. County road commission trucks are helping to haul materials. Kasson township board, headed by Supervisor Charles Noonan, is paying the bills.

winds. It was a successful project. In his building contracts, Dad designed all of the roof trusses with different spans."

Gradual improvements were made at home, as well. A large bedroom upstairs was partitioned to make two bedrooms, which gave us a five-bedroom home. An old screened-in porch attached to the front of our home was torn down and replaced with a recreation room with large-paned windows. Much later, a bumper-pool table was placed in this room. Bernadette remarked how "Grandpa loved to play pool with our brother Larry when he was about five or six years old. They were quite the match, and ended up taking turns winning!"

When I reminded Larry of this, he added, "My head barely cleared the top of the pool table."

An entry door from the recreation room opened to a huge yard where sweet-smelling purple lilacs, on both sides of a narrow sidewalk, bloomed in springtime. Across the road, a wide pathway took you to behind the woods where a relic of a train caboose was found in a pasture for the cows. A ditch filled with hundreds of wild-growing willow sticks lined the roadway. Behind it was our big garden.

On wash days, clothes were hung to dry on clotheslines strung on multiple shade trees in the front yard. If you ever wanted to see Mama upset, Bernadette wrote, "It was on days when clothes were hanging on the line, and the neighbor's cows broke the fence and roamed our yard."

Sometimes that happened in Mama's garden, too, just about the time when the cabbage heads were ready for slicing to make sauerkraut! It was sad when the cows trampled inside her garden. Mama was so disgusted, she would yell, "Get those cows out of here!"

13

Farm Chores, Etc.

DAD PROBABLY HADN'T MILKED A COW since the day he left his father's farm in 1937, a dozen years before, when he headed for Detroit to earn a real paycheck. Dad had become a self-employed carpenter, building a construction business that quickly grew reputable, and probably earning pretty decent money. If he wasn't out bidding a job, he was building!

"At first, Mama milked the cows," Edward recalled. "I went along with her because I wanted to learn how to milk cows. I didn't like seeing Mama having to do this job. I was eight years old when she taught me how to milk a cow. When I decided I could handle the job by myself, I said, 'Mama, let me do this.'

"From then on, I did the milking. We had two or three cows at the time, and many barn chores. There was hay to knock down from the barn loft and cows to milk, feed, and bed each day with a fresh layer of straw, and pigs to feed.

"When it came time to work the fields," Edward said, "Dad taught me everything I needed to know about driving the tractor; besides, Uncle Joe had given me first training on driving straight rows at the O'Brien farm when I was around seven years old."

Early each spring, after the fields were plowed, new stones would be uncovered in the fields. Edward explained to me that the field stones came up to or near the ground surface through the frost heaving. They had to be removed.

"We walked alongside a type of wooden trailer that had no wheels, called a 'stone boat,' pulled by a tractor." Edward continued, "We picked up stones that had fully or partially surfaced and placed them on the trailer. The larger stones were dug out on the spot with a shovel to fully expose the stones, and rolled onto the trailer. Occasionally, we found very large stones, which were pulled by chain onto the trailer with the tractor.

"We hopped on and off the trailer, picking stones until the field was cleared of them." Edward added, "We unloaded them from the trailer and placed them in two separate rock piles at the edge of the field, separating the larger from the smaller stones. The sun was going down by the time we left the fields.

"Dad used these stones in his construction of some homes," he concluded.

Ruth Ann and her friend, Karen Laskey, are picking cherries off the tops.

Pete Sharnowski surrounded by young cherry pickers on the day of the party (circa late '60s)

Tart-cherry-picking season started every year toward the end of July. Mama was the driving force behind us to pick cherries, and we all earned money because of it. The early morning routine before heading out the door to pick cherries at Pete Sharnowski's was as follows:

Chores were done inside and outside. We ate the good warm breakfast Mama had prepared while she was also packing our picnic lunch in a wicker basket. Then we grabbed our gear (harnesses Mom sewed from denim cloth that fit over our shoulders, with ties in front to hold our buckets), and grabbed the picnic lunch before piling in the car. Mama then drove us to the orchard, less than four miles down the road. (The older girls had to take turns staying home and caring for the little ones.)

We walked through the orchard. The grass and the cherry trees were still wet from the morning dew. Pete was on hand and greeted his pickers, assigning each family a row of trees to pick from.

There probably were four large families picking cherries that we knew, but we rarely had a chance to say anything to each other. We talked and sang amongst ourselves, as other families picked cherries in rows farther away from us. The rule was, when you finished picking that row, you moved on to the next available row until the whole orchard was picked, which usually took three to four weeks.

The younger children picked cherries off the bottom branches, and the older children with Mama picked cherries off the higher branches, climbing up ladders to finish off the tops. As we filled our buckets, we dumped the cherries carefully into a rectangular wooden lug that held approximately twenty-five pounds, and sorted through them, removing any rotten ones, stems, or leaves. It was hard work and hot and sticky on most days. We wore clothes that were worn out to begin with, and when the season was over, those clothes were thrown in the trash.

Each day, we kept track of how many lugs we picked. Bernadette remembers picking twenty-five lugs one day, when she was sixteen.

At noon, Pete would ring a loud bell, announcing lunchtime. We children quickly gathered any empty lugs to form a table with benches and covered it with newspapers. Then we ran to the outhouse in the orchard if we needed to use the privy. In the shade, not far from there, sat a tall, new, galvanized cream can with a lid to cover it, containing fresh cold water. A metal ladle hanging from a handle on the side was used for dipping water from the can to drink from or for pouring water over our hands to wash off the stain and grit. Everyone shared the same ladle.

We were past being hungry by the time we sat down on our benches and prayed, "grace before meals," with Mama. She usually served homemade ground bologna or peanut-butter-and-jam sandwiches wrapped in waxed paper. The special treat we all remember was the drink she served—hot coffee and cold creamy milk, much like today's latte or cappuccino. The drink was still warm in a mason quart jar when we passed it around. Each of us took a few sips until the jar was empty. Mama indulged us with a little caffeine, which probably helped us pick more cherries.

After a full day of picking cherries, nothing was better than jumping into Lime Lake and getting cleaned up. By the end of the four-week season, we all had a deep farmer's tan.

When tart-cherry-picking season was over, Pete threw a party for all his pickers. While we sat on the grassy lawn under the shade tree of his farmhouse, he handed out candy bars and soda pop—as much as we wanted.

Pete was a bachelor and never had children of his own, but he sure appreciated the children and their mothers who worked for him. Mama let us pick cherries from a young age until we were well into our teens. Pete rewarded the mothers of these large families with dark, sweet cherries to pick from the trees he saved for the last—as much as they wanted! Mama canned those lugs of plump, sweet cherries, which we enjoyed as a dessert during the months when seasonal fruit wasn't available.

We were always anxious for payday, and Pete would show up when we least expected him, so we were surprised! The pay per lug varied through the years, but I recall being paid fifty cents per lug. It was the first money some of the children earned. The money went into Dad's safe. We might have spent a little, but it was mostly used for shoes and school supplies.

It was fun picking cherries with Mama.

Sometime in August, we harvested wheat and oats. Before Edward took over most of the farming, I recall Dad driving the tractor hauling the binder to the fields. The machine cut the grain and bundled it with binder twine, throwing each bundle to the ground. Dad showed us kids how to rustle up those bundles, forming teepees of three or more with the grain tips pointed to the sky for more sunshine and further ripening.

Then, before threshing, we picked up all the bundles, placed them on a flatbed trailer, and stored them in the barn. All the work was done during the week. The only exception for working on a Sunday was if rain was expected. I don't recall that ever happening.

On the day of threshing, morning dew was still in the air when local farmers gathered in our yard, ready to work. Jacob Bodus, a neighbor down the road, hauled the community threshing machine to our farm by tractor. It was the noisiest contraption ever, sounding something like a train caboose on metal wheels. I always thought Mr. Bodus owned it, until I talked with Roseann (Fabiszak), my former neighbor on the farm.

She explained, "The community threshing machine was owned by Mr. Bodus, Joe Popa, Clemy Mikowski, Barney Schopieray, Tom Witkowski, and your Grandpa Thomas and Uncle Steve Petrowski, and [others]. Other farmers had different situations and got to use it. They helped each other. It was the same with other farming equipment until they could buy their own."

We were lucky, as every year on threshing day, the weather would be sunny without any trace of rain. The weather forecast was watched carefully. It was important that the wheat and oats stay dry without a chance of mildew. This was a tedious, once-a-year job which Dad took charge of, then Edward, and later Ted and Jim. It was the same with the other farming.

Talk about dirt and grime! The threshing machine spun out golden kernels of wheat, then oats, filling burlap bags, which were carried by the men to the old wooden granary and dumped into separate room-size bins: one for oats and one for wheat.

Side Note:

The stalk, after the grain was separated, was straw, which created a high mound on the barn floor. Later, it got transferred to a loft with a mechanical forklift linked to a trolley. There were two lofts: one for straw, and one for hay harvested earlier. Straw provided bedding for the farm animals. Hay fed cows, as did grazing on grass and other growing vegetation when outdoors in a pasture.

Pigs thrived on hay, corn, and grain, apples fallen to the ground from scraggly trees, vegetable peelings, and table scraps, when fed in an outside pen.

"Every few months, a certain amount of wheat, oats, and corn was hauled to a co-op in Lake Leelanau, and ground together into a fine mixture," Edward said, "for feeding essential nutrients to young livestock."

Side Note:

Stored on a high shelf in the granary was an old hand-cranking wheat grinder. We figured Great-Grandma Jozefina must have used it to grind rye into flour, before making bread.

Lunch for the threshers was at noon, at which time the threshing machine was shut down. Mom provided a cleaning station in the side yard, consisting of a large basin of water, and a towel dangling from a pole with a mirror perched above. They washed off the dust and grit and combed their hair. An outhouse was nearby. Lunch was served in our home at the dining room table.

Every one of us girls had a turn at helping our mother with the preparation of food for the threshers—a feast of thanks-giving for their help. The huge meal consisted of meat, fresh vegetables, homemade bread, and dessert. Bernadette recalls "picking bushels of corn and peeling potatoes for Mom to feed the large number of men who came over to work."

In September or later in the fall, it was corn husking season after corn was dry in the fields. It was handpicked, loaded on a flatbed trailer, and hauled by the tractor to the back yard. It was early evening, right after supper, when Uncle Steve Petrowski, his son, Eddie, and other neighbors gathered in the yard to help us. They sat on overturned wooden crates while removing husks off a huge quantity of corn. A yard light hanging from the garage brightened the area when it became dark. They talked and joked with each other until the last cob of corn was husked and stored in the freestanding corn crib.

Ed Fleis and sons unloading crates of potatoes off the trailer at the root cellar

In early October, even if snow hit the ground, it was potato-digging season! The school closed for two weeks to give students time to pick potatoes for their parents. "They called this 'potato vacation,'" Edward stated. "Grandpa was usually out in the fields observing what was going on and supervising.

"I dug the potatoes using the tractor to pull a potato digger, which also shucked off the dirt and vines and left the potatoes in a row to dry.

(The old farm tractor was eventually replaced with a new Case tractor after Dad struck a deal with James Johnson in Empire.)

"Dad helped me load the crates on the trailer and unload them into the underground root cellar. Some years, we had between eight hundred and 1,200 crates." Edward concluded.

Side Note:

Built in 1940, the root cellar had wide wooden bins on opposite ends of a dirt floor for potatoes. The potato sorting machine and crated vegetables took up the middle section. Three outside roofs provided ventilation.

Every kid who was old enough helped with picking potatoes, filling wooden crates one row after another. We would be in the field, dirty from top to bottom, when Mama sent one of the younger children to the field carrying a paper bag full of crisp potato pancakes that she made. We immediately stopped what we were doing, brushed the dirt off our hands, and started eating. They were still warm and moist on the inside. We finished off the bag, and went back to work!

Bernadette recalls an unexpected incident that happened: "One day, as we were picking potatoes toward the end of a row near our property line, which adjoined the Fabe farm, the Fabes had vines of ripe grapes, tempting us to have a taste. After we went through the fence to pick a few handfuls, we heard the echo of a shotgun firing and Raymond Fabe shouting, 'Get out of my grapes!' We exited the fence quicker than we entered."

Edward continues, "In late winter, Ed Petrowski, who bought and sold potatoes on a wholesale basis, would arrange to buy the potatoes. This involved the sorting and bagging of the potatoes to be sold, which also required the lifting of all the potatoes into the sorting machine. I did the heavy work." By late spring, the remaining potatoes in the cellar had sprouted. The sprouts were removed. The potato was cut into sections, leaving at least two eyes (where sprouts were removed) before planting season started over again.

One day, Mama recruited Julie and me to help Edward with barn chores. She told us that we would have to take turns every other week helping Edward with the milking and other chores. Plus, whoever milked had a week off from washing dishes. It was one or the other. I tried to convince Mama that I did not want to milk a cow, but "no" was not a word she would accept.

Before Julie and I took on barn chores, Mama and Edward showed us how to milk a cow. Julie took the first week and scored well. She was kind of a tomboy anyway. The following week was my turn. I dreaded it. When I sat down on the short, wobbly bench, the smell was enough to make me gag; besides that, flies were buzzing around the cow's tail. Then, before I knew it, that smelly tail swung right in front of my face. Ugh! Even though I tried and milked the best I could, I failed.

When I carried my pail of milk to dump into the cream separator, Mama and Edward were standing at the door and stopped me in my tracks to inspect the amount of milk in my pail. They shook their heads in disbelief and Edward said to Mama, "If we allow her to continue milking, the cow will dry up."

Whoopee!! I was relieved from milking cows and reassigned to washing dishes in the kitchen with Mama. Didn't mind that at all!

Julie spent most of her time with chores around the barn. She said, "Growing up on the farm, my brother Edward and I worked as a team milking cows and feeding the animals, spreading fresh straw for their beds, feeding the cows hay in their troughs, collecting eggs in the chicken coop, and whatever else was necessary. I also helped Mama in the garden, planting, weeding, and picking vegetables. I learned a lot of responsibility real fast. I sure don't regret any of it."

Ted wrote: "Every night, Jim or I would go out in the fields to find the cattle and bring them home to the barn. It was a great time to look around and eat all the wild berries along the way. The cows roamed the woods and backfields during the daytime, from springtime until cold weather set in."

Ted and Jim were quite young when they started helping their brother Edward with farm chores. Here's Jim's story about the two of them:

Have you ever volunteered to do something that you would later regret? Ted and I did! We didn't know this was going to be a training exercise for milking cows. We didn't know or understand that our brother Edward was planning on leaving to go to the seminary in his freshman year of school and that he needed to get us trained.

I was about seven years old and Ted was eight when we got a most unlikely present–miniature milk pails. They were shiny, had a handle, probably held about a quart or two. They looked just like the pails Ed and Julie would take out to the barn, only smaller. How cute! We played with them in the snow, put our "stuff" in them to carry around the house. We would sing out, "Na, na ... na," as we walked by our siblings, strutting and showing off! They were cute, and they were ours!

One day, Edward asked us if we wanted to bring them shiny pails and use them in the barn and try to milk a cow. Oh yeah, we were all excited! We're going to play "milk the cow!" How much fun is this going to be? We couldn't wait! We soon found out that playing "milk the cow" was going to be a full-time job.

As things would have it, Ted and Jim assumed full responsibility for the farming after Edward left to study at St. Joseph's Seminary in Grand Rapids. There, he studied Greek and Latin, in addition to other academic subjects. After a year, Edward concluded his vocation was elsewhere, and returned as a tenth grader at Holy Rosary School. He was fifteen. Edward said, "Farming was reduced. I helped my brothers with the farming, and did side jobs helping relatives with their crops. I also sorted cherries at Frigid Foods in Suttons Bay in the summer, so I could earn some money."

14

Feeding a Large Family

WHEN MY BROTHER TED WAS MUCH OLDER, he began entertaining family and friends by singing a "chicken song." It goes like this: *"We had some chickens, no eggs they laid. We had some chickens, no eggs they laid. Then came a rooster into our yard, and caught those chickens right off their guard."* Chorus: *"They're laying eggs now, just like they used to, since that old rooster came into our yard."*

Whenever my mother cooked a tasty chicken dinner, she was the one who fetched, butchered, cleaned, cut, and cooked the chicken. I didn't mind helping her by pulling feathers off the bird. She would pour a stream of hot, scalding water over it so the feathers pulled off easily.

One time, Mom challenged Julie and me to catch and butcher a chicken ourselves. I would have nothing to do with it! Julie didn't mind. She was the fearless and gutsy one in the family. With Mom's help, she fetched the squirmy, squawking bird and succeeded to the end.

Julie remembers Mom saying, "Whoever kills the chicken gets the gizzard. She always made it sound like a delicacy, so I usually volunteered. Turns out, I loved eating the gizzard!"

Twice a day, the older girls took turns feeding and fetching eggs. Mary Jane recalls, "In the wintertime, Mother was concerned about the chickens outside nesting in the chicken coop and would cook up small potatoes to feed them. She knew that warm food might help produce more eggs. I would feed the chickens in the coop when I got off the bus."

I was eleven years old when I heard the first sounds of chirping baby chicks nestled inside a cardboard box Dad set in the center of the wooden dining room table. Every one of us kids huddled with Mama, close to Dad, anxious for him to remove the lid. There they were ... twenty-five or more precious, yellow, fluffy chicks snuggled together.

It was too cold to put them in the coop, so Dad built a wooden framed pen that fit perfectly on one end of Mom's narrow kitchen. She didn't mind. The floor of the pen was padded with a layer of newspapers topped off with a little straw before the baby chicks settled into their first home. Their feed of fine grain and water in separate feeders was their nourishment. They were kept warm by the wood-burning stove by day, and a heat bulb dangling above the pen by night.

Within a few weeks, after one or two flipped over the pen onto the kitchen floor, Mom's patience ran thin. She said, "Enough is enough," and the chicks were moved to the outside coop. Within a couple months or so, they grew to the size of chickens. No matter how good the fencing was, some always escaped and roamed the yard, and even pecked on mulberries fallen to the ground.

The messiest of chores for my brothers was shoveling manure from the barn or coop from time to time to make compost. In the fall, (sometimes, in spring), the manure from the compost was loaded on a manure spreader pulled by the tractor and spread onto fields, providing nutrients to the soil.

In early summer, fields were plowed, disked, and dragged, with an acre or more reserved for Mom's garden. After it was planted, we depended on Mother Nature for warm weather and seasonal rain for seeds to germinate and plants to grow.

"We grew a little of everything," Mom would say. Some years, sweet corn was growing in a back field, and watermelon and muskmelon in a patch near the barn, plus the garden across the road. Depending on our ages, we pitched in and helped with planting, pulling weeds, hoeing, or harvesting. Eating raw peas while picking them off the vine was a treat most of us couldn't resist. Mom spent time alone as well. She would give attention to new plants that needed thinning or fine weeding, transplanting, etc., while an older daughter took care of the younger children and did chores in the house.

During earlier years, Mom raised a large patch of green beans for the sole purpose of earning money. My brother Edward said, "I did the same with pickles in a back field behind the woods when I came home from the seminary. It was a lot of work. I even had help from my friends."

Julie and I picked beans alongside Mama by the pails full and filled one or two burlap sacks. (Beans produce several pickings.) Mama would drive to Cedar and deliver the bagged beans to the Manistee & Northeastern (M & NE) train, headed for Traverse City. I went along one time. I saw the service attendant help her with the bags and set them on a platform inside the train.

Edward hauled pickles there, too. "It wasn't successful. I didn't make much money," he said. Mama never did say how much money she made, but she sure liked finding ways of earning money.

Side Note:

> If not for skipping school one day with two other girls in my grade, we may never have had a chance to ride the M & NE train. With little money in our pockets, we hitchhiked a ride to Traverse City and got dropped off across from (the former) Milliken's department store on Front Street. None of us had ever ridden an elevator, so we went inside Milliken's and rode the elevator up and down until we were satisfied. Then we walked to the *Record-Eagle* and asked for a tour. They obliged us. We watched the whole operation of a newspaper being printed on a bolt of paper on heavy rolling equipment, up to the final cutting stage. The train station was nearby, so we each bought a ticket, took a seat, and traveled the train back to Cedar. The next day, we didn't get into trouble at school. Back then, it wasn't unusual for an eighth grader to take a "skip day" during the final days of elementary education.

Mom was always organized. She knew everything that had to be done on the farm in the absence of Dad working away from home, but when he was home, Dad was in charge. Both of my parents knew "farming alone won't pay bills." Sometimes, we quarreled about jobs Mom designated to us or different things—known as sibling rivalry. When that was going on, she wouldn't interfere. We had to figure things out for ourselves and learn to get along and work together. There were no ands, ifs, or buts about it when Mom told us to do something.

Gardening provided fresh vegetables from the middle of summer through late fall. We enjoyed fresh lettuce, sliced cucumber, and potato salads drizzled with Mom's homemade creamy dressings, besides green-bean soup made with pork hocks and onions, and tomato soup from juiced tomatoes with potato kluskis (dumplings). I learned to prepare all of Mom's recipes, and how to preserve food while working beside her in the kitchen, as did my younger sisters when it came their turn.

When Mom canned, it was an assembly line between the kitchen and dining room table, with jars and lids washed at the kitchen sink. The work consisted of scalding tomatoes or peaches in hot water at the stove to lift the skins; peeling pears; slicing and packing jars at the dining room table; and then processing filled jars on top of the stove or in the oven. Mom canned various fruits, jams, and jelly, beets, tomatoes, pickles, and pickle relish. By the end of the season, basement shelves were full. Cabbage was sliced and salted into a large crock with a plate covering it, and weighed down with a rock. After cabbage fermented to sauerkraut, it was spooned into jars and canned. Extra heads of fresh cabbage and bushels of carrots went into the root cellar for winter storage.

Usually in late fall, butchering of livestock was done. Relatives or neighbors helped Dad, and later when some of my brothers took over. We had our own smokehouse. Ham and bacon were home cured. Slabs of pork, salted down, went into a big crock. Mom made head cheese and fresh liver sausage from pig parts. She canned beef and chicken until meat could be frozen in a freezer unit rented from Ed Kasben, owner and operator of a commercial freezer system at the former Cedar State Bank building. Eventually, Dad bought us a new chest freezer for home. Besides meat, farming provided milk, buttermilk (after making butter), cream, sour cream, eggs, and Mom's homemade cottage cheese.

Bernadette remembers "each of us taking turns hand churning cream in a large jar with a wooden paddle to make butter, and when Mom rendered fat from fresh slaughtered pigs to make lard for baking and frying." She also made lye soap from lard, for scrubbing collars and work clothes.

Mom oversaw the production of cream and eggs, and sold them at Joe Sbonek Creamery in Cedar. "That was her money!" said Edward. "I had built Mom a special box with a light inside for candling eggs. I got the idea after watching the process when I went to market with her. I figured it was better for Mom to find a bad egg at home, instead of being disappointed at the market."

Julie added, "With the money Mom earned from selling eggs and cream, she would buy flour, sugar, and other needed items."

Fortunately for us, on the same day cream and eggs were sold at the market, a free show was shown on a large outdoor screen on the grounds of the (former) Cedar Schoolhouse, across from Solon Township Hall. It was family night, and we'd all pile in Dad's car to go there after dishes were done.

"You girls sure know how to wash those dishes lickety split on free show nights," Mom would say. It's true. We hurried more. Why wouldn't we? We were children and excited to go see black-and-white movies on a big outdoor screen every week during the summertime.

Movies were shown at dusk. It was like going to a drive-in theater, except it was free and no one directed you where to park. Cars were backed up on the hillside facing the movie screen. Some families stayed in their cars, while others spread blankets on the grass to be closer to the screen. Some of the popular shows were *The Three Stooges, Amos and Andy, Gene Autry, Lassie,* and *The Lone Ranger*. Those were special family outings.

15

Dad's Tragic Accident

BERNADETTE WAS THE YOUNGEST IN THE FAMILY when Dad had an awful accident working on a job for the Cedar Fire Department, formerly located next to the Cedar post office. Uncle Joe was working with Dad. They were on top of the roof, coating it with hot boiling tar, when Dad had the misfortune of tripping, and the bucket containing the tar fell and splashed on his face, causing severe burns.

After emergency treatment, his head was completely wrapped in white strips of cloth, with openings for his eyes, mouth, and nostrils.

We had no telephone in the house, and Mama knew nothing of the incident until Dad got home.

Jim was about four years old and was playing outside when the truck that looked like Dad's came into the yard. Jim explained, "The man got out of the truck slowly. The man looked very scary. He had bandages all over his head. All you could see was the cutouts around his eyes and nose and lips. His lips were black. He came closer to the house. I was a little frightened.

"Then, he spoke. 'Go and get your mother.' I knew that voice, but I didn't recognize that person. So, I ran into the house and got Mama. My tears started when I realized it was Dad."

I was standing by the dining room window and saw Dad walking to the outside door. He looked like a mummy with clothes on.

"At first, Dad was confined to bed rest," Jim recalled. "I remember family and friends saying the rosary at his bedside. I remember how sad it was around the house while he was recovering. I don't know how long that took, but it seemed forever."

It was pitiful to see Dad that way, but when he joined us at the dinner table, it seemed to represent some kind of normalcy. Mom diligently treated Dad's wounds and rewrapped his head with fresh cotton strips. When he had his final checkup, the doctor was surprised how quickly his face had healed. Dad said, "I have my wife to thank."

His face was left scarred, and I wondered if he ever would look the same as he did before.

Dad got restless hanging around the house. I think that was the reason why our large living room was remodeled—so he could be home, working at his own pace, and resting, if necessary.

Dad partitioned off our large living room and gave us a smaller living room with French doors, another bathroom, a laundry room, a hallway, closets, and an open staircase. New flooring, knotty pine walls in the living room, wainscoting, and new paint in the dining room were other improvements, in addition to building a niche in the hallway for a telephone soon to be installed—and an alcove in the living room for a piano we hoped for!

Telephone service came from Leelanau Telephone Company, owned by the Sattlers from Cedar. The telephone was an upright wooden, oblong box with a large dial in front. The receiver (mouth and earpiece) hung on a hook along the side. We were on a party line with our neighbors. Each phone had a unique ring. Our ring was "two shorts and two long." The neighbors heard our ring and we heard theirs.

Sometimes, Mom was suspicious that someone was listening in on her conversations with her good friend and neighbor Theresa Zywicki, who was also French. She took care of the matter by switching from talking in English to talking in French, and chuckled when she heard the click-clicks of hang-ups.

In a matter of time, I received telephone calls from a relative in need of a babysitter. I had babysat my younger siblings since the age of ten. I was glad Mom allowed me to babysit for others and earn some money.

Dad's healing and ability to go back to work were family blessings. Mom was pleased with Daddy's remodel job, and so were we!

The first framed picture hung on the wall of the living room was an image of the Sacred Heart of Jesus with the words, "God Bless Our Home."

**Above: Sacred Heart of Jesus
Below: Professional photo of Fleis family. From left: Irene, Edward, Ruth Ann, Julie, and Ed. Front: Ted, Mary Jane, Bernadette, and Jim.**

Soon afterwards, my parents surprised us with an upright piano that fit perfectly inside the alcove Dad built in the living room. Julie and I both knew the piano would be much easier to play than the old pump organ at the O'Brien farm.

Every chance we had, we would sit on the piano bench and try to play the same melodies we heard Aunt Theresa and Aunt Agnes play on their piano. It took a lot of practice before we learned to play a duet called "Chopsticks," with Julie playing the chords and me, the melody, followed by "You Are My Sunshine." Another song was "The Missouri Waltz," one of Aunt Susie's favorite songs she played. Julie and I learned other catchy tunes from listening to music played on the eight-track/radio console player in the dining room.

Dad had taught us how to play chords on the piano and Mama entertained, playing a couple of comical ditties. One tune sounded like this: "Once I saw a pretty girl, who was always chewing gum. She never said a doggone word. She just kept right on chewing gum." We loved it! Our new living room became the center of entertainment.

Mom placed a family photo taken shortly before Dad's tragedy on top of the piano. Many times, I glanced at it and wondered if Dad's face would ever look the same as in the photo. His face was deeply scarred. I don't remember how long it took for his scars to disappear, but in time they became less noticeable, and then disappeared completely.

* * *

Larry was born on August 3, 1951. He was our parents' eighth child and would remain our youngest brother, the last of four boys in the family. He was only a few days old when Dad went back to Grandpa's new house and built him a brick front porch with steps.

Jim remembers the job well. "It was late in the day. Dad was laying up the bricks for the front porch of Grandpa's house, and Ted and I were helping him. We were all excited because we had a new baby brother, and wanted to go home to see him. So, we finished working and headed home.

Young Larry (circa 1954)

"When we arrived, we headed straight for Mom and Dad's bedroom. No baby. No Larry. We went out of the bedroom and told Dad he wasn't there.

"Dad went to the bedroom. He couldn't find him either. So, we went to Mom and asked where he was.

"She smiled that Mommy smile and said, 'Look inside the drawer.'

"We hadn't noticed the slightly opened drawer before in the new dresser Dad had built. We opened it wider to see our brother lying contentedly, tucked inside with his blanket."

* * *

Earlier, on Dad's side of the family:

"My fairytale [came] true," Aunt Theresa wrote, "When my Prince Charming, Boniface 'Bob' Rosinski, age twenty-two, swept me off my feet, and we were married at Holy Rosary Church on July 15, 1950." Aunt Theresa was twenty. After their wedding, they lived in Detroit at his parents' home. Julie was ten and a junior bridesmaid for their wedding.

Aunt Susie, (Dad's oldest sister) had battled asthma and other health issues.

"She traveled with Aunt Theresa and Uncle Bob after their wedding back to Ann Arbor, where she lived. She always had a ride with them whenever they headed up north to see family," according to Aunt Theresa.

Left: Ruth Ann next to Uncle Bob Rosinski. Right (left to right): Phyllis, Susan, Theresa, Sr. Therese, Thomas, Albion, and Betty. In front: Tony, Joe, Agnes, and Leo, taken at Madonna College, Livonia (circa 1950).

Aunt Irene, who had entered the convent in 1943, took the name Sister Mary Therese after becoming a Felician nun at Madonna College (University) in Livonia. When she decided to take perpetual vows of chastity, poverty, and obedience, her immediate family was invited. Mom looked forward to going with Dad. A babysitter was lined up. The day before, one of my siblings became ill. She turned to me and said, "I want you to go take my place." I went with Dad and relatives. It was quite the honor representing my mother at the mass and solemn ceremony at Madonna, where Sister Therese and several nuns spoke their final vows. I was the only niece among many relatives attending this blessed occasion.

16

"Jack-of-All-Trades"

DAD'S CONSTRUCTION COMPANY WAS IN FULL SWING after he resumed work following his tragic accident. A *Leelanau Enterprise* article written by Bill O'Brien, published on October 23, 1997, indicated, "He worked on construction projects from Leelanau to Manistee Counties, building barns, silos, many commercial projects, family homes, plus more." Dad was known as a jack-of-all-trades. He was a general contractor, a carpenter, a plumber, and an electrician. Besides masonry and concrete work, he installed heating and roofing. Some of his crew also had natural abilities, while others were trained.

Through the years, Dad's crew varied. Some, like our Uncles Tom, Joe, and Tony, worked a few years and then worked elsewhere. So did his neighbors, John Zywicki and Walt Novak, and others like Isadore Stachnik and John Garvin from Cedar, and Ray Galla from Lake Leelanau. His uncles, Steve and Joe Pleva, also worked for a time, as did some of my brothers when they were older.

In some business dealings, a handshake or a verbal agreement was all Dad and his customer needed, instead of a written contract.

One time, when he was hired to build a large, beautiful home for friends on the Old Mission Peninsula, he complied with their wishes and wrote up a formal contract.

As the job progressed, the couple asked for extras to be built. Dad obliged, and penciled in the extra cost for time and material.

When the final bill was presented, the couple fumed! They wouldn't pay a nickel over the contract price. They gave no consideration for the extras they asked for. Dad came home disgusted after having to swallow the extra cost, but learned a mighty lesson: "It doesn't matter if it's friend or foe—be upfront and tell it like it is!"

Now ... several more stories:

In 1954, nine housing units were built at the Empire Air Force Base by Dad's construction company. These homes were two- and three-bedroom units built on a slab. They are now occupied by the National Park Service employees.

The same *Leelanau Enterprise* article also stated, "He [Dad] built the home of well-known county lumberman, Pierce Stocking, between Glen Arbor and Empire.

"He [also] constructed some commercial buildings for Stocking for his dune drive in that area, which was later revamped by the National Park Service." Dad did not build the scenic drive, but he did build commercial buildings there for Mr. Stocking, who, according to the US National Park Service, "purchased the forest land in 1948 from D. H. Day, south of Glen Haven." The planning of the drive was in the early 1960s, but it was not completed and opened to the public until 1967.

Dad indicated in his writings: "I worked for the Charcoal Industrial Plant at Glen Haven."

Declared Gordon Plowman of Glen Arbor, "He constructed charcoal kilns. The National Park Service tried to move the old relic, but it's still there!" He was eighty-three years of age in 2017 when I interviewed him by phone.

The September 3, 1998, issue of the *Leelanau Enterprise* stated:
A block and concrete structure is actually a series of charcoal kilns, built nearly half a century ago. They are located near the Alligator Hill Trail (National Park Service) north of Glen Lake. The fronts of the garage-like structure were closed off with concrete blocks when the kilns were in use years ago. Making the charcoal was a long, tricky process.

"I was also employed by Pierce Stocking," Mr. Plowman continued. "I remember your dad, Ed Fleis, doing a lot of work for him. He had terrific muscles handling blocks.

"I hauled blocks, cement, and re-rod for that job. Your dad laid the foundation. Logs were cut up, logs were stacked, good fire going, enough airflow, set for several days until it burned out to charcoal pieces and charcoal packaged. There were twenty kilns. I hauled charcoal in burlap bags on a thirty-six foot trailer to Detroit. The fine stuff went to Boston. Pierce Stocking had about fifty employees at the time."

Dad also wrote, "I did lots of masonry work, building bridges in Kalkaska for Pat [Pierce] Stocking."

He also engineered and constructed the Kalkaska Fish Hatchery for Stocking, with a crew that included Uncle Joe Fleis. The hatchery is now inactive and reverted to state land, which I was disappointed to learn. Dad, Uncle Joe, and others spent a whole summer going back and forth on weekends. It's memorable because I had seen the huge tanks of fish, beginning from tiny minnows. When they reached a bigger size, they automatically went into another tank. Dad took the whole family to check it out.

Dad did some work for the fish hatchery in Honor. I tried to obtain information, but no records were kept of earlier years. However, the fish hatchery is now called Platte River State Fish Hatchery,[56] located on the corner of County Road 669 and US 31. I was happy to learn that the hatchery is in full operation and growing salmon. (In the fall, some eggs are taken from the salmon. Children grow the little eggs at school, and the little fish are planted in the river.)

On M-22 near the village of Empire, St. Philip Neri Church has a memorial altar at the cemetery that honors Reverend Father Joseph Bocek, who served the parish from 1940–55. Dad constructed that memorial. (Father Bocek was an uncle of Ray Watkoski, who later became Julie's husband.)

Left: Ed's business card. Bottom left: Charcoal kilns in Glen Haven. Bottom right: Memorial altar honoring Rev. Father Bocek at St. Philip Neri Cemetery, Empire.

In 1956–57, under the pastorate of Father Herman Kolenda, and Dad's supervision, a new Holy Rosary Convent and private chapel were built. Dad was assisted by his brother Joe, Uncles Steve and Joe Pleva, and John Garvin, some high school boys (as part of the curriculum) giving them

---

56   Benzie Area Historical Museum.

firsthand experience of working in the construction field.[57] Also, many kind parishioners gave time, effort, and financial aid to complete the magnificent building.[58] The Felician nuns finally had a home after sixty years of living quarters in a section of the school.

Blessing of the ground where Holy Rosary Convent was built (circa 1956)

Bystanders watching the blessing included Mary Jane, Bernadette, Thomas, and Ed Fleis

Left: Construction crew: John Garvin, Steve Pleva, Ed Fleis, Joe Fleis, and Joe Pleva (circa 1956)
Right: Holy Rosary Convent (2022 photo)

---

57   Holy Rosary School, 1898–1998, p. 68.
58   *Diamond Jubilee Memoirs*, Holy Rosary Parish, 1883–1983.

17

Mom's Loving Care

IN 1952, I BECAME A TEENAGER. I didn't dare ask Mom for permission to have a party, because I knew she would say, "NO." So, I secretly planned it myself. I had busily and thoroughly cleaned the old wooden dance hall above the woodshed. The hall was rarely used, but was a nice place for the kids to run around and play—especially on a rainy day.

The few girlfriends I invited from school showed up for the party. Mom was pleasant when she saw them, then off we went to the upstairs dance hall. We played games and danced a little.

The party was about over when one of my siblings yelled up the stairs for us girls to come to the dining room. I never expected a birthday cake. Mom surprises me and walks from the kitchen, setting a decorated, homemade cake with thirteen candles in front of me, while singing "Happy Birthday," with everyone chiming in. She told me after the party, she caught onto my mischief when she noticed me cleaning the dance hall.

Mom was a multitasker. She would start off each week by making a large batch of bread. If we ran out of bread, she made another batch. It wasn't unusual for her to have bread rising in the kitchen, and clothes washing in the wringer washer while taking time to sew on the sewing machine.

The following day, clothing was ironed, with special attention given to starched shirt collars for Dad and the boys. There was no permanent-press clothing. The clothing had been sprinkled lightly with water, rolled up, and placed in a basket the evening before. I recall the procedure well.

Mom also took time for rest. Her rule was, "My little ones need a nap, and so do I." Her best time for napping was after lunch. She would lie down beside them and sing a lullaby or tell little stories about the Three Bears, Humpty Dumpty, and Little Jack Horner that she knew by heart.

After the little ones were sound asleep, she would quietly leave the room and have time for herself. That's when she usually sewed. She was afraid if the younger children were around her, they might accidentally stick their little finger near the needle and get pricked. Thank goodness, it never happened!

Besides mending and alterations, Mom made all of her bib aprons, and still made most of the girls' clothing. She sewed dresses, coats, hats, leggings, and hand muffs that kept their hands warm during the colder months. My sister Shirley remembers Mom making her a coat and leggings.

She created her own patterns. Her inspiration for designing clothing possibly came from mail-order catalogs.

Mom rarely needed to shop for fabric. She checked out the clothes closets and would find a garment no longer being used for her next project. Her passion was recreating something new from something old. She didn't waste leftover fabric, either. She saved the pieces and made patchwork quilts. Being thrift-minded, she used worn sheet blankets for the inside lining of her quilts.

Mom overlooked the girls' 4-H sewing projects. My projects were a towel, then an apron, and then a dress. If a seam wasn't straight, I had to rip it out and sew it over. Mom's persistence paid off! She was pleased, as I was, when winning a blue ribbon for a yellow cotton dress that I made.

Another lesson was darning socks. Every month or so, Mom brought out a basket of socks worn out at the heels, along with darning needles and thread to the dining room table. She taught us older girls how to darn socks. We placed a wooden mallet inside the sock where the hole was, and, using a threaded needle, we wove stitches in and out, covering the hole and making our socks good as new again!

* * *

Shirley Irene was the ninth child born in our family, on December 3, 1953. She was blessed to be given the middle name Irene, our mother's first name. In time, she would become the oldest of the "four little girls," as Mom would say. She had four older brothers and four older sisters.

Shirley was several months old when Grandma Jennie came to live with us. It was Mom's turn in her family to take care of her mother. My parents' bedroom was the only bedroom on the main floor. They gave their bedroom to Grandma, while they slept on a sofa bed. Shirley's large crib was also kept in the living room.

Every morning when my parents awoke, they tidied

Seven sisters: Julie, Ruth Ann, and Mary Jane. Front: Shirley, baby Noreen, Bernadette, and Joan (circa 1958) before Rita was born.

up in the living room, setting their bedding aside, and restored the room for family use even before the children came downstairs.

A playpen in the dining room was handy for little Shirley to roam in during part of the day. My brother Jim remembers Grandma Jennie. "Grandma was paralyzed on half of her body and would do dishes with one hand to help Mama. She walked with a cane and couldn't talk, so when we misbehaved, she would hook us around the neck with that cane to slow us down."

Bernadette also remembers Grandma Jennie. "Grandma could only say, 'Dare, dare, me' when she needed something, and when Mama was trying to teach her how to blow her nose into a handkerchief.

"I remember observing how busy Mama was. It was about time for me to start first grade at school. I worried about Mama and told her, 'Mama, I don't think I should go to school. I should stay home and help you instead.' Mama didn't see it that way and I ended up going to school."

I'm not certain how long Grandma stayed with us, but by the time she left our home and was cared for by another of Mom's siblings, Shirley was old enough to remember Grandma saying "Dare, dare."

When Grandma was to be cared for by Mom's brother and sister-in-law, Uncle Cliff and Aunt Theresa (Lamie), in Marlette, Michigan, Mary Jane, at eleven and a half years old, spent a summer there in 1955.

Mary Jane recalled, "Dad and Mom were gone to Traverse City when I was in the garden picking peas for a meal. I saw Uncle Cliff and Aunt Theresa pull into the driveway. They had seen me when driving past the garden, working by myself.

"I quickly left the garden, with shelled peas in my pail, and greeted them at their car. They asked me, 'How would you like to come stay with us this summer?' After I asked permission from Dad and Mom, they let me go, thinking I might be of some help to care for Grandma Jennie."

When summer ended, we as a family took a day trip to Marlette to pick up Mary Jane. Traveling there gave us a chance to visit Grandma Lamie, our uncle, aunt, and cousins. Dad prepared for the trip by clearing out all of his tools from the back end of his panel truck and fitting a daybed for us kids to sit on.

We left home early on a Saturday morning and got as far as Division Street in Traverse City, when we heard the blaring sounds of a siren and saw the bright, blinking lights of a police vehicle trailing our truck. Dad knew he was being stopped for speeding and immediately pulled off to the side of the road.

His rosary beads were strung around his hand at the steering wheel as he rolled down the window.

"What's the emergency?" the cop asked.

Dad was calm and responded, "This is an emergency. My mother-in-law's health is crucial."

We were all sitting on the daybed in the back and were worried Dad would get a ticket. Grandma was paralyzed, but I didn't think of her as seriously ill.

Mom sat quietly in the passenger seat. She had told us to be still.

The officer let Daddy go ... He was lucky! He only received a warning.

We had a nice day visit and then headed for home. Our home had been regularly visited by out-of-town relatives, but it was a rare occasion for my parents to drive that far to visit relatives, let alone take us with them.

We were thankful when we returned home with no further incidents. Dad always had a heavy foot on the pedal, and we were all used to it. I think his rosary beads saved the day!

In a matter of time, more relatives stayed with us. Uncle Steve and Aunt Mary Petrowski, who were elderly, had the misfortune of losing their home in a house fire, less than a mile away. They stayed with us until Dad remodeled their garage into living quarters. Later, Dad built them a new home at the site of the destroyed home.

A couple years after my birthday party, Dad tore down the old dance hall/woodshed after he determined the building wasn't safe anymore. In its place, he built an attached, brick-front, wide single-door garage with a basement underneath. What a convenience that was!

Left to right: Ted, Edward, Jim, and Larry in wagon, and Ed Fleis leveling cement for new garage

18

Music, Music, Music

DAD PLAYED VIOLIN WITH THE ISADORE SODBUSTERS nearly every weekend since 1945, when his band was established. They played at various dance halls for weddings and local celebrations: the upstairs dance hall above Cedar Tavern, Centerville and Solon Township Halls, the gymnasium above Morey's store in Suttons Bay, and the old Lime Lake Hall (the former American Legion Hall) in Maple City.

Mom supported Dad's music through and through, but at some point, she stayed home more often than going to his band jobs. It could have been for the reason of having newborn babies and young children, or the feeling of being excluded. Time and again when she went with Dad, she would sit by ladies she had known since the days Dad courted her. They were friendly and spoke to her in English, but would talk to each other in Polish, excluding her from their conversations. The old Polish-French ethnic divide was still evident.

It was different, though, when she and Dad received an invitation which included the children. Only a few of us could go and we took turns, leaving one of us older girls looking after the younger children. We wore special clothes Mom had ready for us to wear and we got to dance a little. That's what she loved ... having her children with her by her side while Dad was playing music in public.

One day, Dad showed up at home carrying a black leather case containing a man-sized, black-marble accordion. He had just been at Uncle Steve and Aunt Mary Petrowski's home. They had company visiting from Wisconsin. I don't know whether he bartered or paid for it, but that was my first accordion.

It sat unattended for months. With permission from Dad, I tried it on. It was heavy and required a towel behind the back straps to secure it. Playing the piano side of the accordion was easy. Coordinating it with the bass side wasn't. I would look at a reflection of myself with the accordion on in the plate glass window of our recreation room, and could easily spy the rhinestone of the C-base button. That was my start! Slowly but surely, with time and practice, I learned a few tunes, including some polkas. I was fourteen years old.

I made my debut playing accordion on October 17, 1953, with Dad and his Isadore Sodbusters band, when they played for the wedding of Joan Kelinski and John Sassin at the old Lime Lake Hall, in Maple City.

Dad was on the bandstand when he invited me to join him and play a couple tunes. We had never practiced together and I was surprised that he snuck in my accordion. After I slipped it on, he said to "take the lead." I started off playing the "Beer Barrel Polka," as Dad played violin and Uncle Steve Pleva chorded on the piano.

Isadore Sodbusters Band with Ruth Ann playing accordion on October 17, 1953.

Forty-two years later, in 1995, a photo surfaced of the event, when the Kelinski family was sorting through old photos. They were kind enough to give Dad a copy, and he in turn made a copy for me.

19

1954–55

MORNINGS ON SCHOOL DAYS WERE BUSY. Our alarm clock for waking up was usually Dad's voice calling up the stairs, "WAKE UP! TIME TO GET READY!"

Mom fired up the wood stove—part of the combination range, with the other half being a gas stove—and started making a warm breakfast for everyone, while Dad fed coal to the burning furnace in the basement, ate his breakfast, and usually left for work early. There was only one large floor-grate heat register in the whole house, and on chilly mornings, we hovered over it and warmed ourselves after coming down the stairs.

Early-morning barn chores had to be done. Fresh milk from the cows was brought to the shed and dumped into a large, round steel container on top of the cream separator, operated by electricity, which separated the cream from the milk. One spigot delivered cream into a large metal cream can, and the other spigot delivered skimmed milk in a separate container.

Mom was not happy if the cream separator wasn't washed by the time the bus arrived. She would hold back one of the girls, saying, "You're not going to school until the cream separator is washed." Whoever was held back to do the job walked a mile to school. It was a job Mom needed out of the way before she planned the rest of her day, taking care of her little ones and getting her other work done.

One time when I was held back to clean the separator, I recall Mom saying, "You don't know how lucky you are to go to high school!"

I was in tenth grade, and by then, four of my classmates had quit school after ninth grade to help their parents on the farm. "You know," Mom said, "I could hold you back!"

I didn't take Mom's words seriously, because I knew she wanted her children to excel and graduate from high school. I always believed that to be true of both of my parents. Education was a priority.

In 1954, I met Harold Thompson at a Sadie Hawkins dance at the Maple City School gym. I was with high school friends from Holy Rosary School. Some of us dressed up in costumes. The

135

plaid flannel-lined jeans I wore were turned inside out. The boys at school were shy about asking a girl to dance, so the girls danced with each other.

That all changed when three older boys, who were alumni of Maple City High School, came to the dance. One of them was Harold. He walked over to where I was sitting on a bench next to his cousin Ronnie, who introduced us. Harold asked me to dance and came back for another dance. I was only fourteen years old. I felt flattered dancing with him because he danced so well.

I saw Harold a few months later, at a dance in Copemish, thirty-two miles away, where a crowd of young folks gathered and danced. It was a double date for Julie and me, with a couple of nice boys from Kingsley. As soon as my date and I danced ... I discovered he had two left feet!

Harold must have noticed because he rescued me with a dance. Then, off he went and danced with other girls, then came back asking for another dance. Before the evening was over, he asked for a date. I couldn't say yes because I needed permission from my parents.

I asked Mom first if I could go on a date with Harold. She said, "Go ask your dad. If he says it's okay, it's okay with me." I went to the living room and asked Dad. He told me, "I know Harold's aunt and uncle (Anna and Leonard Armstrong). I built their barn." Harold was a young boy when he came to live with them from Detroit. His parents were divorced. Dad didn't say "yes" either. I had permission after they talked it over and determined I could go.

Harold was five years older than me. He was twenty, and I was fifteen, when we had our first date was in Copemish—the popular place for dancing. I got so sweaty from dancing that my shirt got stained blue from the bleed of my jumper.

Shirley was the baby in the family when I was offered my first summer job after my freshman year in 1954. Mom didn't hold me back. I think her reasoning was all about learning the ways and means of earning a paycheck, just as she had when she was my age.

I met Carol Konieczka, a fellow cheerleader, at a basketball game between Holy Rosary School and Glen Arbor School. Her parents needed help at the Dinette Restaurant in Glen Arbor.

Ruth Ann standing in front of the building now known as Art's Tavern in Glen Arbor, across from the (former) Dinette Restaurant. (circa 1954)

I worked there for two summers, waitressing, handling sales at the cash register, cooking when they were shorthanded, and cleaning. A jukebox in the corner was entertaining. I loved hearing the music! Then I worked for the Barczaks, who owned a commercial laundry service in Glen Arbor, ironing white shirts for waiters. I was provided room and board at both places, and was fortunate to come home for visits.

* * *

Back at the farm, Dad surprised us when he brought home our first television in the early '50s, and set it in a corner of the living room. We could hardly wait to watch the first show on the black-and-white screen. It was in the middle of the day and a business meeting was taking place in Cadillac. It wasn't what we expected. We could see people talking to each other on a live screen.

The reception wasn't the greatest. It had rabbit ears for an antenna and we could only pull up one channel, Channel 13 from Cadillac. Later on, Dad installed an outside antenna.

Soon, Channel 7 from Traverse City was available. Frequently, in the evening, after chores were done, we watched TV as a family. Some of the popular shows were: *The Arthur Godfrey Show, Ed Sullivan, Liberace, I Love Lucy, Groucho Marx, The Lawrence Welk Show*, and Bishop Fulton J. Sheen on *Life Is Worth Living*. On Saturdays, Julie and I would watch *Your Hit Parade*, a show playing a variety of music.

Mama let us be teenagers and have the TV on as we worked and listened to the popular tunes. Julie and I took turns scrubbing either the living room or dining room floors on Saturdays.

"Mom loved to hear us singing and signed us up for talent shows and offered our talent for numerous community functions and events, including many television appearances," Julie recalled.

We called ourselves The Fleis Sisters when we entered our first competition at Maple City High School. The Schramski Sisters from Suttons Bay won first place, and we won second.

The following year, we competed again and sang a song called "Sisters," and won first place. The lyrics of the song fit us perfectly, as we pointed a finger at each other and sang, "I'm there to keep my eye on her."

Another opportunity for Julie and me was singing at a regional Farm Bureau meeting at Twin Lakes, near Traverse City, after our parents volunteered us to supply the entertainment as members of the local Farm Bureau group in Isadore. We wore matching blouses and jumpers that Mom sewed for us. Our cousin, Gertrude Ann Pleva from Cedar, accompanied us on the piano.

Ruth Ann, Gertrude Ann Pleva, and Julie at Gilbert Lodge (circa 1956)

We entertained more than we planned, singing three top country songs we had learned from listening to *Your Hit Parade* on TV, never paying attention to the words. All we cared about was learning a song that we could harmonize to, as Julie's voice was soprano and mine was alto or tenor.

The song titles we selected were "Softly," "Slowly," and "More and More." It's beyond your imagination how the audience responded. Julie and I finally understood what all the laughter was about. The ridiculous song titles made everyone laugh out loud.

What an evening it was, with my parents in the audience and everyone laughing. We talked and laughed with Dad and Mom all the way home. What did we know as teenagers? We were still learning.

Another event was Dairy Days, held at Clinch Park, sponsored by the Grand Traverse Dairy Council to raise funds for Northwestern Michigan College. The invitation for Julie and me to perform came from Uncle Joe and Aunt Lucille (Lamie) Harpe, Mom's sister. They owned Green Acres Dairy, a business on Old Mission Peninsula, that sold and delivered milk in glass bottles. Their daughter, our cousin Faye, used to help her parents by washing those bottles.

We sang at the event, and the next day, the *Traverse City Record-Eagle* had an article about it! "The most hilarious feature of the Dairy Day program was a demonstration of hand milking by Rep. Arnell Engstrom, who proved that he hadn't forgotten how. He was assisted by Ruth Ann and Juliette Fleis, who sang a rendition of "Bessie the Heifer." It stated, "$25.70 was added to the

Northwestern Michigan College building fund. Participants drank all the milk they wanted for 10 cents. A total of 416 half pints of white and chocolate milk was consumed."

Channel 7 had heard about "The Fleis Sisters" and were looking for entertainment for a brand-new children's show called *The Deputy Don Show*. I was old enough to drive Dad's car, so Mom and Dad gave Julie and I permission to be in the show.

Mom went with us on a little shopping spree to J.C. Penney's store, where we purchased our duds: Levi jeans; long-sleeved, plaid, cotton, Western-style shirts; and cowgirl hats! Whoopee!

We performed on TV twice a month for several months after school. We practiced before the show with our cousin Gertrude Ann Pleva, who played piano and accompanied us.

She rode with us to the television station on M-72 for the show. Julie and I sang and used motions with our words, singing for the children our favorite songs: "Sisters," "There's a Little White Duck," "I've Been Working on the Railroad," and "Tennessee Wig Walk." We never expected to be paid, but we did receive boxes of doughnuts, compliments of the sponsors. Another time, we performed at an outdoor Western show on Channel 7, when Aunt Agnes (Fleis) accompanied us by playing her banjo.

20

The Siblings Remember Life on the Farm

LIFE ON THE FARM SETTLED INTO ROUTINES that lasted two decades, spanning the lives of those who lived there from 1949–69.

Following are memories of farm life from my siblings.

Mom was a superb cook. She would assign small chores for the girls to help her as she prepared a meal, such as setting the table, peeling a kettleful of potatoes, or making a simple one-egg cake for dessert.

Shirley said, "Mom always made dessert special by serving it in special dishes. She never served dessert on a plate we had eaten dinner from.

Thomas Fleis enjoying one of many meals with the Ed Fleis family

"One of my favorite memories is coming home from school, and Mom made a fresh batch of homemade bread, and she remembered to save some of the dough so we could fry it up in a pan of hot oil, and slather it with fresh churned butter and homemade jam. Mmmmm. My mouth is watering just thinking about it.

"Another favorite was on Fridays during Lent, and Mom would make French toast and sprinkle it with enough cinnamon and sugar-yum! How about her famous potato pancakes? We were all very spoiled!"

Bernadette recalls: "Breakfast was always hearty, but I also remember the oatmeal and cream of wheat in the winter months.

"We always sat down at the table before we ate and prayed a blessing. The large family we were, we all ate our meals together. We always had full meals that included meat, potatoes, a

140

vegetable, and dessert. I remember one of our favorite desserts was canned peaches with graham cracker crumbs sprinkled on top, or when peaches were in season, Mom would slice fresh peaches, sprinkled lightly with sugar, and topped off with homemade whipped cream. Delish!"

Joan adds: "I remember Mom making Polish paczkis for us. She would flatten the dough and form circles in the dough with a glass, and after the dough was raised, she dropped one at a time into hot boiling lard, until they were nice and brown. They were light, airy, and delicious, filled with jam, or sugar-coated when we shook the paczkis in a brown bag with a little sugar."

Ted said: "Mom and Dad both had a sweet tooth, and we seemed to always have dessert at the evening meal. Fresh strawberries and cake … topped my favorites! (That's if you cleaned your plate first! That was Pa's rule.)"

Jim: "How did Mom and Dad determine how we sat at the dinner table? It seems like I was always the last one to get the potatoes. Mom was serving more food than Burry's Restaurant in Cedar. I don't know how she did it."

Burry's was a restaurant with fine dining, served family-style, and was the only place in Cedar where you could buy an ice-cream cone. Whenever Dad gave us a few coins and told us to buy an ice-cream cone, we lined up in front of Burry's ice-cream counter. There had to be four or five of us. Mr. Burry would smile when he saw us, and thanked us when he served our cones.

Julie: "Although living on the farm required much work, it was also fun. During these times, I learned to sing some of my favorite songs. Whenever there was work, there was also singing.

Shirley remembers "when we younger girls would be in the kitchen doing the dishes (which always took hours, of course), we would be fighting and Mom would come into the kitchen and say, 'Girls, quit fighting and sing!'"

Joan: "Mom never let us cook with her. She must've enjoyed preparing the food. It was our job to set the table, and then, the big job was to clear the table and wash many dishes. If Mom saw us girls bickering or fighting, she would get us singing. Time went quickly, and the dishes got done."

Mom trained all her daughters to wash and wipe dishes properly. We learned very quickly what her expectations were, because as soon as one of us stirred a little fuss, she would start singing.

It took two girls to do the job, and sometimes three—one to wash, one to wipe, and one to put away. As soon as Mom heard arguing coming from our mouths …

"I want to wash."

"No, I want to wash."

She didn't say a word, she just started singing to distract us. We would laugh at ourselves and join in. That was Mom's routine.

We learned several songs at the kitchen sink. "Tell Me Why," "You Are My Sunshine," "Que Sera, Sera," "Let the Sunshine In," and "Have Faith, Hope, and Charity."

I think if Mom had been in the barn when the boys were doing chores and not getting along, she might have started singing there, too! She did say, "I can't be in two places at the same time." My brothers learned the songs from hearing us singing, when they came into the house from doing their barn chores.

With the size of our family, we had piles of dishes to wash, and it wasn't always easy. But what is cherished the most is the time we spent in the kitchen with Mom, who instilled in us ... the ability to work together, get along with each other, and to sing together!

At least once a year, my parents hosted the Isadore Farm Bureau meeting at our home. Several relatives and neighbors gathered for a business meeting. Living on the farm, eggs and fresh cream were plentiful, so Mom would serve scrumptious homemade cream puffs filled with whipped cream. They never failed her.

Then came a little entertainment from the older children, singing one or two familiar songs they had learned in the kitchen with Mom.

I recall one of the members saying afterwards, "I can hardly wait for the next meeting at your house."

"Will there be entertainment next year?" asked another.

Our home wasn't the only place my siblings entertained. Mary Jane, Ted, and Jim danced with a 4-H group called "The Student Kolo," at Holy Rosary School. The idea for organizing a dance group started when one of the nuns, Sister Mary Leonette, was playing records for the class. She trained those three, along with seven other students, making five dancing couples to dance to Yugoslavian folk music. The group first danced for the school, then for the Isadore Farm Bureau group, before entering competition. They won first place when they competed against seventeen other groups throughout the state on the campus of Michigan State College on April 24, 1959.[59]

---

59   An educational program called "The Spring Songfest" held on the campus of Michigan State College (now Michigan State University). My siblings were in grades ten, eight, and six. The event was sponsored by the University of Michigan Broadcasting Service.

Thanks to the *Leelanau Enterprise*, the group was identified as the "Homestead Larks" when they won the blue ribbon.

THIS PHOTO, taken during the 1958-59 school year, shows Leelanau County 4-H'ers entertaining an audience with some traditional dances at a 4-H program. The participants are Raymond Brzezinski; William Walters; Vincent Zywicki; Theodore and James Fleis; Mary Jane Fleis (Steup); Dorothy Fabiszak (Fritz); Germaine Fabiszak (Schmidt); Barbara Zywicki (Sister Mary Theresanne); Bernadette Mikowski (Winowiecki) and Christine Mikowski (Schlueter).

Discipline

How did our parents handle discipline? No matter the age, they disciplined us when we were caught misbehaving. Are spankings fun? NO! Did we get spanked? YES!

I don't think our parents wanted to face the Lord at their demise and have to admit they spoiled their children. Younger ones faced each other sitting in chairs—no fun looking at the one from whom you just tried to take away their toy! Then the giggling would start. When they finally had permission to get off their chairs, they hugged each other and said, "I'm sorry," and off they went, content.

As we got a little older, the remedy was, "Stand in a corner," or, "Kneel in a corner—and say some prayers while you're at it!"

When we thought our time was up, we would ask, "Can I get up now?"

Sometimes Mom said, "Yes, you can." Other times it was, "No, not yet!"

When more than one was involved, we apologized and forgave the other.

If Mom caught us saying a bad word, such as "sh*t" (even though there was plenty of it in the barnyard), a little taste of soap in our mouths cured us.

When we were older and should have known better, we got a whack on the seat of our pants, and, depending on the reason, Mom added, "Dad's gonna hear about this when he gets home." She and Dad talked about what was going on each day. We knew Mom was in charge when Dad wasn't home, but he took over when he was.

I got in trouble when I forgot to unplug the iron after ironing my school clothes one morning. Mom was angry when she saw the plug still in the outlet and gave me a good scolding. Dad was home at the time and heard all the commotion. That was the only time he gave me a whack on my seat with his belt, warning, "You could have burnt the house down."

"One time," Shirley says, "Mom found a pack of cigarettes in my bedroom, and I explained to Mom that I was not smoking (and, at the time, I wasn't), just holding them for a friend and trying to help them quit smoking. But Mom, in her wisdom, said, 'You are who your friends are,' meaning, you may not be smoking today, but if you hang out with those friends long enough, you'll be doing the same thing. How right she was!"

Mom had a lot of sayings. Shirley remembers, "When you point a finger, there are three fingers pointing back at you"; "If you have your health, you have everything"; and "Be a good example to your younger sisters." Mom never thought she was very smart because she only went through the eighth grade, but she was the smartest and wisest woman I ever knew.

Some situations called for more discipline, as Jim explains: "Only on special disciplinary sessions would Mom first talk to you and try to reason why you did what you did; then second, make you go across the road and pick out your own switch from the willow sticks that grew wild there. You would then take the switch to her so she could find out if it was deserving of the butt it was about to meet.

"Sometimes I would pick thin switches, sometimes thicker ones. I remember one time I left the leaves on the end of it, thinking that this would cushion the blow. However, I found out the leaves on the end of the switch actually inflicted more pain.

"Sometimes I would get across the road and take my time, hoping Mom would forget what I had done. That never happened. Then the suspense as I knelt over her knee. … Then the blow came! Sometimes soft, sometimes hard! I know Mom never tried to hurt us, she only tried to make us learn."

Mom enforced modesty as well, as Jim explains: "As a child, I didn't know what a bra or women's underwear looked like in the Sears and Roebuck catalog or magazines. When we could look at a catalog or magazine, all the women were wearing clothing. Mom had taken a ballpoint pen and sketched in any areas of the model's clothing that wasn't appropriate for us to see."

Mom's traditional screening of catalogs left an impression for Bernadette's boyfriend, Ken Denoyer (who became her husband). Bernadette said, "I was behind in being ready, so Ken sat in the living room, waiting and looking through magazines. When we got in the car to leave, Ken asked me, 'Who colors the clothing on the pictures in the catalogs?' I said, 'Oh, that's Mom that does it. She doesn't want us to see anything indecent.' Ken said, 'She does a pretty good job.'"

I believe discipline serves as a warning for us to remember that life won't always be easy!

21

Weekend Routines

IN THE MID-FIFTIES, we often called Mom and Dad "Ma and Pa."

Rita said, "Saturdays at home on the farm meant cleaning the house and getting church clothes ready, polishing shoes ... and CONFESSION at church."

Ma's routines were down pat. Every Saturday morning, floors were often scrubbed by hand and sometimes got a "lick and a promise," as she would say, when she wanted floors washed in a hurry. About once a month, the floors were waxed with a homemade cotton pad attached to a handle. The floors shined and looked like new!

Ma made sure all our Sunday church clothes were ready by Saturday. One of the children polished shoes and lined them up on top of newspapers spread on the floor.

When we girls were too young to style our own hair, Mama would wrap our hair in rags. After we washed our hair, we took turns sitting on a chair next to the dining room table, where Mama stood near a pile of long, thin, white cotton strips she had torn from worn bed sheets.

She combed through our hair first to remove all the knots and tangles. Then she sectioned off enough hair for one curl. The one whose hair was being curled held one end of a cotton strip on top of her head. With the remaining strip, Mama twirled the section of hair for a single curl downward, around and around the cotton strip, then twirled the remaining cotton strip over the twirled hair until it reached the strip held by her daughter and tied both ends together. That held the ragged curl in place. Then, she sectioned off another small portion of hair, and so on. The result on Sunday morning was the look of Goldilocks or Shirley Temple with ringlets galore!

"Mom saved ribbons from packages or whatever," Shirley remembers, "washed them, ironed them, and fashioned them to make pretty bows for our hair."

Mom loved having one of her daughters curl her hair. I was probably twelve when she allowed me to cut her hair and give her a home permanent, such as Tony or Lilt. She got compliments, and had me do the same for Aunt Mary Petrowski and Aunt Josie Pleva, who lived near us.

Mom was like that, wanting us to help others. She always had a daughter on whom she could depend to beautify her hair.

On Sunday mornings, Ma made certain we were dressed properly for church. The boys wore their best trousers and shirts, usually with a tie. The girls wore dresses and covered their heads with scarves or hats. "At Easter time, we always wore a bonnet," Joan said. The girls also wore white gloves.

Pa was always first to be ready. He headed for the car and waited for us. Ma would dress the youngest children before she got herself ready. By then, Pa was already honking the horn. Kids piled in and waited for Ma. Then Ma came. We were never late for church, thanks to Pa.

Sundays were the most relaxing and playful, with minimal chores to do. Also, meals on Sundays were different from weekday meals. We had two meals rather than the usual three. Since we were fasting for Communion, we had our big breakfast after church, and dinner was served around 4:00 p.m.

Ma planned a Sunday meal in advance. She did the nitty-gritty work on Saturday. When planning a chicken dinner, one or two chickens were butchered, feathered, cleaned, cut up, and soaked on Saturday. You might ask, "Wasn't that a lot of work for your mom, preparing those big dinners on Sundays?" The answer is "Yes!" But she never took a day off from cooking! She loved to cook for her family. Ma's kitchen was the heart of our home.

After Sunday breakfast, all the children trailed behind Pa to the living room. They knew he was about to entertain them, and waited patiently while he slipped out the bow from his leather violin case and slicked it up with a piece of golden rosin, up and down the strings, then draped the violin across his left shoulder and started plucking the strings. If the sound wasn't right, he called out to Julie or me to play an *A* on the piano, then an *E* as he adjusted the tuning pegs. Pa always made certain his treasured violin was tuned properly before he entertained.

The children partnered off with each other and danced to the count of "one-two" when Dad played a polka, or "one-two-three" when he played a waltz. Larry was dancing with his little sister, Shirley, when he was four and she was two years of age.

Sometimes Dad entertained us by bouncing a wooden marionette up and down on his knee to the rhythm of piano music played by Julie or me.

That was Dad's special time with us. Mom could hear music, laughter, and giggling from where she worked in the kitchen preparing dinner, and every now and then, she would come into the living room and stay awhile. Her face would light up with delight to see the children dancing and having so much fun!

Our home was known for having lots of company, especially on Sundays, with warm hospitality extended by Pa and Ma, besides delicious meals, music, laughter, playing cards, and Pa's "shot and a beer" offered to the men folks. "*Na Zdrowie!*" (Cheers!)

When you came to the door, you were greeted. When my parents talked with you, it was, "What's going on in your life?" They uplifted your spirit with humor and made light of things.

As children, we were taught to mind our manners and to be polite and address adults with their proper title: "Mr." or "Mrs.," "Aunt" or "Uncle," and to say, "please" and "thank you" at the proper times.

The youngest children never had to wait to be fed. A smaller table set up in the dining room was where they sat down on small chairs and ate their meals. After their little tummies were full, they went off to play.

The girls set the table with a fine, white tablecloth and the blue-willow dishes that were brought down from an upper cabinet of the kitchen.

When it was time to eat, Dad led the blessing before meals, as everyone stood near the table and prayed together, "Bless us, O Lord, for these Thy gifts, which we are about to receive, from Thy bounty, through Christ, our Lord. Amen."

Ma often served food in courses, just like a restaurant. She would serve chicken soup with homemade noodles or czarnina—a sweet-sour soup made with pork instead of duck, homemade bread or rolls with churned butter, fresh vegetables, scalloped potatoes or mashed potatoes with gravy, and the best fried chicken you ever tasted! Then, to finish off a meal, she would serve dessert.

We never ran out of food. The one or two chickens Ma cooked for a Sunday meal fed all of our company, as well.

After every meal, the girls knew their routines well. We might have felt a little sorry for ourselves, having to clean up and wash the dishes. We had a little help sometimes, but the company usually played cards with Dad after dinner; euchre, pepper, or poker at the dining room table. Ma joined in fun at some point! Often, there was entertainment for our company, whether it was singing or playing instruments.

Sunday Drive

At least one Sunday each summer, Pa would ask out loud just before going outside, "Who all wants to go for a ride?" and we'd yell out, "I wanna go!" and pile into his car, even though it was always the same road trip on M-22 through Port Oneida. We loved it!

Driving past Little Traverse Lake on M-22, the first stop was Lund's Scenic Garden, where we walked along a pathway in the woods and viewed several billboards depicting biblical scenes of the life of Christ. They were amazing! We never met Mr. Lund, but he was the painter of those scenes. It was sad to see the scenes fade over the years, and eventually to see Lund's Scenic Garden close. If Mr. Lund only knew how much we appreciated his beautiful artwork.

Next stop was Shalda's Grocery, not far from the Bi-Centennial Barn, where Dad picked up a few cigars. Then off we went to the roadside Dairy Freeze before Port Oneida Road, where he treated us to ice-cream cones.

Ma would entertain us along the way, telling jokes or testing us on our spelling. She would say, "Mississippi River, can you spell it?" or "Railroad crossing! Watch for the cars; can you spell "IT" without any r's?" The younger children would try hard to spell the big words, but the answer for both was "i-t"!

If anyone ever acted up in the backseat, Pa would say, "If you don't straighten up, I'm pulling off the road." He meant what he said, and it wasn't fun sitting on the side of the road ... before he drove off again.

22

More of the Fifties

WHEN I TURNED SIXTEEN IN APRIL OF 1955, I felt older than I was, perhaps because I heard so much about "Busia marrying Dziadzia" when she was my age. Dad and Mom held a party for my sweet-sixteen birthday. They invited a few relatives, including Grandpa Thomas, but not any of my friends, except for Harold.

I figured my parents thought Harold was a good catch for me. He was Catholic, had a good job in the Upper Peninsula as a lineman, drove a decent car, and played cards. He and Dad seemed to hit things off really well from the start!

For our dates, we frequented places where there was dancing, usually traveling thirty-five to forty miles to the dance halls in Summit City or Buckley. It was also common practice to attend the wedding dance of an acquaintance and just walk in and dance with no invitation. Sometimes, we went to the State Theater in downtown Traverse City to watch a black-and-white movie, and enjoy a root beer at the J&S Drive-In afterward.

Occasionally, Harold's friends threw a party. They were old enough to drink, just as he was, and had a beer party. That didn't seem strange, as there was always beer at home whenever we had a gathering. I never touched a drink. I had learned my lesson when I was a kid sneaking that taste from Dad's bottle of whiskey.

All the same, it was never wise of me to overlook Harold's drinking. I was lovestruck and somewhat flattered dating someone older. I didn't think to discuss these things with my parents either. I relied on myself to figure things out.

It served me well to have the mindset of finishing high school, responsibilities at home, music to enjoy, and the privilege of a summer job.

While I was working during the summertime of my high school years, I didn't realize how hard times fell on Ma, and even took for granted how more work was expected from my two younger sisters, Mary Jane and Bernadette. This was especially true the summer of 1956, a few months after my baby sister, Joanie was born, when both Julie and I were working in Glen Arbor. Julie washed dishes at the Old Orchard Inn and had room and board there. Julie said, "The countertops were full of dishes after Sunday brunches, but I enjoyed working there."

My parents' tenth child, Joan Francis Cabrini, born on February 5, 1956, was blessed with two middle names honoring Saint Francis Xavier Cabrini. Born in Italy, she was the first American canonized saint in 1946.

Joan was born three weeks early, three days after our mother's fortieth birthday. "You weren't due until the end of February," Mama once told Joan, "But, I went into labor when I was at a dance at Solon Township Hall."

Joan's First Communion (1963) with Shirley, Rita, and Noreen

When Joanie wasn't talking by the age Mama expected, she mentioned that she was afraid Joanie might be "tongue-tied." I dreaded hearing Mom say the words "tongue-tied," but didn't ask what those words meant. Instead, I secretly took my little sister aside every now and then, and spoke a single word clearly up to her ear. Just Joan and I—no one else was around. I did that for a while. It might have helped, because it wasn't long before she was talking! Mom was so surprised to hear little Joanie ask for things, instead of pointing to what she wanted.

Our younger sister, Bernadette, said, "I could tell when Mama was frustrated, and I couldn't understand why you girls were working somewhere else when Mama needed your help at home." Bernadette took it upon herself to help Mama all she could when she was a few months shy of eight years of age.

Mary Jane, at twelve, "spent a lot of time in the kitchen helping Mama," Bernadette added. "She helped her prepare large meals and [did] any job that needed to be done."

Mary Jane said, "One day, when Mom and Dad went to Traverse City, my sister Julie was home and in charge, and I said to myself, 'Today is the day I bake bread.' My mother baked ten to twelve loaves of bread at a time, and I stood beside her asking to knead the dough and bake the bread. She just did it herself while I stood by watching.

"So, they were out of the driveway, and I proceeded to get out the *Home Comfort Cookbook* and used it as my guide. I doubled and quadrupled the recipe and the bread was baked when they got home.

"Mom asked, 'Who baked the bread?' and I owned up to it. There was no fanfare; I just took on the job of baking bread for the family.

"The lesson for me was the teaching Mother did while we were under her wings and how she let us make choices and follow through with them. I have always been thankful for the opportunity to succeed or fail under my parents' guidance."

Julie met her husband-to-be around this time. "When I was about fifteen years old, in the tenth grade," she says, "I attended a wedding at Solon Township Hall, where Ray Watkoski from Grand Rapids was playing accordion in a family band called The Pokacenos.

"He played in a band with his father, his brother, and his cousin. The band was new to us, and was beginning to play at a lot of weddings in the area. Our parents knew some of Ray's relatives who lived in the Traverse City area, where Ray's family visited and stayed whenever they were up north.

"Just as I was leaving the dance, Ray asked me where I lived, and I quickly said, 'Go past Holy Rosary, over three hills—the farmhouse on the right with all the kids.'

"A couple days later, Mom and I went to Cedar to sell the cream in a cream can that was collected from milk on the farm, and [I] saw Ray again. He explained that he had been looking for my house all day and he followed us back to the farmhouse."

* * *

In my senior year of high school, I worked at the R&S Shoe Store in Traverse City on Saturdays, making fifty cents an hour, plus extra coins when I sold additional footwear or accessories. I had permission to drive Dad's car to Cedar and rode with Mr. Al Laskey Sr., to Traverse City, as he worked at the furniture store across the street from the shoe store.

Ma helped me find this part-time job. I was wearing a pair of high-heeled shoes when we walked together downtown as I looked for a job. I saw a sign posted on the shoe store window and went inside to inquire, and was hired.

I think it was the high heels I was wearing that got the owner's attention, because one day he asked me, "Why aren't you wearing your high heels to work?" I told him, "My high heels were more for dressing up, not for working in."

With income of my own, I bought some school clothes and shoes. I also set aside money for savings in Dad's safe from the time I started earning a paycheck in high school. When I was invited to stand up as an attendant for three family weddings, I was able to pay the expenses for the three separate formal dresses I was to wear.

In my sophomore year, I was a bridesmaid when Uncle Joe Fleis and Lucille (Zywicki) were united in marriage on September 3, 1955, at Holy Rosary Church. At the end of my junior year and Julie's sophomore year, we both were bridesmaids for the wedding of Aunt Agnes Fleis, as she and Ron (Williams) married on June 2, 1956, also at Holy Rosary Church. In my senior year, I was a bridesmaid for my cousin, Lucille Rahe, on the Lamie side, and Elmer (Zenner), when they were married on November 10, 1956, at St. Mary's Church in Hannah. My brother Larry served as ring bearer and Shirley was the flower girl.

During high school years, Julie and I sang for many weddings at church and special occasions at school. The beautiful hymn, "On this Day, Oh Beautiful Mother" was always sung near the end of the nuptial mass when the bride placed a small bouquet of flowers on the altar at the foot of the Blessed Virgin Mary's statue. Then, she and her newly married husband prayed for intercession from Her for blessings in their marriage.

During my junior year we had no music teacher. Sister Domitilla, the principal, asked if I would take charge of the high school choir and accompany them on piano. I was happy to help out. In earlier grades, Sister DeChantel and Sister Noel had given me basic instruction on how to read musical notes, but I didn't know enough to proceed that way, and played music by ear.

Rehearsals took place during recess. Julie was always the first to show up and sat beside me; then the other girls came. The boys wouldn't give up recreation outdoors for singing, so I convinced Sister Domitilla that I needed regular school time for practice and she allowed it. I was pleased with the choir's performance at the Christmas program and at the spring graduation ceremony.

Before graduation day, my parents invited me to go to Traverse City. When we got there, Dad parked his car in front of a music store. We walked in, and Dad said to the salesperson, "We want our daughter to try on some accordions." I tried on several. The one I liked best was a lady's white marble, 120-bass accordion. I couldn't believe it when Dad and Mom bought it for me! I thanked them. They encouraged me to keep on playing music, and I did.

Soon afterwards, they took me to Maple Tavern in Maple City on a Sunday afternoon. Dad asked the owner, Glen Noonan, if it was okay if I played a little music? He said, "Sure!" There I was, playing polkas on my brand-new accordion for folks hanging out in the bar on a normally quiet afternoon.

My favorite place for entertaining was at home in front of my family or when company came over, and I considered myself lucky to be able to play this beautiful instrument.

 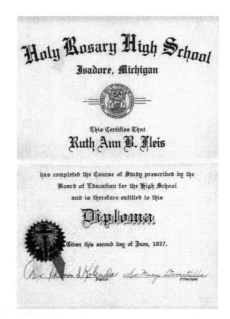

Ruth Ann, Rev. Fr. Kolenda, and Mary Ann Laskey (circa 1957)

In June of 1957, the day of my graduation, with my friend and only classmate, Mary Ann Laskey, the newly finished Holy Rosary convent was blessed by Rev. Father Kolenda. We reached a goal at a time when other classmates dropped out of school to work on their parents' farms, got married, or transferred. I couldn't help but notice how proud my parents were to have the first of their children graduate from high school; a goal my mother had yearned for.

My parents' eleventh child, Noreen Dolores, was born on April 24, 1957. My mother had developed gestational diabetes during her pregnancy and worried that it might affect her baby, but it didn't. Another blessing! However, diabetes impacted Mom's life eventually.

Noreen's birth occurred six weeks before my graduation. I had taken Mom to the hospital as Dad wasn't home, and stayed with her until he arrived. My baby sister was the bundle of joy I held on my graduation day.

"I was born two days before Dad's forty-second birthday," Noreen wrote. "Dad was a man of few words and talked fast, and, for a while, people thought my name was Dienne. Apparently, when asked shortly after my birth what the new baby's name was, Dad jokingly muttered, 'The End.'

Young Noreen (1961)

"Having our birthdays so close worked out swell for me. Even though our family didn't go overboard celebrating birthdays, Mom always made a big deal about Dad's special day, so Dad and I always blew out birthday candles together.

"Dad was strong, and the dozens of golf-ball sized mounds that lay under the skin of his arms and stomach made him seem even more so. (Those mounds were called fatty tumors and were an inherited trait in Dad's family. Grandpa also had them.)

"As a small child, I loved to curl up on the recliner with him. He'd watch the Detroit Tigers play baseball on TV, and I would lodge myself comfortably along his massive arm. I loved how he made me feel safe.

"Sometimes, I would show him the big muscle of my biceps. He would playfully squeeze the skin on the bottom-side of my arm. 'That's chicken fat,' he'd say. I knew Dad loved me, chicken fat and all."

* * *

The Isadore Sodbusters played well into the late '50s, but "faded out," to use Dad's words, "after other big bands started coming to town with better equipment." Ray Banasiak, owner of Sugar Ray's Tavern on M-22 in Cleveland Township, brought in Ray Tobaczka from Muskegon, Frankie Yankovic and his Yanks from Cleveland, Ohio, and the newly formed Pokacenos band from Grand Rapids. (He sold his business to a corporation, known as Sugar Loaf, in the 1960s.) Another place for dancing was Maple Tavern owned by Glen Noonan, in Maple City. Bobby Atkinson was a sixteen-year-old accordion player there. Later, he became a musical part of our family.

* * *

On Christmas Eve in 1957, Harold (whom I dated since age fifteen) had jokingly draped a colorful peacock bedspread on the living room floor in front of my parents and siblings. I couldn't tell if it was my present or not … and went off to the kitchen. He followed me and asked if I would marry him. I said yes, but was stunned at how he planned his proposal. We decided to be married on June 21, 1958.

Meanwhile, life went on for the siblings. Mary Jane entered a Mother's Day contest at Holy Rosary School called, "Mother is the Queen of May." She won first place for submitting this essay:

"My mother is the greatest because of her bestowment of tender love and sincere devotion, and mostly, her gratitude and justifiable discipline given to us."

Mary Jane won twenty-five dollars' worth of merchandise from a local dress shop, Joyce of Leland, and took Mom shopping for a dress to wear for my wedding. Mom selected a beautiful pastel-blue dress adorned with rhinestones and imitation pearls, with jewelry and a shawl.

Mary Jane occasionally bought other dresses for Mom because one day, before she was seventeen, she was looking inside Mom's closet and made an observation. "Mom, these clothes don't fit you," she said.

"I'll just keep them," Mom replied.

When Mary Jane asked Mom what size she was, Mom replied, "Fourteen and a half."

One day, Mary Jane was going to Traverse City with Dad and said, "Dad, I need some money to buy Mom a new dress."

Dad gave her the money and she bought a dress.

"That was the start," Mary Jane said. "From then on, I always knew Mom's size, and when I was able, I would buy a dress for her."

Meanwhile, Julie graduated from Holy Rosary School in early June of 1958. At a May ceremony she had the honor as class president of placing a crown of fresh flowers on the Blessed Virgin Mary statue at Holy Rosary Church. For the occasion she wore Aunt Agnes's wedding gown and veil.

I lived at home until the day of my wedding and worked a desk job as cashier/clerk for Coca-Cola Bottling Company on West Front Street in Traverse City. I paid for my wedding dress and accessories. Harold and I paid for our wedding cake, flowers, and photographer. He was working for Cluff Well Drilling, on the peninsula.

Ray and Julie became engaged on the eve of my wedding. When she announced her exciting news to Mom and Dad that evening, Mom's rather flustered and confused response was, "Go give that ring back to Ruth Ann!"

Mom probably thought that Julie was just teasing, but the thought now of having to plan a second wedding must have been somewhat of a shock.

The morning of my wedding, I was alone in my bedroom, when I slipped on my wedding gown and looked in the mirror. My eyes teared up and revealed a troubled heart. I had only myself to blame as I hadn't ever gone to my parents for advice or talked to a priest in preparation for marriage. There were some things I wasn't content with in making a lifetime commitment. I knew in my gut to call off the wedding, but I didn't have the courage. It seemed too late. All the preparations were done. Chickens had been butchered, and food prepared for a double reception. My parents had sacrificed much to give me a nice wedding.

At nine in the morning, one year after my high school graduation, the church bells rang as I walked down the aisle, holding onto my father's arm. My floor-length, white-satin wedding gown with its lace overlay, full skirt, long sleeves, perfectly scalloped neckline, and long, flowing veil, secured by a small cap of beaded pearls, all stayed in place, as did I. Harold and I said our marriage vows at a very solemn ceremony during a nuptial mass at Holy Rosary Church, officiated by Reverend Father Herman Kolenda.

By ten in the morning, I was Mrs. Harold Thompson.

Julie was my maid of honor and Ray Watkoski, her fiancé, was best man. My bridesmaids were my cousins, Barbara and Faye, and Harold's cousins, Arlene and Jeanette. Groomsmen were Harold's friends: Philip; Bob; a good neighbor, Leonard, and my brother Edward. Larry was our ring bearer; the flower girl was Shirley.

Immediately afterward, breakfast was served to a select group of close family and a few guests. Later, a feast of homegrown chicken cooked to perfection, with sides of mashed potatoes and gravy, homemade dinner rolls, and other tasty food was served to about one hundred guests at the Centerville Township Hall.

Thomas Fleis and Jennie Lamie were the honored guests.

Our honeymoon took us to Engadine, in the Upper Peninsula, where Harold had worked a few years back as a lineman installing electricity and had stayed at a rooming house there. He wanted me to see the place. It was dark outside when we arrived after a three-hour drive.

It wasn't at all what I expected from the way he described it. I had pictured something more lavish. It was more of a man-cave, with several rooms upstairs where everyone shared one bathroom. I suspected I was the only woman there.

I was right. The next morning when we had breakfast, the only people I saw were men.

From there, we went to see the famous Tahquamenon River waterfalls. It was an amazing sight, as Harold said it would be. Then, we ventured quite the distance—a seven-hour drive to the Wisconsin Dells, where we boarded a boat for a long, close-up tour, which I loved. From there, we went to Milwaukee, Wisconsin, and visited Uncle Roman and Aunt Virgie Fleis. They were known for showing guests a royal time and we were not disappointed. It was the first time anyone ever ordered me a drink; I believe it was called a "Pink Lady."

Upon returning home, we settled in a furnished upstairs apartment on Second Street in Traverse City, which cost us thirty-five dollars a month. I resumed my job at Coca-Cola, which was walking distance to Front Street downtown. Harold resumed work at Cluff Well Drilling, on the peninsula. As a newlywed, I found out he had a habit of stopping for a drink after work. I wondered if he even loved me when he would come home so late for an evening meal.

Sometimes, I got tired of waiting for him and walked over to Uncle Leo and Aunt Betty Fleis's home nearby, on Randolph Street. I played cards with Uncle Leo. He was as good of a card player as my dad and I knew the game pretty well, so he didn't always win.

The great thing about Harold, though, he never quibbled about attending mass on Sundays and visiting family afterwards.

The greatest blessing of our marriage was our nine children: Stephen (1959), Karen (1960), Janice (1961), John (1962), Edward (1963), Mary Lou (1965), Victoria (1966), Donald (1970), and Christine (1974).

Julie and Ray followed us down the wedding path, right on our heels. That summer, they set their wedding date for May 2, 1959. She moved to Grand Rapids and lived with Ray's sister and brother-in-law. Julie said, "We were planning to come home to visit my parents on Thanksgiving, when I received a letter from Mom. It read, 'Dear Juliette, I know you are planning to come home this weekend for Thanksgiving and I know you are planning to get married in May, but I think August would be a better month, because I'm going to have a baby in June. Love, Mom.' Ray looked at me and I looked at him ... and he said, 'WE'RE NOT WAITING TILL AUGUST!' We rearranged our wedding date and were married on January 3, 1959, at Holy Rosary Church."

23

Babies

AT THE TIME OF JULIE AND RAY'S WEDDING, I was very pregnant, expecting my first baby in March. Mother and I were pregnant at the same time. I was nearly twenty and she was forty-three. It would be my first child and her last. Sometime later, Julie and Ray announced they were expecting a baby in October.

Close to the due date of my firstborn, I wasn't feeling well and didn't know if I was in labor. Harold decided it was best for us to go to my parents' home. As soon as we arrived, Harold and Dad went to Sugarfoot's Saloon for a drink, presumably to celebrate my baby-to-be. In the meanwhile, I helped Mom peel potatoes while my younger siblings were playing nearby. My parents' home was my refuge. I tried my best to stay positive about my marriage, and never spoke of any troubles. Now that Harold and I were expecting our first baby's arrival, I could only hope and pray that things would get better for us.

I was thankful to be near my mother. She never told me how worried she was that she might have to drive me to the hospital until years later. I was relieved that Dad and Harold made it back in time, and Harold drove me straight to the hospital.

We became proud parents when Stephen was born on March 23, 1959.

It was good that Aunt Anna and Uncle Leonard invited us to stay with them, as she was a big help in getting me adjusted to care for my newborn baby. We had gone directly from the hospital to their farmhouse in Maple City.

My mother and I created a beautiful white lace gown, satin coat, and cap, all made from my wedding dress, for Stephen's baptism. Eight of my babies would wear the outfit at their baptisms. One of my babies never made it home, but was still baptized.

Two months after my baby's birth, we rented a small two-bedroom cottage on Lime Lake that my parents owned and which Dad had built a few years before, but rarely used. Dad did give us a chance to buy the cottage. By then, we had purchased a lot near Cedar, and decided to have a house built.

Dad was our contractor. His crew was Uncle Joe Fleis and Ray Galla. Uncle Leonard also helped a lot. Harold did all the sanding on wood trim, doors, and cupboards. I did the finish work.

While there, I was able to observe Dad's work ethic firsthand. It was a wonderful experience from start to finish.

Our youngest sister, and my parents' twelfth and last child, Rita Antoinette, was born on June 14, 1959, just days before my brother Edward graduated as valedictorian of the senior class at Holy Rosary High School, and three months after grandson Stephen's birth (my son).

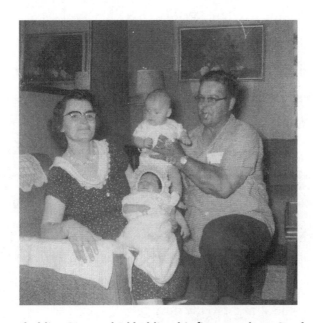

Irene holding Rita, and Ed holding his first grandson, Stephen

Rita was as pretty as could be! Her thick, dark hair poked through the holes of the crocheted yellow bonnet she wore as a newborn.

Dad would say, "It's cheaper by the dozen." My parents never complained about raising a large family. Dad typically held the youngest toddler on his lap at the table to feed her a few bites of food.

My sister Mary Jane remembers how things usually were for Mom with a newborn baby. "Mom's kitchen was always a flurry of activity, with making meals, baking, or warming the milk in a baby bottle. The warmed oven was a place Mom sat in front of with the baby in her arms when it was cold outside and drafty inside. She had it set up with warm water and towels and a change of clothes for the baby. Remembering it brings back the smell of the soap she used and a warm bath."

Soon after Rita's birth, Mary Jane, now entering eleventh grade, started to experience joint pain. She also suffered from strep throat and was ultimately diagnosed with rheumatic fever, needing to be hospitalized for a week.

As she was recuperating in the hospital, Mary Jane overheard Mom talking with another woman and expressing how nice it would be if one of her daughters became a nurse. She had already seen the tender, loving care Mom had given Grandma Jennie after her stroke. Being a nurse might be her path to follow, as she had considered becoming a nun.

This decision meant that Mary Jane would need to take chemistry at an accredited high school, which Holy Rosary did not offer. This meant that she would have to leave home and no longer be able to help Mother with the baking, which Mary Jane had done since she was twelve. Mama "made the sacrifice to let me go," Mary Jane said.

Wondering how she might earn money to live elsewhere, she thought she might get a job as someone's housekeeper, just as our mother had done in her younger days. "Working in the kitchen with mother," Mary Jane recalled, "Mom would tell how she worked for a family in Traverse City as a mother's helper and housekeeper. She got paid enough that she saved a dollar a week for a suit of clothes, which she said she wore when she met Dad, which I thought was really something."

Mary Jane found a position through an ad in the newspaper and lived with a family in Traverse City for three years while she attended St. Francis High School in her senior year, graduating in 1961. She then attended Northwestern Michigan College. The decision to leave Mother to care for eight younger children without her help did weigh heavily on her.

By fall of 1959, Edward attended college. He saw no future in farming. Somewhat influenced by his father's general contracting business, he began his pursuit of a degree in civil engineering at Northwestern Michigan College (NMC). He was awarded a five-hundred dollar Laura Olmsted Memorial scholarship for his aptitude in math, which greatly offset the cost of tuition. He was deficient in college prep courses in math and science and took remedial courses, loading up to twenty to twenty-two credit hours each term in order to catch up.

Edward also worked part-time in the college cafeteria during the school year and at Dad's construction company during the summers while he went to NMC.

***

Ruth Ann's story:

Both mothers of babies, Mom and I became very close. We accompanied each other to our doctor visits. I relied on her for advice and learned many of her home remedies. One remedy in particular was treating my baby when he was congested from a cold, with a warm-to-the-touch-of-my-finger light rub of camphorated oil on his chest, and covering the area with a slightly warm cloth diaper. We spent a lot of time together, and in doing so, I learned more about her ways. I started making bread from scratch, canning foods, and sewing. One summer, we picked wild blueberries found along the roadside near Lime Lake and the back hills on Bodus Road. The preparation of just sorting and cleaning these berries to can was long and tedious. Another attribute was that Mom cared how I looked. When she noticed my face looked pale, she suggested adding some rouge to my cheeks to give color. Upon seeing me wearing a plain housedress Aunt Anna had given me, she showed up the next time with a stylish pair of black and white cotton slacks she sewed. In some ways, I was aging sooner than her. My long, dark hair had a few gray hairs. Her dark, fine hair had none. *I loved Mom. She was there for me … time and again.*

***

Grandma Jennie had been well taken care of by her family since having a stroke ten years earlier (1948). When her health declined, she began receiving care at Solem Nursing Home in Traverse City; then in June of 1959, she was transferred to Grand Traverse Medical Care Facility. At the time of her death on August 26, 1959, "Grandma Jennie pressed the crucifix to her lips as all of her family were praying the rosary."[60] She was seventy-four. Rev. Father Robert Plamondon, her nephew, was the celebrant for her funeral mass at St. Francis Church, in Traverse City. Her burial took place at St. Mary's Cemetery in Lake Leelanau, next to Grandpa Lugie.

What I remember about Grandma Jennie was her wavy, thick hair, thick glasses, and prayerful disposition. One time, she called to me with urgency, "There, there" when her rosary beads dropped from her hands to the floor while lying in bed. After I found her rosary and placed it in her hand, she was peaceful again.

Less than two months after Grandma's funeral, on October 21, 1959, Julie and Ray's joy in anticipating the birth of their first child turned to sadness when their baby boy, Joseph, died at birth. He had exceeded his due date by nearly three weeks and Julie developed toxemia (preeclampsia)

---

60   *Lamie/Lamy Book*, p. 584, stated by Aunt Lucille (Lamie) Harpe.

during labor. Baby Joseph had movement throughout labor, but suffocated at his birth. He weighed ten pounds, seven ounces. Julie and Ray endured great sorrow, but were blessed with five more children: Dale (1961), Diane (1962), Debra (1964), Douglas (1968), and Dawn (1972).

My second born was Karen Marie. She came into this world on February 22, 1960. She appeared healthy when I held her in my arms, except for a bluish tinge to her tiny fingers. Within twenty-four hours of her birth, we had her baptized at the hospital before she was in an hours-long exploratory surgery performed by Doctor Cline at Munson Hospital in Traverse City. Afterward, we received the shocking news that our precious infant daughter was born without a pancreas and needed a transplant, which was extremely rare. She was placed in an incubation unit at Munson Hospital.

I blamed the cause of my baby's defect on a free chest x-ray I had taken at a mobile unit in Cedar, when I wasn't aware of being pregnant.

Just as our parents had shown by example, I prayed through difficult times, along with being grateful that I had a healthy one-year-old son, Stephen (Steve), who was already walking, to care for.

We moved into our new home in Cedar the day after Steve's first birthday. I would visit my infant daughter at the hospital every chance I had. When our baby Karen's weight dwindled to nearly two pounds, I felt overwhelmed, and sought the Sacrament of Reconciliation with a priest to clear my conscience. Two days later, on April 23, 1960, our precious baby Karen died after two months of hospitalization. I was saddened by her death, but was at peace.

24

Entrepreneurship

WHEN DAD HEARD OF CEDAR GENERAL HARDWARE STORE going up for auction, he decided it was something he might like to buy. After discussing his intention with Mom, she agreed. He showed up the day of the auction and ended up being the highest bidder. It was May of 1960, when Dad purchased the Cedar General Hardware store from Lewis D. Commins.

At the same time he bought the hardware store, Dad was finishing a construction job for the United States government. He was awarded the contract to build the Cedar post office, with interior space of 1,270 square feet, with brick masonry and block sides. It was to be completed by May 1, 1960.[61] So, Dad went from one big building project and ventured into another.

The Cedar General Hardware Store consisted of two buildings: an old wooden structure and a concrete-block building. The original store had its beginnings in 1945, after Mr. Commins purchased a blacksmith shop from Anton "Tony" Svboda on Sullivan Street (County Road 616) and had it moved to Cedar. The front of the store had hitching posts where customers had tied their horses or parked their cars. The front section inside had creaky floors, and the back section only had a dirt floor, which included an in-house, similar to an outhouse.

The concrete-block building was large and unoccupied. It had been purchased by Mr. Commins in 1949 from Ed Mikowski, who had Dad build it for the sole purpose of establishing a second bar in town. Unfortunately, when the census was done for Solon Township, the population didn't allow for another liquor license. The mainstay, Cedar Tavern, had existed since the early 1900s.

There wasn't much inventory—only a "few rusty nails and some seed corn," Dad wrote later.

Dad still worked full-time in the construction business, but was at the store every morning to start off the day, sometimes showed up in between, and always closed at the end of the day.

I helped Dad when he first opened for business in the old store while Mom babysat Steve, who was fourteen months old. I didn't expect any wages; it was a favor for a favor between Mom

---

61   *Leelanau Enterprise*, March 24, 1960: "Cedar's new post office will remain under ownership of Clarence L. Burry, and was leased for five years with option of renewal. Postmaster was Mrs. Helen Kucera."

Northern Michigan's Biggest Weekly > **The Leelanau Enterprise and Tribune**

VOL. 83 — NO. 24   LELAND, MICHIGAN   THURSDAY, MARCH 24, 1960

Building Contractor Buys Cedar Hardware

Edward V. Fleis, Cedar building contractor, has purchased the two buildings and stocks of Cedar hardware and will operate the business as a farm and family store.

He plans to remodel the newer building, move the business there, then remodel the present store for use as a warehouse.

The buildings and stock were sold at auction by their former owner, Lewis D. Commins.

Left: Article from Leelanau Enterprise. Top right: Blacksmith shop before it was Cedar General Hardware, early 1900s (photo from Leelanau Historical Museum). Bottom right: *Leelanau Enterprise* headline.

Learn New Postoffice To Be Built At Cedar

Must Be Ready For Occupancy By May 1; Clarence Burry Bid Accepted

Cedar residents, who have been trying for more than a year to get a new post office, learned this week that the Post Office Department has signed a construction and lease contract with Clarence L. Burry of Cedar and that construction will begin as soon as weather permits.

Completion and occupancy are set for May 1. The new building will be next door to the fire station and about 450 feet west of the present post office.

The new post office will be situated on a 64 by 120 foot lot. The building will provide 1,270 square feet of interior floor space, a 28 square foot platform, and hard surfaced parking and maneuvering area totalling 4,416 square feet.

Built of masonry, it will have brick front and block sides and back. Specifications call for new modern lighting and equipment, including a low, open patron-service counter.

Cedar's new post office will remain under ownership of Mr. Burry and will be leased to the Post Office department for five years, with a renewal option for an additional five years.

The Post Office Department had been trying for more than a year either to secure an acceptable lot on which a new structure could be built or to lease an existing building which could be remodelled.

The postmaster at Cedar is Mrs. Helen Kucera.

Fleis Gets Contract To Build Post Office

Clarence L. Burry of Cedar, who will build a new post office there and lease it to the federal government, announced this week that the construction contract has been awarded to the Edward Fleis Construction Company of Cedar and that completion date is June 1.

The new post office will be built on a 64 by 120 foot lot just west of the fire station.

Left: *Leelanau Enterprise* articles. Post office under construction (circa 1960). Lower right: Cedar post office (2022 photo).

and myself to help Dad get his business up and running. My job was to greet customers, enter sales on written receipts, tend the cash register, and keep things tidy.

Those were long days for me because only a few customers were coming in every day, and Dad didn't have much inventory to offer, except for heavy bags of farming supplies and some tools. Later that fall, Dad decided to close the original store and re-establish the business in the newer concrete-block building, north of the same property. (He also had use of an old, vacant warehouse behind the store for setting aside building supplies and bulky merchandise.) My parents renamed the new store "Cedar Hardware and Farm Store."

Dad depended on his children's help: Ted at first, then Jim, eventually Larry, and later, Shirley, Joan, and Noreen filled in the gap. Occasionally, Mom helped.

"I never had anything to do with the hardware store," says Bernadette. "I was twelve years old, in the sixth grade at Holy Rosary School, the oldest girl at home when our parents first opened the store. I remember every morning before leaving for school that the cream separator had to be washed; and as soon as I got home from school, I

Cedar Hardware and Farm Store in downtown Cedar with pickle warehouse behind it (Where Cedar Area Fire and Rescue is now.)

quickly changed from school clothes into my everyday clothes and went downstairs to help Mom.

"There were many daily chores besides weeding the garden. I remember picking big fields of cucumbers behind the woods facing west, and then they were sold to the co-op in Lake Leelanau. We had two big gardens. I loved eating raw peas.

"On Saturdays, we always had to completely clean the house, wash floors, and put everything away. Mom sewed during the week, but I rarely saw her sew. I expect she did her sewing at night. On Sundays, Mom's sewing machine was always put away.

"Mom stayed home quite a bit until the little ones were older, before she started helping at the store, which usually was on Saturdays. Then she would take some, or all, of the little ones with her to the store and leave a list for me. I would make the supper meal; the meat part of the meal was usually already cooking. I was busy," Bernadette concluded.

Meanwhile, Dad's construction business accepted one of the most dangerous jobs—digging a basement under the two-story building of the former Jakielek's Drug Store—now Wool and Honey—next to the Cedar Tavern. My cousin Ray Pleva explained: "Your dad, Uncle Steve Pleva, and my father, [Uncle Joe Pleva], hand dug the dirt with round pointed shovels, dumping dirt on a conveyor belt which took the dirt outside through the only opening on the backside of the building."

***

The old, wooden store still standing was a concern for my brother, Jim. One day, he asked Dad, "What are you planning to do with the old store?"

"Burn it down!" Dad answered. He was a volunteer fireman and had already obtained permission from the Cedar Fire Department to do so.

Jim explained what happened next. "I immediately rushed over to the old store and lit a match to a board that was dry as a bone, and the old wooden store quickly went into flames. Heiney (Frank) Zimmerman's gas station was next door (now Cedar Lefleur & Gifts), and he rushed over yelling, with his hands in the air. 'What the heck is going on?'

"I thought he was going to kill me!" Jim said, adding, "The Cedar Fire Department was there, and within two hours, the old store burned to the ground without a mishap."

Dad was known as the local fixer-upper guy and could help anyone with almost any problem. Besides selling merchandise, he would replace screens and windows. He always had lumber and plywood available. He would custom cut any lumber for a customer.

One of his customers was Roy Romanowski, a fellow Lions Club member. Roy said, "I had a front step at my house go bad. Your dad came over, took a look at it, didn't even measure it, and came back later with a new step that fit perfectly! We still use the step to this day."

Another customer, Carl Lautner from Solon Road in Cedar, bought roofing from Cedar Hardware. His son, Jim, remembers how pleased his father was with the job. Jim said, "Your dad and some of his sons helped with the installation of the steel roof. The barn and two other buildings were roofed the first week of December, in 1960. It was sixty degrees that whole week. The roofing is still in good shape because your dad sold good quality steel. The barn was forty-by-sixty, and thirty feet to the eaves. The other buildings were two stories and thirty-by-forty."

25

The Early '60s

MY SISTER JOAN, WHO WAS SPEECHLESS AS A TOT, was learning so quickly that she started first grade in 1960, when she was only four and a half. "Sister Mary Luke told Mom that I was ready," Joan relates. "I was so excited to ride on the bus!"

Mom's little ways of teaching us helped. "She used to spell so many words out to us as she was talking to us," Joanie explains. "That's probably why all of us are such good spellers today!"

In 1960, when Mary Jane was a seventeen-year-old student and living in Traverse City, she won another contest: top honors in a cherry pie baking contest sponsored by the Grand Traverse Cherry Producers Association. She competed with twenty-one contestants from all over the region.

An article in the December 3, 1960 issue of the *Traverse City Record-Eagle* stated:

Mary Jane Fleis, Grand Traverse Cherry Pie Queen (circa 1960)

> The contestants were judged on the basis of preparation for baking, the pie itself and upon appearance and deportment. The contest was held at Michigan Consolidated Gas Co.'s Traverse City office and was followed by a banquet at the Park Place Hotel. James Beckett served as toastmaster and John Williams, local radio and television personality, crowned the queen and presented gifts on behalf of Traverse City Bank. She won a $50.00 scholarship and a lovely dress from Milliken's Department Store in Traverse City.

Mary Jane represented Grand Traverse County in the state competition in Grand Rapids six months later, but didn't win.

In the fall of 1961, Jim left the farm and went to Holy Ghost Seminary in Ann Arbor when he was in the ninth grade. On occasion, he would sneak off and visit our Aunt Susie Fleis, who lived there in Ann Arbor. He also discerned that the priesthood wasn't his vocation and returned as a tenth-grade student to St. Mary's School in Lake Leelanau.

While Jim was gone, Ted was responsible for the farming. He said, "Besides working the farm, I worked at Dad's construction sites as a brick tender and in the hardware store during my teenage years. In the summer, on the farm, I worked on the community traveling threshing machine as a representative of our family. We went from farm to farm, threshing the wheat and oats. I believe it was the first time I drank a Stroh's beer. The men said, 'When you work like a man, you drink like a man.' Working in the hardware store was great training for gaining sales experience."

Our youngest brother, Larry, was thirteen years old when he began working at the store for Dad, after school and during the summer months. He said, "The first time Dad asked me to help at the store, he told me to come to Cedar on the bus from Holy Rosary. The bus dropped me off at Pleva's Market (now Polish Art Center). I didn't have any idea where the new hardware store was, so I started walking and had to ask for directions. That person sent me up the hill. I ended up at the Gambles store (now Cedar River Coffee Co.). Obviously, Cedar Hardware was not well known—at least not yet!"

Larry Fleis standing in front of a display at Cedar Hardware

Our parents were fortunate when the Gambles store closed. They accumulated a good amount of inventory for their own store. Dad and my brothers paid close attention to what merchandise customers asked for and didn't have. They only had to ask once. It took pleasing one customer at a time and saving them a trip to Traverse City. Mom suggested items as well. I recall how pleased she was when showing me a display of children's dolls and toys on a large wooden table, and another display of various school supplies.

Whenever Mom was at the store, she greeted and assisted customers, dusted shelves, and rearranged merchandise. If the floor needed attention, she grabbed a broom or wet mop. She set an example to her family to keep the store clean.

"One of my worst jobs was dusting," my younger sister, Joan, said. "Every little item had to be lifted, dusted, and placed back on the shelf. Mom showed us how, then assigned us to work alongside her."

Dad still used the old warehouse behind the store for twenty-pound gas tanks and rental equipment after he built additions to the store, doubling its size. He created space for building supplies: cement; concrete blocks; lawnmowers; gardening, plumbing and electrical supplies; propane tanks; and more. A small addition near the front of the store kept refrigeration for night crawlers and a large water tank for minnows. Another addition stocked paint and painting supplies. The store quickly became a popular family store.

Ted and Jim both worked on and off at the store until each graduated from high school.

Jim recalled: "Besides working the store, we also did the farming, milking cows, chickens, etc. Dad would call Ted and me whenever he would get in a semi-load of cement and we helped unload the heavy bags, which were labor intensive. Dad had an allergy to cement and his hands would break out and bleed. He also relied on others."

Even our cousin, Al Fleis (from Wayne, Michigan), helped. Al wrote, "I think Uncle Ed would call my dad [Albion Fleis] to find out if we were coming up, because he would have a semi-load of concrete (600 bags) to unload. Working at the hardware store was all part of the fun in growing up with my cousins!"

Meanwhile, Edward received his associate's degree at NMC in May 1961, and was then enrolled at Michigan Technological University in Houghton, Michigan, four hundred miles away in the Upper Peninsula. To help pay for his expenses, he worked as a soda jerk at the college cafeteria and later as a bartender and waiter at a hotel.

During the summer of 1962, he worked for Collins Engineering in Milwaukee on a federal program of evaluating existing buildings for suitability as fallout shelters. The summer of 1963 was spent in Houghton on a very extensive land-surveying program.

When Edward came home to visit family and friends in Cedar, he often hitchhiked or arranged for a ride with Michigan Tech students from the Traverse City area. "The shared cost for the five or six passengers was one cent per mile, and taking turns in paying the four-dollar toll to cross the Mackinac Bridge." Edward continues, "One time, when I was hitchhiking home for Christmas, I got a ride for much of the distance from a guy who worked for a cigarette distributor company as their business salesman … heading for Traverse City. The several cartons of cigarettes and box of cigarette lighters that he gave me ended up as Christmas gifts."

A couple younger siblings recalled Christmas stories of their own: Joan said, "I think I was nine when Santa didn't have anything for me, and I was sad. Then, out of the clear-blue sky, another Santa came back into the house. He had found a little purse that apparently was dropped in the snow from the bag of Christmas gifts Santa carried on his shoulder.

"The following year, I found a bag of gifts in the laundry room and stuck a wrapped Bonne Bell perfume set in there, just to make sure that it would never happen to me again."

"Another time," Joan said, "It was late at night and I couldn't sleep. I sneaked downstairs and I could see Mom busily sewing on red material. To my surprise, on Christmas Eve, my three other sisters, Shirley, Noreen, and Rita, and I received beautiful identical fuzzy red shirts, along with leggings, as a gift from our parents."

Noreen's unusual story happened when she was five and a half, and after the Christmas trimmings were down. She said, "In front of one of the living room windows on the farm was a desk decorated to look like a chimney at Christmastime, but during the rest of the year, it was a handy place to sit and watch the coal truck make its deliveries. We had a coal-burning furnace in our basement and the chute for the coal was directly below the living room window.

"I remember one delivery in particular. Mom was in the kitchen; all the older kids were in school and Rita (three and a half) and I were alone in the living room. We were sitting on the desk when the coal truck showed up. The driver was backing up the truck and I was waving at him to come closer and closer. Suddenly, I could see he was getting too close, and I shouted, 'Stop!' but he didn't stop. I threw Rita on the floor and jumped and laid on top of her just as the coal truck crashed through the window! We didn't get hurt, but never sat on the desk for coal truck deliveries again."

Over the course of many years, Christmas celebrations at the farm home were plentiful. A decorated spruce tree had a string of colorful electric lights strung on its branches, instead of metal clip-ons holding small candles, used in earlier years, and the nativity scene was adorned with leftover, fresh green branches tucked behind it on a library table in the living room. Santa's visit took place a few hours before attending midnight mass.

One Christmas Eve, (Dad's sisters) Sister Mary Therese and Aunt Agnes, dressed as Santa Clauses. They rode four miles in an old-fashioned sleigh pulled by a tractor, on a cold wintry day. We figured it was Santa's arrival when we heard bells ringing, and rushed outside, dressed warmly, to greet them. It was easy to recognize them … by their laughter, and cheerful voices.

Typical of every Santa we ever had, the same questions were asked, "Do you say your prayers every night? and "Were you good or naughty this year?" If you answered no or naughty, you were reminded to try and do better the next year. Then the whole family gathered in the dining room, where Santa called out your name before handing out a present.

Hours later was midnight mass at Holy Rosary Church. Not everyone went with Mom and Dad, but most of the family did. The younger ones, fast asleep in their beds, were looked after by an older sibling. Over time each member of the family, from the oldest to the youngest, experienced this wonderful tradition.

After mass, Mom headed straight for the kitchen to prepare an early morning breakfast with help from the girls. When the table was set, and the food was ready, our family gathered around the dining room table, joined hands with Mom and Dad, and Dad led the blessing. Before the meal of Polish kielbasa, scrambled eggs, fruit, homemade frosted cinnamon rolls, or a Polish cuisine called *chruscikis* (angel wings), we shared *oplatki,* a thin, oblong wafer, like those used at communion. (The wafer in the form of pieces broken off was considered a family blessing celebrated only at Christmastime.) The gift of *oplatki* started when one of the Fleis nuns sent the thin rectangular wafers in a mailed envelope as a Christmas gift to the family.

The feast day of the Three Kings, on January 6, had its own tradition. Using blessed epiphany chalk obtained at church, the initials of the Three Kings, "19 + C + M + B + 62," were inscribed on the wood trim above the entrance door facing the dining room. The initials represented Caspar, Melchior, and Balthazar. The plus sign in between represented the cross, and the nineteen at the beginning and sixty-two at the end represented the year. Epiphany is also known as Three Kings Day, and doing this was considered a blessing on our home and to all who lived, worked, or visited there.

* * *

Side Note:

When my third child was due, and I needed to go to the hospital, Harold was ice fishing miles away, so I phoned Mom. Fortunately, my brother Edward was home from college on term break, and he took me. Thankfully, Harold arrived in plenty of time before the birth of our healthy daughter, Janice, on January 22, 1961.

A year to the date of her birth, we welcomed our newborn son, John, in 1962. His birth created the first double birthday in our family. I didn't have help when I came home from the hospital. I thought I could do it all, and had a nervous breakdown when my baby was about six weeks old. At the time, a babysitter was watching the children. I was with Julie and Ray in Traverse City, when sudden numbness swept over me, and thinking, "Surely, I'm going to die." I asked to see a priest, and gave him (what I thought would be) my last confession. After receiving emergency care at Munson Hospital, I was sent home with medicine. My sister Julie stayed with us a full week, and Mom and Aunt Anna took turns helping us. Certainly, Harold must've been worried. My health was restored in time. *The grace of God was with us.*

26

Shared Memories

JOAN'S SUMMERTIME MEMORIES: "The four little girls, Shirley, Joan, Noreen, and Rita (as Mama called us) played a game upstairs that included Larry. The girls always wanted to be altar girls, but since it wasn't allowed in church, we'd make believe upstairs. Larry was always the priest. We pressed bread with a whiskey glass to make the host.

"We played a lot of card games too! There was always euchre if you had four players. Other games were Kings in the Corner, pinochle, canasta, rummy, 7-Up, Crazy 8, and gin rummy. When we didn't play cards, we played Monopoly.

"When we were outdoors, playing baseball was fun, as well as hula hooping. I never had much luck with it, but some of my siblings were able to keep the hula hoops above their waists for a long time, just twirling. We'd play in the granary with the rye, or in a little house that we made from leftover cement blocks Dad had behind the garage.

"We always had plenty of kids at the house, especially on the weekends when cousins would come over and as some of our nephews and nieces got old enough, they would play too," Joan concluded.

Bernadette remembers "many cousins staying with our family during the summer months. There were always extra heads at the table during school vacation time. Even though Mom was cooking large meals, I don't recall that she complained.

"I do remember her joy in having the extra company. She would joke around and genuinely be interested in their young lives. She also assigned chores to the cousins. They were part of our family ... not freeloaders! When I was doing dishes in the kitchen, I was thankful when I had the help."

Cousin Gene, (son of Uncle Cliff and Aunt Theresa Lamie) was about fourteen and a half years old when he stayed on the farm. He told me, "I helped with farming, gardening, and picking beans. I don't remember much about that, but I do remember going to the cherry orchard and making no money picking cherries, but your mom [Aunt Irene] helped me out. The owner of the orchard [Pete Sharnowski] was short on help with picking up lugs and asked your ma if she knew anybody who could do the job. She told him, 'I sure do! My nephew Gene would be a good help for you.' From that day on, he kept me on the job and that's where I made good money, thanks to your ma."

(Left to right): Cousin Al Fleis, Ted holding Noreen, Mary Jane, Lamie cousins, Cliff and Joyce, Irene holding Joan, Bernadette and Shirley in center (taken at the farm, circa 1958)

Cousin Joyce was about eleven years old when her parents (Ben and Agnes Lamie) allowed her to go to Traverse City for part of her summer vacation. Joyce wrote, "I stayed a couple of weeks with Uncle Med and Aunt Gertie Lamie's family, then went on to Aunt Irene and Uncle Ed's. They were kind enough to let me come to the farm and visit, even with all the children they had. It was a very memorable stay with them. Everyone had to pitch in with daily chores, so the household ran as [smoothly] as possible.

"I remember one day I was assigned to pull weeds in a few rows in the vegetable garden. I think Mary Jane had a few rows to weed, also. It seemed like it was the most boring, time-consuming, and slow job I ever had to do and I did not like doing it at all.

"Well, I finally got my rows finished that day, and, guess what? I must have done a good job, because I was assigned a couple more rows the next day. I tried really hard to trade with someone, but no one wanted to trade chores. Imagine that.

"I told Aunt Irene it was too slow and boring, but she said, 'Joyce, you can do it. While you're on your knees pulling those weeds, pray to God; not the regular prayers we all say, but just talk with Him about anything, like how your day is going, if you're sad or lonely. Talk about anything that comes to your mind and heart and before you know it, you'll be done and you'll feel much better about your day and yourself.'

"So, I went to the garden and started weeding in my row and began my first conversation with God. It was beautiful! And you know what? I was done before I knew it.

"To this day, I love being on my knees, praying and talking to God as I weed my own garden. I thank my dear Aunt Irene every day for teaching me how to talk with God. I'll never forget her for that and I have a very special place in my heart for her."

Cousin Sharone wrote, "After much discussion, I convinced my parents, Cliff and Theresa Lamie, to allow me to spend the summer with my cousins [at Uncle Ed and Aunt Irene's] so I could pick cherries and strawberries to earn money for school clothes.

"My parents left for home Sunday afternoon. What fun we had Sunday night! However, about 6:45 Monday morning, a loud voice from the bottom of the stairs at the Fleis house said, 'Everybody up! Time for breakfast!'

"Well, all feet hit the floor except mine! I was used to sleeping in. After all, it was summer!

"In about five more minutes, the voice now said, 'Sharone, get up! We are all waiting for you to come down for breakfast!' I got up immediately and came down to see everyone dressed and waiting for me to say grace and eat breakfast! Oh, the looks [from] my cousins; I was never late for a meal again. When Uncle Ed says, 'Get up!' you get up!! There is something to be said for fear and respect!

"One thing that we all looked forward to was the Isadore Chicken Dinner. Well, that day it seemed that everyone had a job scheduled at the chicken dinner, either waiting on tables or working under the big red-and-white tent where games were played, so I stayed back with the three little girls, Joan, Noreen, and Rita. I was supposed to get them ready and Uncle Ed would pick us up and take us to the chicken dinner.

"Well, I had them ready on time. We waited and waited. Uncle Ed must have been busy and didn't come. We didn't want to miss the fun, so we walked a little over a mile. When my Uncle

Ed saw us, he was happy we made it. He didn't say anything about not picking us up, and neither did I! We got there and had fun. It was all good. Life is good with the people we love!

"One Saturday morning at breakfast, Uncle Ed said that he and Aunt Irene were going into Traverse City and three of the children would go … with them and [then] go to the movie theater. Uncle Ed asked if I would like to go. I was so excited!

"That day, we all worked hard getting our chores done. I hurried to get ready. Uncle Ed had said earlier that day that we would be leaving at six sharp. I was ready in time, or so I thought, but I went back upstairs to get something. It took a little longer than I anticipated. I got outside and the car was going out the driveway. NO TC, NO MOVIE for Sharone. If we don't follow directions, we might miss out on fun adventures!"

Cousin Faye, a godchild of my parents and daughter of Joe and Lucille (Lamie) Harpe, said: "I just loved going to Aunt Irene and Uncle Ed's home. They had girls. We had fun! Good cama-raderie. I didn't get in on the music much because I was a helper in the kitchen with the girls as we had to wash the dirty dishes. It was good to be together. I pray for Aunt Irene and Uncle Ed every day."

Cousin Kasia, (daughter of Roman and Virginia Fleis), said, "Your mom and dad always had room for me to stay, no matter how many kids were in the house."

Bernadette added, "Kasia would stay with us one or two weeks during the summer months, for a few years starting about the age of twelve. She got to enjoy a little farm life as a city girl from Milwaukee. We were about the same age. Sometimes she and cousin Al Fleis were there at the same time."

Cousin Al, (son of Al and Phyllis Fleis), recalls farm life: "I was just a shy guy," he admits. Then, I met my Uncle Ed Fleis's family. I had fallen in love. ...

"Two of the boys in particular, Ted and Jim, kind of took me under their wing. They showed me more hiding spots on that farm than you could shake a stick at. These spots were great when my dad and mom were coming to take me home.

"I'll never forget my first time down the hill in that wooden cart we built. Awesome. Felt like one hundred miles per hour. And when there was sneaking out in the evening and spending the night on the hill behind the house. (It rained that night.)

"Fun times for a shy little guy. The boys gave me an education on electric fences, too. Drinking water from the creek was neat. Eating little green apples was not so cool. Grabbing a jar of fresh strawberry jam and a loaf of bread, we ran to the barn. Mmm-mmm, good. Grease-gun fights were fun.

"Their sisters liked to tease. Mary Jane said if I helped with dishes, I could have an extra cream puff. I said yes. I didn't realize that all the milk pails, cream separator parts, and twelve peoples' dishes had to be washed. I was learning.

"Chasing cows or running from them—bulls—[was] exhilarating.

"Picking cherries, hauling hay—fun, no matter what.

"I'm not so shy anymore."

* * *

The first time my brother Edward was introduced to Barbara Duperon of Lake Leelanau was at a county employees' picnic at Lime Lake Hall. She was there with her parents, and he was with Dad and Mom the summer after returning home from the seminary.

They met again at a Holy Rosary Chicken Dinner in the summer of 1957. Edward was in charge of the ring toss game, and kept luring her back ... by giving free rings to toss. They dated on and off through high school. Their love rekindled when Barbara came as a "casual invite" to our parents twenty-fifth wedding anniversary.[62]

It was at that celebration on September 4, 1962, when Dad, Uncle Steve Pleva, and Stanley Mikowski with the Isadore Sodbusters played as a band for the last time for family and friends at the reception and dance of Dad and Mom's anniversary party at the Centerville Township Hall, the same place where their wedding dance took place in 1937. All of their wedding attendants were present.

> MR. AND MRS. EDWARD V. FLEIS
>
> REQUEST THE HONOR OF YOUR PRESENCE
>
> AT THEIR SILVER WEDDING ANNIVERSARY
>
> ON SEPTEMBER 2, 1962
>
> MASS OF THANKSGIVING
>
> HOLY ROSARY CHURCH, CEDAR
>
> AT 10:00 A. M.
>
> AND
>
> RECEPTION: 5:00 P. M.
>
> CENTERVILLE TOWNSHIP HALL

---

62   *Lamie/Lamy Book,* p.539.

Left: Ed and Irene's wedding attendants from 1937. Left to right: Agnes (Fleis) Williams, Louis Lamie, Susan Fleis, Irene and Ed, Leo Fleis and Lucille (Lamie) Harpe. Right: Ed Fleis and Steve Pleva provided entertainment at Centerville Township Hall.

Even though Dad's band retired, he never retired from playing his treasured violin. He would gladly pick it up and play a tune for family gatherings and whenever invited elsewhere.

Beginning in the fall of 1962, Jim and Bernadette were both attending St. Mary's High School in Lake Leelanau. Bernadette said, "Jim and I had to wait an hour at John Kelinski's, at the corner of French Road and Hohnke Road each morning, from the time we were dropped off by the Glen Lake school bus and picked up by the St. Mary's school bus. It was a long wait, and Mr. Kelinski would invite us to come inside—when it was cold and stormy out.

"The following year, we stayed warm in a small shed a local farmer brought over and placed on the corner where we stood. When school ended each day, we also transferred from bus to bus with long waits in between until Jim got a car of his own in his senior year."

* * *

In January 1963, Edward invited Barbara Duperon to attend the famous Winter Carnival at Michigan Tech. She made the long journey. "It was a long, thirteen-hour trip on the bus," Barbara said.

"We enjoyed a weekend of entertainment and dancing," Edward stated. "We were able to see the newly popular Peter, Paul, and Mary in concert, and enjoyed walking around viewing gigantic ice sculptures constructed by the fraternities."

In December 1963, Edward received his bachelor's of science degree in civil engineering. He then started his career with Williams and Works, an engineering firm in Grand Rapids, Michigan.

Rayaires Band from Grand Rapids: Ray, Edward, Julie, and John.

Meanwhile, music was ever present in the family. After Julie's father-in-law, John Watkoski, retired, the Pokacenos changed its name to The Rayaires. Julie's husband, Ray, played accordion; Julie played keyboard; his brother, John, played banjo, and my brother, Edward, played drums. All the band members lived in Grand Rapids. They traveled up north to Leelanau County whenever they were invited to play for a wedding, anniversary, or a public event. Edward was a band member for seven years.

* * *

Back to the hardware store. My sister Shirley said she was eight when she started working. She recalls, "I knew in no uncertain terms that Dad had to be diverse in order to provide for his family. He worked his tail off and entrusted his children. He opened up houses before folks returned to their summer homes and did carpentry on the side. I went with him on jobs and handed him tools." She also observed, "I think people must have thought we were well-to-do, because we were dressed well, but we weren't."

Joan was seven or eight years old when she and her younger sister Noreen spent quite a bit of time at the hardware store. She said, "We would sit on the cement porch in front of the store as people would come in to buy items. Then, before you knew it, Dad put us to work.

"Dad was doing side jobs. I was with him when he was putting in the new bathroom in the basement of the Centerville Township Hall. I learned quickly the difference between pliers and wrenches!"

Noreen was Dad's little helper, as well. She said, "I was maybe five or six years old when Mom would send me with Dad to 'help' him. Some of my siblings would dispute this statement and simply say that Mom wanted me out of her hair, but I can attest to the fact that Dad gave me hands-on training in the world of carpentry. For example, I would need to get my hands on the broom and sweep the sawdust from the worksite. Sometimes I had to wiggle into small places to get my hands on a wire that he couldn't reach.

"Mostly," Noreen continued, "I needed to get my hands on the tool he wanted. I can remember him calling for a pipe wrench. I went back and forth, and I think I brought just about every other tool from his red toolbox before I found a pipe wrench. Eventually, though, I learned the names of the tools.

"Besides knowing the tool names, Dad's hands-on training provided another unexpected memory. One day, when I was about sixteen years old, I was at my boyfriend's house, and his family was watching home movies. I looked up and saw Dad on the screen. Come to find out, theirs was one of the homes Dad had helped build, and one [where] I had tagged along as his helper. That home belonged to Willard and Irene Savage on Little Glen Lake, and their son, Tom, became my future husband."

My youngest sister, Rita, was a toddler when she was with Mom driving to the hardware store during winter to deliver a home-cooked meal for Dad, which was less than four miles from the farm. Schomberg Road is nothing but hills. Mom didn't realize how slippery it was until she hit an icy spot while attempting to drive up the hill past Popa's driveway.

The tires spun, the car slowed until it wouldn't budge forward, and started skidding backward over a snowbank and dropped at least one hundred feet, landing right-side up in a ravine pillowed with deep snow.

Little Rita, standing in the front seat, asked, "Mom, what are we doing down here?" She never cried or fussed.

Mom opened the car door on her side. Miraculously both were unharmed and able to get out. They trudged through the deep snow and made their way to the main road, where Mom stuck her hand out to hitchhike, and a passerby gave them a ride to the store.

When they arrived, Dad was shocked to hear their story. It stuck with him and was retold many times. Mom continued to make food deliveries but limited herself to driving in good weather.

After working nearly three years for Dad, both after school and during the summertime, Ted graduated from Glen Lake High School in June 1963. Soon after graduation, he joined the Marine Corps and reported for duty on June 26, 1963.

Ted explains, "I was the first to leave the farm and join the military service. Mom had tears in her eyes as I got in the car with Dad as he took me to the bus station in Traverse City. My dad did not display his feelings often. As I was stepping on the bus steps, he suddenly grabbed me and hugged me. For the first time, I felt that, even though there were twelve of us, each of us held a special love from Mom and Dad.

"Boot camp was at San Diego and advanced infantry training at Camp Pendleton in California. From there, I was stationed for eighteen months at Twenty-Nine Palms, California, in the 1st LAAM Division. On January 16, 1965, I shipped to the 3rd Tank Battalion, 3rd Marine Division, in Okinawa. In early June of that year, our division was given orders to move to Danang, Vietnam, to protect the air base from mortar shelling."

What helped our family during the time Ted was in the service were the frequent letters exchanged back and forth between him, Mom, and some siblings. Instead of worrying, my parents entrusted his safety to God, by praying for him.

Jim said, "1964 and 1965 were tough years for me. After Ted left, I was running the farm alone, helped Dad at his hardware store, and worked as a busboy at Sugar Loaf Ski Resort … my life was starting to take its toll on me! My grades weren't that good, my attitude wasn't that good, and my disposition wasn't the best. My father and I had it out over the farm work, and the principal of the school wasn't too thrilled with me either."

With all that, Jim graduated from St. Mary's in 1965. However, having had it out with Dad, "It was time to move on … and so I did," he states. "Within a week of graduation, I packed my bags and headed to Grand Rapids. ... Once there, I lived in several apartments and with Julie's family. Her husband, Ray, got me a job at a machinery shop, cleaning and painting mills and lathes, but the toxic paint fumes gave me headaches.

"I woke up one morning and told Ray, 'Nope, ain't doing this anymore,' and quit that job."

Then Jim found a job he liked, as an "elf," working the night shift at the Keebler cookie factory, where he worked his way up to equipment operator. "Great job," Jim commented. "I loved it."

On January 16, 1965, it was festive, almost like Christmas, when Edward married Barbara Duperon at St. Mary's Church, Lake Leelanau. They made their home in Grand Rapids, where Edward resumed his position at Williams and Works, and Barbara was employed as a licensed practical nurse at Sunshine Hospital (Spectrum Health Special Care).

Their children are: Jeffrey (1965), Gerard (1966), Michelle (1969), and Brian (1971).

Meanwhile, Mary Jane finished her requirements to become a registered nurse. Her class of fifteen was the first class to finish a twenty-seven-month nursing program begun at Northwestern Michigan College by Mr. Les Biederman. "We were the pioneers of this nursing class with associate's degrees," Mary Jane declared, "whereas previously [registered] nurses graduated from hospital programs or colleges with a four-year degree." She passed the registered nursing exam.

Mary Jane, RN

Side Note:

My blessings doubled when my sister Mary Jane had put on her cap and gown at Munson Hospital and assisted me in both labor and delivery of a healthy newborn son for Harold and me, on February 5, 1963. Three Edwards now circled in the family: my dad, my brother, and my son. Mary Jane was a student nurse at the time.

27

Music, Family Life, and a Turning Point for Grandpa

LIFE CHANGED FOR LARRY AT AGE THIRTEEN, after Dad brought home an accordion for him. "Not that I wanted to play the accordion," Larry commented, "because I was much more interested in playing the piano.

"This accordion was heavy, but I practiced with it in my bedroom and sometimes downstairs in the living room. Mom would always tell me if something didn't sound right."

One day, Larry came to my home and asked if he could borrow my white marble accordion, because the one Dad gave him was "old and bulky," he said. Up until then, Larry was my only sibling interested in learning to play the instrument. Of course I would lend him my accordion, even though I didn't want to part with it.

Besides listening to Frankie Yankovic records and music recorded for him on cassette by his brother-in-law Ray Watkoski, Larry also used a self-teaching book, *How to Play an Accordion*. He practiced diligently and not only learned to play the instrument well, he formed a band with his two younger sisters.

Larry explained, "Joan, Noreen, and I would try to play songs together. We had an upright piano in the living room, and my brother Edward gave us drums that he wasn't using anymore.

"The three of us spent every day in that living room, playing our instruments and learning to harmonize the songs. Mom and Dad were always encouraging us. They would always have us play whenever we had company at home. It was good practice for us. Our little combo went over well."

Joan recalls, "I started drumming using the beater on the big drum, and the stick on the snare. It was so important to keep the beat, and if I didn't, I would hear it from brother Larry... slow down ... speed up!"

Noreen added, "Larry taught me how to play chords on the piano. I was eight years old at the time, and I remember the first song I ever learned to play was the "Tic Toc Polka," known as Cedar's national anthem, in the key of *C*. Larry was bound and determined that I could play a whole octave on the bass chord. He'd keep telling me, 'Stretch your fingers,' and I'd say, 'But my fingers are little!'"

* * *

Now, young Rita's story: She tried to be grown-up one day. "In 1965," she wrote, "I was in kindergarten at the Cedar schoolhouse. After school, I got on the bus. Mr. Lawicki, the bus driver, asked me, 'Are you supposed to go to the hardware store or the farm?' I answered him in my small five-year-old voice, 'The farm,' even though I knew Mom had told me to go to the store that day.

"I was dropped off next to the mailbox in front of the two lilac bushes and took the sidewalk to the farmhouse. I went to the living room, rocked my baby doll, and kissed my baby good-bye, then started to walk to the store, which was about four miles away. After walking over three or four hills, I started to cry. I sat down near the stop sign at Holy Rosary Church, I turned around, and looked at the school.

"Inside, my sisters and brothers were in school. My sister Shirley saw me from the upstairs classroom and soon the principal and Shirley came to me. A phone call to Mom was made in the principal's office. And ... that was my first day in first grade, because the nun decided to keep me in school and then I went home on the bus with my siblings. Dad was working away from the store and Mom couldn't leave the store to pick me up."

* * *

Mary Jane explains how she went about finding a good spouse. "In August 1965, I went with coworkers from St. Mary's Hospital to Sainte Anne de Beaupre in central Quebec, Canada. My intention was to pray for a good Christian Catholic husband. I then took a vacation around Thanksgiving and went home. I stopped at the hardware store and giddily said, 'Dad, are there any single guys that you sold licenses to?' Dad said, 'Yeah, there's one in the box.' I went to the license box and found a license for Roger Steup, Fort Wayne, Indiana, six feet tall, twenty-eight years old, and two hundred pounds. Mom and Dad said they were going to the Maple Tavern that night and I went with them. Mom and Dad knew a couple of the hunters that were friends with Roger. I did some dancing and had a good time. Around 1:00 a.m., on November 21, 1965, Roger and his friend arrived at Maple Tavern, and sat with us. I invited Roger and his friend to the Fall Festival at Holy Rosary Church the following day, since I was waiting tables there. They didn't show up, but I went back to Maple Tavern that evening with a girlfriend. Lo and behold, the guys were at the tavern. Roger came up to me and asked me to dance. Since I had my own car, Roger followed me home and asked me out for the next day.

"My little sister Rita, who was about six years old, answered the door when Roger arrived and asked if he could see her sister Mary Jane. Rita slammed the door on him. We went on a bingo date that night and then to the Kingsley Bar the following night. He went back to Fort Wayne and came back in the middle of December and talked marriage."

Mary Jane went to Fort Wayne to meet Roger's family on New Year's Eve, and they were engaged that weekend. They married on April 23, 1966, at Holy Rosary Church, and made their home in Fort Wayne, where Mary Jane accepted a registered nurse position at Parkview Hospital, and Roger resumed his job as manager at Gator Trailers.

Their children are: Rebecca (1967), Jennifer (1968), Maureen (1970), Roger Jr. (1975), and Natalie (1978).

Mary Jane and Roger were newlyweds when they took a trip up north to spend a few days with Ma and Pa in August, recalled Roger.

"Pa asked if I could help out at the hardware store in the morning. Of course I could. I was thinking, 'What a good chance to bond with my new father-in-law.'

"Next morning, after a fine breakfast prepared by Ma, off Pa and I went to the store. Much to my surprise, there was a flatbed semi-trailer with bags of cement waiting to be unloaded. While Pa waited on customers in the store, there I was getting a workout unloading the bags of cement. Pa always was able to recruit help, and that was some bonding or getting to know one another!" Roger concluded.

Larry adds to this story. "For those special friends and sons and sons-in-law, there was sometimes 'a shot and a beer' available in the backroom. I remember a couple of times when my brothers-in-law, Ray Watkoski and Roger Steup, were out together. They would spend time with Dad, playing cards in the store, sometimes doing some fishing, and maybe hit the bar later, while I took care of the store."

Julie's husband, Ray, has another story: "After a long weekend, Roger and I went with Dad to the Cedar Hardware Store on an early Monday morning. It was a slow morning, so the three of us parked ourselves at the cashier counter and played Setback, a card game that requires ten points to win. Back and forth, we evened out playing seven or eight games."

The final game was called "Lucky Dad." "Roger was on eight and bid two with the possibility of going out. Ray was sitting on seven and bid three-that would put him out. Dad was dealing. He was in control and the last bidder.

"The interesting part of Setback is you get one point each for high, low, jack, and game, with the possibility of winning four points. The jack must be retained and not taken away with an ace, king, or queen. The fourth point is the count of cards in addition to trump—from ten on up is worth ten points each.

"Dad was on six points and said, 'I shoot the moon.' Normally you lead higher cards to draw out trump ... Dad couldn't, because all he had was a bare jack. Roger and I had NOTHING to stop him. Dad made the four points he needed and won the game. How can you forget lucky Dad?" Ray concluded.

Edward Fleis, first president of the Cedar Chamber of Commerce, also was the first person to launch his boat Saturday at the new concrete ramp on the Cedar River. The project was financed jointly by the Chamber and the Department of Natural Resources.

Record-Eagle photo by David Averill

Undated *Record-Eagle* article: Ed Fleis launching the boat after the new concrete ramp was built at Cedar River

The Cedar River, just five hundred yards from the store, provided the perfect outlet for early-morning fishing. Dad launched his boat off the ramp at the river, and after a long, winding boat ride, he'd drop a fishing line in Lake Leelanau. Noreen remembers accompanying him one Saturday. She steered, while "he spent most of his time untangling the motor and his lines from the weeds."

Things became more eventful when Mary Jane's husband, Roger, went fishing with Dad. It was dusk and they were heading back along the river when they came around a bend and saw three guys chest-deep in the cold water. Their boat had overturned. Roger and Dad pulled them into the boat, gave two of them their jackets, and tried unsuccessfully to upright the boat. Finally, they took the three back to Cedar, where they made a phone call from the tavern, and "Dad bought each of them a shot of whiskey."

* * *

At a family picnic in Solon Park, Dad and Mom stayed on shore. Rita was quite young and wading in the water ahead of me. All of a sudden, I saw her head bobbing up and down! I didn't know if she was just having fun, but I quickly grabbed hold of her and lifted her out and put her next to me. She had accidentally stepped into the deep drop-off past the dock and was in water over her head. Rita reminded me of this story after she blurted out to me, "Ruth Ann, you saved my life!"

In another incident, Shirley recalled, "Ruth Ann, you probably don't remember when I fell off the dock where you were sunning yourself, and you quickly jumped in the water and saved me." She further stated, "I'm still afraid of water."

Mom feared water and would only wade in a lake up to her knees. That was the reason she enrolled her children to take Red Cross swimming lessons, from beginner to advanced, during the summertime, at Solon Township Park on Lake Leelanau.

* * *

Side Note:

The blessing of our daughter Mary Lou's birth was on February 5, 1965. Now, we had two double birthdays in a household of five children. She and her brother Edward shared the same birthday, two years apart. Janice and John's birthdays were on January 22, a year apart. Within a month, Mary Lou was wheezing in her bassinet. I phoned Mom for advice. She came over as soon as she could and placed an onion poultice on my baby's chest. With constant vigil between us, Mom stayed overnight to help care for her. Mary Lou got well and nothing more had to be done. I thanked God for the blessing of my baby's health and my nurturing mother.

Meanwhile, Harold got help for his drinking. When he returned home, he was glad to be healthy, as we all were. It was a fresh start in our marriage of nearly seven years. We enjoyed a new life as a family and faced things that needed to be done. The following spring though, he figured out how to make homemade dandelion wine, after picking hundreds of tiny, yellow flowers that grew wild in our yard, with help from the kids.

Turning Point in Grandpa's Life

Grandpa Thomas was a strong presence in our lives. He always said a Polish blessing upon entering my parents' home, and was a frequent guest at the table. He could be a tease at times, but we all loved him. He liked hearing any Polish words we knew. One time, when I invited him to the table for a meal, I should have said "*Przyjdz i usiadz,*" meaning "Come and sit down," but made a mistake, saying, "*idz do domu,*" which means, "Go home." He looked at me startled heading for the table. That's when I knew I messed up.

Thomas Fleis relaxing in the front yard at the farm.

Grandpa's health had taken another turn in the late 1950s. "He developed diabetes," Aunt Theresa explained. "I suspected something was wrong when I noticed he lost a lot of weight."

She continued, "Then in approximately 1961, Grandpa was alone at home when he felt a stroke might be coming on. He went to his car and drove to Uncle Tom and Aunt Betty's, who lived right behind him. They weren't home, but when he arrived, their daughter Nancy was there. She recognized something was seriously wrong and called your dad."

I recall Dad telling me about the ordeal. "I knew right away my father had a stroke; I couldn't make out a word he was saying. I drove so fast with your mom to see him and took him straight to the hospital. It was confirmed he had a stroke."

"From then on," Aunt Theresa said, "Grandpa was cared for by various family members: Uncle Leo and Aunt Betty, Aunt Agnes and Uncle Ron, Aunt Susie in Ann Arbor, where he could walk across the road to go to church, and Uncle Bob and me. He couldn't talk, but sometimes words would dribble from his mouth. His mind was good, and he could play cards.

"He had a longer stay with Uncle Roman and Aunt Virgie in Milwaukee. They had a nice apartment for him on the main level of Uncle Roman's jewelry store."

Meanwhile, the youngest of Grandpa's children, Uncle Tony, married Patricia Barczak on October 21, 1962, at St. Augustine's Church in Milwaukee, Wisconsin. They made their home in Wisconsin, then in Cedar. Grandpa had decided to part with his home near the time of Tony's wedding when most of his family was present, and sold it to the newly married couple.[63]

---

63   Information from Aunt Theresa (Fleis) Rosinski.

All twelve Fleis siblings in age order after Thomas Fleis's funeral. (Left to right): Leo, Ed, Susan, Roman, Albion, Thomas, Clemence, Sister Therese (Irene), Joseph, Theresa (Rosinski), Agnes (Williams), and Anthony (circa 1965).

When Grandpa's health declined, he was brought back to Leelanau County and resided at Maple Valley Nursing Home, Maple City, where he died on May 13, 1965, at the age of seventy-seven. His funeral at Holy Rosary Church was officiated by Rev. Aloysius Ulanowicz. His burial plot is near his beloved wife, Agnes (my busia), who preceded him in 1944.

In the same time frame, Uncle Tom and Aunt Betty and their children moved to Traverse City after selling their farm to Joe Roth, the proprietor of Frigid Foods, Inc., in Suttons Bay. Later, he sold the farm to Glen LaCross, of Leelanau Fruit Company, Suttons Bay. Now, you'll see acres of cherry trees cover the fields at the former O'Brien farm where we once lived.

Side Note:

Another blessing for Harold and me was the birth of our daughter, Victoria, on March 21, 1966. She was two days shy of her seven-year-old brother Steve's birthday. At this time, Mom was sewing baby quilts for her grandbabies. She gave quilts to baby Victoria, and to our one-year-old daughter, Mary Lou. Those two little girls were inseparable from the start! Whenever Victoria was in her playpen in the living room, I would find Mary Lou right beside her. With Victoria's birth, Harold and I had three boys and three girls, besides our precious angel Karen in heaven.

* * *

A couple years after Grandpa's death, the family grieved the tragic loss of my aunt, Sister Mary Therese, on May 7, 1967, at the age of forty-two. Earlier, on a Sunday morning, she attended First

Holy Communion services at Holy Rosary Church for three young relatives: my son Steve, my sister Rita, and cousin Cindy, daughter of Aunt Agnes and Uncle Ron. We celebrated Steve and Rita's event at my home. Cindy's was celebrated at her parents' home in Cedar.

Before Sister Therese said her goodbyes, her voice was recorded on a cassette tape as a musical session was held at Cindy's event. Aunt Agnes played piano, followed by Sister Therese playing a classical melody. She was the emcee also, and encouraged everyone to participate. At least fifteen relatives sang or told a funny story before she headed back to Detroit where she was a choral director and business teacher at St. Andrew's Parish.

Sister Therese in front of Holy Rosary Convent with First Communicants: cousin Cindy Williams, Steve Thompson, and Rita Fleis (circa 1967)

Tragedy struck on her drive back to Detroit. She was southbound on I-75 near Clio with her friend Sister Martin as a passenger when suddenly traffic slowed, and so did she. *The Flint Journal* dated May 8, 1967, states that "Sister Martin heard screeching tires behind them and believes Sister Therese heard this and pulled over to the median to avoid being hit from the rear." The car lost control and ended up across the northbound lane, hitting a utility pole. Both nuns were ejected out of the car. It took her life and paralyzed her good friend, Sister Martin.

Sister Therese's loss dimmed the light of a life that radiated warmth, joy and dedication.

A solemn requiem mass was held at the Felician Sisters motherhouse chapel in Livonia. Auxiliary Bishop Joseph M. Breitenbeck celebrated the mass.

As a choral director, Sister Therese composed musical notes and lyrics for an entire Latin mass, which was given to her sister, my Aunt Agnes. She held onto the composition for five years before showing it to me. A thirty-fifth wedding anniversary was coming up for my parents and a mass was scheduled. She and I purposely learned the sacred music with Mary Narlock, the organist at Holy Rosary Church, and sang the Latin liturgy for their mass.

28

Mid-to-Late Sixties

Family photo taken when Ted was on military leave. Standing (left to right): Jim, Ted, Edward, Larry, Mary Jane, Shirley, Julie, Bernadette, and Ruth Ann. Sitting (left to right): Joan, Irene, Rita, Ed, and Noreen.

ON JANUARY 20, 1966, TED RETURNED HOME for a twenty-five-day leave after serving in Vietnam. He surprised Mom by giving her a twelve-piece set of china dishes. From then on, she began using those dishes for Sunday dinners. Ted said, "While on leave, I helped Dad at the Cedar Hardware Store. Mr. Patrick Fitzpatrick, from Cedar, walked in the store with his daughter, Mary Lou. I asked him if he needed anything and he said, 'No, I just wanted my daughter to meet the new Marine in town.' He also said, 'This store has everything you need.' That day, I met my future wife. We began dating by the end of the week."

Ted's next assignment in the Marine Corps was at the Marine Air Base in Cherry Point, North Carolina. He said, "I convinced my brother Jim that he needed a change in life and if he moved with me, we would live off base. So together we went and had a great time." Ted had six more months in the Marines.

Jim remembers Ted's return home on leave very well. "The family was full of excitement when he came home," explained Jim, who drove back to Cedar from Grand Rapids to spend some time with Ted. "We got together several times while he was home on leave. We were like twins when we were younger. We weren't just brothers; we were best friends.

"Ted looked increasingly stressed until, about a week before his scheduled return, he finally spoke up and said, 'I don't think I can do this. I can't go to that base and live in a barracks without going crazy.'

"Ted said that he might be allowed to live off base if he lived with a relative within fifty miles of the base, and he would have separate rations and a housing allowance. He looked at me and asked me if I would move down there with him.

"The following week was crazy!" Jim declared. "The day I quit my job," he said, "I learned I had just qualified for a great benefit package. I was eighteen. I quit, sold my car, sublet my apartment, and on and on, jumped in the car with Ted, and off to North Carolina we went.

"What a drive!" Jim recalled. "The time went by fast as we reminisced about our childhood ... and conversed about his time in Vietnam and Okinawa."

They drove into a town called New Bern and found a furnished apartment in the paper for thirty-five dollars per month, including utilities. The brothers couldn't believe their luck. When Jim explained to his new landlord that he would be looking for a job, Mr. Bell replied, "You're looking for a job?"

"I told him I was," continued Jim. "He told me to be up and ready to go at six the next morning. He said his nephew was working at a mine and they needed workers. I told him I'd be up.

"Sure enough, at 6 a.m., this pickup truck pulled into the yard, but the front was full. He told me to get in the back. Well, the back had a makeshift tarped enclosure on it, and when I opened it up, there were another three or four guys back there. So, off we went.

"We pull up to this massive construction site. The contractor was Rea, Brown & Root out of Houston, Texas. At that time, they claimed to be the sixth-largest construction company in the world.

"Those guys I rode with went in through the gate and went to work. I was told to go to this trailer and fill out an application for employment. I no more than filled it out, and they said, 'Okay, here's your badge! You are now a tin knocker. Go and see that foreman over there.'

"WHAT THE HELL IS A 'TIN KNOCKER?'" Jim asked himself. "I was just a farm boy from Cedar, Michigan, who also spent time as an elf at Keebler's!"

Fortunately for Jim, the foreman delegating work for the day looked around and asked, "Does anyone know how to make coffee?"

Jim raised his hand.

"He told me to go into this shack and make a pot," he continued. "I remembered Mom making coffee, and I remembered her saying, 'When you make coffee, put in a pinch of salt; it takes out the bitterness.' So, I did, and he loved it.

"From then on, over the next few months, I got paid TIN KNOCKER wages, but I never knocked tin. I was the official coffee-making, blueprint-straightening, go-fer.

"Things went along well for a while, until one day, Mrs. Bell called me downstairs and told me I had a phone call.

"Hello," I said. The lady on the other end sounded intimidating. "'Mr. Fleis, this is the United States Selective Service! We are under the impression that you are avoiding the draft, and if you don't show up at the bus station next Wednesday at 8:00 a.m., we will be sending the police to pick you up!'

"She said that all in one breath, but by the time she stopped talking, I was the one that couldn't breathe. So, guess where I was the following Wednesday at 8:00 a.m.? Off to Raleigh, North Carolina, I went. Got in line, like the rest. Got poked, picked, and tested. Finally, I got called in for an interview.

"The sergeant started, 'After looking at your test results, you qualify to go to Officer Candidate School. There, you will be trained, and upon completion will be given the rank of second lieutenant.'

"I asked him, 'Where do I sign?' and I did, for a three-year enlistment. I felt pretty good and proud. That farm boy from Cedar, Michigan, is no longer an elf or a tin knocker ... This is big....

"I had these great thoughts going through my mind, when I noticed this sergeant kind of looking up to the ceiling, down to the floor... He asked, 'Are you Mr. Fleis?'

"I [nodded] my head yes. 'Step into my office ...' and I did. (This guy was sharp.) He whispered, 'YOU ARE QUALIFIED!'

"'Qualified for what?'

"'For the A ... S ... A ...'

"'The what?' I asked.

"'The ARMY SECURITY AGENCY. You know, cloak-and-dagger, spy stuff ...'

"I suddenly recalled an evening I had spent with Dad. I had to be twelve to fourteen years old when Dad asked me if I wanted to go with him to the Knights of Columbus Hall in Traverse City for a father-son dinner. So, I went. They had an FBI agent as a guest speaker that night. I left there with exciting thoughts of the cloak-and-dagger spy stuff that he spoke about. All the way home, my mind raced at thoughts of what I would experience if I ever became a F...B .. I ... SECRET AGENT MAN.

"As time passed, I often thought about that night, but they were just that, passing thoughts.

"The officer told [me], 'The only thing you have to do to get a cloak and dagger is to just sign up for one more year,' so I did.

"No one else in the family knew what had happened. I think Ted was the only one who knew I was drafted ... I wrote Mom and Dad a letter when I was in basic training."

Jim was on his way to making his dream come true.

* * *

Bernadette graduated from St. Mary's, Lake Leelanau, in 1966. She met her future husband, Ken Denoyer, on a double date. Bernadette explained, "My brother, Jim, [a senior at the time] asked if I would double date with him, as he was dating Ken's sister Carol. Carol's mother would not let her single date. Jim and Carol dated for a short time, and Ken and I continued dating throughout my junior and senior year of school. We were engaged on July 9, 1966, and were married on October 1, 1966, at Holy Rosary Church.[64] It was a great celebration for everyone! That evening of the wedding, my brother Ted surprised us."

Ted explained how that happened. "In June, I was told I was not going to be discharged, and my enlistment was arbitrarily extended for up to four months. They needed to build up the soldier strength for the Vietnam War. I then learned in September that we would be finally discharged sometime in October. I was hoping to be home for Bernadette and Ken's wedding.

"Retired Chief Hospital Corpsman Patrick Fitzpatrick (Mary Lou's father), sent a letter to the Marine Corps commandant asking for my early discharge because of the wedding. Well, that woke up my captain! He was less than happy and called me a 'congressman's son.' In the end, I was discharged at 12:01 a.m. October 1, and drove straight through from North Carolina to be there for Bernadette and Ken's wedding day. At 9:30 p.m. that same day, I arrived at Solon Township Hall."

---

64   Father Ulanowicz officiating, and Father Donzilla and Father Voss assisting at the nuptial mass.

Bernadette and Ken's children are: Keith (1967), Scott (1968), and Brian (1971). (Scott and Brian were born with congenital birth defects. Scott lived for five months and Brian lived until age five.)

* * *

On January 27, 1967, Ted married Mary Lou (Fitzpatrick) at Holy Rosary Church. The weather was blizzardy. Some relatives couldn't make it to the wedding. Jim was Ted's best man.

Jim's story: "I was in the army, stationed at Fort McClellan, Alabama. I was waiting for orders to be transferred out to my new duty station; so, my commanding officer would only give me a three-day leave. I figured that should be enough ... two days to spend before the wedding and then leave late the day of the wedding. I left the fort and flew into Atlanta, Georgia ... everything was going okay ... we no more than got in the air and they informed us a major storm was about to hit Michigan, so we had to land in Cleveland, Ohio. I slept on the floor that night, awaiting the flight news for the next day. None of the airports were open the second day. Next morning, I was informed there were only two airports open in Michigan ... Detroit and Traverse City. I landed in TC about an hour before the ceremony. I got to the church about a half hour before the service ... then went to Mary Lou's parents' house for the reception ... then was taken from there to the airport and flew back to Alabama."

Ted and Mary Lou moved to Grand Rapids after their wedding. "My brother Edward helped us get a start," Ted said. "I joined Bell & Howell as a technician and worked my way up to regional sales manager.

"During the early years of marriage, I used the GI bill to go half-time at Grand Rapids Community College, and then attended Aquinas College."

Their children are: Jeanette (1967) and Christopher (1968).

New Family Band

Larry played accordion at a talent show at Glen Lake School when he was a sophomore. Right around that same time, in 1966, he, on accordion, together with Joan, eleven, on drums, and Noreen, ten, on piano, formed Larry and His Larks. Mom came up with the name because she thought Joan and Noreen sounded like larks. Mom made matching polka dot shirts for everyone to wear.

Larry & His Larks: Joan the drummer, Larry on accordion, and Noreen playing piano keyboard (circa 1967)

"Dad started a [public relations] campaign for the band," Larry wrote. "We played a few freebies, and I remember playing in front of the Cedar/Maple City Lions Club for their monthly meeting."

Dad also arranged for them to play at a graduation party, and Joan and Larry were paid twenty dollars each. (Noreen only did a little singing.) That's when they realized they needed to buy her a keyboard. Dad took them to Fiedler's Music Store in Traverse City. The salesman at first didn't take them seriously because of their ages, but once he did, Dad bought new drums, a new keyboard, a small amplifier, and microphones. The new equipment made practicing fun.

In 1968, Larry brought Joan and Noreen, as part of the Larry and His Larks combo, to Glen Lake School's talent show. They got a standing ovation.

"The first real full-paying job," Larry recalled, "was playing for a fiftieth wedding anniversary party at Centerville Township Hall." Although they didn't specify a fee, the family paid them seventy-five dollars. By then, they knew enough songs for a full set, Noreen was on a portable keyboard, and they were fully amplified. "Our claim to fame began," Larry proclaimed.

* * *

Dad became a dealer for Chaparral snowmobiles in the mid-to-late sixties. He purchased some to rent out through the hardware store.

Larry said they were nothing compared to the current models: they broke down all the time, would overheat, the spark plugs would foul, and the belts would come off or break. Whenever you went on a trip with others, somebody in the group always seemed to have a breakdown.

Chaparrals for sale at Cedar Hardware (circa 1967)

Around 1967, either Dad approached management at Sugar Loaf Ski Resort or they approached Dad, but Larry spent many winter weekends renting out four to six Chaparral snowmobiles over there by the hour. The people renting the machines would run them almost wide open, going as fast as they could along the private airport runway. Of course, in those days, wide open was probably thirty to forty miles per hour.

The Chaparrals did have continual breakdowns, broken windshields, and they overheated. Still, Dad made money renting them to Sugar Loaf and when the management saw that, they rented out their own snowmobiles the following year.

On the weekends, Dad would bring a couple snowmobiles home from the store for the family to enjoy on the farm. One time, Julie's husband, Ray, Larry, Ted, and his wife, Mary Lou, took a couple of snowmobiles on trails Larry had been on a few days earlier. A lot of snow had fallen since then. One snowdrift was ten or twelve feet high.

Ray and Larry caught air going over the top of a drift, landing fifteen feet down the trail and swiftly moved out of the way, because Ted and Mary Lou, trailing behind them, landed in exactly the same spot. They were thankful no one got hurt.

However, that night, Ray began to experience chest pain. By Monday morning, he was in the doctor's office, hardly able to move. The doctor found no fracture, but it took six months to heal.

* * *

"Money was sparse in wintertime," Larry said. "In order to supplement the income, Dad started selling NaChurs fertilizer and DeKalb's seed corn."

EDWARD V. FLEIS
Leelanau County Representative

NaChurs Liquid Fertilizer

                                    P.O. BOX 38
PHONE 228-5602   CEDAR, MICH. 49621

Ed showing strawberries produced by a local
farmer, Joe Czerniak, from Cedar

Dad sold NaChurs fertilizer, out of Ohio, through the farm supply arm of the hardware business. The product was used by farmers for strawberries, cherries, apples, and other crops. Dad and Don Witkowski called on farmers and presented the program. If a customer was interested, they tested soil for them during the winter months of February and March, going by snowmobile into the orchards, shoveling the snow, and scooping out dirt, then used a probe to get into the ground for a soil sample, which was sent to the lab in Ohio to see what nutrients the soil might lack.

Paul Watkoski, an Elmwood Township cherry grower, served as regional manager for the company. Dad handled business in Leelanau County as district manager under Paul. Don Witkowski, Paul's son-in-law, was directly employed in sales alongside Dad. "When the results came back," Don explained, "Your dad and I went back to the farmers and showed what was needed for their soil. In the spring, I went back, driving Paul's big, converted gasoline truck and delivered the fertilizer to the farmers' tanks, from which the farmers would spray the crops themselves. One farmer was also a pilot and sprayed his fields from his plane.

"Farmers had a discount when they paid up front, otherwise, your dad had to go back and collect the payments," Don added. "I worked with your dad for five years, 1967 to 1972, and he was a good guy and fun to be with."

Dad also had an outdoor storage tank and pump at the store, and customers could purchase smaller amounts of liquid fertilizer.

One job of Joan's was removing labels with a knife from gallon glass jars, so Dad could pump the liquid NaChurs fertilizer in them to sell. Joan said, "I used a knife one time and instead of removing the label, I gashed my right middle finger. That was the end of that job for me!

"I also helped Dad with invoices and statements. Noreen and I would actually send out the statements at the end of the month. We were young to be helping with the bookkeeping!"

Larry recalls helping with unloading semi-truckloads full of cement at the store. "This happened maybe two or three times a year," he said. "So, Dad asked me to round up a few friends. My macho friends got a workout, made a couple of bucks, and I think they enjoyed it."

Once, when Joan and Noreen were helping Larry move a cement mixer, there was quite the mishap. Noreen explains, "Somehow, that heavy mixer came down and flattened Joan's finger. I never ran so fast in my life as that day, running up to Jakielek's Drug Store to get some bandages."

Joan added, "The middle finger on my right hand split in half and was gushing with blood. Larry wrapped [it] with a cloth first and Noreen came back with the Band-Aids. I never did see a doctor to this day, and my finger never regained its muscle."

Shirley remembers multiple assignments. She said, "At times, I was assigned to wax and polish floors … I would watch Dad mix paint or replace a window or screen, and learn those jobs … I could get customers whatever they needed, whether it was nails or plumbing fixtures.

"Dad sold minnows; I helped clean the bait tank. I packed night crawlers in little boxes for customers. One time, my cousin Christy [Pleva] helped me. We used the adding machine and checked out customers at the cash register. We all learned by watching Dad," Shirley concluded.

Noreen continues, "Brother Larry, my sisters, and I learned life skills, like waiting on customers and counting inventory at the store. Besides packing night crawlers, three dozen to a carton, Joan and I cleaned out the fish tanks, bathroom, pop containers, burned trash, and mailed invoices. It was also common for Dad to send me up to the bar to get a hamburger or go to the post office right around the corner to buy some five-cent stamps.

"It wasn't all work, though. There were the daily treats of a root beer or 7-Up, popsicles from the ice-cream cooler, and Heath bars that Dad kept behind the cash register counter."

Young Rita said, "One time, when I was at the store, Dad lifted me up to his lap and allowed me to punch the sale of a customer into the cash register. It took longer than usual, and the customer got impatient and uttered some cuss words.

"Dad looked at the customer and told him firmly, 'You don't talk that way in front of my daughter.' I was five years old. Those words Dad spoke made a lasting impression for me."

Another memory for Larry: "During the summer, we maintained long hours, to about 7:00 or 7:30 p.m., and were open on Sundays, too, for a limited time. Fridays seemed to be special. Mom would sometimes bring meals from home while trying to keep them warm. This was before microwaves. Some Fridays, Dad would go to Maple Tavern and bring us fish. I loved that fish! Of course, for some reason, he would leave early and it would take about two hours or more for that trip, so I was pretty hungry by the time it arrived.

"The older I got, the more I was left to run the store alone. Dad and Mom felt comfortable taking off for short trips … Being in customer service for seven years, in addition to having the band, [Larry and his Larks], really helped my career development in my ability to handle customers. I have to tell you that in all the years that I worked with Dad, I only remember him losing his cool one time, but he said nothing until the customer left.

"Mom didn't get very involved in running the hardware [store]. She still had five of us to raise and was busy. In addition to the store, Dad was very active in the Cedar Chamber of Commerce, the Cedar/Maple City Lions Club, the Knights of Columbus, and was a volunteer firefighter," Larry concluded.

**Ed, Tony, and Dave before departing on a trip promoting cherries, circa 1970
(photo courtesy of Dave Taghon)**

Dad joined the Cedar Chamber of Commerce in 1960. He was given the opportunity to promote the cherry industry ten years later, with fellow chamber member Tony Galla. Local historian Dave Taghon, from Empire, wrote this story: "During the summer of 1970, your dad, Tony Galla, and myself joined the Traverse City Chamber of Commerce for a three-to-four-day trip. We took ten Oldsmobile convertibles from Traverse City to southern Michigan and Indiana. Our trunks were full of cherry products, which we proudly delivered when we stopped at smaller towns to spread the news of the cherry industry.

"We also hit several breweries, as well as prominent businesses, including the Studebaker Plant in South Bend, Indiana, where they were still building the Studebaker Avantis, as I recall.

"Mr. Jim Beckett, along with his daughter Barbie (Beckett) Houghton, who was ending her reign as 1969 Cherry Queen, came along on the trip.

"Your dad, Tony, and myself were always in the same car. It was a great bit of fun for all," Dave concluded.

Dad was one of twenty-two charter members of the Cedar/Maple City Lions Club when it formed in 1964.[65] A podium he built to use for meetings is still in use.

(Photo courtesy of Pat Hobbins)

Kneeling, left to right are Art Finch, Basil Jankowski, Fred Taghon, Mr. Ditmer, President Nash Isadore Stachnik and Reymond Brow. Standing,, Glen Noonan, Lowell Cate, Albin Rosinski, Edward Fleis, Raymond Salisbury, Larry Novak, Harold Sweeny, Anthony Mikowski, Gerald Salisbury, Adolph Novak, Robert Stacknik, Charles Flaska, Clarence Burry, Frank Winowiecki, LaVern VanHorn, Paul Miller Clintion Meewenberg and Russell Bevelthymer.

65   The Cedar/Maple City Lions Club is a part of Lions Clubs International, a network of volunteers who work together to answer the needs that challenge their community. They provide eyeglasses and hearing aids to community members, besides collecting thousands of glasses sent to Central and South America. They hold fundraisers for community families in need, distribute food baskets, and provide three annual scholarships to Glen Lake School graduates, and much more. In 1980, their community building was built for holding meetings and community events. They assumed management of Old Settlers Park in conjunction with Myles Kimmerly Park.

Dad's fellow Lions Club member Pat Hobbins provided this information: "In 1971, the Cedar/Maple City Lions Club leased and developed Myles Kimmerly Recreation Area, a 143-acre park belonging to Leelanau County. The Lions built the tennis courts. Your dad helped a lot with that … he helped with most of the projects, which included building baseball diamonds and trails, and putting in cement floors for the pole barn, picnic shelters, and toilets.

"The Lions developed the Kasson Township Park as well, and then turned it over to the township. Your dad was a hard worker. Your mom worked at most of our dinners.

"At club-sponsored bingo nights, whenever your dad called bingo, he was quite the character, making people laugh when he called out some numbers, especially "'sickety-six' for 'O 66,'" said Hobbins.

Monday evening was the usual day for bingo. Mom would go with Dad. She loved to play bingo, and when Dad wasn't calling, he played the game too. They also played bingo at other places. One time when Harold and I went along with Mom and Dad and played bingo at the VFW Hall in Lake Leelanau, my husband won the jackpot. We still owed Dad money after he built our home. When we got home, Harold gave Dad his winnings.

"That will take care of the balance," Dad responded, "as I am grateful for Ruth Ann's help when I first got started at the store."

Left: Ed with his brother, Joe Fleis, as Knights of Columbus color guards at Holy Rosary Church. Right: The Elks Flag Day, 1986. Back row (left to right): Ed Drzewiecki, Everett Burkholder, Leo Riskey, Phil Walters, Ed Fleis, and Gordon Larch. Front (left to right): Tony Zywicki, Paul Watkoski, and Glen King (photo courtesy of Glen and Frances King).

In the mid-sixties, Dad became a member of the Knights of Columbus. The Knights maintained the K of C Hall on M-22 in Greilickville for many years. Eventually, Dad became a fourth-degree member and joined the Color Guard.

In a conversation with Dad's fellow knight, Glen King, and his wife, Frances, they stated: "The Knights volunteered with their wives and prepared and served meals for Traverse City Iron Works, Cherryland Electric, and credit union functions. Your mom and dad worked at those dinners. This was a way for the Knights to earn charitable donations.

"Your dad also participated in Cherry Festival parades for approximately ten years. He was the nicest guy ... he always stood up straight." Dad belonged to Council 1213, affiliated with Immaculate Conception Church in Traverse City.

* * *

Meanwhile, the combination of the talent show and the anniversary party opened the door to a lot of bookings for the Larry and His Larks band. "We were very, very busy," Larry reminisced. "Friends would call us to find out our open dates before they called the church to set up the date of their wedding. We played hundreds of weddings and some high school proms." At seventy-five dollars per event, we were making big money in 1968–69.

"Mom and Dad drove us everywhere we played, until the girls were a little older," said Larry. "Mom and Dad had a small car, a Dodge Dart, into which we crammed the drums, accordion, amplifier, piano, and the five of us."

* * *

For years, my Dad smoked cigarettes and cigars. "He smoked, but I don't think he ever inhaled," Joan said. "I recall his cigarette bobbing from his mouth—with an ash of an inch or two long, and he was able to talk at the same time!"

She continued, "Larry, Noreen, and I went to a band job, just the three of us. Noreen and I were 'shenanigans' smoking. Larry was driving the car while Noreen and I were cramped in the backseat with the big bass drum. We put a newspaper in front of us, pretending we were reading, lit a cigarette, and you could see the smoke going up above the newspaper. Larry turned around, did a double-take and said, 'Put that cigarette out before you start a fire.' Noreen and I never smoked in Dad's car again going to a band job. It wasn't long afterwards that Dad bought a green station wagon. Now we even had more room!"

Joan also remembers riding in Dad's station wagon one night about one in the morning, coming back from a job. "We usually played for four hours, until midnight or 1:00 a.m.," Joan said. "Noreen and I were tired and fell asleep. We were just going around the last curve by Holy Rosary Church, when, all of a sudden, we woke up to the smell of a skunk. A car was coming right at us and hit the rear end of the driver's side, even though Larry headed for the ditch to [try to] prevent the accident. We were fortunate that Larry was on the ball! It was a hit-and-run with little damage [to] the station wagon."

Shirley was fifteen when Larry taught her to drive. Then, one day, she begged Mom to let her drive from the hardware store to the farm. Shirley said, "I thought I was so cool, and Mom, sweet Mom, gave in to my begging and let me drive the Dodge Dart. She was a brave soul. I did pretty good until I turned in the driveway and did not slow down enough and drove right into the ditch. Mom never yelled at me or made me feel bad about it. Of course, it was quite a while before I drove again."

* * *

Larry played my white marble accordion for five years. He saved enough money to buy himself a wonderful accordion from his brother-in-law, Ray Watkoski.

"He gave me a deal I couldn't resist!" Larry exclaimed.

Of course, I was glad to have my accordion back, and to play music again.

Larry graduated from Glen Lake High School in 1969. He received the Dr. Alonzo A. Norconk Scholarship award and grant, which he used to attend Northwestern Michigan College in the fall. He continued to work at the store until 1971. Larry said, "Dad and I spent lots and lots of time together over the years. We got to know just about everybody in the local community. He made a lot of friends and purposely stayed out of politics."

Jim recalled Dad's words of wisdom: "Remember, when you're in business, you aren't a Democrat or a Republican ... you're an Independent!"

Dad and Mom gifted customers at Christmas with calendars and matchbooks. The advertisement on the matchbook read:

The front cover read:	The back cover read:
Phone Number 228-5417 CEDAR HARDWARE NA-CHURS Liquid Fertilizer, Sporting Goods, Live Bait CEDAR, MICH.	Quality vs. Price–Don't try to buy a thing too cheap from those with things to sell, because the goods you'll have to keep, and time will always tell. The price you paid you'll soon forget, and the goods you get will stay; the price you will not long regret–The quality you may!

29

The End of Farming

IN 1965, AFTER JIM LEFT HOME, FARMING CEASED. My parents were thinking about moving closer to Cedar. Mom was spending more time at the store, as was the rest of the family.

I was aware that our parents were thinking about moving closer to the store because they approached Harold and me about switching homes with them. I couldn't imagine us going back to living on the farm after living close to Cedar for nine years.

Dad sold the largest parcel across the road from the farmhouse to a couple from Detroit, who built a large two-story home in the middle of the property. The rear of their parcel goes back to where the old railroad train tracks used to be. Another chunk of land behind the barn sold; there are three homes on it, with many trees across that property.

The opportunity for our parents to make the big change in residence came in 1969, when the John Sattler home in downtown Cedar went up for sale. The two-story, yellow, Victorian-style house, located on the corner of Whitman and Kasson Street, had five bedrooms, an open staircase, and high ceilings. The kitchen window had a view of the downtown area.

Originally owned by M. A. Culver, it was the first home to have electricity in Leelanau County when a Delco light plant was installed in the house and in Culver's business in 1917.[66]

Beginning in the mid-1940s, a *Leelanau Enterprise* article dated June 9, 1949, indicated, "The Sattler house occupied the first Leelanau Telephone Company, a private telephone service serving southwestern Leelanau County and Suttons Bay Telephone Company."[67]

Mom and Dad bought the home, and in the late summer of 1969, my parents and younger siblings made the move to Cedar. They rented out the farmhouse for a couple years. By then, half of us were married: Julie, Edward, Mary Jane, Ted, Bernadette, and me. Jim was overseas in

---

66   Odom, S., *Leelanau Enterprise*, "Cedar Home and Business Leads County Toward Electrification," March 10, 2011.
67   Hubbell, A. "Party Lines Were the Pits."

Taiwan with the army and Larry would soon be off to Northwestern Michigan College. The next two—Shirley, nearly sixteen and a junior, and Joan, a freshman at thirteen—were both attending Glen Lake School in Maple City. The youngest two, Noreen and Rita, were both going to Holy Rosary. Noreen, twelve, was in the eighth grade, because she had skipped a grade; Rita, ten, was in grade five. The youngest two transferred to Glen Lake after eighth grade.

Noreen commented, "I remember the night we moved from the farm into Cedar. I wish there would have been a picture taken. I'm sure we looked like something out of *The Beverly Hillbillies*, packing up the old, green pickup truck and moving into town. I was sitting in the open back of the truck with my sisters, holding on to some of our belongings so they wouldn't blow away. We waved as we passed Holy Rosary Church. I don't recall any of us kids having advance notice that we were even moving, but move we did! What an adventure!"

Our parents' home was situated in the middle of town, kitty-corner to Vlack's Market, later, Mikowski's Market, and currently, Buntings Market. "Mom would send me there for a gallon of milk or a loaf of bread," said Noreen. "Mr. Mikowski would write it up on Mom's tab, which she'd pay at the end of the week."

The telephone company had installed phone jacks in every room. That meant the girls could plug a phone into any of their bedrooms upstairs. "In fact," Shirley recalled, "Dad gave us a phone to use upstairs. We were teenagers. … How cool was that!"

Joan said, "After living out on the farm, it was convenient to live within walking distance to the grocery store, pharmacy, gas station, and post office. Even Dad's hardware store was just two blocks down the street. My friends, Donald Mikowski and Sue Peplinski, were our new next-door neighbors!"

Noreen rode a bike all over town during her teen years. She said, "I traveled just about every square inch of road in Cedar on our family's blue Schwinn bike. My cousin Agnes Fleis was my best friend, and I often rode to her home, a short distance from the Cedar River."

Rita loved the new activities in town. "I learned to hunt night crawlers, fly kites, drive a mini-bike, play chess and football, and ride a bike," she said. "I loved living close to my friends."

One thing the home didn't have was a

Ed and Irene's Cedar home (the former Sattler house) after Ed built the attached garage

garage, so Dad built a large two-door garage with a convenient, walk-in breezeway connecting it to the house. He had no more than finished the job when Shirley suffered a mishap driving Dad's car. As she tried to pull into the newly built garage, she misjudged and hit the middle blocks between the two garage stalls. She cried as she tried to explain to Dad and didn't dare ask permission to drive his station wagon for a while after that.

Shirley started dating David Mikowski in high school, where they were named king and queen of the prom in their senior year. David's parents were owners of Mikowski's Market. Our parents became close friends with David's parents soon after moving to Cedar. Their homes were across the street from each other. Many good times were spent playing cards at either home.

Meanwhile, Shirley was helping at the store a lot. "Dad gave me a key to the store in my senior year," she said. "At times, I was responsible for opening or closing the store. One time, a friend from school and I went to the hardware store to pick up some supplies to decorate for a dance. Dad was gone to lunch at Cedar Tavern, and, since I had my own key, I opened the door, and as I entered, I noticed some smoke and sparks. I sent my friend down to the fire department next to the post office downtown. The adding machine had shorted out and caught fire. I believe God sent us there at [that] precise time, so there was very little damage."

An article in the *Leelanau Enterprise* stated:[68] "A fire in a short-circuited adding machine was estimated to have caused $2,000.00 damage at the Cedar Hardware and Farm Store, according to Al Rosinski, Chief of the Solon-Centerville Volunteer Fire Department."

A couple of my children recalled memories of Grandpa's store.

Mary Lou wrote, "I must have been about five and was hanging out at the store with Grandpa one day, when he taught me a lesson in honesty and consequences. He noticed something in my mouth and asked where I got it? Grandpa didn't miss a thing, and soon realized I was eating a piece of candy that I hadn't paid for … He put me to work sweeping the floor."

Her older brother, Edward, said, "I bought a bottle of orange soda for a dime from the machine in front of the store and dropped it. I hoped Grandpa would give me a dime for another one but was afraid to ask."

---

68   "Leelanau History," published twenty-five years later on December 4, 1969.

Side Note:

"We have another 'tax deduction,'" Harold said after the birth of our son Donald on April 15, 1970. I was thankful for our healthy baby boy. Just a couple weeks before, I had one of the best surprises. I was sitting in a chair relaxing after a small baby shower when my little daughters, Mary Lou and Victoria, ages five and four, walked up to give me a gift. Each had carefully folded their blankies and handed them to me for the expected baby-to-be. They were the blankets my mother had given them, made from soft cotton material lined with flannel. They were still in good shape, and I used them for the new baby.

As a toddler, Donald found his happy place in the kitchen, playing with smaller pots and pans stored in the drawer below the oven, while Mary Lou and Victoria had a lower cupboard in the kitchen to store their play stuff. My oldest son, Steve, learned to wash dishes while kneeling on a chair. Janice learned to measure and blend ingredients and roll the dough for a pie crust. John and Edward dug for worms with their older brother in the summertime to go fishing with their dad. They learned to go fishing on their own, too. Some of the children picked mushrooms and helped with the garden: planting, weeding, and picking produce. They also went cherry picking with me.

* * *

Mom was a silent disciplinarian. Shirley and Joan occasionally skipped school. One time, Joan recalled, "There was a bad snowstorm. We came home at the usual time. Mom was ironing clothes in the kitchen and she asked if we had a good day at school.

"Naturally, we said, 'Yes!'

"Then Mom said, 'That's funny! School was called off at noon.' She didn't scold us; she didn't have to say a word. We knew we did something wrong … and we made sure and listened to the weather report the next time!"

On another occasion Joan added, "Dad gave us girls fair warning that if we missed the bus, we would be walking to school." He said this just about every day.

"Well," Joan continued, "my sisters Shirley, Noreen, and I missed the bus one day. There was no vehicle to drive and no one to hitch a ride with, so we started walking to Glen Lake School, at least ten miles away. Come to find out, one of the townspeople went to the store and told Dad that he saw us girls walking to school.

"I don't think we were [yet] to the Third Creek heading to Maple City, a mile away, when a car stopped on the road and the driver said sternly, 'Get in the car, you girls!' It was Dad! He [had] locked up the store and came to get us. He never said a word to us all the way to school. He was so upset. I know he was one worried Dad."

Shirley said, "One time, I was coming home with Mom. We left Maple City, heading for Cedar in the Dodge Dart. About three miles from Cedar, Mom noticed the gas gauge was on 'E', so she put the car in neutral and turned off the engine. We were flying!" Shirley recalled. "Woohoo! We coasted all the way to the hardware store.

"Another time when Mom was driving," Shirley said. "She wanted to say a rosary on the way to Traverse City, and I was begging her not to. So Mom settled with, 'How about one decade of the rosary?' I agreed. "We prayed one 'Our Father,' ten 'Hail Marys,' and one 'Glory Be to the Father.'"

For years, Mom talked about wanting to visit the Basilica of Sainte Anne de Beaupré, a major Roman Catholic pilgrimage landmark in central Quebec, Canada, on the north side of the St. Lawrence River. The shrine honors the Grandmother of Jesus, the Mother of Mary.

Mom's mother, (Grandma Jennie), was very devoted to the saint, so much so that she had a statue of Sainte Anne de Beaupré displayed on a small altar in her bedroom after her stroke. "Don't think for a moment Grandma wasn't praying, even though she was only able to utter words of 'Oh, dear me,' and 'dare, dare,'" my sister, Mary Jane said.

Mother's wish came true in 1970, when my parents planned a pilgrimage there. Bernadette was asked to stay at the house with her four youngest sisters, Shirley, Joan, Noreen, and Rita. "Little did I know the teenage girls had already spread their wings," Bernadette commented, "and there was no way they were going to listen to their older sister. They were used to their independence now."

The trip took my parents to the land of Mom's grandparents, Alfred and Regina Lamie, in Quebec. Even though they didn't take time to explore Mom's ancestry, this trip was fulfilling in itself, as they did get to the shrine, satisfying that deep desire planted there by her own mother.

Bernadette was happy when our parents returned home, and the girls were still alive with the house still standing—and clean. Most of all, she said, "I was done with my responsibility."

Jim finished his tour with the United States Army Security Agency in 1970, after twenty-seven months in Taiwan. He returned home wondering about the next step in his life.

He didn't have to wait. "I no more than got home," he shared, "then the NSA (National Security Agency) contacted me." They offered him a job in a related field, with a good wage and benefits that even included a clothing allowance. But it would all be overseas. Jim, who hadn't been home in over two years, didn't feel ready to turn around and leave, so he turned it down.

Wondering what else was out there, he went down to Grand Rapids to visit family and see what kind of work was available. An ad in the paper for a position as a private detective with Pinkerton's caught his eye.

"Pinkerton's," he thought. "Isn't that the wild-west company that chased Jesse James? I better check this out." He worked for them for about three and a half years, first in Grand Rapids, then in Lansing, and eventually Chicago.

It was very exciting work. One day, he was called in to see the company president, who said they wanted him to move into investigation management—a great promotion. "You do have an associate's degree, don't you?" asked the president. "That is one of our prerequisites."

When Jim answered that he didn't, the president offered him a job in security division management.

"I told him no," Jim said. "I told him if I needed an associate's degree, I would quit my job and go to college.

"Moving home was an adjustment for me. I went from carrying a gun, chasing and investigating people that were doing bad things at all times of the day and night to 'Jim, what time did you get home last night? You stayed out pretty late! Don't forget today is Sunday ... church time.'

"'Yes, Mother.'

"Actually, it was great reuniting with my parents," he admits. "I think it healed an old wound that I had with my father since the age of seventeen years old."

It only took a few weeks and Jim had his own place. He rented a house Dad bought across the street from the hardware store. He worked at Sugarfoot Saloon and attended Northwestern Michigan College in Traverse City. Jim earned his associate's degree in 1976.

Larry continued helping Dad at the store, even while he was a student at Northwestern Michigan College. "I worked with Dad until I graduated with an associate's degree," he stated. "Once I went to Michigan State, my brother Edward got me a job as an intern in the summer at Williams & Works, an engineering firm in Grand Rapids, so I didn't go back to work in the store."

Dad needed other resources. He hired Dale Gauthier in the summer of 1971. Dale said, "When I was eighteen years old and graduated from Glen Lake, I stopped in the store and asked your dad if he needed some help. He hired me on the spot, and I worked until the spring of 1972. During that time, your mom and sisters, Shirley, Joan, and Noreen, also worked at the store. I remember your mom waiting on customers and handling sales at the cash register." Then, Larry Petroskey came on board, under Glen Lake's work release program, until he attended college in the fall. Dale and Larry were the only employees Dad hired outside the family.

Shirley graduated from Glen Lake High School in 1971, and soon after, attended Northwestern Academy of Beauty. She had desired to become a cosmetologist since eighth grade. Shirley explained, "My hair was rather long, and Mom took me to the beauty school in Traverse City. After I got my first professional haircut and perm, my hair was short and curly, but after a few washes, it became short, fuzzy hair. Then I began using a hair straightener that I purchased at the five-and-dime. God bless Mom, she never said a word about my hair the whole time. Mom was cool.

"After having the courage to ask Dad to borrow money to move to Traverse City into an apartment with three other girls," Shirley related, "and needing money to go to cosmetology school, he opened a checking account for me and shortly after, I started school. I also found a waitress job at Bill Thomas's Restaurant. Eventually, I paid Dad back." Shirley received her cosmetology license in 1972.

Dad took Shirley to buy her first car, "a 1970 Ford Mustang, three on the floor," as she described it. "It was cool, and of course, I had to borrow money from Dad again, but eventually, I paid him back."

* * *

Dad and Mom were contemplating the sale of the hardware store at the same time as selling the farmhouse, farm buildings, and the remaining 5.9 acres to Gordon and Betty Hughes from Milwaukee, Wisconsin, in 1971.

Their daughter, Deborah, was thirteen when they moved to the farm. She said, "Just coming out of winter, my parents, brothers, and [I] drove into the driveway to look at the house and property. The outbuilding where the workshop was sealed the deal for my father [Gordon]. Besides, the home was large enough for a family of five ... a garden and plenty of room for us to play."

* * *

"The Last of The Farm Dust," written by my son, Steve:

I was twelve years old when Grandma and Grandpa sold the farm. The granary had to be swept out. Uncle Larry and I tackled the job.

The granary was very dusty. I got thirsty. We went to the house and a couple glasses of water were sitting on the counter. I drank and almost choked on it, as my mouth was full of gritty dust.

My uncle said, "Don't you know, you have to swirl the water in your mouth and spit out the first swallow?" I learned a good lesson that day.

* * *

Our parents exercised their freedom. Maybe it wasn't the wisest thing for them to subdivide the homestead, but none of the older children were interested in farming. We have no regrets. What we do have, though, are the great memories of living there.

In 2012, the Hughes family invited the Fleis family to visit the farmhouse and property. I had visited them earlier, but several family members took the tour.

Ted recalled the occasion: "Looking at the kitchen window, I remembered Mom baked bread several times a week. When she did, the kitchen window was open, and as you walked by, you could smell the bread. You were immediately hungry. There was nothing better than fresh bread and homemade butter.

"The old potato sorting machine was still in the root cellar. I remember we grew potatoes as a cash crop that was dug in October and stored in the root cellar, sorted, and sold in the winter. The work was hard and I hated sorting rotten potatoes, but the best memory was Mom would always make potato pancakes during harvesting time. I don't know if the taste came from freshly dug potatoes or the recipe, but nobody ever made better potato pancakes than Mom."

* * *

In November of 1972, after owning and operating the Cedar Hardware and Farm Store for twelve years, my parents sold the store to John and Sharon Baxter from Glen Arbor. The Baxters operated the store for twenty-two years and sold it to Ron and Kit Novak from Cedar in 1994. The Novaks sold to Richard and Jen Zywicki, also from Cedar, in 2007, who remain the current owners. The store still maintains the tradition of family working together.

Larry stated, "I always thought I would be buying Cedar Hardware, but when I was at Michigan State, Dad and Mom found a buyer. That obviously changed my thoughts entirely. Owning a store does not give a family flexibility to take vacations or time off. The store was successful for Mom and Dad. With the sale, they received a monthly payment via a land contract, and they were able to retire early. They lived modestly. Good for them! Dad was fifty-eight and Mom was fifty-seven."

After the sale, Dad and Mom's lives slowed down for the first time since 1937 when they were married. I wondered what decision they would make moving forward, but realized how much they had accomplished in thirty-five years.

They began attending monthly luncheons sponsored by the Commission on Aging (now Leelanau County Senior Services) held at the Cedar/Maple City Lions Club Hall in Maple City. They met folks their age or older, and played cards with them after the meal. They played cards with friends and family. They played bingo. They loved to dance, and the (former) Maple Tavern in Maple City was a popular place for dancing on Saturday nights. They were on the go, while still raising their three youngest teenage daughters: Joan, Noreen, and Rita.

Our free-as-a-bird parents would jump in the car and go, and that's what they did when they heard Ray and Julie were having a party on Halloween night at their home in Grand Rapids.

Our petite mom was in costume when they made a couple of stops on the way, one of them at Edward and Barbara's home. My sister-in-law, Barbara, was giving out treats to neighborhood trick-or-treaters. "The doorbell rang and I went out with the candy," Barbara said, "handing it out by handfuls. This one kid was tapping her foot and pointing to her basket for more candy! I gave her more, but when she tried it a second time, I said, 'We only have enough for everyone to get some.' So, she peacefully left with the group.

"It wasn't until we arrived later at Julie and Ray's house for a party that we found out that the trick-or-treater was Mom."

Dad purchased a good, used Winnebago motorhome. It became our parents' home on wheels in Cedar. A honk of the horn, and you knew they were in your driveway offering you a ride. The more the merrier!

When you joined our parents, you could count on a little music as Dad plugged in an eight-track tape, beer or soda in the fridge to quench your thirst, a deck of cards on the table ready for a game, and a drive down the road you'd never forget.

I remember those rides with my children on board, on beautiful sunshiny days, thinking how lucky we were. Dad didn't drive long distances; it was more about taking up the scenery in Leelanau County. It was carefree and pure fun!

My daughter Victoria remembers going for a ride in the Winnebago with Dad. She wrote: "Grandpa was a pedal-to-the-metal kind of driver. We were laughing so hard. I said, 'Grandpa, you're driving too fast.' He said something like, 'I've got somewhere to go, and if I'm going there, I want to get there.'

"It was a riot! Grandpa was just fun, even though I felt nervous. He had no fear."

That Winnebago came in handy getting Larry and his Larks to their music gigs.

"Polka music was a big deal back then," Joan explained. "Everyone hired a polka band for their events, and we played at many weddings, proms, and credit union parties. When we were in our teen years, Mom and Dad went with us all of the time. We played for many occasions in Gaylord and Petoskey and got to know some of the regulars that came to the events. It was quite comfortable traveling in the Winnebago motorhome, and Larry was old enough to take over the wheel when Dad got tired of driving in the wee hours of the morning.

"I still can't figure out how we made it to Sunday morning mass, when we didn't get home until early in the morning.

"It didn't matter if it was rain or shine, snowstorm or blizzard … we had a job to perform, no matter what. There was one time when it was snowing and blowing so bad that Mom made sure we had enough extra warm clothes, blankets, a shovel, and sand in case we went into the ditch. We made it to the wedding at Garfield Township Hall in Traverse City, and we noticed people shoveling the bride and groom's car out of the ditch. The party still went on!!

"We also played for a Waslawski wedding at the Solon Township Hall on a Saturday evening when only a dozen or so guests were able to make the reception because of the winter storm.

"The VFW Hall in Lake Leelanau was a hot spot for wedding receptions, where we played frequently. Maple City Tavern held weekly open dances, and when Noreen and I were fifteen and sixteen years old, they finally allowed us to play. We were young, and Mom gave us instructions: 'Never cross your legs, and don't go outside during break.'"

On January 20, 1973, David and Shirley were married at Holy Rosary Church. They lived in Grand Rapids after their wedding. Within a couple years, they moved back to Cedar. Their children are: Stephanie (1974), David (1975), Douglas (1976), Shaun (1980), and Sarah (1982).

Beginning in February of 1973, my parents ventured to Florida in their motorhome to visit friends and relatives for a few weeks. Joan, seventeen, Noreen, nearly sixteen, and Rita, fourteen, were still in school. "We tried to assure Mom and Dad that we felt very capable of looking out for ourselves," Joan said, "but Mom and Dad saw it differently and weren't taking any chances. They hired Mrs. Eitzen from Cedar to be in charge and, let me tell you, that didn't go over very well! We were your typical rebellious teenagers and resisted taking orders from her.

"Before our parents returned home, we made sure the whole house was clean and had all the clothes washed; even those that hung on the door of Mom and Dad's bedroom.

"The house looked great when they got home, but then Dad asked, 'Where are my clothes that were hanging on the door in the bedroom?' He had left his lottery tickets in his shirt pocket. It was one of the first tickets Dad bought for the lottery in Michigan."

In 1973, Larry received his bachelor's degree in civil engineering from Michigan State. That same year in June, Joan graduated from Glen Lake High School.

Joan had dated Dale Gauthier on and off throughout high school, having met him the first time when she and Noreen sang with Larry and His Larks at Glen Lake School when she was still in the eighth grade at Holy Rosary.

The summer after Joan's high school graduation, she worked at Leelanau Pines Campgrounds on Lake Shore Drive in Cedar, getting ready for a move in the fall to Grand Rapids, where she would attend Davenport College of Business.

Dad helped Joan pack her belongings in the red station wagon, and together, off they went to Grand Rapids. Dad had her drive since she was moving to the big city, and never had driven on an expressway. Joan lived with her brother and sister-in-law, Ted and Mary Lou, and their children. They had already built a small bedroom for her. She had lots of family nearby as the newlyweds, Shirley and David, were renting the upstairs apartment.

Soon, Dad sold Joan a yellow Ford Maverick, so she had wheels to drive in Grand Rapids. "Between studying," Joan said, "I went back and forth almost every weekend to Cedar to play band jobs. There were times that Larry, who lived in Grand Rapids also, would pick me up and we would take the 260-mile round trip together."

In 1973, Noreen, at sixteen, was one of the first employees of Cedar Treats, a new ice-cream shop (now called Blue Moon Ice Cream Shop) in downtown Cedar. She earned one dollar an hour plus lots of free ice cream. Customers lined up down the street after summer baseball games.

Noreen met Tom Savage for the first time when she was thirteen, at Glen Lake High School, even though their paths crossed multiple times before. Noreen wrote: "For starters, Dad had built an addition on Willard and Irene Savage's [his parents'] home on Little Glen Lake, where I had gone as a helper for him. Another time, I was in the band playing at his sister Sharon's wedding reception held at the Savage home. Other times, my sister Shirley's best friends, Jean and Joan, [twin sisters of Tom's] were in high school and would stop at our home. I remember seeing him sitting in the car waiting for them.

"Nope, the time wasn't right to meet each other, until the first day of high school in 1970. Entering the side door of Glen Lake High on that day, my eyes locked with the eyes of a boy who was walking towards the door a short distance down the hall. At that moment, I said to myself, 'I'm going to marry him someday.' Tom later told me he thought the same thing." Noreen's romance with Tom Savage didn't last at first. "We were in the same grade and became a couple our freshman year … but broke up later that year."

Noreen's relationship with Tom Savage resumed "when he asked me to go to homecoming in my junior year, 1972." She wrote: "He was the quarterback for the varsity football team, and I told him that I would go to the dance with him if he scored three touchdowns during the game. He did, we went, and the rest is history!"

* * *

Side Note:

In March of 1974, Harold and I would soon have eight children in the house, as I was expecting a baby. We had three small bedrooms, and one of our children was sleeping on a cot in the utility room.

A couple months before, Mom and Dad showed up unexpectedly. Dad asked, "What are you going to do?"

Family photo of Harold and Ruth Ann's family: Victoria, Mary Lou, Janice, John, Steve, Edward, Ruth Ann holding Christine, and Harold holding Donald (1975)

Dad had a plan for us. He explained that if we could have an open stairway in our living room to the basement, we would have a hallway, a bathroom, a family room, and two bedrooms with a drop ceiling. We liked his idea.

We went along with Dad to pick up materials and carpet remnants. He worked steadily on the construction. One day, my son Steve, nearly fifteen years old, asked his grandpa if he could help with the job of trimming the new door frames with knotty pine.

Grandpa said he could, handed Steve a hammer and a six-penny finish nail, and said, "Okay, pound that nail!" Steve tried to pound it into a knot and, of course, he couldn't. He didn't realize it's impossible to pound a nail into a knot.

Grandpa watched and said, "DRIVE IT AGAIN!" Steve succeeded.

The job was done well before our daughter Christine's birth on March 3, 1974, at (the former) Leelanau Memorial Hospital in Northport. Upon discharge, my baby and I needed a ride home, and I couldn't get a hold of Harold by phone. (In those days, telephones weren't equipped to take a message.) Fortunately, a patient being discharged at the hospital was someone I knew well, and had a vehicle to drive himself to Cedar where he lived. He was Izzy Stachnik. As we pulled into the driveway, my children rushed outside to greet us! When Harold came home, he was surprised to see me holding our newborn baby.

My four boys shared rooms in the newly finished-off basement, while my girls shared rooms upstairs on the main level. We kept baby Christine's bassinet in our bedroom. What a difference it made to have a five-bedroom home for our large family, and all because Dad and Mom were looking out for us.

* * *

Joan returned home in the spring of 1974, where she was hired at WGTU TV-29 in Traverse City. "That was one of the best and most interesting jobs I ever had," Joan said. "I was also in a couple commercials. The pay was not good, however. I made ninety dollars per week, and when the receptionist quit, they gave me an extra five dollars per week for doing her job as well.

"In July, Dale asked for my hand in marriage. On his own, he began taking religion classes at St. Rita's Church in Maple City. He was baptized, received his First Holy Communion, and was confirmed. Harold and Ruth Ann were his godparents."

Joan and Dale were married on October 19, 1974, at Holy Rosary Church. After the wedding, they moved into a nice two-bedroom mobile home they had purchased prior to their wedding.

It was located near Chums Corner in Traverse City, where Dale was employed as a machinist at Cone-Drive Gear, and Joan returned to WGTU-TV 29.

Their children are: Robert (1979), Russell (1981), and Dale (1982).

* * *

Noreen graduated from Glen Lake High School in June 1974. That same summer, she moved to Traverse City, rented an apartment with three other girls, and worked at the Big Boy. She and Tom were engaged in July 1975.

In the fall, Dad and Mom took Noreen and Rita on a trip to Florida. Noreen wrote, "After Dad drove the Winnebago for twelve straight hours, he told me he was going to take a nap and it was my turn to drive. It wouldn't have been a problem, but at seventeen, I had never driven the Winnebago. Even so, I didn't question him and got behind the wheel.

"I recall my bare, white-knuckled hands on the wheel, somehow maneuvering my way through downtown Fort

Noreen and Rita, with Ed and Irene posing in front of the Winnebago

Lauderdale, while Dad never even stirred from his nap in the back. That's the way Dad was."

Side Note:

On February 20, 1975, school resumed for my six oldest children, after spending a few days at home due to a wintry ice storm and school closings. Their time at home was well spent working on school projects for a bicentennial contest at Holy Rosary School. Everyone remembered to take their project back to school, except for Edward. The picture he drew leaned on the wall at the top of the sofa in the living room.

He called home, "Mom, would you please bring my bicentennial entry? Today is the deadline." Then he added, "You don't even have to come inside. I'll be looking for you."

Harold was home. I asked him if he would drive. He said no. I was so frustrated when he refused to drive that words slipped out of my mouth never before spoken to him. I slipped boots over my shoes, put on a winter jacket, and tied a babushka (headscarf) over my head. I was planning to drive the car when Harold said, "Take the Bronco." The Bronco was a blue, short-bed truck. As I was about to leave, Donald, nearly five, was begging to go with me, and Christine, nearly one, was still in her crib.

On the way, I noticed my side of the road was heavily sanded; the other side wasn't. When I got there, Edward was outside in the freezing cold waiting for me in front of school, just as he said. I handed him his bicentennial entry and he thanked me. He waved good-bye as I left.

On the return trip, I hit an icy spot on a sharp curve only three tenths of a mile from school. The truck spun around and went up over a snowbank, rolled over, and landed upside down in a ravine. While in motion, I said an act of contrition, thinking I would die, and was sorry for the words I uttered to Harold.

I was pinned underneath the truck, lying on snow-covered ground, and thankful to God I survived.

I could hear cars driving by. Then I heard sirens. The Cedar fire department was on the scene. Strong men lifted the short-bed truck off me, and carefully lifted me up. With assistance, I was able to walk the distance to the ambulance parked on the road.

The other men picked up the scattered cement blocks that weighed down the bed of the truck.

They rushed me to Leelanau Memorial Hospital in Northport. X-rays showed I had double whiplash and would have to wear a neck support, besides having numbing sensations on my right arm and leg.

I felt blessed to return home the next day wearing a neck collar for support and to resume life with my family. As imperfect as my marriage was, I had much to be thankful for. My children needed rides. I continued to drive, even though the accident played over in my mind. Then I purposely took a part-time job at Vlack's Market for a change of pace, which helped pay for groceries. My daughter Janice babysat after school, or an aunt from close by during the daytime. The physical repercussions of the accident faded over time. I was thirty-six.

* * *

Larry had known Jackie Norconk from Empire while attending Glen Lake School. They both graduated the same year, in 1969, but never dated until two years later. On April 5, 1975, Larry and Jackie were married at the Immaculate Conception Church in Traverse City. Jackie, as a fine seamstress, created her own wedding gown. After their wedding, they made their home in Wyoming, Michigan, where Larry resumed his civil engineering position with Williams & Works, Inc. Their children are: Ben (1976), Chelsea (1978), and Jodie (1981).

* * *

My Dad's sister, Aunt Agnes (Williams), was a self-taught accordion player. She told me how she got her start playing music in public. "Your brother Larry invited me to play at Sugarfoot's Saloon in Cedar, back in 1973. I played a cheap accordion and sang four songs. Lee Jones, the owner, asked if I would play another gig. I had two weeks to prepare. I borrowed Bobby Atkinson's accordion and had a forty-watt used amplifier. My first big job was New Year's Eve at St. Rita's Hall in Maple City. My son, Joe, played guitar alongside me." She formed her own band, Agnes and the Polka Dotz. She played at Cedar's first Polka Festival in 1975, as did Larry, Joanie, and Noreen with Larry and His Larks, and Bobby Atkinson with Bobby and His Polka Pals, besides other bands.

Cedar Polka Festival parade, Jim and Doris on the tractor with Larry & His Larks

Left: Agnes Williams playing accordion at 1976 Polka Festival. Right: Leonard Mikowski, owner of Vlack's Market, with Ed, Irene, and the Rayaires Band (1976).

Shelby Pendowski's article from the *Leelanau Enterprise*, dated July 3, 2014, titled "Cedar Polka Fest: All About Heritage and Music," described how the first festival came about. "The idea of having a polka festival was conceived by five members of the Polish Legion of American Veterans with help of Cedar community members. Lawrence Novak, Ed Fleis [Dad], Adolph Novak and other members helped create the Cedar Polka Fest."

Back on August 27, 1975, the *Traverse City Record Eagle* article, "Thousands At Polish Fete," by David Averill, summed up the first polka festival, sponsored by the Cedar Chamber of Commerce, on August 26, 1975. The festival also celebrated the upcoming bicentennial (the year of 1976) and honored the Polish Legion of American Veterans, culminating in a convention they held for several days at Sugar Loaf Village.

In describing the first Polka Fest, the article stated: "An evening parade featured the drum and bugle corps of the Polish Legion, local polka bands and a marching band, followed by dancing in the streets and hay rides. Thousands of supporters descended upon the village of Cedar on a Tuesday and enjoyed a beautiful summer evening—just right for eating kielbasa, drinking and dancing."

It was a busy time for Dad, his fellow chamber members, and other volunteers.

* * *

On October 4, 1975, Noreen and Tom Savage were married at Holy Rosary Church. They made their home in Columbus, Ohio. Noreen attended Columbus Business University, and Tom was at Ohio Institute of Technology. Eventually, they made their home in Grand Rapids, Michigan.

Their children are: Angela (1978), Heather (1981), Jenna (1985), Mark (1986), and Ashley (1994).

With Noreen living in Ohio, there was talk that Larry and His Larks might need to disband. Instead, Joan and Larry decided to ask their spouses, Dale and Jackie, to join the band. "Jackie learned to play the piano," Joan said, "and Dale learned the guitar."

"Now it was different," Joan explained, "because one couple always had to travel the roads. Larry and Jackie were living in Grand Rapids and we lived in Traverse City. In the beginning, most of our band jobs were in Traverse City, and eventually Larry got some band jobs in the Grand Rapids area."

In December of 1975, Mom and Dad took Rita on another Winnebago trip to Florida. She was just sixteen, with a new driver's license.

She begged Dad while traveling, "Can I drive the motorhome?" After she asked him several times, Dad pulled into a rest stop. She learned to drive in traffic through the six-lane freeway on I-75 through Atlanta, Georgia.

"Quite a few family members went along," my brother Edward wrote, "When Mom and Dad were making plans to drive their Winnebago to Florida, Ted and Mary Lou, and Barbara and I decided to accompany them. We rented a twenty-eight-foot Champion motorhome to travel in comfort. In addition to our children—Jeff, Jerry, Shelly, and Brian—and Ted and Mary Lou's children—Jeanette and Chris, [Mary Lou's sisters] Terri and Kathy came along to babysit and have fun together.

"Rita and my boys, Jeff and Jerry, traveled with Mom and Dad when we left from Grand Rapids on Friday, December 19, 1975," Edward stated, "equipped with state-of-the-art walkie-talkies for communicating between motorhomes. By Saturday night, we were just fifty miles north of Atlanta. Early Sunday morning traffic was bumper to bumper in the middle of Atlanta, amidst others heading for a warmer climate for winter break.

"About twenty miles south of Atlanta, Dad was in the lead. He signaled and moved quickly into the middle lane to pass the car in front of them, just as I was experiencing a noticeable and unusual vibration from the rear of the vehicle. I slowed down and pulled over to the shoulder to check the tires. We immediately tried to contact Mom and Dad with the walkie-talkies, but they were quickly out of range.

"In checking out the tires, we found that the wheels for the two tires on the left rear tandem were about to fall off. Calling road service on a busy interstate on Sunday morning at 7:00 a.m. was pointless. We jacked up the vehicle and tightened the two remaining lug nuts and traveled on the shoulder of the road for about three to four miles to the next exit and found a service station that was open. They had no facility for parts and labor to replace the lugs, but recommended a business in Atlanta, which we contacted. After giving them all the information on the wheels and tires, we were told to expect a mechanic by 11:00 a.m.

"He finally showed up at about 4:00 p.m. on Monday. We were on our way at 5:30 p.m. and headed to the Disney World area, arriving in the wee hours of the morning. We stopped at a rest area for the night.

"We had discussed with the folks plans to go to Disney World, and so we decided to go there for the day, hoping to run into them. While the kids were enjoying the rides and amusements, Ted and I were scouring the area, looking for any sign of my folks or Rita and my boys. Disappointed with our futile efforts, we headed for the parking lot. [We] were among the last leaving the park. To our amazement and surprise, as we approached our motorhome, we really got excited to see the folks' motorhome parked next to ours. They had spent a good part of the day searching for our motorhome. One of my boys had to be lifted up to confirm our belongings. The joyful reunion included a couple of shots and beers as we discussed the adventures of the trip and the day.

"Earlier that day, my folks had allowed my boys, Jerry, nine; Jeff, ten; and Rita at sixteen, was to look after the two minors at Disney World, but the boys managed to get away from her."

"During all the excitement," Jeff said, "Jerry and I got separated from Aunt Rita. Imagine that! We ended up being discovered by Disney staff as unaccompanied minors and were escorted to the human lost and found. Aunt Rita eventually came and rescued us. Although it was a safe ending, it's a painful memory. I remember arriving at the Winnebago and getting a good hair pull on the back of my neck from a worried but relieved Grandpa."

Mom and Dad stayed on in Florida, while the rest traveled home to Michigan. The children had to go back to school. Shirley and David moved temporarily into our parents' Cedar home and looked after Rita until Mom and Dad returned in early spring.

* * *

Jim met his sweetheart, Doris (Dorie) Milasavlejich, at Sugarfoot Saloon, where he was working. She was visiting her sister, Mila MacNaughton, who had just had a baby.

"While in Cedar," Dorie said, "I went to a softball game, where Tom [her sister Mila's husband] and Jim played on the same team. After the game, we all congregated at the saloon. I went to lunch again at Sugarfoot's that week. I thought Jim might be working and hoped that he would show up, as he had offered to give me a ride on his motorcycle, but he didn't.

"I drove back to my sister's house to say goodbye, and Jim showed up when I was shutting the trunk of my car to go home. I got on his motorcycle with him, and the rest is history."

Jim and Dorie were married on July 24,1976, at the Greek Orthodox Church in Kalamazoo, Michigan. Jim was the manager at Sugarfoot. They made their home in Cedar, but soon moved to Rogers City, Michigan, where they bought the TNT Bar. Their children are: Jason (1977), Melissa (1980), and Travis (1993).

Rita was a senior during the 1976–77 school year. That winter, Joan and Dale stayed with her while Mom and Dad spent a few months in Florida.

Rita was a cheerleader when Glen Lake School won the Class D state basketball championship that year in Ann Arbor, against Detroit East Catholic. Geoff Kotila, from Glen Lake, was the hero in the championship game, scoring the final five points as Glen Lake overcame a 68–65 deficit in the final thirty seconds. Coach Don Miller was only four years into a forty-one-year Hall of Fame coaching career.[69]

Mom and Dad, home now from Florida, took the Winnebago to the final basketball game, with Larry and Joan traveling with them, surprising Rita. What a reunion that was! There was so much screaming and yelling because of the excitement of the game that the next day, when Larry and His Larks played in Muskegon, everyone had hoarse voices.

In the spring of Rita's senior year, the *Leelanau Enterprise* described her as "pretty and articulate" when she won the Polish Princess Pageant held at Solon Township Hall in Cedar. Pageant judges were Susan Jo Deering, Miss Leelanau County of 1976; Steve Barber, a radio announcer with WLDR-FM from Traverse City; and Probate Court Judge Betty Ann Weaver, who would later become chief judge on the Michigan Supreme Court.[70]

As winner, Rita won a fifty-dollar savings bond and represented the Cedar Chamber of

---

69   "Laker Legacy: 1977 Glen Lake boys basketball team celebrates 40th anniversary of state championship by Dennis Chase," Traverse City Record Eagle, 7/5/2017.

70   Newspaper article found in Mom's scrapbook (undated).

Commerce in Traverse City's Cherry Festival parade. She also presided over the Third Annual
Polish Festival.

**Left: Rita as Polish Princess, and her court, Lisa Hill and Cindy Drzewiecki (background is Ed and Irene's home).
Right: Rita dancing with her dad, Ed, on the street (1977).**

In June of 1977, Rita graduated from Glen Lake. She and my son Steve celebrated their
graduations together at St. Rita's Hall in Maple City. While growing up, Rita was determined
to learn a musical instrument. She started playing the alto saxophone in fifth grade, played the
instrument throughout her high school years, and was a member of Glen Lake's marching band.

To commemorate Rita's graduation, brother Jim built a large wooden picture frame which
held all twelve of our eight-by-ten professional graduation portraits through the years from 1957
to 1977, with Dad and Mom's photo placed in the center. They proudly displayed it on a wall of
the living room.

Ruth Ann (1957)

Julie (1958)

Edward (1959)

Mary Jane (1961)

Ted (1963)

Jim (1965)

Bernadette (1966)

Larry (1969)

Shirley (1971)

Joan (1973)

Noreen (1974)

Rita (1977)

Left: Ed and Irene showing off new T-shirts. Right: Family photo taken by Solon Township Hall.

Left: Jenny, Maureen, and Becky Steup on violins. Middle: Ted Fleis and his son, Chris, singing the "Chicken Song." Right: John and Steve Thompson on accordions.

On September 4, 1977, our parents celebrated their fortieth wedding anniversary by repeating their wedding vows during a mass at Holy Rosary Church, officiated by Rev. Father Mulka, followed by a reception at Solon Township Hall. The occasion brought many of their siblings and other relatives traveling from a distance. A feast of food, along with drinks, music, and dancing was enjoyed by many. Dad played violin, family bands performed, my

Ed doing the limbo with some of his grandchildren.

brother Ted with his son Chris sang the hilarious "Chicken Song," and grandchildren of all ages entertained. It pleased our parents to see their grandchildren spread their musical wings.

Mary Jane and Roger's children learned to play the violin and/or the piano. Mary Jane explained, "My love of music came from early exposure to instruments and singing in my home growing up. I shared my love of music with each of my five children, Rebecca, Jenny, Maureen, Roger, Jr., and Natalie. They learned to play the violin by ear, through the Suzuki method. They would listen to countless records and cassettes of the recordings of the songs to become familiar with them. They attended weekly lessons for refinement, and we as parents were expected to be participants in the lessons and the teachers at home. The children performed on Saturdays at the local college, for family groups, festivals, and at church. When Roger Jr. was two to three years old, he was given a small violin, thus joining the family adventure. He eventually began lessons in classical guitar. My youngest daughter, Natalie, took piano lessons when she was old enough. The high school the older girls attended did not have an orchestra at the time, nor a violin program, and so the family retired from the program. It was a wonderful experience for our family and united us in a shared adventure," Mary Jane concluded.

Several of my children got their start in music by taking piano lessons from a music teacher in Empire, who drove to my home for one full summer.

Steve and John were ages fifteen and thirteen when they began teaching themselves to play my accordion. They would sneak it out from its case, help each other strap it on, and take turns playing it; all the while, I was away from home. Even my other children didn't tell me what was going on.

One day, the boys surprised Harold and me as we pulled into the driveway. Steve had the accordion strapped on and played a polka, then John took a turn playing another familiar tune. They sounded great! They played the same tunes I did, but each son developed a style of their own.

Illustration of Steve and the Polka Kids in one of Steve's Leelanau Memories coloring books.

Within a few years, they formed a band, Steve Thompson & the Polka Kids. Besides playing the accordion, John taught himself to play the button box, bass guitar, and trumpet. Everyone sang along to the music, sometimes solo, or duet. Janice stated, "I was sixteen years old when we had our first gig at Maple Tavern on New Year's Eve in 1977, when they didn't have a band." The band played for a few years until going their separate ways. Music continued for my sons playing with other bands, and for my daughter playing piano.

The Rayaires Band transitioned to the Ray Watkoski Family Band, after their children learned to play instruments. Julie's husband, Ray, played accordion, and Julie played bass guitar and piano, along with all their children-from the oldest to the youngest. Dale played trumpet, accordion, and bass guitar; Diane, piano; Debbie, drums; Doug, trumpet; and Dawn sang. This band recorded "One to Remember"[71] dedicated to Ray's father, John Sr. Little Dawn, age five, was featured singing "Dzien Dobry Polka."

Left: Dale, Ray, Debra, Julie, and Doug. Dawn and Diane are in front of the drum. Right: Larry, Dale, Joan, and Jackie.

The music of Larry and His Larks continued at weddings, dances, and festivals, traveling as far as Florida to an event hosted by Marion Lush. Fortunately, Dad and Mom were there to see the family's musical accomplishment.

---

71   Recorded at River City Studios, Ltd., Grand Rapids. Engineer, John Fritz.

They also played in-state at festivals in Boyne Falls, East Jordan, Frankenmuth, Muskegon, Grand Rapids, and of course, the Cedar Polka Fest.[72] In 1979, Larry and His Larks recorded an album, *Traveling the Roads,* dedicated to Mom and Dad. They were assisted by local musician and friend Bobby Atkinson, accordion player for Bobby and His Polka Pals. The picture for the album cover was taken on Wayne Hill, overlooking Traverse City. The recording was made into albums, eight-track tapes, and cassettes.

Beginning in the fall of 1977 through 1980, Rita attended nursing school at Northwestern Michigan College. During her first year, she played saxophone with the jazz band. Being thrifty, she was the apartment manager for a couple of years. Her nursing training was completed at the Traverse City Medical Care Facility. She became a registered nurse in 1980.

Meanwhile, Rita married her high school sweetheart, James Cwengros from Cedar, at Holy Rosary Church on September 14, 1979. Their first home was in Big Rapids, Michigan, where Jim was attending Ferris State University in pursuit of a pharmaceutical career, and Rita acquired a nursing position at Mecosta County General Hospital. Their children are: Eric (1982), Andrew (1987), and Laura (1990).

Rita, RN

72   The *Traverse City Record Eagle,* Sept. 1, 1979.

Ruth Ann and Harold (1958)

Julie and Ray (1959)

Edward and Barbara (1965)

Mary Jane and Roger (1966).
Back, from left: Edward, Ed, Irene,
Mary Jane, Roger, Ted, and Jim.
Bottom left: Noreen, Joan, Shirley,
Bernadette, Julie, Ruth Ann, Larry,
and Rita in front.

**Ted and Mary
Lou (1967)**

**Jim and Doris
(1976)**

Bernadette and Ken (1966)

Larry and Jackie (1975)

Shirley and David (1973)

Joan and Dale (1974)

Noreen and Tom (1975)

Rita and Jim (1979)

Snow Birds

After the last of my siblings graduated, Dad and Mom made plans for a longer stay in Florida. In 1977, they started wintering there for six months, usually leaving during the middle of October. Dad's remark was, "It's cheaper for us to winter in Florida than to stay home." My brother-in-law, Ken (Bernadette's husband and owner of KD Plumbing & Heating, 1976 to 2008 in Lake Leelanau), winterized their home. He drained pipes and turned off the furnace, and then made sure everything was up and running again in the spring.

They saw as much family as possible before leaving, receiving warm hugs from us close by, and families living in Grand Rapids and Fort Wayne, places which were also stayovers. Mary Jane (in Indiana) would sometimes take Mom shopping, something she had done since being a teenager. She said, "If Mom mentioned she needed a dress or a pair of shoes, Roger and I would buy it for her."

The Winnebago (home on wheels) was upgraded to a good, used fully furnished, mobile home in Swift's Trailer Park in Fort Myers, where friends from Leelanau County were wintering nearby. They were Izzy (Dad's former employee) and Josie Stachnik from Cedar, Emil and Martha Bunek, and Richard Forton from Lake Leelanau.

The whole bunch got together often. They played cards, bingo, shuffleboard, and enjoyed a little music from time to time when Dad brought out his violin and played a few tunes with Richard Forton playing guitar. Sometimes, the group met up for church, followed by a senior lunch buffet. Occasionally, they went shopping at a flea market.

I was fortunate to visit my parents. Harold surprised me when he said, "We should go see your mom and dad." It was a short trip. We took a flight instead of driving. Our daughter Janice, a senior in high school, looked after the children for the two or three days we were away.

It was my very first time in sunny Florida and the only time Mom and I were both barefoot when sitting on a white sandy beach near the gulf collecting seashells for her projects, while Dad and Harold admired the ships sailing in the vast water.

Mom learned crafts from women in the park and had a portable sewing machine from home to sew on. A couple projects she completed over time were: burlap wall hangings trimmed with twine and a flower motif of tiny multicolored shells besides small bouquets of roses from shells resembling rosebuds that were painted in a pastel rose color and attached to a long, floral green stem with leaves. Mom made things to give to the family.

My parents' newest delicacy was shrimp. Dad bought it fresh from a man selling it down the street after a catch in the gulf. It had to be cleaned and deveined before Mom cooked it in seasoned water. That was my first time eating shrimp, and it was "delish" dipped in sautéed butter.

A three-wheeled bike was convenient for them to ride around the park, or for Dad when he shopped at a local grocery store. He also went fishing, as my brother-in-law, Ray Watkoski, stated.

Top left: Ed taking Irene on a joy ride. Top right: Irene and Ruth Ann shelling by the gulf in Florida. Bottom left: Richard Forton on guitar and Dad on violin having a heck of a good time! Bottom right: Richard Forton showing the catch he and Ed caught for the day!

Ray said, "Richard Forton had a boat safe enough to fish in the Gulf of Mexico. Dad would go fishing with Richard on the gulf every two to three days and venture out maybe three miles. They kept what fish they needed and sold the rest at the fish market. Dad told Ray, 'We covered our expenses for bait and had spending money left over.' It was nothing for them to get six to eight good-sized fish. They were easy to sell at the fresh-fish market. They did that for a few years."

* * *

Dad and Mom decided to sell the historic (former Culver/Sattler) home in Cedar in the spring of 1978. During that summer, they gathered what possessions they no longer wanted and sold them at an auction they held. The buyer of the home was Scott Flaska, owner of a local insurance agency. His son Corey, is the current owner. Instead of settling at their new destination by Lake Leelanau, my parents headed for Florida, and waited until spring.

Back in Fort Myers, they spent the Christmas season of 1978 with my brother Edward, his wife, Barbara, and their children: Jeff, Jerry, Michele, and Brian. Edward's family traveled in a motorhome from Sanford, North Carolina.

Edward recalled, "Dad and Mom were so fascinated by a magnificent Christmas display they had seen and took us to see it. It had at least ten thousand lights displaying life-size figures of the nativity scene."

A couple of their children wrote memories of this visit.

Brian recalled a special gift. "Grandma was very sweet and was always crafty. She gave me one of the stuffed blue-jean-fabric people named Otto."

Jerry recalls asking Grandpa if he and his sister, Michelle, could borrow the three-wheel bike and go for a ride. Jerry wrote, "Michelle rode on the front fender, which made it a little difficult to steer, but we still had much fun laughing and cruising around the trailer park. The turns got a little sharper and I started getting us up on two wheels. Then I realized we warped the wheels so badly that we had to wobble the tricycle back [to my grandparents'] home and explain what we did! No one was very happy. My mom and dad felt responsible for the damage, so they bought the bike and took it home. Dad had the bike fixed and then gave it to Grandma and Grandpa as a gift. By then they had moved to another park in Killarney. I remember seeing Grandma riding it there, with a big smile on her face!"

Edward also said he had a conversation with Dad and observed him with a sense of nervousness. "He seemed more humble. I couldn't think of a time when Dad wasn't healthy, except when hot tar burned his face years ago. Now, it seemed as if something was wrong with his health. He said he hadn't been feeling well. He indicated that he wanted to get his state of affairs in order." He concluded, saying, "It was the first time Dad talked to me about such a serious matter."

By January of 1979, Dad became critically ill. He found out he had cancer of the colon and needed emergency surgery. Mom immediately notified the family. Shirley and I decided on the spot to leave for Florida while working side-by-side at Mikowski's Market in Cedar. Julie joined us in Grand Rapids, where we departed on a flight to Fort Myers.

Thankfully, Mom wasn't alone during Dad's crisis. Our elderly great-aunt, Sister Augustine, was visiting my parents at the time. Her kindness, and prayerful and helpful disposition, was just what Mom needed.

When we arrived in the lobby at the hospital, we were met by Mom and Sister Augustine. I asked Mom, "How did you get to the hospital?" She said, "I drove."

"Unbelievable," I thought. If Dad only realized how independent Mom could be. Her will-power to be strong when Dad depended on her showed, but his critical health was stressful and "took a toll on her" as Edward reminded me.

Seeing Dad under these circumstances was difficult. He was in rough shape. At one point, he expressed to me and others that he experienced seeing a bright light during surgery and wanting to stay there. He was thankful for his doctor and prayers, he said.

Dad's health improved the few days Julie and I were there. Shirley was able to stay longer. She continued to support Dad's healing, was helpful to Mom, and "finally got to know Sister Augustine," said Shirley. "I couldn't get over how cheerful she was!"

Shortly after Dad's discharge from the hospital, he again became deathly ill. After going through another surgery, he found out the infection was caused by a stitch left in his incision. Now he had a drainage tube inserted there. He was in worse shape than ever, but by the grace of God, he survived. His doctor told him he should be able to live five normal years.

Several family members came to support Dad's healing, as well as some of his siblings. Joan was seven months pregnant with her first baby and "wanted to go to Florida," she said, "but Mom didn't want me risking the long trip and told me to stay home," so I did. "I called Mom daily to make sure everything was okay."

Three months after Dad's initial surgery, he celebrated his sixty-fourth birthday on April 26. He wasn't fully recovered and still had a draining tube attached to his incision. However, that didn't stop him from driving the 1,500 miles to take Ma and himself back home, but there was no rush. They would take their time and rest as much as possible.

Before leaving Florida, Mom wrote a letter to Joan:

We expect to be home in early May. Hope our house is all set. As you know, we haven't lived in it yet. Hope you'll be able to go swimming this summer. We hope and pray that all will be well with you. Dale will have to learn to sing some new lullabies. When we are traveling, we do most of our praying.

Love to you, Dale, and baby-to-be.
Mom and Dad

While traveling and visiting family members, they heard of the exciting news of Joan and Dale's son Robert's birth on April 30. After arriving in Traverse City, Dad and Mom stopped at Joan and Dale's to welcome their newest grandbaby, who was two weeks old. They stayed with them a few days before moving into the cottage.

30

The Lake Cottage

IN MAY 1979, MY PARENTS SETTLED INTO A LOVELY, brand-new, three-bedroom modular home on Lake Leelanau. This lakefront property near Solon Park in Cedar was purchased from Harold Lautner. The cottage was seasonal, as Dad and Mom continued winter stays in Florida.

The first time I visited them, Dad was outside putting away something and Mom was in the kitchen, cooking a meal on the stove. She seemed flustered when I came in to say hello, and all of a sudden burst out, "I can't do this anymore!"

I wasn't sure what was going on. I hadn't planned to stay long, just coming straight from work; I wanted to give each a warm hug now that they were back from Florida. Yet, Mom asked me to stay for dinner. I couldn't refuse. I would have offended her and Dad if I had not stayed. Family was important. What was the rush for me that day? More than anything, it was important to spend time with my parents.

The timing was perfect, as she needed a helping hand. I found out Mom was extremely tired. Besides getting acquainted with all the new appliances, she had difficulty finding things in her new kitchen. The one thing she loved the most was seeing the gorgeous view of the lake in the slider window above her kitchen sink.As for Dad, it seemed his healing and ability to resume normal activities happened for him in no time.

Julie and her husband, Ray, bought the cottage next door shortly afterwards, and would travel with their children back and forth from Grand Rapids, spending as much time there as possible. In fact, it brought a lot more people out, especially on the weekends. "When our parents moved to the cottage, they hosted many picnics for family and friends," Rita said.

That's how it was—food and drinks, along with boating, fishing, bonfires, music, and playing cards. The grandkids loved wading and swimming, paddle boating, tubing and water skiing, etc. We were all fortunate to have both places to visit for summer fun!

I remember one summer when Dad went tubing. He was determined to try it out! As Ray pulled him from behind his boat, Dad sat on the huge tire tube, bobbing up and down as it flew

Top left: Admiring a "catch" from Bernadette and Ken's pond in Lake Leelanau. Top right: Ed with grandsons Brian and Chris. Bottom right: Ed with grandsons Dale and Edward.

across the lake. Dad held on for dear glory, sometimes hidden by the deep waves, as Ray drove his boat full circle, hitting his own wake over and over.

When he came to shore, Dad said, "Unbelievable!" He never let on that he was afraid. I had been afraid for him. He seemed to inject humor no matter what! I think he was relieved he got through the wakes and safely got back to shore, as I was. What a ride!

Another time, it was no laughing matter for Dad the time he returned home from fishing with his friend Richard Forton, only to find his car gone! What he couldn't figure out was how in the world his car could be gone when it had been blocked by Mr. Forton's car. Even stranger, when he went inside the cottage, Mom was gone too!

One thing about Dad—he believed no one would ever steal his car, so he had the bad habit of leaving his keys dangling in the ignition. Lucky for Mom, who seldom drove but always kept her license renewed!

Tired of waiting for the guys to return, she had decided to take Dad's car for a ride. Because it was blocked by Mr. Forton's car, she couldn't back it out of the driveway, so she drove to the front of the cottage, across to an open area between mature pines along the lot line between the cottages, then along the side of Julie and Ray's cottage, to the driveway, and then headed for Lake Shore Drive.

I was so surprised when Mom showed up unexpectedly at my door a few miles away, giggling as she told me about the mischief she got away with.

Dad got his share of laughter when Mom came home and told him, too. Shaking his head in disbelief, he said, "I couldn't figure out how in the world you got out of that driveway."

"Where there's a will, there's a way," Mom used to say. Well, she sure walked that talk. Both of our parents were like that. They found the ways and means to do what they wanted to do. And it did us good to see our parents laugh and make light of times in their lives.

Dad needed a place for his boat and car, so he built an attached double-door garage behind the home, with plenty of help from family. He also had help when he laid a new wooden dock from shore to deeper water to anchor his boat. He loved fishing. He would go by himself or take Mom, or others, including his grandkids, for boat rides around the lake.

Many grandchildren wrote their stories, remembering special times at Grandpa and Grandma's lake cottage. One special memory for some was fishing with Grandpa. "He taught me patience and how to put a worm on my line," said Julie's daughter Dawn. "He would go up and down the lake until we would catch one."

Shirley's daughter, Stephanie, said, "Grandpa was a great fisherman. I loved the boating trips with him!"

Joan's son Robert went fishing with Grandpa and his brothers. "He would lift us all in the boat with one arm. He was my version of Popeye ... big arms and fearless, in my eyes," Robert said.

Here is his brother Dale Michael's story, "A Drowning Boat":

> Grandpa and I were going fishing at Solon Park.
>
> Grandpa backs up the boat. Fishing gear is in the boat.
>
> The boat fills up with water.
>
> I said to him, "Grandpa, the boat is drowning!"
>
> "Just a minute, hold on!" Grandpa said.
>
> Grandpa pulled out the boat to shore again, and the water all drained out.
>
> He forgot the boat was unplugged.

My daughter Mary Lou remembers, "Grandpa could be spontaneous and a real jokester," she wrote. "… on the dock with Grandpa behind you … big mistake! Guaranteed to get pushed in. Every time." The bigger lesson? "He taught me to laugh a little more and not take life too seriously."

My daughter Christine remarked, "When Grandpa would take the grandkids for a ride on his boat, he would have a heyday blowing the air horn."

My son Donald described the way a typical fishing day would unfold in the summertime. "My dad [Harold], would drop me off at Grandpa and Grandma's house … We would have some lunch. Grandma would make some Campbell's chicken noodle soup with crackers. Grandpa would have his shot and beer, then head out for the lake. We would troll in about ten to fifteen feet of water. I remember Grandpa pointing out fish on his little sonar, then having a fish on! I never could figure out how he would see them on it."

Donald continued. "One time, Dad and I were fishing and went out and got Grandpa. We had a few dozen crawlers for bait. We caught rock bass, bass, perch, and bull head all out of the same spot. We cleaned fish for hours!! We never could find that hole again.

"The only time Grandpa would turn down a day of fishing was if the boat didn't run," which was seldom. "My grandparents taught me to appreciate family and the outdoors."

Many favorite memories of grandchildren surround Mom's cooking. Dawn, Julie's daughter, remembers "strawberry picking with Grandma down the road at Skeba's [for ten cents a quart] then cleaning the berries and waiting for Grandma's strawberry shortcake after dinner."

Melissa, Jim's daughter, would ask Grandma if she would make her delicious rice pudding, and she did. "She added a sprinkle of cinnamon on top of the pudding, just for me. Grandma made me feel special when she did this. But, looking back, she did this for all her grandchildren."

Sarah, Shirley's daughter, said she "loved pistachio pudding on angel food cake … Grandma was always feeding us! She was sweet and always happy!"

She introduced my Christine to liver and onions.

Mom taught Mary Jane's daughter Maureen how to scramble eggs. "She told me to get two eggs, crack them open in the pan, and stir them around."

Angela, Noreen's daughter, recalls Grandma peeling an apple in one long strand, regardless how small or dull the knife she used. "Then she'd have us eat the skin," she comments, "telling us it was the healthiest part of the apple."

Heather, Noreen's daughter, remembers, "Grandma would offer us juice. We would always say, 'Yes, please!' very excitedly, but it never failed that the juice she poured into cute little glasses was grapefruit juice. [We] always [had] high hopes that it would be orange juice!"

Mary Lou, my daughter, always felt welcomed at her grandparents' home. "Food was usually being prepared, and sometimes Grandma put me to work slicing carrots or peeling potatoes. No matter the occasion, potlucks, cooking, or sharing a meal was an expression of love for me."

Douglas, Shirley's son, associated food his grandma gave him with her "quiet little laughs, and warm hugs."

Shirley's daughter Stephanie also tied food with hugs. "I remember Grandma always giving wonderful hugs. She was the best meatball maker too! I loved her pistachio cake."

My Victoria remembers Grandma offering her "cookies and hard candies, and feeling special."

Family parties were special, said Julie's daughter Diane. "While I was a teenager and young adult, I thought of such happy times—parties at the farm, the house in Cedar, and especially at the cottage on Lake Leelanau. During those get-togethers, there was always plenty of food, loud laughter, music, bonfires, euchre, and even a little drinking, all [of] which usually lasted well into the early morning hours.

"It's amazing, but I don't remember a single time when Grandma complained or told anyone to be quiet or to go to bed—something a mother would naturally do. Family was so important to her, and she never interfered with their time together by trying to control the situation. Perhaps her difficulty hearing played a role, but I believe it was because she was an incredible mother who knew that relationships and memories are built during those times.

"When I met the love of my life," Diane continued, "Grandma couldn't remember Tom's name. Who could blame her? She had many grandchildren, and I just added one to the mix. For the first few years she would say, "Hello, Dave!"

We would laugh and say, "Grandma, it's Tom!" She would put her fingers over her lips and chuckle.

"One day, when we arrived at the cottage, we walked into the house and, just like always, Grandma said, "Hello, Diane and ... Dave!"

Tom looked right at Grandma and said, "Hello, Grandpa!"

She chuckled, then never forgot his name again.

"Now that I'm older, I realize how instrumental Grandma was in the special bond her children have with each other. What a gift she gave us all!"

Mother loved playing bingo with her grandkids. She would call out a number and watch the older grandchildren help the younger ones find the number before she called the next number. There was no rush. It was Mom's way of teaching numbers to her young grandchildren. Whenever a winner called out, "BINGO!" you could hear it throughout the cottage.

Edward's daughter Shelly recalled, "When I was with my cousins at the cottage, Grandma would want us to play bingo when we were together, so she would wrap up prizes in wrapping paper, and mark them 'boy' and 'girl.' You might unwrap a prize that said 'girl' and find a little figurine or a fishing frog or something like that."

Shirley's daughter Sarah said, "The back bedroom at the cottage was loaded with prizes for bingo, including paper dolls and games."

My Mary Lou said, "Grandma was prepared for bingo games with household, white-elephant prizes, or inexpensive finds from Florida flea markets. Just playing bingo was a hoot, and there was always something to win. I loved Grandma's thriftiness!"

Then there were other times when a grandchild accompanied Grandma to bingo elsewhere, as my daughters tell. ...

Mary Lou continued, "Grandma even drove us to bingo, stacking Sears catalogs on the sunken driver's seat so she could see over the steering wheel. She slipped me some play money once we arrived and had a ball! While I don't play bingo often, when I do, I always think of Grandma."

My daughter Victoria said, "Grandma would take my sister Mary Lou and me to bingo at the Holy Rosary Church basement. I remember Grandma was a snappy dresser, wearing high heels and her famous red lipstick, and not winning. I think I was around ten years old and my sister was eleven at the time. Neither of us won."

We were entertained by talent shows. One memory of Noreen's daughter Angela was the talent show held in the garage of Uncle Ray and Aunt Julie's cottage one summer. She sang, "On top of spaghetti, all covered with cheese ... I lost my poor meatball when somebody sneezed..."[73]

"I loved how so many family members shared their talents that day," said Angela.

I recall my niece, Debra, with my girls, Mary Lou and Victoria, singing "Rainy Days Polka," a song they created while spending time together on a rainy day.

Occasionally, Dad brought out his beloved violin and played for us. His audience was a bunch of us gathered at the picnic table or sitting on lawn chairs in the front yard. Whenever he played the fishing song, it was reminiscent of years gone by when we had such a good time giggling as

---

73   Written by Tom Glazer

kids, just hearing him play and sing this silly tune. Over time, we learned the words and even came up with actions. This is our version:

THREE LITTLE FISHIES

Down in the meadow in a little bitty pool
Swam three little fishies and a mama fishy too
"Swim," said the mama fishy. "Swim if you can."
And they swam and they swam all over the dam.
Boop boop dit-tem dat-tem what-tem Chu!
Boop boop dit-tem dat-tem what-tem Chu!
Boop boop dit-tem dat-tem what-tem Chu!
And they swam and they swam all over the dam.
"Stop," said the mama fishy. "Stop if you can."
"Stop," said the mama fishy. "Stop if you can."
"Stop," said the mama fishy. "Stop if you can."
And they swam and they swam all over the dam.
Boop boop dit-tem dat-tem what-tem Chu!
Boop boop dit-tem dat-tem what-tem Chu!
Boop boop dit-tem dat-tem what-tem Chu!
And they swam and they swam all over the dam.[74]

74　Composed by Saxie Dowell, words by Josephine Carringer and Bernice Idins (1939).

Left: Ed playing a little music with his sister, Agnes. Right: Ed and Irene's grandchildren (left to right): Shaun, Robert, Chelsea, and Angela.

Left: Clem as minister, Irene, Janice as bride, Julie as groom, and Ed at the mock wedding. Right: Ed and Irene surrounded by friends and relatives at the cottage.

One time we were entertained by a mock wedding. Uncle Clem and Aunt RoseMarie (Fleis) and Uncle Roman and Aunt Virgie (Fleis) from Wisconsin were visiting when our parents were celebrating a wedding anniversary. Julie and my daughter Janice brainstormed the idea of a mock wedding and surprised our parents and all of us as they paraded on the front lawn of the cottage. Janice dressed as the bride, wearing her grandma's wedding gown and veil. Julie dressed the part of a groom and wore a dark suit, white shirt, and white bow tie. Uncle Clem was the preacher, with made-up vows. What a hoot it was!

* * *

Meanwhile, musical band changes occurred in January 1982 for Larry and His Larks due to distance and raising young families. Joan, the drummer, and bass guitar player Dale teamed up with long-time accordion player Bobby Atkinson and formed a band called Bobby, Dale & Joan. After expanding with piano player Cheryl Dezelski from Cedar, they renamed their band, Joanie and the Polka Tripps, and recorded *Polkas from the Cedar Swamps* in 1983.[75]

Left: Album of *Polkas from the Cedar Swamps* (1983), Dale, Joan, Cheryl, and Bobby. Right: *Family Style Polkas* (1985), Larry, Noreen, Tom, and Jackie.

As for Larry, the accordion player, and Jackie on guitar, they regrouped with original piano player (sister) Noreen in 1983 (after a seven-year absence) with her husband, Tom, playing drums. Both couples conveniently resided in Grand Rapids. Larry and His Larks recorded *Family Style Polkas* in 1985. One of the songs, "Polka Hero," was sung by their combined children, with help from Noreen. The album was dedicated to polka kids of all ages.[76]

---

75   Recorded at Multi-Media Productions, Traverse City.
76   Recorded at River City Studios, Grand Rapids, Michigan. Engineer, Tim Helt.

Snow Birds, continued:

By spring of '82, Dad and Mom's winter destination was Killarney, Florida, twenty minutes from Orlando, where Edward's family had relocated a couple years earlier from Sanford, North Carolina, after he accepted a senior associate position with a major engineering and planning firm. My parents purposely moved from Fort Myers to be closer to them and other relatives, Joe and Marcella Pleva (Lake Leelanau), and Andy and Irene Pleva (Cedar), all from Leelanau County.

This central location in Florida brought many relatives and friends from out of state to visit. A two-bedroom, double-wide mobile home offered comfortable space for company, which Mom indicated in a letter written to Joan and Dale: "We have quite a bit of company, and that makes the time go faster."

A memorable visit for my brother Larry occurred that same spring. He wrote, "My wife, Jackie, and I, and our kids went several times to Florida to get a break from the winter and see Mom and Dad. Between Jackie and me, we often would drive all the way through in our station wagon or van-usually a twenty-plus-hour trip. We would play cards, sit in the sun by the pool, and play a little shuffleboard with them, and then join Edward, Barbara, and family for a couple of days.

Larry and Jackie with their young children, Edward and Barbara with their children, and Ed and Irene.

The Space Shuttle Orbiter Columbia — riding piggy back atop a modified 747 jet called the Shuttle Carrier Aircraft — arrives at KSC after a two-day journey from the Dryden Flight Research Center in Ca. Two weeks prior Columbia returned to Earth from the first flight into space.

POST CARD

Address

Postcard below the inaugural flight: "It was kind of nostalgic," Larry said, "when Dad sent us Easter greetings on a postcard several years later, which featured the inaugural flight of April 12, 1981."

"One trip that I remember well was after my brother Edward recently moved to an existing new home in the Orlando area. He had a project for Dad and me when we visited. We spent the first couple of days working on landscaping. You can imagine how much fun this work was, since we were on vacation, and besides, it was very hot.

"The third morning of our visit, Dad was loading up a bunch of stuff in the car to head for Edward's. I said to Dad, 'Enough is enough! We are goofing off today.'

"So Dad and I; my daughter Chelsea, age three; and son Ben, age five, drove to Cape

Canaveral. We were pleasantly surprised by a ton of people that were at Cape Canaveral. It happened to be the inaugural flight where the space shuttle was strapped on a 747 and flown back to Cape Canaveral. It was an awesome experience with Dad. Jackie and Mom stayed home with my nine-month-old daughter, Jodie.

* * *

Back to memories at the cottage ... Joan's son Robert stated: "Life runs in generations, patterns, and memories. Generations live on stronger as time progresses. I've tried to think back to twenty-five years ago and even further.

"It was every summer that I could remember going to the lake at Grandma and Grandpa's cottage. There was always so much family. My cousins would circulate throughout the entire summer. Swimming, waterskiing, you name it, we did it!

"Uncle Ray and Uncle Larry played accordions around a campfire, singing, 'Put Another Log on the Fire.' If you wanted to play cards against Grandpa though, [you didn't] count on winning. Those were times never forgotten and treasured forever.

"Grandpa used to think WWF wrestling was real. Cracks me up! One thing that kept me uneasy was when I was riding in the car with him. He would drive fast ... ride on people's bumpers. I remember praying he would slow down," Robert concluded.

* * *

The Cedar River Project:

By the 1980s, nothing had been done to the Cedar River since the days of sawmills and train tracks. It was an eyesore to the community, with all its overgrowth; it looked like a muck hole. So in 1983, the Cedar Chamber of Commerce needed to hire an engineer/foreman to head up the Cedar River Project.

Dad, a fellow chamber member, volunteered. He wanted the job. "I can take on this project and be foreman," he said, "and get the help I need!"

The chamber negotiated and decided that Dad was the man for the job as engineer/foreman. They trusted his ability from his many years of working as a building contractor; besides, his knowledge in construction was a great asset to the Cedar community. The chamber also knew that he would save them lots of money and take the bull by its horns!

Dad was sixty-eight years old and semi-retired at the time.

Left: Start of Cedar River Project (1983). Top right: Wooden form boards ready for concrete. Bottom right: Concrete hardened.

Ray Pleva said, "I had to first petition the Solon Township Board with the idea of a Cedar River project." Besides dredging the riverbed, the project would widen the river, install a new footbridge, remove trees, and clear the land afterwards, opening up more space for the public and the adjoining ballpark.

After the project met the board's approval, Ray's second step was to approach the Cedar Chamber of Commerce. With Dad as foreman, it was full steam ahead, and the new Cedar River project had its start in June of 1983.

Ray and Dad collaborated on the whole project from start to finish. The Department of Natural Resources and units from the 46th Engineers Group of the Michigan National Guard from Manistee were both involved. The DNR paid ninety percent of the cost of this project.

When the project began, no one had any idea of what was on the bottom of the river, but in the process of dredging, they removed wire, barrels, several thousand wood shingles from the old wood mill which once stood near the edge of the river, wooden pilings and old posts from an old railroad track which crossed near the road bridge, and big logs from an old sawmill. Some of the remnants from the logging industry were seventeen inches wide. Silt was also removed from the swamp that comes from the forest and washes down the river. Silt can plug your boat motor and ruin it, and fish can't swim in it, so it had to go.

Donated By:
Ray & Julie (Fleis) Watkoski
of Grand Rapids, Mi.
1983

Engineered & Construction
Supervised By:
Edward V. Fleis
Cedar, Mi.

Top left: Bridge delivered. Top right: Ray Pleva presenting a sign to Julie and Ray in gratitude. Bottom left: Cedar Bridge refurbished in 2021. Bottom right: New manufactured sign donated by Ted and Mary Lou Fleis in 2021.

This was all swampland. The engineering project involved creation of a new current control for the river flow. Lastly, a new iron footbridge was donated by Ray and Julie Watkoski from Grand Rapids. Ray acquired a heavy-duty shop overhead crane bridge through a contracting job associated with his company, Midway Machinery of Muskegon. Their son, Dale, and others had constructed the new bridge assembly. They cut it lengthwise, separated it, rewelded it, and put in supports and decking. The bridge was painted red before it was delivered.

It was a community collaboration. Don April did the excavating. Others working on the project were Paul and Walt Galla and Uncle Tony Fleis (Dad's brother). Tony's pontoon boat in the river was a platform Dad and his crew stood on while they worked.

Logs removed from the river were hauled to Ed Kasben's sawmill, where they were cut into planks and later used as form boards for the cement work.

Dad poured the walls. If the bolts had been off by even a half-inch, it would not have worked.

When it came time to place the bridge, the Leelanau County Road Commission provided a loader with cables to pick up the bridge. Accidentally, the bridge ended up in the water. Don April, with his backhoe, hooked up cables on the other end, and the bridge was picked up again and slowly set in place.

"We just stood there and watched, with our mouths hanging open as the six-foot-by-sixty-two-foot bridge was lowered onto the four bolts and fit precisely," said Ray Pleva.

To finish off the landscaping, Charlie and Jerry Flaska hauled in 150 yards of black dirt, and Ray Popp from Elmer's Crane and Dozer leveled it off, while Henry Gatzke spread grass seed.

Butch Couturier made both signs between the river and County Road 645. A plaque located near the location credits Dad and his daughter and son-in-law, Julie and Ray Watkoski.

The bridge over Cedar River serves as a pathway for walkers, hikers, and snowmobiles in the wintertime. Many people enjoy fishing and kayaking the river under the bridge.

After all was said and done, Ray Pleva remarked, "Your dad had good work ethics." (This story was based on conversations I had with Ray, and a photo album and newspaper articles of his.)

31

And Now, Ruth Ann's Story

By 1983, HAROLD HAD BEEN SELF-EMPLOYED as a well driller for five and a half years. He operated his business from home: had a single rig, one or two employees, and an accountant.

Our marriage of twenty-five years had held up. Through the years, we took our children to visit my parents regularly and had the best of times. On a recent Sunday, when Harold and I visited them, they seemed unusually quiet. I found out why ... on the next day ... when I came home from work.

As I pulled into the driveway, I saw a foreclosure notice posted on the garage door. Dad showed up immediately. He said, "Your mother and I want to help you and the children."

I told Dad I never interfered with Harold's business.

He said, "It's time you did."

After Dad left, I searched through Harold's filing cabinet and discovered recent years of unfiled taxes that he never mailed. Fortunately, Dad and Mom paid the debt and were repaid after Harold sold his failing business. Our home was saved, but our marriage wasn't.

By then, half of our family—Steve, Janice, John, and Edward, had jobs and were living elsewhere. Mary Lou entered MSU in the fall, Victoria was a senior at Glen Lake School, and Donald and Christine were in grades eight and four at Holy Rosary School. Their ages ranged from twenty-four through nine.

For over a year, I had been employed as a part-time teller at Pacesetter Bank (changed to Old Kent, and then Fifth Third) after working a couple years at Maple Valley Nursing Home as a social and activity director.

Making a decision to separate from Harold was one I never wanted to make. Our Lord knew the efforts of trying to save our marriage. Joining Al-Anon was one of them. When I went to my first meeting, my intention was to help Harold stop drinking, but found out the program was for me to get healthier. My children would ask, "Mom, why are you going to meetings?" I would say, "If I can't help myself, I hope I can help someone else." After a while, by going to meetings and practicing daily prayer and meditation, I had a better grip of serenity.

Although, the closer it got to the date of a legal separation from Harold, the more fearful I became. I was at the point of backing out, when our family endured the tragic death of my son John, on February 3, 1984. It was declared a suicide at age twenty-two. He was a multi-talented musician … inspired as a child strumming a toy guitar. His talents were shared with the Nu Sonics polka band from Grand Rapids, traveling back and forth from Cedar. He was employed as a machinist with Subco in Traverse City.

Overwhelming sadness prevailed in my family. We comforted each other the best we knew how.

My refuge was a crucifix hanging on a wall facing my bed. When I looked at the cross filled with anguish and crying, the sufferings of our Blessed Mother Mary were visual to me all night long. She was kneeling at the foot of the cross after her Son Jesus died. I knew She understood my anguish as a mother.

By morning, my head was clear with a sense to move forward with the legal separation.

John's funeral was at Holy Rosary Church. His burial plot was next to our infant daughter Karen's gravesite at the parish cemetery.

The day after, I found courage to drive to my place of part-time employment and told the manager my status, and the need to provide financial security for my family. Soon afterward, I qualified for a full-time position at the bank.

Through the grace of God and our Heavenly Mother, strength overcame strife.

Aloha

Within days of returning to work, Julie invited me on a trip to Hawaii, saying, "It'll be good for you to get away. It won't cost you a dime, but you'll have to sing." Things worked out where I was able to go. The five-day vacation to Oahu (February 17–23) was a blessing I never imagined.

Julie wanted to become a travel agent for Breton Village in Grand Rapids. She planned this whole trip with assistance from an agent. She brought family, friends, and four family bands together for a vacation that focused mostly on music and optional side tours.

Dad and Mom were among 112 travelers, besides Uncle Leo and Aunt Betty Fleis, from

Traverse City. The group included cousins Joe and Marcella Pleva from Lake Leelanau; Larry, Jackie, Noreen, and Tom, with Larry and his Larks; Joan, Dale, Bobby Atkinson, and Cheryl Dezelski, with Joanie and the Polka Tripps; Aunt Agnes and son Joe Williams with Agnes and Her Polka Dotz; and Julie and Ray with the Ray Watkoski Family Band, besides many polka-loving friends from Leelanau and Grand Traverse Counties and the Grand Rapids area.

Upon arrival at the Oahu airport, we were greeted "aloha" by Hawaiian ladies presenting colorful leis of flowers to wear around our necks. At the hotel, neither a fly nor a mosquito could be seen, even though entry doors and windows were left open all day long in weather of perfect humidity, but closed at night.

A room in the hotel designated for the dance parties also provided a place for hula dancing lessons, which Mom, my sisters, Aunt Agnes, and I enjoyed. We learned to sway our hips and move our arms gracefully while Hawaiian music played in the background.

At the dance parties, Dad entertained, playing violin from time to time with some of the family bands. Each band was known for playing a popular polka, waltz, or music for slow dancing.

Couples twirled white handkerchiefs high in the air while dancing to "Twirl Your Hankies Polka" which Larry and His Larks played with accordion player Larry as lead singer. When keyboard player Noreen sang "A Polish Lullaby," it was as if a hush went through the room as everyone listened attentively. Her song of endearment was one Mom always loved to hear her daughter sing.

Joanie and the Polka Tripps excited the crowd with a peppy tune called "Uptown Saturday Night," with Dale playing guitar as lead singer, and drummer Joan harmonizing with her husband. A softer melody, "The Rose," was sung in harmony by Joan and keyboard player Cheryl. Accordion player Bobby's singing of an upbeat tune, "Gotta Have a License," was another crowd pleaser.

Agnes and Her Polka Dotz had everyone cheering upon hearing their hometown mentioned in the lyrics of "Dear Hearts and Polka People" sung by accordion player Aunt Agnes. Her son Joe's singing of "Polka Tickles" while playing bass guitar was hilarious!

The famous "Beer Barrel Polka" sung by accordion player Ray with The Watkoski Family Band had everyone chiming in and singing the catchy chorus: "Roll out the barrel, we'll have a barrel of fun. Roll out the barrel, we've got the blues on the run..."

Julie played keyboard while she and I sang "Sisters." It was a popular song, reminiscent of the '50s, when we were known as the Fleis Sisters. I sang with Aunt Agnes, too! We didn't sing at the event. Instead, we strolled the streets one day in search of a place to sing, and found a bunch of folks sitting in an outdoor area. We asked them for permission to entertain, and they happily said yes. It was much fun for both of us, singing tunes for folks we didn't know, while Aunt Agnes strummed her banjo.

Another time at the hotel patio, the accordion players Ray, Larry, and Bobby drew quite the crowd when they started playing polkas one afternoon. The music put Mom in the mood to dance! We sisters took turns dancing with her, then Larry came by with his accordion and started playing familiar songs Mom taught us as children, and we all sang with her. Our all-time favorite was "The Bible Tells Me So."

Top left: Julie and Ray with Irene and Ed upon arrival in Oahu, Hawaii. Top right: Larry Fleis, Ray Watkoski, and Bobby Atkinson entertaining the crowd at a patio party. Bottom left: Ruth Ann dancing with Irene and enjoying the music. Bottom right: Marcella and Joe Pleva and Irene and Ed at the masquerade party.

The final event was a masquerade party. Dad, with his cousin Joe Pleva, showed up wearing dresses, wigs, and makeup, along with red-painted fingernails. Come to find out, Mom had helped

Dad dress up, and Joe's wife, Marcella, helped her husband. Neither Dad nor Joe had a shy bone in them. Dad even stepped up on stage, sat on a chair, and played tunes on his violin. It goes to show that my parents were never too proud to take advantage of a good time—no matter where they were—and that's what kept them going.

A couple of side trips were a luau with tropical food and entertainment by grass-skirted hula dancers accompanied by drums and chanting, and a boat tour of Pearl Harbor and the USS *Arizona* Memorial, a 184-foot memorial honoring the 2,388 Americans who died during the Japanese attack on Pearl Harbor on December 7, 1941.[77] The day was balmy and chilly for me and my friend, Jean Lawson from Suttons Bay, when we took this historic tour.

Besides dance parties and side trips, I spent quiet times alone, which helped me think through what was going on in my life. By the time I was ready to return home, I was at peace with a sense of direction.

Continuing my story:

The legal separation took place in June of 1984. Our three youngest children lived with me, but soon, I was down to two after Victoria graduated and found a job in Traverse City. Harold lived with his elderly Aunt Anna in Maple City.

In less than a year, I realized I made a mistake and should have filed for a divorce. I took my faith seriously, and feared the disgrace it would bring upon me, my children, my parents, and the church community. I was at God's mercy, and sought wise counsel from an elderly priest at a Carmelite Monastery. After he suggested I go through the court, then go through the church, I followed through. My marriage with Harold of twenty-eight years ended in divorce in June of 1986. (My church annulment, six years later, was a healing process that traced back to the early state of marriage.)

Harold and I did our best in maintaining a good relationship with each of our children. He blessed our family when he found sobriety in AA, which lasted his lifetime.

Goodness prevailed, through God's mercy.

* * *

A memorable occasion in the summer of '86 for my children, Donald and Christine, and me was an unexpected weekend camping trip to the D.H. Day State Park in Glen Arbor after my

---

77   "Survivors Mark Pearl Harbor Anniversary," CBS News.

good friend and neighbor, Karen Laskey, invited us to go with her and her two sons, Allen and Lee, friends of my kids. She brought the camper, a tent, and food. It did us all good to sit around a campfire and laugh over silly things. One cloudy morning, the boys cast fishing rods near the shore of Lake Michigan. When the rain came down, they stayed there, just for fun, and didn't catch a fish!

* * *

The children and I were doing great, when suddenly in December of 1986, we had a house fire. I had no idea that a snow blower I bought a few months earlier at a rummage sale needed repair. Donald and his friend were working on it in the basement in an attempt to plow the driveway. When they tried starting it, it suddenly backfired and ignited a pile of papers. Donald quickly grabbed the gas can to prevent an explosion, and ran to the neighbors with his friend to call 911. Donald stated, "It seemed a long wait, as I was hurting with third-degree burns on both hands, and later treated by EMS."

Christine and I heard the siren go off in Cedar, not knowing where the emergency was until we headed for home, a mile away. I drove behind the Cedar Fire Department and saw flames pouring from my home. I worried about Donald. We didn't see him anywhere from where I was parked alongside the road. Seconds later, the Leland Fire Department responded. It was a long wait for my daughter and I to be reunited with my son. That was all that mattered.

Good neighbors, Al and Karen Laskey provided shelter for us. The only clothes we had were the ones we were wearing, and we received gently used clothing and bedding from Glen Lake Community Church in Burdickville, which we were happy to receive. Later, we had privacy after Julie and Ray offered the use of their cottage.

The day after the fire, we checked out the damage with Al, our neighbor, who wouldn't let us go inside by ourselves. Upon entering the kitchen, we saw the Sacred Heart of Jesus picture still intact with color, lying on the table, with no wooden frame or glass when blackened remnants were everywhere. I considered that to be a miracle. Al was working as a fireman the evening before. He said, "When I saw that picture lying on the floor and being trampled on in water, I immediately picked it up and set it on the table."

Thankfully, we were covered by insurance. The interior was gutted from the rafters to the basement floor with a new cross beam except for several feet of flooring exposed on each end. Windows and doors were replaced. The brick exterior and roofing were fine.

Monetary blessings came from Holy Rosary Church parishioners, as they insisted on helping us ... besides cousins David and Rebecca Fleis, who made it their mission to assist us.

My parents also kept us "close in prayers" at their winter destination, and wasted no time visiting us upon their return in May, as we were back living at home. After Dad did an inspection of the reconstruction, he said, "They did a good job!" That meant the world to me, since he had built this home twenty-seven years before.

Donald had turned seventeen the previous month, in April. We were blessed by his bravery and safety. (He contributed to this story.) *I believe faith is tested when we have struggles. ...*

More from the '80s

After Julie's successful trip to Hawaii, she became a travel agent. She arranged for Dad and Mom to do more traveling. They went with a group to exotic places such as the Virgin Islands and on a Caribbean cruise.

Ted, his wife Mary Lou, and their teenage children, Jeanette and Christopher, were on the cruise with Dad and Mom. Ted recalls, "There was a little gambling on the ship. We were with

Caribbean cruise in 1985. Couples, left to right: Ray and Julie, Ed and Irene, Edward and Barbara, Ted and Mary Lou, Dale and Joan, and Roger and Mary Jane

Mom and Dad at the casino. After a few hours of gaming, I was walking around and saw Mom sitting on a bench in the corner, and could tell she had lost all the money she came with. I sat down by her, and as we talked, I took five twenty-dollar bills from my wallet and held them in my hand. I asked Mom if I was her favorite of all my brothers and sisters. With a smile on her face and a twinkle in her eyes she said, 'Yes, you are my favorite!' Then she took the money and immediately left me for a slot machine so I could savor her unforgettable wonderful words."

Ted's daughter Jeanette commented, "They had a game on the cruise to find out who had the most kids, grandkids, pictures, etc., and I think Grandma won everything. She enjoyed winning!"

* * *

My niece Diane stated how Grandma helped her put motherhood in perspective when she and her husband Tom's firstborn daughter Jennifer entered the world in 1984. She said, "The day after coming home from the hospital was hectic. Baby Jennifer was a bit colicky and crying most of the time. I didn't know what to do.

"The mailman knocked on our door, and in our bundle of mail was a letter from Grandma. In it, she congratulated me on the birth of our first child, a girl, just like she had. She told me to cherish those first few months when that child needed me so much. She shared her memory of how beautiful babies smelled, and how, when they were first born, they had fuzz on their ears and how you can almost watch their eyelashes grow. Then the best part: she said I should drink a beer a day while I was breastfeeding because it would relax me, and the more relaxed I was, the more relaxed the baby would be. I just loved her for that! That letter helped me put motherhood in perspective. I read it many times when our children were babies."

* * *

The idea of a sisters' get-together was initiated by the youngest of us—Rita. We had no clue what to expect when we arrived for a stayover at a motel in Cadillac in 1984. Mary Jane came from Indiana; Julie, Noreen, and Rita from Grand Rapids; and Bernadette, Shirley, Joan, and I from Cedar.

Shortly after we arrived, we phoned Mom and Dad. Hearing the news that all eight of us girls were together was quite the surprise. The same for our brothers when we phoned each of them. How could we not forget them? That was the first thing on our minds!

With no spouses and no children, there were no responsibilities. We prayed together and shared plentiful food and drink we brought with us.

Later in the evening, we dressed for our first-ever pajama party, where we relaxed and listened. Each of us took turns talking about past and present stages of our lives, along with our dreams and aspirations. Through laughter and tears, sharing our lives was bound to change us and bring us closer than ever before.

Some of the sisters continued to talk past sundown, while others settled down for the night. We doubled up and slept in the four queen-size beds in the two adjoining rooms.

No one paid attention to the clock, yet somehow, we all awakened at sunrise, got dressed, and walked downstairs to the motel restaurant, where we enjoyed a nice warm breakfast. Afterward, we packed our bags, said our goodbyes with warm hugs, and headed home with cherished memories.

One evening spent at a motel with all eight sisters present was a real-life blessing. First, it was all about getting there; then lifting our minds and hearts to prayer; then being there for each other. Even though there was an age gap of twenty years from the youngest to the oldest, we were united.

It only took a single occasion for all of us to realize we wanted a sisters' get-together to be an annual event. We continued to bless ourselves with overnight stays for thirty-plus years, at various places, including events hosted in our homes. We have drawn strength and perseverance from each other.

Not to be outdone, our brothers began getting together as well. "Don't remember the year, but I do remember the situation," Jim wrote. "The brothers were at a get-together at Ray and Julie's cottage on Lake Leelanau. There was a campfire with a lot of conversation going on.

"Don't remember how it started, but the brothers' conversation alluded to the fact that with

Left: Sisters singing at a niece's wedding (1990). Right: Brothers singing at "The Old Course" at Sugar Loaf bar pub (2011).

Ed living in Florida, Ted in Pennsylvania, Larry in Grand Rapids, and Jim in Rogers City, we were only getting together about every two to five years.

"'Life is too short,' was the comment made.

"That's when we made a pact to get together and go somewhere at least once a year, with or without our wives. To the best of my knowledge, there hasn't been a year without us getting together since."

First Fleis Golf Outing

About thirty members of our family showed up for a round of golf when the Fleis Open was held for the first time in the summer of 1984. Bernadette explains, "It all happened after my husband, Ken, and I and our fifteen-year-old son, Keith, took golf lessons and knew of other family members already playing the game. After talking it over with a few members of the family, we took charge, bought a couple tee shirts for the top winners, and planned the whole event at The Dunes golf course in Empire.

"We picked teams by drawing names from a hat. The winners were our nephew, Tom Pelak [Diane's husband], and myself. The way we set it up, the winners had to plan the following year's event, the place for the outing, and buy the prizes.

"What began as a fun golf outing became a family tradition and has been held every year since," Bernadette concluded.

Group photo of the first Fleis Open at The Dunes golf course in Empire. It shows the first-place winners, Bernadette and her nephew, Tom Pelak. Right: Ed and Irene having a great time riding the golf cart and passing out refreshments.

Our Parents' Golden Wedding Anniversary

Dad and Mom's core values of faith, family, and music were completely captured in the celebration.

It was warm and sunny on August 8, 1987, when our parents renewed their wedding vows: "For better or worse, in sickness and in health, till death do us part," during a polka mass to celebrate their golden wedding anniversary at Holy Rosary Church. The ceremony was officiated by Rev. Father Al Gietzen.

Mom's usual saying: "Many hands make light work," was certainly true for all the preparation it took to make this day special. Shirley lined up a kitchen crew that helped her make dinner rolls and cut up fruits and vegetables. Others gathered gladiolas for altar flowers, made a picture board, hauled a keg of beer or soda pop, played music, or did the cleanup when it was all over. Everyone helped in some way.

Mom looked especially nice wearing a soft-aqua dress with short flaring sleeves with an oval neckline and sequined bodice. Her fine dark hair, sprinkled discreetly with gray, was styled perfectly by Shirley, the beautician in the family. Dad looked handsome wearing his dark suit, short-sleeved white tux shirt, and white bow tie. Both wore corsages of white mini carnations trimmed with a gold-colored leaf.

They were surprised when Bernadette and Ken showed up at the cottage and offered them a ride to church. Ken was wearing a chauffeur's black top hat, vested gray suit, and white shirt with black tie. Bernadette wore a poufy black hat and an ankle-length dress of creamy satin with Juliette sleeves.

They had definitely dressed the part for what happened next, which Bernadette described. "Escorted to the car, sitting in the backseat, our parents had a footrest and a little roller shade on the back window as Ken drove the burgundy-with-black-trim 1930 DeSoto four-door car. Only two days before, I had gotten a call from Loretta and Larry Ludka from Traverse City, who were strangers to our family, and offered the use of their antique car for a day after hearing about the upcoming fiftieth anniversary of our parents from mutual friends. Mr. Ludka even loaned his black top hat to Ken."

At church, a white runner placed on the center aisle led Dad's fellow Knights of Columbus Color Guards to the front of the church, marching and carrying swords downward. They included Uncle Joe Fleis, Joe Pleva, Paul Watkoski, Tony Zywicki, Glen King, and Ed Drzewiecki. They then turned and faced each other and stood erect when Dad and Mom passed through, taking their seats in the church pew, followed by attendants from their 1937 wedding: Uncle Leo (best man) and Aunt Betty Fleis, Aunt Lucille (maid of honor) and Uncle Joe Harpe, Aunt Agnes (flower girl), altar boys (five grandsons) Roger Steup Jr., Ben Fleis, David and Douglas Mikowski, and Jason Fleis, and lastly, Rev. Father Gietzen, celebrant of the mass.

Jim and Bernadette read the gospel readings. Larry, Joan, and Noreen sang the liturgy while playing instruments, assisted in singing by Julie and me. The closing hymn, "May the Dear Lord Bless and Keep You" was sung by everyone as the Color Guards preceded Dad and Mom in the procession after mass to the back of the church.

A reception for family, relatives, and friends was held at Solon Township Hall in Cedar. A delicious family-style dinner was served by Tony and Marge Zywicki of Traverse City and their family, as a favor between them and Dale and Joan. The Zywicki family also decorated the hall with ribbons of gold and white crepe paper strung from the ceiling to the walls, and trim on top of the white cloth-covered tables displaying bouquets of flowers. Typical of a wedding day, Mom and Dad cut the first piece of a tiered, white-frosted cake and gave a bite to each other when it was time for dessert.

After the tables were cleared, Aunt Agnes played the "Anniversary Waltz" on her accordion, honoring Mom and Dad's first dance, then couples from our immediate family joined in. I had the honor of dancing with my son Steve.

Entertainment was provided by all of the family bands: The Ray Watkoski Family Band, Larry and His Larks, and Joanie and the Polka Tripps. Dad played violin as well. Ted sang the hilarious "Chicken Song" with nephew Jason. Uncle Tony added to the mix of laughter and tears when he sang "Old Shep," the old song from his childhood.

The biggest surprise for our parents was the twelve of us singing a comical rendition of "The Twelve Days of Christmas," which was more like "The Twelve Children of the Fleis Family!" We made up the words on the spot. It started out like this: "Through fifty years of marriage, my true love gave to me …" with each one of us, by age, singing our own rendition. Mine was "One only oldest daughter" and "a partridge in a pear tree."

Top left: Preparing veggies and fruit during the work bee held in front of the cottage. Top right: Ken and Bernadette with Ed and Irene in front of the 1930 DeSoto, upon arrival at Holy Rosary Church (1987). Bottom: Ed and Irene with grandchildren.

Top left: Ed and Irene Fleis's great-grandchildren. Top right: Ed and Irene's twelve children singing their own rendition of "The Twelve Days of Christmas" at Solon Township Hall. Bottom: Irene throws the bouquet to the married gals.

Here's the song:

Ruth Ann – one only oldest daughter

Juliette – two thousand headaches

Edward – three polka bands

Mary Jane – four handsome boys

Ted – FIVE NIGHTS OF BINGO

Jim – six new babushkas

Bernadette – seven days of dirty dishes

Larry – eight loving sisters

Shirley – nine million diapers

Joan – ten games of euchre

Noreen – eleven hundred garage sales

Rita, the youngest of the bunch – great, fantastic, loving, wonderful ....

We roared, "More, more, more!" and then I ended the song with, "One promise that will last a lifetime."

Roger, our brother-in-law, sang another song, along with his family:

We were taught to work since the day we were born,

We had patches on our britches, but Mama kept us neat,

We had food on the table, and shoes on our feet.

We sat down at the table, and thanked God in prayer,

We had plenty to eat, and plenty to wear.

Also, in the mix of fun were older tunes: "Have Faith, Hope, and Charity," "Playmates," "Daddy's Whiskers," and a song called "Mother."

Mom meant the world to us!

While singing the following song, Mom joined us:

M is for the million things she gave me.

O is for only that she's growing old.

T is for the tears she shed to save me.

H is for the heart of purest gold.

E is for her eyes with love light shining.

R is right, and right she'll always be.

Put them altogether, they spell Mother, the word that means the world to me.

Mom had a shy side when it came to talking in front of an audience; however, she surprised us when she stepped onto the stage and told a little ditty about a couple with a large family, and the wife was deaf. It was the perfect story for Mom, as she did have a hearing deficiency.

The story went like this:

"As you know, Ed and I have a large family, and people always ask, 'How come you have such a large family?'

"Well folks, you see," she said, "I am quite deaf, and when we would go to bed at night, Ed would ask, 'Do you want to go to sleep or what?'

"And I would respond, 'What?'"

Laughter and huge applause followed. God bless Mom! She had such a sense of humor and was so true to herself.

Dad got up on stage and thanked everyone for coming and said, "I really enjoy our children, every one of them."

* * *

A thank you received from our parents, dated August 20, 1987:[78]

We, your father and mother, appreciate very much what you and your brothers and sisters have done for us. You have all worked together and put on the most fabulous Golden Wedding celebration that ever has taken place in Leelanau County. The ride to church provided by Ken and Bernadette in the DeSoto really put us in the mood of 50 years ago. When we got to church, Larry [was] playing on accordion, Noreen [was] on the piano, Joan [was] on the drums, and Ruth Ann and Julie [were] singing. The Polka Mass was enjoyed by all attending. The church and Cedar Town Hall were beautifully decorated by all of you.

The dinner was so delicious that if we did eat too much, we danced the calories away! We were blessed with good weather. We also heard that all arrived [at] their homes safely.

---

78   Letter to Joan, Dale, and boys intended for family.

We want to thank you, one and all, for all the pictures taken, the beautiful flowers, for all the good musicians, and also the many songs you had prepared for our entertainment.

God Bless you all and reward you for your generous heart and soul.

Love, Mom and Dad

Snowbirds

In February of 1987, Joanie and the Polka Tripps were hired to play music for a festival in Ft. Lauderdale, Florida, after receiving an invitation from Marion Lush. It was their second time around as Joan and Dale had played there several years before with Larry and His Larks.

Joan's story:

Before making the long trip from Cedar, we purchased a small, rusty white school bus. We added a table and benches with seating for four, and called it the "swamp buggy." Our friends, Lucia Novak and Joe and Ed Wisniewski, traveled with us. We got as far as Georgia when the rear end axle [of the swamp buggy] went out. Luckily no one was hurt, but the question was, 'How are we going to get to our band job in Florida, besides all the equipment?'

I called Mom and Dad. They graciously rented a U-Haul, which Dad hauled behind his station wagon all the way to Georgia to pick us up [approximately 352 miles]. There wasn't enough room in the station wagon for eight people. We were fortunate. A young man we met at the rest stop while waiting for Dad and Mom agreed to follow Dad with three passengers in his vehicle. We got to the band job. Mom and Dad and the young man stayed with us for the entire festival. We had a great time!

The next day, at Mom and Dad's mobile home, we walked up to the Killarney Bar nearby, and asked the owner if we could set up our instruments and play for his patrons. He excitedly agreed. He cleared tables and chairs and provided a dance floor. Mom and Dad contacted Florida friends, and they also joined the party. Bobby on accordion, Dale on guitar, and me playing drums entertained the crowd for a few hours. It was the first time Mom and I celebrated our birthdays together since I was a teenager. I turned thirty-one that year, and Mom turned seventy-one. Our birthdays were three days apart: Mom's on February 2, and mine on February 5.

The following day, Dad and Mom with the U-Haul behind the station wagon and the young man with his vehicle drove us back to Georgia to pick up the "swamp buggy." The repair job was done. (We ended up having to buy a cheap ambulance to replace the rear-end axle that went out.) It seemed good to be back on the road going home to Cedar.

In February 1988, Aunt Theresa (Fleis) and Uncle Bob from Detroit visited Dad and Mom in Florida. "The timing was perfect!" Aunt Theresa said. "Your mother was celebrating a birthday. I honored her birthday by cooking a meal of roast beef, mashed potatoes, gravy, etc., and topped it off with freshly baked homemade sweet rolls and bought a birthday cake. I was happy to do that for her. I remember how happy she was. Edward and Barbara came over and joined us for the meal."

The following year, (brother) Jim, Dorie, and their children Jason and Melissa, ages twelve and nine, traveled from Rogers City, Michigan, during spring break to see Mom and Dad in Florida.

Melissa's story:

My best memories of Grandma and Grandpa were from our family trips to Killarney, Florida. Not only because we left the state for a holiday, but because of the alone time we experienced with them. We lived further away from them than most of our family growing up. I truly treasured those trips to Florida.

The most vivid memories I recall were how they dressed, and how they acted so seamlessly with one another.

Grandma loved to wear her little floral dresses with lace trim, with some darker-than-her-skin-tone knee-high socks, [and] open-toed leather sandals. She carried her 1950s-style handbag around her wrist, and always wore the biggest smile on her face.

Grandpa on the other hand loved his shorts with socks, and leather Velcro shoes. He wore his striped soft jersey polos or Hawaiian shirts while drinking a beer and showing me his 'Popeye' arms. Grandpa was the best storyteller and could always make me laugh. What I'll never forget about Grandpa was watching him ride his three-wheeled bike. I remember how the two of them were so sweet together, and always had fun. They both made all of us feel so loved.

When I turned fifty in April of 1989, my family was dwindled down to Christine and me. I decided to challenge myself and take piano lessons to learn how to read music instead of only playing by ear.

After receiving instruction, I began practicing childrens' lessons on the spinet piano in the living room for an hour every day, and eventually practiced classical melodies. It was repetitive. I was lucky that Christine, as a teenager, never complained. I took lessons for five years. My daughter was twenty when I had my last recital, and played the classical piece "Ah! Vous D'jerais, Maman Variations" by Mozart at the Glen Lake Community Church, as a student of Yvonne Daly. I was the only middle-aged person among children of various ages.

* * *

Meanwhile, my parents sold the cottage after owning it for ten years. They lived full lives and seemed to always predict the right time to move on. They chose to downsize to a smaller home while maintaining winter stays in Florida. Even though Dad would often say, "My best days were when I retired," we knew that was true for Mom as well. Ray and Julie sold their cottage shortly afterward.

32

Counting Family Blessings

NESTLED IN THE HEART OF CEDAR was Martha Novotny's home. In 1989, my parents purchased her smaller, two-bedroom home of eight hundred square feet that was in need of repair. They moved in and the work was tackled later by the family.

A roof-covered small porch had a slider swing. It was the perfect spot for either one or both to sit contentedly. They had privacy. Trees and bushes blocked the view of neighbors' backyards. That part of the house near an alley was a trail Dad walked every day to pick up mail at the post office he had built thirty years before, a block and a half away.

Both of my parents thrived on the companionship of family, and counted their blessings at this stage of their lives, to see all of us practicing our faith, getting along with each other, and having fun together!

They looked forward to us visiting them-especially on Sundays after they came home from church and had breakfast. They even planned for a meal and stored a kettleful of peeled potatoes the day before in the refrigerator. Other food and drinks were brought in by us. Out-of-towners were always welcomed to stay, as a sofa-bed in the living room and a spare bedroom provided ample comfort.

Card games played at the kitchen table were competitive with lots of enjoyment for the grandkids as well as the oldsters. In spare time, Dad and Mom played a game of gin rummy, or Dad played solitaire.

The largest room was the living room. Daylight streamed through multiple tall windows that had open blinds and white lace valances. Pictures of four generations were displayed proudly in various places; even the wooden-framed collage of twelve portraits of our high school graduations with Dad and Mom's picture encased in the middle hung above the sofa. We and our children would browse through a pile of photo albums leaning against the TV cabinet any time we wanted.

Mom's oldest and treasured blue-leather photo album, bound together by a narrow black cord, had been around since I was a young girl. It contained black-and-white photos of her younger life...eighth-grade graduation, courtship and wedding with Dad, her siblings' weddings when she was a bridesmaid, and some of me and my next oldest siblings. After many years, the album fell apart. Some loose black pages with photos glued to them still remained intact, and provided us photos for this book.

Dad was the family photographer. Over the years, he had a Kodak camera requiring a roll of film that produced black-and-white photos, a Polaroid making instant-colored photos, a movie camera producing reel to reel movies in color, and another camera using a roll of film that was developed into photos or slides. He usually showed movies or slide films on an early Sunday evening when most of us were there. (More recently, the old movies and slide films dating back to the late '50s have been shown at family Zoom meetings by my brother Larry.)

Top: Painting porch; Scraping and painting one side of the house; Scaffold needed for the upper part; Painting even higher. Bottom: Completed job.

It was Labor Day weekend and the occasion of our parents' fifty-second wedding anniversary when our family gave them the gift of a work bee and got all the repairs done on the house. Everyone had a job! My job was working in the kitchen with Mom, preparing, cooking, and serving food for the hungry bunch, and keeping up with washing dishes and kettles. Besides food, there were plenty of refreshments of beer and soda pop to quench our thirst. It was one full, exhausting day with everyone working side by side.

The loose, painted siding was scraped down before it was repainted a shade of yellow. Loose or missing roofing shingles were replaced, as a stack of leftover shingles was found in the basement from when the roof was originally shingled. The yard was cleared of tall weeds and received a fresh mowing of grass. Windows sparkled after they were washed inside and outside; walls and cupboards were washed down.

By the end of the day, our parents expressed gratitude for the work that was done. Everyone was sweaty and worn down as they headed back to their homes with some still having a long distance to drive.

* * *

Mom never lost her wit! She saw the chance for a getaway when Dad's car was home. He had left with someone to do a job, which took more time than usual. She came up with a notion of where she wanted to go for a joy ride, but she needed a driver and phoned my daughter, Christine.

Christine's story: "I had just gotten home from school and Grandma phoned and asked if I was driving yet. I told her I was, but I only have a driver's permit, not a license and can only drive with one of my parents. She said, 'That's okay.' Then Grandma said she wanted to go for a ride and asked if I would drive Grandpa's car. I said sure!

"I got on my bicycle and biked over to Grandma's house. She was at the door and happy to see me. We got inside Grandpa's station wagon. I turned the key and the car started right up. Away we went down the road. First, Grandma wanted to see her parents' farm on French Road. Then we went a few more miles further down the road where she saw the Martin School property where she attended school. After Grandma was satisfied, we went back home. It was the one and only time I drove Grandpa's car. I was fifteen years old."

* * *

Mom's latest hobby was crocheting. On top of their bedroom dresser was a doll figurine wearing a full-skirted yellow crocheted dress that she made. When my daughter Janice wanted to learn more stitches in crocheting, she talked to her Grandma.

Janice explained: "I had learned from Aunt Anna how to double crochet an afghan. When I talked to Grandma, I never expected her to pay for me to take a class at NMC, 'How to Read Patterns,' a two-hour class. After the class, I learned to crochet a rose for a centerpiece. I learned to make booties, scarves, and hats. I can pick up any pattern and read it. It taught me how to crochet beyond one stitch. I learned to add crocheted roses to my afghans."

* * *

Dad was seventy-five and Uncle Joe was sixty-three when they began working side by side for granddaughter Diane, and her husband, Tom, in Grand Rapids. Of course, Mom went along, too.

Diane wrote, "Six years after the birth of my daughter Jennifer, Grandpa and Grandma spent fifteen days helping us renovate our barn into a beautiful home. When I look back and think how much work we got done in a short time under Grandpa's supervision, I can't believe it! I was in the final weeks of pregnancy, so I wasn't much help on the project. Instead, I worked most days with Grandma, cooking and cleaning for the crew.

"During those fifteen days, our fourth child, Lauren, was born. Just before I went to the hospital, Grandpa asked how I wanted the stairs leading to the upper floor to be arranged. I didn't know and couldn't answer. I was in labor and told him that whatever he came up with would be fine with me. When I got home from the hospital, he had a beautiful two-level staircase built and ready for carpet, right under the skylight window that he suggested we install instead of a barn cupola.

"That summer, I was able to spend a great deal of time with Grandma. I learned so much from this petite woman who had incredible knowledge of life and love. She taught me things that made a big impact on me. She gave me much advice about childrearing and life ... like a drop of peppermint in a baby bottle will soothe the baby's stomach; how warming a cloth diaper slightly in the oven and wrapping it around the baby's stomach would help provide comfort. (Make sure the temperature is comfortable on your own skin first.) I miss Grandpa and Grandma, but I am thankful for the time I was able to spend with them. They were amazing role models who fully loved God, family, and each other."

My sister Rita's son, Andy, was about three or four years old when "Grandpa and Great Uncle

Joe came down to Grand Rapids to help my dad [Jim] remodel the basement of our old house," Andy wrote. "My dad mentioned that when he got home from work, he was surprised that Grandpa and Uncle Joe had framed and drywalled two rooms in the basement. I think my dad asked them not to do that without him. Just shows how quick and hardworking Grandpa was."

Three of Noreen's daughters also have stories:

Angela wrote, "One summer while Dave Helder [future husband] and I were dating, we were up north and Dave mentioned to me that he had never been to my grandparents' house. So, we decided to just stop in. Grandpa was home; he invited us in, gave Dave a beer, and we sat in his living room reminiscing and going through many old photo albums for a few hours. Grandma and Grandpa always had an open-door policy. I'm so glad that Dave and I stopped on that day. It was a special time we will always remember."

Heather wrote, "I was about ten years old, staying at Grandma and Grandpa's house for a week in Cedar. This was the week that Grandpa taught me how to play cribbage. Long story short ... he whooped me! There was no beginner's luck or 'freebies.' He had no mercy. We must have played until midnight one night, just him and I at that small dining room table. He beat me every game with a laugh and a smile. I came close a few times, but still no success.

"I will never forget that night. Grandpa not only taught me how to play cribbage, but also to keep trying, to never give up, to never expect anything handed to you, and to hold your head high and laugh it off!"

Jenna wrote, "When I was about nine, my cousin Jennifer and I were spending the night up north. We took some of Grandpa's beer cans from the shed and went to Buntings Grocery Store to cash them in and get a snack. The next day, when Grandpa found out what we did, he made us clean out all of the cans from the shed and cash them in for him!"

* * *

Mom and Dad's lives hadn't slowed down much even though both had developed heart conditions in recent years. He carried a small bottle of tiny nitroglycerin pills in his pocket in case he needed one. Mom was diagnosed with angina (reduced blood flow to the heart) besides being a diabetic for years. Her simple remedy for relaxation was drinking a warm cup of water with a little milk.

33

A Civic Leader

A FELLOW CHAMBER MEMBER AND COUSIN, Ray Pleva stated, "Your dad was a sparkplug in the Cedar community; he set the example. You shouldn't be afraid to give a little of your time and of yourself."

After thirty years of membership and dedicated service with the Cedar Chamber of Commerce, Dad received the honor of grand marshall for Cedar's Polka Fest in 1990. He and Mom were both featured in the parade.

Irene and Ed in the 1990 Cedar Polka Festival parade

Leading the parade were veterans from the VFW Little Finger Post 7731, Leelanau County, carrying the American flag and flags from all branches of military service. Following close behind were Dad and Mom. They were happy as could be, as they waved their hands to a cheering crowd on both sides of the street. Polka music was heard throughout, played by an out-of-town band and a couple of our own family bands. The Knights of Columbus, local businesses, antique cars, and politicians were all part of the parade, which was about four blocks long.

The main festivities took place under a huge white tent on the tennis court behind the former train depot, two blocks east of the main part of town.

Every polka fest since 1975, Dad worked at designated booths during the multi-day festival, as did other chamber members/volunteers. Mom knew Dad would be busy, yet never hesitated to go with him. She once said to me, "Why should I stay home and miss out on all the fun?"

Mom was always surrounded by family members at a large table. Many stopped by to say hello. When Dad showed up on break, it was always a treat to see my parents dancing to a nice slow waltz, played by one of our own family bands. Then came the usual invite for dad to join the band and play a few tunes. After a quick tune-up, he played his beloved violin just like a fiddler, and pleased the crowd!

The Cedar Polka Fest was like a homecoming to celebrate Polish heritage…to indulge in food, drink, dance a polka, and attend a mass with liturgical Polish music on Sunday, under the tent. The usual celebrant was the diocesan bishop from Gaylord and Polish lectionary readings by Mr. Joe Janik from Cedar.

Side Note:

Cedar Chamber of Commerce sponsored its fortieth Cedar Polka Festival in 2022.

Ed playing the violin at the Cedar Polka Festival in the 1990s

My niece, Shelly (Edward's daughter), has memories of the 1990 Cedar Polka Fest. She said, "Grandpa and I often celebrated our birthdays together after they became snowbirds in Florida. Mine is April 19, and his was April 26. In 1986, I turned seventeen, and he turned seventy-one, so we both thought that was pretty cool. Fast forward to sometime when I was twenty-one-plus, and we were up north and Grandpa was manning the admissions table at the polka festival. I got there and wanted to buy a ticket to get in, and for some reason, I didn't have my driver's license with me. Back then, people were less concerned about those things than they are today, but not Grandpa. He was not going to let me get that adult ticket without my ID. Finally, I was like, 'Grandpa, remember I turned seventeen when you turned seventy-one?' I watched Grandpa quickly do the math in his head and then turn to the guy next to him and say, 'She's okay.' This taught me two things; Grandpa could still do math quickly in his head at age seventy-five, and he was still a stickler for the rules."

* * *

The Cedar/Maple City Lions Club would host social events for members and their spouses. Mom loved those invitations from Dad and would prepare a dish to share with others for a potluck dinner.

In August of 1990, when a dinner was held, Dad's fellow members were in for some unexpected entertainment.

After dinner, Lion Pat Hobbins had interviewed several couples. When he came to my parents, they talked about their family. Dad described himself as "energetic and a troubleshooter; a carpenter, bricklayer, and mason." When Dad mentioned he played the violin, Lion Pat asked, "Where's your violin, Ed?"

"In the car," Dad answered.

Lion Pat then asked, "Would you play a tune for us?"

Dad said, "Sure, I'd be glad to" and went to his car, retrieved his violin, and brought it to the room and played several tunes for his fellow Lions and their guests.

Side Note:

After watching a DVD of this event given to me by Lion Pat Hobbins, I couldn't help but think that his fellow members never knew the musical side of Dad until that evening.

From spring through fall, Dad and Mom kept up with community events like playing bingo and senior luncheons. Mom's only affiliation was the Ladies' Rosary Society at church, whereas Dad attended multiple meetings. Whenever he was at a meeting, she would phone me if she wanted company. My home was less than a mile away. It was easy for me to come visit her, bring her to my home, or go wherever she wanted.

One time, Mom agreed to go with me to a spring concert at St. Gertrude's Church in Northport, where I was singing for the first time as a member of the Leelanau Choir in May of 1991. We also talked about taking a nice slow walk before the concert, near where I worked.

This experience was new for Mom. I wasn't surprised when she hesitated to go when I arrived to pick her up, then changed her mind and convinced herself to go.

We spent the whole evening together...beginning with walking the boardwalk at the Suttons Bay Marina. We took our time and held hands as we walked a ways, admiring the bay, the natural wildlife with birds flying above, and creatures in the wetland, and seeing many boats anchored at the marina. When we walked back to the car before heading to the concert, Mom remarked, "I never did anything like this before."

At the concert, I sang in the alto section of the choir of about twenty members directed by John Glover. While singing, I noticed a familiar gentleman from Suttons Bay standing in a far corner and enjoying the concert.

Afterward, Mom and I mingled with choir members and guests for a while. As we were about to leave, that same person, Keith Smith, was standing at the end of the line waiting for cookies and refreshments. He smiled and said hello to us, so I introduced Mom to him ... and walked away blushing.

The following work day, Keith walked straight to my teller window instead of his usual teller, which was noticed by my co-workers. He was friendly and inquired where I lived. I didn't mind telling him, "Cedar." He then asked about Cedar's polka fest. He seemed genuinely interested in me. Yet, I didn't have the nerve to tell him I was transferring to the Glen Arbor branch the next day.

I would think of our sudden encounter often during the following months. So, one day, I dug up the courage and phoned him, after finding his number in the telephone book, and offered him a friendship, after which he replied, "That would be really nice." He asked for my phone number. Shortly afterward, he phoned me and we had our first date in the fall of 1991. Little did we know—our friendship would lead us to marriage.

This joyful time of my life intertwines with a wonderful evening with Mom, and a new life awaiting for Keith and me.

34

Snow Birds

EDWARD'S FAMILY HAD RESIDED in the state of Florida since 1980. The distance between them and our parents never mattered. Edward explained, "Dad and Mom would pack up their things and be on the road for a weekend stay at our home, arriving on a Saturday afternoon and returning home on Monday morning, usually every three weeks. The weekends were leisurely, as I never had any work lined up for Dad. I would rent a boat and we went on boating excursions. We watched sports on TV, played cards with Dad's usual offerings of a shot and a beer, and enjoyed meals together. Mom was pleased whenever Barbara served her favorite dessert, Pistachio Delight. We celebrated birthdays and holidays at either place, along with relatives visiting from up north."

Family members from up north visiting Ed and Irene and Edward, Barbara, and family.

In the early 1990s, Joan and her husband, Dale, gave Dad and Mom plane tickets to travel to and from their winter destination, instead of driving down. They were both excited and relieved not having to make the long road trip.

A few days prior to their departure, Dale drove Dad's station wagon down to Killarney, Florida, and got a ride to the airport to fly back to Michigan the following day. Ted did the same. He stated, "For a few years, we flew Mom and Dad to Florida. I drove their car there, and then my wife, Mary Lou, and I would fly back home. It was great! We always had a day or so with them and would go to mass together and go somewhere to play bingo. They both loved to play bingo."

While Dad and Mom were in Florida, Mom's health took another turn. Her angina was painful. She had a blockage to her heart that required a stent. By the time of her surgery, several family members were there to support her ordeal: Mary Jane, from Indiana; Shirley, Joan, and Rita from Michigan; and Ed and Barbara from Florida. All of the family kept Mom close in prayers for her recovery.

Shirley recalls "the long trips to the hospital back and forth, three toll booths each way, and Dad's driving. Most of the time was spent in the hospital."

Joanie recalls good times: "In the evening, when we returned to Dad and Mom's home, Dad was in good spirits. It was rare for four of his daughters to be alone with him. We played cards, drank beer, and laughed a lot. It helped Dad wind down from full days at the hospital. He would just look at us and say with a smile 'You girls …' because we were so full of the dickens!"

In the fall of 1992, Edward and Barbara helped Dad and Mom find a mobile home in Shady Rest Mobile Home Park in Sebastian, located near the Indian River on the east coast of Florida. They now lived closer to their home in Melbourne and my brother's newly established civil engineering firm, Fleis Associates, Inc.

With our parents spending winters in Florida, keeping in touch kept our family close. Phone calls were more frequent from some and less from others, due to long distance calls being charged by the minute. Sending letters back and forth or a note on a postcard were more common.

A postcard Joan received from Mom said, "We miss everyone when we're away, but it is healthier for us to be here." A weekly letter Mom could always count on came from her son-in-law, Roger. Mary Jane commented, "I would sit across the table from my husband and tell him what to write."

Back when granddaughter Michelle (Edward's daughter) made her first communion, she received a letter from both her grandparents, as they were unable to attend the blessed event. An excerpt from Mom's letter said, "We will be praying for you and hope you will pray for us." Dad wrote, "I hope you have a beautiful First Communion day."

A beautiful Christmas letter Mom wrote one year was sent to each of the twelve families. After writing the original letter, she had eleven copies made. The letter was found in Bernadette's album.

> *Dear Family,*
>
> *As we are approaching the glorious season of Christmas and the New Year, we set aside our other activities and extend our deepest greetings of Love. We wish each and everyone A Happy, Holy, Holiday season. We hope you are all in good health, as this leaves us in good health and Spirits.*
>
> *You are all in our hearts and prayers every day; our children and their spouses, also our grandchildren and their spouses and great-grandchildren. You are all precious and lovable. The more we have, the more we love them.*
>
> *Have a Joyous Holiday Season. We love you all very much.*
>
> *Your Dad and Mom, Grandparents, and Great-Grandparents.*

A valentine that Ed sent to Irene before they were married

Other times, Valentine's and Easter cards were also exchanged in the mail, and our parents always remembered all of our birthdays and wedding anniversaries.

My niece, Jeanette, relates, "I always received a birthday card from Grandma. It always amazed me, with so many grandkids (and great-grandkids), that she remembered my birthday. She made me feel pretty special.

"The last time I saw Grandma, she stopped at Aunt Noreen's store [The Gift Basket in Grand Rapids, 1987-2004] looking for birthday cards. She found a card that had a man and a boy sitting on a dock looking at the sunset. She comes up to me and says, 'Jeanette, this card reminds me of your father.'

"I am looking at it and see that the man and the boy were pretty bald. (At that time my dad had a full head of hair.) I asked Grandma, 'You know who my dad is, right?'

"She gets that giggle going and says, 'Yes, I know your father is Ted.'

"I said, 'But Grandma, my dad has a full head of hair.'

"Her response: 'He does now, but not for much longer,' and she giggled some more. I gave her a big hug and kiss and we said, 'I love you' to each other. I still have that card."

In January of 1994, Bernadette and Joan took a trip to Florida "with the intention of helping Mom and Dad with anything they could." They were aware Mom's health had declined. "Dad was doing most of the cooking, laundry, and cleaning by now," said Joan.

"One evening, while sitting down at the table and playing a game of euchre, Mom seemed very upset. Come to find out her health insurance policy had been canceled due to her diabetes just prior to us arriving. We knew our parents couldn't afford to pay for her diabetes and heart medicine, besides risking the need for healthcare.

"The next morning, we all sat down and had a meeting with an insurance agent. Mom now had a new insurance plan. Both parents were relieved. The timing was perfect for us to be there."

Bernadette decided when our parents returned to Cedar, she would clean and tidy up their home once a week. It would give her an opportunity to visit them more often. She followed through with her decision.

Shortly afterwards, the whole family decided unanimously to support our parents financially, to help them live comfortably and not worry about expenses for the rest of their lives. Larry was designated to be in charge of the bookwork for the fund and keeping us informed. Each family contributed according to their means. Dad and Mom were most grateful. It was a family blessing they never expected.

When Shirley, the beautician in the family (Shirley's Hair Salon, 2000-present), traveled to Florida in April of 1994, Mom was in for a treat! She said, "I brought perm and rods, manicure stuff, and was able to give Mom a perm and manicure while visiting there.

"We went to the beach where Mom and I looked for seashells. Dad was under the umbrella the whole time. I asked him if he wanted some sunscreen, but he didn't want any. Well, you should have seen his belly when we got home. Talk about a lobster ... he got burnt!"

The following month, Dad and Mom's return flight from Florida took them to Grand Rapids, where they welcomed their newest grandchild, Ashley Rose Savage, daughter of Noreen and Tom. She was born on February 11, 1994—nine days after Mom's seventy-eighth birthday. Ashley remained the youngest of Dad and Mom's fifty-one grandchildren, with forty-seven remaining, as five had passed away.

 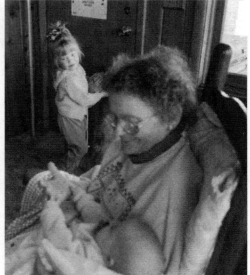

Left: Ed holding youngest grandson, Travis (1993). Right: Irene holding youngest granddaughter, Ashley (1994), with granddaughter Laura (1990) observing. These three grandchildren were born after Ed and Irene's golden wedding anniversary in 1987.

When Dad and Mom arrived in Cedar, the weather was unusually hot. Mom was soon uncomfortable, as they had no air conditioning in their small home. A cooling fan brought in from Joan and Dale gave her some relief. When they stopped by to see me, Mom seemed frail and had difficulty remembering things. I felt sorry for her, and suggested to Dad, "It might be helpful if you kept track of things going on in a small notebook for Mom to read." I was told that he did buy a notebook.

Later that month, at Larry and Jackie's home in Ada, Michigan, Mom and Dad were excited upon seeing a huge trampoline set up in the backyard, providing recreation for their son Ben's graduation party. Mom noticed how much fun it was for the children. She simply had to try it out! She held hands with my sister Julie and a grandchild, Eric, to feel safe while bouncing on the jumping surface multiple times. She was thrilled to have so much fun! That same evening, however, Mom had issues with her breathing and her heart. Dad took her to the doctor soon after they arrived home, only to find out the doctor wasn't too concerned. That same weekend, I had a big surprise … when Keith proposed marriage, and I happily accepted. At this time of my life, I was willing to take a chance for happiness with a wonderful man. Even though he wasn't Catholic, he never hesitated going with me to a family event held in a Catholic church. I couldn't wait to tell my parents.

When I told them, they impressed upon me that they liked Keith, and the most important bond of their marriage was being united in the same faith. It was the one time I heard the powerful statement, "Faith sustained us," expressed by Dad while his arm rested contentedly on Mom's shoulder as he spoke. She nodded in agreement and repeated his words. They looked supremely happy as they looked at each other while speaking the truth of their nearly fifty-seven years of marriage.

I cherished their love for each other, but my heart sank with their disapproval. I decided to say nothing to Keith at the moment. I was fifty-five years old.

Shortly after, Edward and Barbara were out from Florida and took Mom and Dad and relatives Joe and Marcella Pleva, to Sugarfoot Saloon for a Friday fish fry of walleye and whitefish. Enroute home, they stopped at my home.

Keith was sitting out front with me when Dad's car pulled into the driveway. Dad seemed to be in a hurry, and only Mom got out after Keith rushed over to open the car door. Mom and I went inside and she told me, "I saved some fish for you," and handed me the white carton with the fish. *I thanked her for the fish, and we hugged each other warmly before saying goodbye.*

35

Mom

THE FOLLOWING DAY, SATURDAY MORNING, June 18, 1994, I was at work in Glen Arbor when I received the sorrowful news in a phone call that Mom had died. As it happened, Dad awakened earlier than Mom that morning and went to the kitchen to prepare breakfast. When the food was ready, he went back to the bedroom to let her know breakfast was ready and playfully touched her toes, only to discover that she had died during the night. In his state of shock, he made phone calls. He wasn't alone for long before family was at his side. Our beloved mom was seventy-eight. When our family gathered, we prayed the rosary for her eternal rest, Mom's faithful, daily prayer.

Irene and her daughter, Ruth Ann, admiring their resemblances of each other (taken by Keith).

Dad and Noreen arrived early at Martinson Funeral Home in Suttons Bay. Noreen explained, "While waiting for others to arrive, Dad quietly turned to me and said, 'Noreen, go sing to your mother.' I felt honored by his request, walked a few steps to the casket where Mom was laying, and sang 'Tell Me Why,'[79] a song Mom taught us as children." These are the lyrics:

Tell me why the stars do shine.

Tell me why the ivy twines.

Tell me why the sky's so blue

And I will tell you just why I love you.

Because God made the stars to shine.

Because God made the ivy twine

Because God made the sky so blue.

Because God made you, that's why I love you.

Mom's funeral, on June 21, was at Holy Rosary Church and officiated by Rev. Charles Zeeb. We honored our mother by celebrating her life with a polka mass, with family members playing instruments and everyone singing the liturgy. I felt privileged being at my father's side the whole time. As we left church and were walking to the cemetery, accordion music was played while family members sang the lighthearted song "Irene, Goodnight." A Christian burial followed at Mt. Calvary Cemetery on the parish grounds.

A Tribute to Mom

Our mother held the family together. She was strong and resilient. A fabulous cook, she served a multitude. She was "Mom" to many, including cousins who stayed over with arms open wide for hugs. She knew how to laugh and have a good time. She cherished all the generations of her family. She served her church and community faithfully.

When we were infants, Mom, you hummed or sang a lullaby; instilling the first sounds of music.
When we were little, you taught us simple prayers; instilling the first lessons of faith.

---

79   *Wikipedia*, written by Marty Gold, lyrics by Al Alberts, published in 1951.

You never allowed us to disrespect you or Daddy and told us to be respectful of others, especially the elderly; instilling manners.

You taught us to be helpful to you and Dad, and to always look out for the younger children; instilling expectations.

You provided instruction and oversaw all of the household and many farm chores; instilling responsibilities.

You avoided any squabbling by us girls working in the kitchen by singing and before you knew it, we were singing with you; instilling fun and laughter.

You allowed freedom to explore music by ourselves, but work came first; instilling discipline.

You allowed us to make mistakes and to fight our own battles; instilling independence.

I finished high school when you could have used my help at home and learned perseverance.

Because of you, I do not fear water and would think of you when I swam to the deep end of a pool; instilling confidence.

The same for driving a car a long distance. How could I ever forget how much you yearned to have more freedom to drive and go places?

You were selfless. Always thinking of others. Even with having little money in your purse, you willingly parted with some when you thought someone needed it more. I was that person once, when you parted with a ten-dollar bill and snuck it in my hand when I was going through hard times. I tried to give it back, but you wouldn't take it. You instilled generosity.

Your unfailing discipline and spirit of determination contributed to the success of all of us.

Shortly after our mother's death, my brother, Ted, established an education fund called "The Irene D. Fleis Education Fund," honoring her memory. Dad inquired as to why his name wasn't attached to it. Ted had to remind him, "But, Dad, you are still alive!"

Ted explains why he did it. "I believe if not for Mom, I may never have graduated from high school. My high school years were challenging, to say the least. Many times, when I talked to Mom about stuff I was involved with, she would listen, ask me what I was going to do, and sometimes offer advice. After we were done talking, she would look at me and say, "Theodore, and this too shall pass." Three times, she also added ... we don't need to tell Dad."

After Ted held a 50/50 drawing at his home, the memorial fund began with a total of fifty-six dollars. The family held polka dances, euchre tournaments and other informal events to build up the fund.

More Tributes

Dad came to visit Bernadette, handed her a box, and said, "I have this gift for you."

Bernadette explains, "I opened it and there sat three broken pearl necklaces. I was so pleased that Dad entrusted me with this beautiful gift.

"Shortly afterwards, Ken and I were planning a trip to Milwaukee to visit my cousin Linda [Fleis] Schulte. I told her about the necklaces and asked if she could take me to a jeweler to get them fixed. The jeweler looked at the pearls and told me immediately that there was no value to them. I quickly replied, 'Oh yes, there is ... they were my mother's.' I had the jeweler repair all three necklaces. Sometime later, I presented two of the necklaces to my sisters, Shirley and Joan."

Grandson Eric (Rita's son), said, "The year Grandma passed away, I was jumping on the trampoline with her at Uncle Larry's place. I remember she was so tiny and always had those sugar-free candies. They weren't the best, but I would eat them. Grandma always seemed to have a rosary."

Grandson Andy said, "I recall my mother, Rita, telling me how Grandma always had a smile on her face and loved seeing all of her grandchildren. My father, Jim, mentioned how she was always cooking and feeding guests and was always a great host. I wished I would have had the opportunity to know her better. From what I know she was a very kind, loving, and faithful person. Unfortunately, I was very young when Grandma passed away."

Granddaughter Diane said, "Grandma was by far one of the sweetest women I've ever known. She was always happy and a great cook. I loved playing gin rummy with her. She would kick my butt often."

Granddaughter Angela (Noreen's daughter) said, "Whenever I rocked my babies in my arms, I would always think of Grandma as I would hum or say 'Uh ah uh, uh ah uh' ... I knew that Grandma loved to hold and rock little ones, and she would be humming the same thing over and over."

"A Little Walk with Mom," by Noreen

Sometimes, on a day that seems far from perfect, you learn a lesson that can last a lifetime. For me, that day was February 2, 2015. Outside, it was bone-chilling cold and snowing. Inside, I'm sitting on a crowded, hot bus, riding home from work, when I realized, Oh great! I missed my bus stop! Can this day get any worse? My car wouldn't start, so I had to take the bus to work. I'm trying to get a bachelor's degree, and I have a great big bag filled with homework to finish

… AND this morning, I woke up late, so I missed going to the gym. That makes three months in a row! Now, I'm a half mile away from where my husband's waiting for me, and he doesn't have a cell phone. He says he doesn't "NEED" a cell phone. I tell him, "Yes, you do need a cell phone, FOR ME!"

Do you want to know why I missed that stop? I was daydreaming, because that day was my mother's birthday. It had already been twenty years since I lost her.

Her name was Irene. She was feisty, funny, and about four feet nine. In fact, she was so tiny, a doctor once told her she'd probably never have any children. Well, I'm number 11 out of 12. People would say, "Irene, why did you have so many kids?" And she'd say, "Well, I'm a little hard of hearing. Every night, my husband Ed would say, 'Well, do you want to go to sleep or what?' And I'd say, 'What?'"

Society would have called my mother "uneducated," because she only went to school through the 8th grade. Oh, she loved learning, but she grew up during the Depression, and just like the stock market of 1929, Mom's dreams of getting an education crashed.

But to me, Mom WAS educated! To me, she was a teacher!

When I was just a little girl, she taught me to sing, "You are my sunshine, my only sunshine." She taught me to read and to spell, and as I grew older, she taught me about life, and her values, and the world, as well. She knew so much about the world.

Looking back, I'm amazed that with all of us kids, she had time to teach me anything, and to play with me every day. We played follow the leader. All. Day. Long. I'd follow her to the clothes-line, where she would be hanging out the clothes, and then I'd follow her to her bedroom. While she was folding the laundry, I'm sneaking a peek in her closet, where she hid a white shoebox.

"Mom, what's in that shoebox?"

"It's the world, honey."

"The world?"

I remember once following her footsteps in the snow out to the chicken coop, and then I'd fall in the snow. I can still hear her giggling.

So, I was daydreaming, but now I'm off the bus. I'm a half mile away from my husband. Did I mention, he doesn't have a cell phone?

I think to myself, I can do this. I've walked a half-mile before.

Yeah, genius, but not in the freezing cold and snow, carrying a heavy book bag.

Cold wind is slapping my face, the smell of gas fumes in the air, cars flying by, and shoes damp, sidewalk not shoveled. There's no path!

If I didn't have this book bag, I'd be fine. What am I trying to prove by going back to school anyway? I'm too old for this.

And just then … I could hear my mother giggle. It was as if she was walking right beside me, saying, "Noreen, don't be so hard on yourself. You'll get there."

But Mom, I should have finished that degree years ago!

And it was at that moment that I remembered the shoebox, that box my mother kept in the closet. When she died, she left that box for me. And do you know what was in there?

The world.

There were newspaper clippings of world events, like politics, vaccines developed, and the man on the moon. This box showed me my mother never quit learning, and she found a way to get an education.

As I looked ahead in the snow, I saw a fresh trail of just two footprints. It was as if my mother was leading me, and it was then I knew I could follow her once more. I could follow her example.

I like to think that my mother left me that shoebox so that I would learn its lesson, but I don't think the box was meant just for me. I think she wanted me to share the secret of the shoebox with you, and it is this: In all you do, do the best you can with the resources you have, right where you are.

When I finally reached my husband, he said, "I'm sorry I didn't have a cell phone." Yesssss! The funny thing is, this once, I was glad he didn't. I would have missed a little walk with Mom.

"You are my sunshine, my only sunshine."[80]

---

80   In August 2017, Noreen competed in the Toastmasters International World Championship of Public Speaking in Vancouver, British Columbia. The contest involved over 30,000 contestants from 142 countries. Noreen reached the top 20 in semi-finals with the speech, "A Little Walk With Mom."

36

Life Goes On

AFTER MOM'S FUNERAL, I told Keith what happened when I had talked to my parents about his proposal of marriage. He said, "If your parents had said it any other way, I would have been surprised, because of how they were raised."

While grieving the loss of my mother, I questioned my decision to marry Keith. He remained patient and supportive; qualities that I loved about him. After a while, when he said, "I will wait for you," that affirmed it for me. I didn't wait any longer. We talked to my parish priest to prepare for the sacrament of marriage and Keith took Catholic instruction to support my faith.

Keith and Ruth Ann on their wedding day

It was the season of brilliant fall colors when Keith and I spoke our wedding vows at Holy Rosary Church, on September 30, 1994, officiated by Rev. Al Gietzen. We were honored by the presence of Dad and our immediate families, which included Keith's three adult children, six of my seven adult children, plus spouses and a few grandchildren. A reception followed at the Riverside Inn in Leland, with an informal reception the next day at his home in Suttons Bay, where our newly married life began. (My home in Cedar was sold before the end of the year to Joe Brzezinski.)

No Slowing Down

None of us predicted what was next for Dad when he was alone after Mom's death, until he was offered a huge construction job from his son-in-law, Ray, and accepted it. It was just what Dad needed to occupy his time.

In regard to his father-in-law, Edward V. Fleis, and the Morton Building in Muskegon Heights, Michigan, owned by Ray and Julie Watkoski, Ray wrote:

"Just a little background—this building had approximately 80,000 square feet of floor area. Our desperate challenge started in late June of 1993. A high percentage of the population in the City of Muskegon Heights were black people. This came about because of the foundry operations in the Heights and Muskegon before and during World War II. Black people were brought in by trainloads to work in the foundries.

"After the war, the heavy production came to a halt. By the mid-60s and 70s, a large number of great companies left the city. To name a few ... Norge, Continental Motors, Bennett Pump, Shaw Box Crane, and Morton Manufacturing. After the 70s, the unemployment rate for blacks in the Heights hit twenty-five to thirty percent. Something had to be done.

"Enter the great Edward V. Fleis. The only gentleman I knew that could make it happen! At the time he was an unbelievable seventy-nine years old.

"In the middle of June in 1994, three black women walked into my office and asked: 'Could we rent some space from you?' My reply was, 'Please, come in and sit down and tell me what you need.' Classes for adults learning a trade to find a job had to be in session by September 4th. These women were the head people of the Heights about education.

Ray Watkoski hired his father-in-law, Ed, as foreman for the project at Morton Building in Muskegon Heights.

"We spent about forty-five minutes discussing what was required. They needed eighteen classrooms and two working areas for the students. One of the women said, 'We need an answer in a day or two!' I said, 'I will get back to you this afternoon.' After they left, I called Dad and told him the story. At the time, he was in good health and knew he could make it work.

"I had bought the building in 1981, and by this time, Uncles Tom and Joe Fleis, and my nephew, Steve Thompson, [my son,] all did different things to the building. Now it was time for the "master" to take over.

"I called the head gal of the Heights Adult Education and gave her the news that we could have it open for class on September 4th. I told her, 'We could get it done for a cost of $4,900 per month.' She said, 'That works for us.'

"Dad had about three days to get everything ready for the project. The fun finally began! Through the years, I had witnessed several projects that Dad put together, and I believe he had a divine connection with St. Joseph, patron of carpenters. Dad put together a crew of seven or eight guys, including my brother-in-law, Tom Savage, and Dad's grandson, Roger Steup Jr. I think the oldest of the crew was about sixty.

"We [were] about a week into the project when Dad heard someone cussing up a real storm. He stopped everybody from working and called an immediate meeting of the whole crew and said, 'If I hear anyone using God's name in vain or the F-word again, you will be fired instantly.' I want to emphasize how that bunch had extreme respect for Dad and everyone else involved.

"They were putting in ten to eleven hours a day. A couple of times I was told they were ahead of schedule and cut back their time to half days. I know this job could never have been done without the leadership of my great father-in-law, Edward Fleis, from Cedar, Michigan. He has a permanent job in HEAVEN."

Tom (Noreen's husband) worked on the project. He remarked, "In the morning, I would stop over [at] Julie and Ray's and [ride] with Dad to Muskegon. He and I worked side by side, framing and drywalling; whatever needed to be done in transforming the upper part of the old building into classrooms. Dad knew what he was doing. It was a joy to work with him. After work was done, it was my turn to drive us back to Grand Rapids.

"It wasn't the only time Dad and I worked together. A couple years later, he helped me install the trusses on a new workshop I was building on the property Noreen and I

Ed with Tom Savage holding his daughter, Ashley

purchased, on which we later built a new home. I built the workshop first," Tom concluded, "to make sure I got one!"

The summer also provided special memories of Dad for Noreen. She said, "Dad had a broken heart after Mom passed away. I could see his hands trembling sometimes as we spoke of her. He missed her so much and hated to be alone, so I offered to drive him back and forth from Grand Rapids to his Cedar home, so he could be home for a change.

"Up until then, I could not recall Dad and I having anything close to a deep conversation, but the road trips gave us time to talk about what was important. He spoke about selling his Florida place; he had no more use for it without Mom. I urged him to give himself time and not rush to decide anything. We talked a lot about faith and family. I'll never forget this precious time with Dad."

* * *

Earlier, in May of 1994, Shirley divorced her husband, David Mikowski, after twenty-one years of marriage. She explains, "Shortly after Mom's funeral, at the age of forty, I sat across from Dad, crying my eyes out, and asked him to consider me moving in with him temporarily. I was soon to be homeless, since I could not afford to make payments on the married home. I would pay seventy-five dollars per week until I could find a suitable and an affordable place to house myself and my children still at home. Dad agreed to a temporary arrangement and I moved [into his home] in early July

Ed with his daughter, Shirley

with help from my sweet sister Joan. I was not able to have my children with me all the time.

"By August, I had found an apartment to rent in Maple City. I gave Dad a phone call and told him I had the apartment, but in the next breath, he told me, 'You're not moving.' I argued that my children had to come and live with us too. Dad said we would work it out.

"Dad made a bedroom for Shaun in the basement, and Sarah shared a bedroom with me. I paid three hundred dollars a month rent, and eventually took over all the household bills."

Snow Bird

In the fall of '94, Dad made up his mind to go to Florida by himself. Joan didn't want him traveling alone so she went with him. She said, "I spent a full week with Dad. It was an eye-opener since I had never spent quality time with him except for playing cribbage. I noticed he had mellowed out. He wasn't the disciplinarian he once was. He was thoughtful and caring. I had time to play euchre with Dad and the boys at the clubhouse ... and drink a little beer too ... no shots!

I did some cleaning, but made a decision right then and there; I would hire a cleaning professional the following year because I fully intended to take Dad again to Florida ... and I did!"

Ruth Ann's Story:

I was able to retire from Old Kent Bank (now Fifth Third) in November of 1994 after Keith told me, "If you want to work, fine. If you don't want to work, fine." Both of us were now retired and free to come and go as we pleased.

We headed for Florida in January to give Dad some help. When we arrived, Dad greeted us at the door, but I missed Mom already. Why wouldn't I? She was the parent I spent most of my time with. As mothers raising children, we always had much in common besides our special outings. I loved Dad. He helped me during significant times of my life, besides the musical bond we had, but he and I rarely engaged in a personal conversation for any length of time. Now that we were there, I wanted to make the most of it and see how things went. Dad could never replace Mom but he was the only parent I now had.

Keith tackled the worst job first! He shoveled a massive amount of Spanish moss deposited on Dad's mobile roof, filling garbage bags full. I started in the kitchen and went room to room, doing whatever needed to be done, until the last window with blinds was washed. Even though I was there to help, my mission was more about getting to know my father.

Every morning Dad awoke early, started breakfast, and set the table. One morning when I was late getting up, I fully expected Keith and Dad to have eaten breakfast by then, but they had waited for me. That was a habit of Dad and Mom's–to always have breakfast together. *He was patient and thoughtful.*

Immediately after breakfast, Dad quickly cleared the table and started washing dishes. I grabbed a towel and wiped the dishes. *He was prompt and organized.*

In the afternoon, he took time for rest. He sat in his reclining chair and watched TV for a while. Then he turned it off, lifted his prayer book from the end table beside him, and prayed quietly. *He was faithful to rest and prayer.*

When he noticed I looked tired, he said, "Why don't you take a break," and thanked me for helping him. *He was concerned and appreciative.*

Dad occupied some of his time playing a game of solitaire, playing shuffleboard with Keith, or the three of us played cards in the evening. *He took time for recreation.*

One time when we took a walk, Keith noticed how fast Dad walked for a man his age. He asked him, "Dad, how come you walk so fast?" Dad replied, "I don't feel my age." *He still felt young.*

When we attended church during the week, Dad was ready and out the door before me. I fully expected to hear him honking the horn like the younger days, but he didn't. He just waited in the car for me. When I was beside him in church, it was just as it was at Mom's funeral; *a grace and a blessing I have cherished ever since.*

Ed with his daughter, Ruth Ann, in Florida

My life changed with this visit. I felt blessed with knowing my father better than ever before. He had many traits I still hoped to achieve. No longer did anything press on my heart. I trusted that if anything were to happen to Dad, I would be fine.

On January 23, 1995, Dad sent a note of gratitude to Larry, regarding the family fund that was set up the previous year.

> I sure am glad Larry that you are willing to help with all the book work and financing with the family of sons and daughters.
> May our Dear Lord Bless You All,
> Sincerely, Dad

Shirley and Joan were both in Florida when Dad turned eighty in April of 1995. Joan explains: "The morning of Dad's birthday, he went straight to his closet and pulled out a Burger King hat to wear for the day. Then off we went to the horse races and won one hundred dollars. We took him shopping to Walmart and bought him a couple pairs of plain-colored shorts to replace the plaid shorts that he often wore with striped or plaid shirts. Our next stop was the post office. We

Left: Ed in his plaids. Right: Ed celebrating his eightieth birthday.

mailed a box to Larry, containing a pair of Dad's plaid shorts and a striped shirt as a souvenir of his wardrobe. Dad got a kick out of that. You can't imagine how much laughing was going on."

Later, "Shirley and I planned a birthday party for Dad. We walked around the park and invited anyone we saw outside of their mobile home. We decorated the clubhouse, ordered a cake. At least thirty people had joined us.

"When the party was over, Dad was driving us to Melbourne Beach to meet up with Edward and Barbara and their children. Dad was heavy on the gas pedal and driving a little too close to the car in front of him, and so I was a wreck sitting in the front, and told Dad I couldn't take his driving anymore. Shirley was in the back, praying…

"We met Edward's family at a local restaurant and were treated to a delicious meal. The evening was spent playing euchre at their home, and then we stayed overnight.

"The day after, Dad remembered what I said to him when he was driving. Now, he sat on the passenger side when I drove us back to Sebastian. He KNEW he scared the living daylights out of me!"

I agreed with Julie that she and I travel with Dad on his return trip to Michigan. We took a flight, arriving the day before the long road trip. I couldn't help but notice how timely and efficient Dad was.

His luggage was already packed in the car for the early morning departure. After breakfast, we washed dishes. Dad wiped down the refrigerator, closed blinds, shut off the electricity, and locked the door behind us. That was it!

We took turns driving. When it was Dad's turn, Julie quickly moved to the backseat. "No way," she said, when I asked if she would take the front seat. I sat in the front seat and held onto my rosary beads the whole time.

We were bumper to bumper in traffic when rain was pouring down. I looked at the speedometer. It registered eighty miles per hour. I said, "Dad, you're going eighty." With a grin, he said, "I am eighty!"

It was nerve-wracking. He had aged but there was no stopping him. He had a fearless energy and a quick wit all his life. Had he been a race car driver, he might have been a champion!

Sometime later, Dad wrote the following note to Larry:

It brings me new life when the family comes and visits me as I enjoy them all.

Sincerely, Dad

* * *

Shirley's story continues: "Living with Dad for two years was a huge blessing for me and my children. He was such a great example for us. He was very disciplined in his daily routine. He would get up at the same time every morning, say his prayers, eat his breakfast, clean his house, and work on a project until 11:00 a.m., until *The Price Is Right* would come on TV. Then he would sit down and watch it and have his first beer. Then he would have lunch and continue with some project or leave and help someone out until dinnertime.

"My children saw and lived with his self-discipline, and his great faith and faithfulness. Dad would motivate them to be self-disciplined by getting them to help out with chores, not sitting around or laying around, but being useful. I so appreciated Dad for all he gave by just being who he was. David, Douglas, Shaun, and Sarah would tell you they would get mad at their grandpa, but in the long run, [they were] so appreciated and blessed by his authority."

Shirley's son, Shaun, wrote the following letter (undated) as a student at Glen Lake School:

Dear Grandpa,

I'm writing this letter to you as a project for Composition Class. The assignment is to write a letter to someone who you feel is your hero. And since I'm very inspired and look up to you, I'm writing this letter to you.

In my opinion, a hero is defined as someone you respect, admire, and look up to. I feel you more than suffice for that description. The reason being that I feel that you easily qualify as a hero is because of what you are always doing, building and working and helping others. You're always there when someone needs to talk or be serious, and when someone wants to relax and play cards. You never waste time, and you're always willing to show me new things and new ideas that I wouldn't understand. You're always willing to take me under your wing, and try to mold me into a better person.

I'm glad that you're around when I'm at [Mom's] and your house because I have someone to hang out with and talk to. You're the only person that understands me, and you're the only one that can beat me in cards.

I wish that you didn't have to go to Florida every winter, but I understand that you have to because the cold weather can make you seriously ill. If you were younger and still as kind, witty and still so easy to talk to, you would be my best friend in the whole world. Actually, you almost are my best friend in the whole world. I hope you're doing okay.

Sincerely,

Shaun Mikowski

Shirley's daughter, Sarah, wrote:

"Grandpa was a little different to me because I lived with him for a while, so I got to experience him as a father figure. He never let us kids sleep in, even when I was twelve and had nothing that I had to do. He would make me get up and wash all of the dirty dishes in the sink. My mom said that when she was a kid growing up, she was never allowed to sleep in. She either had work to do on the farm or at the store, and he looked at me and Shaun the same way. He was also really rough with all us grandkids, not gentle like Grandma."

Shirley continued: "I shared a house with Dad until I purchased my home in July 1996. Dad was not too excited about me buying this home because I had tried talking to him before about buying his house with him just living there. Well, when I asked Dad to come look at the house and to get his blessing, he still did not want me to buy this house. So, here I was, sitting across from him at his kitchen table. I'm breaking down with tears ... looked at him, and told him, 'I need to start somewhere, just like [you] and Mom in [your] beginning days.' From that point forward, Dad was my cheerleader. I knew he had given me his blessing for my decision to buy the house.

"He came with me to the title company on the day of the house closing, and signed as a witness. Dad also had said I couldn't move in because there was no way to get my stuff moved over because the house I purchased had a fence all around and there was no gate in the back fence near his house. So lo and behold, when I got back, Dad, my son David, and nephew Robert (Joan's son) had installed a gate."

Shirley's son David wrote:

"When my cousin Robert (Joan's son) and I went to install a gate between my mother's house right next door from Grandpa, we were sizing up where to place the door. Grandpa came around and just snapped the fence and said, "[G]et going." ... Although that snap still remains, we helped him with the job. It is a great memory of my grandfather. The years of worn turf created a pathway between homes, [and] showed it was worthwhile.

"Another time, Grandpa needed a new well. If you don't know how to do it, you have to pound the pipe into the ground. Well, I will tell you, my grandfather and Uncle Joe supervised my cousin, Dale Michael (Joan's son), and myself, and would chime in when it came time. This man would not quit, and I respect him so much for that. It has created our family's work ethic through the generations.

"I was lucky enough to spend an exceptional amount of time with Grandpa in his elder years, and watched him build doll cradles for his granddaughters, and him and Uncle Joe fixing the concrete at the driveway for my mother. He could be a stern man though.

"When I was on break from college, I spent some time at Grandpa's house, and he would literally kick me off the couch for church every Sunday. He was a very devoted man to his church, community, and family," David concluded.

Shirley's son Doug wrote:

"So there I was, the only laborer with not one, but two foremen, Grandpa and Uncle Joe. I learned a lot that day; how to hold a hammer for one. Thanks to comments like: 'You're holding it all wrong' and 'It shouldn't take so many hits to drive a nail in.' Needless to say, there was a lot of laughing and some work done that day! I had a blast!"

Shirley's tribute:

"I will treasure forever the greatest blessing any child or household could receive. Our home was God-centered. I recall being a wee child, waking up in the morning and coming down the stairs seeing my Daddy on his knees by a chair in the dining room, and opening the door to my parents' bedroom; finding Mom on her knees. That has left an imprint on my soul, forever. Then years later, living with Dad after my divorce, what a true witness he was, for it was his prayers in the morning that took priority over work and play."

Heirloom Quilt

My daughter, Janice, created a unique scrapbook quilt for her grandfather. She said she used a computer to scan the images of dozens of photographs and reprint them on iron-on transfer paper, which was used to convert the pictures to fabric for the quilt. She estimates that "more than 130 faces are included" of her grandparents' twelve children and their spouses, forty-seven grandchildren, and all of their great-grandchildren.[81]

---

81   Bill O'Brien, "Computer Adds Images to Fleis Quilt," *Leelanau Enterprise*, October 23, 1997.

Four generations of the Ed and Irene Fleis family of Cedar were displayed on a family quilt created by Ruth Ann's daughter, Janice (left). Janice is holding her two-and-a-half year old son, Jacob. Also pictured are Ruth Ann and Ed (1997).

Janice writes: "I have very fond memories of Grandma and Grandpa. The old farmhouse, the piano playing, playing spoons on the living room floor, playing pool, the scary root cellar, Grandma making bread, cooking dinner in that long narrow kitchen, etc. Her love of family and talent [in]sewing and crocheting I believe is in me today. In the year 1997, I used my talent and decided to make Grandpa a family scrapbook quilt for Grandparents' Day to show and share my love for the family. I pulled it off!

"Grandpa was in Florida at the time when I started the process, and I needed some photos from his albums at his home to include Grandma and Grandpa when they were younger. Aunt Shirley helped me out on that one! Then the big process of gathering photos from all my aunts and uncles. What a task! I took pictures at the cousins' outing at Solon Beach, making sure to include everyone. On Grandparents' Day, Grandpa was at his house when I presented his gift. The expression on his face was priceless! He saw the quilt; even said he was wondering where his photo albums went! Photo albums were returned and Grandpa could literally sleep that night with his family wrapped around him. I miss you, Grandma and Grandpa, but fond memories I have … with both of you!"

Dad proudly displayed his scrapbook quilt on a wall in the hallway of his home.

Shirley writes:

"I had a beauty salon for a short time in the married home. So, I had all the equipment I needed to open up a beauty salon in my own home. On Labor Day weekend, I asked my brothers, Ted and Jim, if they would drop by and give me their opinion. Ted came by. He asked if I had talked to Dad about turning the backroom into a hair salon. I told Ted that Dad had been depressed and his health wasn't the best. I didn't think Dad would be up for doing the remodeling. Ted, in a very stern voice, replied, 'Don't bury the dead until they're dead.' So, I went to see Dad the next day and he literally ran over to my home with his tape measure. You talk about bringing back spark into someone's eyes. So, I was only going to do part of the back area, but the next day, we both thought about it and agreed to use the entire space. Boy, I'm sure glad I did. So, Dad had a new lease on life. He had purpose again, and a project that he could just walk across from his yard to work on whenever he wanted to. My sister Rita brought leftover paneling. Ray and Julie provided a light for the adjacent laundry room. Dad had all kinds of helpers—Uncle Joe, Keith, Julie, Ray, my sister Joan, and my daughter Stephanie. We all learned a little about handling drywall, electrical, etc. Keith and Ruth Ann purchased a new entry door for me.

"God's hand was in all of it, as it always is, so Dad had gotten as far as he could before he left for the winter [in] Florida. So I prayed for a miracle for God to send an angel to do the finish work, and He sent my brother-in-law, Tom Savage (Noreen's husband), and his brother Ray, who did all the finish work. They installed the sink, trim, door, etc. All that was left to do was the painting and installation of some type of flooring. Well, I did the painting through the grace of God, with a lot of tears, and had carpet installed the day before the salon opening. The opening for Shirley's Salon was [in] April 2000. Dad's face was priceless when he saw the completed project for the first time upon his return home."

37

Dad

DAD'S WORKSHOP IN THE BASEMENT wasn't convenient to get to. He had to lower his head underneath ductwork from a huge furnace taking up space in the center of it. He was building birdhouses, doll cradles, napkin holders, and miniature wood-slatted rocking chairs (adding festive, miniature figurines of Mr. and Mrs. Santa Claus on the seats). His handcrafted doll cradles were sold at Basket Expressions in Lake Leelanau, which Bernadette owned and operated from 1987–2000, besides fulfilling family requests.

My son Steve was working in construction for Grand Traverse Log Homes and brought his Grandpa scraps of wood, cedar, and oak. He said, "It was amazing how Grandpa kept himself so busy."

Ted wrote: "At our house on a lake, outside Grand Rapids, we wanted to attract purple martins that thrive on mosquitoes. I asked Dad to build me a house for them and gave him a set of plans. A couple weeks later, he dropped it off. I liked it so much that I had him build several, including a couple of pump houses [used to cover outside pumps] for the neighbors. I still have one left but it will never be installed.

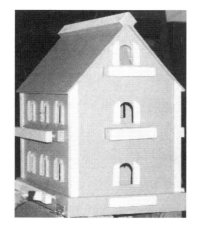 

A couple craft items Ed made: a bird house and a doll cradle

307

"At retirement, Dad was always looking for something to keep himself busy. I had several remodeling and repair projects that needed to be done. Whenever I called him, he seemed to drop everything to come and help me.

"Dad and Uncle Joe built our firepit out of brick. Here was Dad in his eighties and Uncle Joe working together as block layers one last time. It took me back to when I was a teen and worked at Dad's construction sites as a block/brick tender when they were laying blocks. (A tender is a 'go get it for me person' in the business.) It didn't take long before I heard them yelling, 'More mud, more bricks, the mud is too soupy.'

"After we finished the project, we went fishing. I brought crawlers and worms. The night crawlers caught fish, the worms caught weeds. Needless to say, as soon as we ran out of night crawlers, we were done fishing.

"Dad loved to play cards, and euchre was his game. It was amazing, we never seemed to sit down and have a family discussion. We would start playing euchre, cribbage, or setback, and before you knew it, the conversation opened up. My best memories of Mom and Dad were their humor and positive attitude. They both knew how to laugh and laugh out loud."

Granddaughter Jeanette said, "My dad, Ted, number five of the twelve, taught my brother Christopher and I at an early age to be go-fers—you know, go fer this and go fer that. Well, one day I went over to my parents' house and heard some noises coming from the backyard. I decided to walk around the house and see what was going on. I could not believe what I saw. Grandpa and Uncle Joe were working on bricking my dad's firepit. What surprised me was that my dad was Grandpa and Uncle Joe's go-fer. Theodore (Ted) go get us this, Theodore go get us that, and so on. I stayed there watching for quite a while, enjoying it. At one point, Grandpa noticed me and had a big smile on his face. I then realized we were both enjoying my dad being his go-fer."

Joan wrote, "When I saw the beautiful martin house Dad built for Ted, I asked Dad if he would make one for me. He said, 'Go get a long post and a base to clamp the post to.' Dad built the martin house, brought it over, clamped it onto the post, and supervised erecting it to the sky. How beautiful! And the martins started coming!"

Another story of Joan's: "The house my husband Dale and I bought near Cedar was old, and needed a lot of repair. The previous owners installed a washer and dryer in an unheated entryway. On a very cold evening, the washing machine froze up. I told Dad about it, and he called his brother, my Uncle Tommy. They gutted the entryway and bathroom. It was roughed in within a week or so, and others did the plumbing, heating, etc. It was such a blessing. Whenever I needed help, my Dad was there."

Now, more stories about fishing and playing cards, among others:

Dad appreciated it when he went fishing and had family on board to help launch his sixteen-foot fiberglass boat at the boat ramp at Cedar River. He used a trolling motor to get past the winding river that flows into Lake Leelanau. That's where the fish were ... and they caught lots of fish!

Roger (Mary Jane's husband) recalled, "Over the years, Pa and I had some memorable fishing excursions, cribbage games, and just some real good times together. He had a wonderful sense of humor and loved to tease everyone. He was like a father to me, and I miss those good times that we had. He was always glad to see our family visit, even if we got him out of bed at midnight to let us in. I always looked forward to the big bear hugs we shared when we arrived. I miss the card games, the conversations, the cold beers, and the eye openers, but more than that, I miss him."

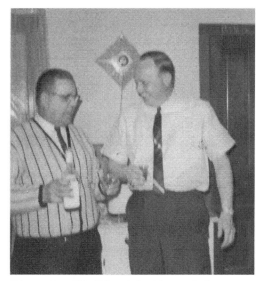

Ed toasting *"Na Zdrowie"* with son-in-law, Roger Steup (circa 1967)

My brother Larry wrote, "Dad enjoyed playing cards, and of course I do too. Dad liked to win. I remember playing cribbage lots of times with him, whether we were at Mom and Dad's house or they were visiting us. We had some very competitive games, though he seemed to be on the winning side much of the time.

"When I was at Dad's place, it seemed like a shot and beer was the usual offering. The shot went down pretty easy.

"The best memories of the card-playing with Dad [were] the good conversations we had while we were playing cards."

Dad taught Joan the game of cribbage. She said, "We would sit for hours playing and many times he would help me with my counting. He could tell the total points by looking at the cards, while it took me a while to count my hand and crib. It was simple when it was 15–2, 15–4, and three and seven, but as I got better cards, such as two runs of [jack, queen, and king] it got much more difficult. Dad would always say, 'I shouldn't tell you that,' and I would always say to him, 'Yes, you should, Dad. You are my teacher!'"

Grandson Eric (Rita's son) said, "I loved to hear Grandpa play the violin. I always loved his laughter and that silly, big-mouth Billy Bass wall ornament. Whenever you walked by it, it activated a motion sensor and would either shimmy or flap its tail and sing, "Take Me to the River." I remember when I was a young kid, Grandpa's arms had bumps on them and I asked him what they were. He said they were muscles. I was convinced he could pick up a car by himself and told everybody about it. I remember him helping my dad with remodeling our basement and that he worked so fast!

"I remember Grandpa always giving me a hard time about not eating all my breakfast and giving me a really hard time when we played euchre because I wasn't fast enough! But it was all in good fun!

"I was a teenager riding with Grandpa in his car when I tried to give him directions to Uncle Larry's place. I really didn't know what I was doing, but he followed my directions anyway, even though we got lost. This was before cell phones, but Grandpa knew what he was doing so we made it there okay."

Grandson Andy (Rita's son) remembers how "Grandpa always used to joke with us little ones. He liked to tease us by taking out his dentures in front of us. I also remember how we all thought he had giant Popeye forearms.

"I played cribbage and euchre with Grandpa in my older childhood years. I remember how there was no mercy. I was not yet up to his playing speed for counting points for cribbage.

"I think of Grandpa as a man who worked hard, played hard, loved his family, and loved music. He passed away when I was a freshman in high school."

Granddaughter Laura (Rita's daughter) was too young to remember Grandma. She said, "But I remember Grandpa playing the violin and spoons, laughing and letting me always sit on his lap. My memorable time with him was at my brother Eric's graduation party when I beat him at cribbage. Of course, I was thrilled, and later I was told that he never lost to anyone. Grandpa must've let me win that game."

Granddaughter Ashley (Noreen's daughter) said, "One of my fondest memories with Grandpa happened at a dance. I was going up to give Grandpa a hug, and before I knew it, I was 'dancing' on his toes … my little shoes on his shoes. I remember feeling so tiny next to him. Such a sweet memory."

Granddaughter Debra said, "Grandpa had a tough façade and I was always a little intimidated by his big muscles. As I grew up, I learned they were fatty tumors. But honestly, he was a pillar of strength to me.

"When Grandma and Grandpa would stay at my parents' house (Julie and Ray's) or we stayed at their house, I remember sneaking past their bedroom and seeing both on their knees at the foot of the bed saying their nightly prayers. Their faith in God was their top priority, and that dedication made a difference in the lives of all of their children, grandchildren, and great-grandchildren. Their love and commitment to God and to each other will carry on for generations to come!"

Mary Lou (my daughter) said, "Grandma and Grandpa were a great example of love and working together as a team. I cherish the years I had with them and hope their legacy of faith, family, and fun lives on for all future generations. When I think about how important Grandpa and Grandma were in my life, I realize the life lessons they instilled in me at a very young age."

Grandson Christopher (Ted's son) said, "I believe Grandma and Grandpa can be described in three easy terms: FAMILY, RELIGION, and COMMUNITY. They were very proud of their family, kids, grandkids, and great-grandkids. They were devout Catholics. They were very active in their community and contributed to its growth."

Granddaughter Maureen (Mary Jane's daughter) said, "When it came time for my wedding, I asked Grandpa to walk me down the aisle and give me away, along with my father, Roger. When he got into town, I got a call from my dad saying Grandpa wanted to wear his own black tux. He looked very sharp, but he stepped on my dress most of the way down the aisle. Aside from this, having my father on one arm and my grandfather on the other as I walked down the aisle was one of the most precious moments of my life.

"Then, when my son, Bradly, was born, my husband, Jay, and I were struggling with choosing his middle name, but then it dawned on me to give him Grandpa's middle name, Vincent. Shortly after his birth, I received a card with a little note from Aunt Rita saying, 'Bradly Vincent, what a strong name!'"

Granddaughter Natalie (Mary Jane's daughter) wrote:

"My favorite time with Grandma and Grandpa was when they came to Indiana for a visit. Grandpa often played cribbage with all of us. One night, as he was watching *Wheel of Fortune*, I asked him if he would play cribbage with me. He, of course, agreed. What made this more special than any other cribbage game? I won. I ACTUALLY won against the Cribbage Legend, at least in my eleven-year-old eyes. I couldn't believe it! I kept asking, "Did you let me win?" and Grandpa just responded with hearty laughter. I don't remember the score, or how many games we played, or if he did let me win, but I will forever treasure the joy of hearing him laugh."

Side Note:

If not for Mom, I may never have learned how to play cards. I was in my twenties when she said, "If you don't learn the game, you'll be sitting on the sidelines watching everyone else having fun." For starters, I watched several games, then was asked to take someone's place if they wanted a break. I made mistakes and found out that was all part of the game. Playing a game with Dad was more challenging. He was sharp with numbers and knew every card played.

Victoria, my daughter, wrote:

"Grandpa's game was euchre. One time, I walked in and said, 'Grandpa, do you want to play cards?' Since there were only the two of us, we played gin rummy instead of euchre. It seemed like we played twenty games. Grandpa was a card shark!

"I loved visiting my grandparents, and felt close to both of them. They made every grandchild feel blessed and special. I loved them! They were a blessing to me."

Christine, my daughter, wrote:

"Grandpa and Grandma loved to play cards. One of the games I played with them was called 'Screw Your Neighbor,' a game you play with pennies. Another game was euchre, and I remember Grandpa saying, 'If you don't get euchred, you're not playing the game.' He'd say, 'You gotta call it!'"

Cousin Ray Pleva remarked, "The one thing about the Fleis family: they all were born with a deck of cards in their hands. They could sit there for one hour, two hours, three hours, and have more fun, and when they got done nobody was mad at each other."

38

Military Service

Uncle Leo Fleis.

Uncle Roman Fleis.

Uncle Tom surrounded by family members. From left: Susan, Leo, Grandma Agnes, Irene, and Grandpa Thomas.

Uncle Clem Fleis

Uncle Joe Fleis

Ted Fleis

Jim Fleis

Ruth Ann's husband, Keith Smith

Mary Jane's husband, Roger Steup Sr.

Victoria (Thompson) Nicholls

Chris Fleis

CHRIS IS THE SON OF TED AND MARY LOU FLEIS. He joined the US Navy in April 1987. After training in Florida and Idaho, he was stationed on the USS *Seadevil* (a nuclear submarine) and the USS *Billfish*. In 1994, he was transferred to Norfolk, Virginia, and served on the USS *Cincinnati* and then the USS *Key West*. In 1996, Key *West* changed home ports, where he finished his service in Hawaii. Christopher was honorably discharged in December 1996 with the rank of petty officer first class electronics technician.

* * *

Victoria is the daughter of Ruth Ann Smith and Harold Thompson. She joined the US Navy in January 1988. After basic training in Orlando, Florida, she transferred to the naval base at San Diego, California. She served on the USS *Acadia AD-42*, a US Navy combat vessel, as a signalman with tasks of flashing light by Morse code, semaphore, and flag duty during Operation Desert Shield and Desert Storm in the Persian Gulf War from August 2, 1990, to July 31, 1991. Forty countries entered in the alliance against Iraq. After the war, each crew member received a Sea Service Ribbon, two Southwest Asia Service Medals with two bronze stars, a National Defense Service Medal, an Armed Forces Expeditionary Medal, and a Navy Unit Commendation Ribbon. During her time in the service, she also went on two Western Pacific tours before and after Operation Desert Storm. After serving four years and one month, she separated from the US Navy with an honorable discharge as signalman 3rd class in February 1992.

* * *

Roger Jr. is the son of Roger and Mary Jane Steup. He served in the US Army from 1995–99. He attended basic training at Fort Knox, Kentucky, Quarter Master School at Fort Lee, Virginia, and Hazardous Material Handling Vehicles School at Fort Leonard Wood, Missouri. From there, he served in a combat engineer unit out of Fort Stewart, Georgia. He was deployed to Kuwait in 1996 to protect the country from neighboring Iraq. He was in the country at the same time Osama Bin Laden bombed the Air Force barracks in Saudi Arabia and was further extended to stay in Kuwait. He left the army with an honorable discharge in March of 1999 as an E4 specialist.

* * *

Roger Steup Jr.   Douglas Mikowski   Doug's wife, Niki Mikowski   Shaun Mikowski

Douglas is the son of Shirley Mikowski and David Mikowski. He was enlisted in the US Air Force for twenty-three years as part of active duty, reserves, and the Michigan and Wyoming Air National Guard. He entered basic training January 4, 1996, at the age of nineteen and retired January 14, 2019. During his career he worked on the Predator Unmanned Aerial Vehicle (UAV), F-15, F-16, A-10, KC-135 and C-130 as an avionics sensors mechanic, an aerospace ground equipment (AGE) mechanic, and as crew chief. Also, during his career, he performed the duties of a biomedical equipment technician (BMET), a budget analyst, an acting first sergeant, and a unit deployment manager. He started his career as an airman basic (E-1) and retired as a master sergeant (E-7). During his career he was stationed at Lackland Air Force Base, Texas; Sheppard Air Force Base, Texas; Nellis Air Force Base, Nevada; Indian Springs Air Force Base, Nevada; Osan Air Base, South Korea; Selfridge Air National Guard Base, Michigan; Fort Sam Houston, Texas; and the Wyoming Air National Guard Base. He deployed to Hungary, Australia, Okinawa, England, Germany, Turkey, Crete, the Azores (Portugal), Spain, Qatar, Hawaii, Alaska, California, Maine, Florida, Kansas, Arizona, and Washington DC.

While in the military he graduated from Lawrence Technological University in May 2008 with a bachelor's of science in architecture, attended three tech schools, and graduated at the top of his class as a Distinguished Graduate from the AGE and BMET tech schools. He received numerous medals, ribbons, and awards, including the Air Force Meritorious Service Medal, the Air Force Commendation Medal, and the Air Force Achievement Medal. He also met and fell in love with Niki (who became his wife). She currently serves as a senior master sergeant (E-8) in the 153rd Wyoming Air National Guard Medical Group.

* * *

Shaun is the son of Shirley Mikowski and David Mikowski. He joined the Marine Corps in October 1998, graduating with honors from the Marine Corps Recruit Depot, San Diego, in January 1999. He trained at Marine Combat Training, Camp Pendleton, California, and then Fort Leonard Wood, Missouri, before reporting to H&S Battalion on Parris Island, South Carolina, where he served for almost three years, earning a meritorious corporal promotion, becoming a Marine Corps martial arts instructor, and performing a special assignment as base security after 9/11. In February 2002, Shaun reported to Marine Corps Air Station (MCAS) Iwakuni, in Japan. Attached to MWSS-171, Shaun deployed to Thailand for a multinational joint-combined land, sea, and air Cobra Gold exercise, and later conducted a unit-level training (ULT) exercise at Camp Fuji, Japan, that included advanced training in patrolling, weapons firing at the base of Mt. Fuji, and later climbing to the top of the mountain.

In May of 2003, now Sgt. Mikowski reported to MCAS Beaufort, South Carolina. Attached to MWSS-273, in July he reported to Yuma, Arizona, for training in preparation for deployment to Iraq. Upon returning to Beaufort, he was assigned as the squadron commander's personal assistant in preparation for the upcoming deployment. In February 2004, MWSS-273 deployed to Kuwait, then convoyed up to and remained at Camp Al Asad, Iraq, in support of Operation Iraqi Freedom (OIF). MWSS-273 completed its mission, and in September of 2004 returned to MCAS Beaufort. Sgt. Mikowski was selected for staff sergeant, and was honorably discharged in October 2005.

* * *

Mark is the son of Tom and Noreen Savage. He joined the US Army on June 14, 2005, at the age of eighteen, as a communications specialist. He was stationed at Fort Hood, Texas, and served three deployment tours of Iraq in support of Operation Iraqi Freedom 2006–08, Operation Iraqi Freedom 2009–10, and Operation New Dawn 2011–12.

He became a noncommissioned officer (NCO) in January 2010 and served as the communications noncommissioned officer in charge in the Forward Support Company, 1st Battalion, 82nd Field Artillery Regiment. He installed, maintained, and troubleshot signal support systems and terminal devices to include radios, wire, and battlefield automated systems and was accountable for over three million dollars' worth of military equipment. He provided technical assistance and unit-level training for automation, communication, and user owned and operated signal equipment. Sgt. Savage was honorably discharged on June 14, 2013.

* * *

Mark Savage   **Todd Klotz**   **Zachary Fleis**

Todd is the son of Maureen and Jason Klotz (grandson of Mary Jane and Roger Steup). Todd enlisted in the Indiana Army National Guard on April 9, 2009. His promotion to sergeant was on February 1, 2013. He reenlisted on April 8, 2015, and participated in a training event in Australia from June to August 2018. He reenlisted again on October 13, 2020. Todd completed the basic leader-training course and was placed on the Commandant's List in December 2020. He served a deployment in Washington, DC, from January 14-28, 2021. Todd's MOS (military occupational specialty code) was 88M20. His job title was heavy motor transport operator, and his title was ammo team leader. His main job was to distribute ammunition.

On April 1, 2023, Todd was promoted to the rank of staff sergeant as an 88M30 (heavy motor operator). He will be transferring units to the 1638th transportation company in Remington, Indiana.

* * *

Zachary is the son of Jeff and Kerry Fleis (grandson of Edward and Barbara Fleis). Zachary enlisted on September 8, 2021, into the US Coast Guard. He graduated from the Coast Guard Training Center in Cape May on November 5, 2021, where he earned awards for Best Shipmate and Best Yeoman. He is a seaman E3 and is stationed in Port Townsend, Washington, on the CGC *Osprey*.

39

Polka Fame

ACCORDING TO AN OCTOBER 9, 2000 ARTICLE, "Love of Music Lands Couple in Hall of Fame," by Cymbre Sommerville Foster in the *Leelanau Enterprise*, "Ray and Julie Watkoski celebrated their induction into the state Polka Music Hall of Fame with some two hundred friends and family-among them, eighty-five-year-old Edward V. Fleis of Cedar, Julie's father, who played his violin for the event."

Julie had sent information about their band to the Michigan State Polka Hall of Fame committee. The committee ultimately voted to confer the state's highest honor on them on October 1, 2000, in recognition of the generous and spirited service they contributed to the polka music industry.

"Ray and Julie's lively polkas have sent couples spinning the dance floor for decades," at weddings, family gatherings, and benefits and, "for years" they were part "of the musical line-up at the Cedar Polka Festival."

Also in Cedar, "five local weddings had [us] coming back playing for their twenty-fifth and fiftieth anniversaries," Ray said.

Besides their children, Dale, Diane, Debra, Doug, and Dawn in the Ray Watkoski Family Band, other musicians played on occasion, including three son-in-laws, Tom, Dan, and George, besides Jim Farhat, Tom Engeman, and Bobby Atkinson, and vocalists Ted Soho and grand-daughter, Kayla.

Ray Watkoski and the Harmony Sounds "THAT WAS NICE"

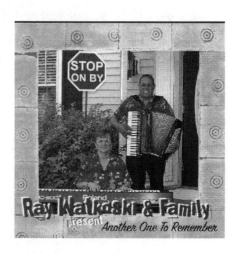

Ray Watkoski & Family present *Another One To Remember*

The band recorded two more albums: *Another One to Remember*, and *That Was Nice*.

Another Hall of Famer was my brother Larry. The *Leelanau Enterprise*, "Polka-Playing Engineer, a State Hall-of-Famer," written by Amy Hubbell, published on October 24, 2010, stated:

> Polka-loving County native Larry Fleis was inducted into the Michigan Hall of Fame, on October. Larry's brother-in-law Ray would tape songs for him to learn. He would practice them, until his playing duplicated the original recordings, besides taking instruction from a book that came in the mail.
>
> His mother came up with the name "Larry and his Larks" in 1966, when Larry at age 15, formed the band with his sisters, Joan (11) playing drums and Noreen (10) playing keyboard, because she thought the girls sounded like "larks."
>
> The trio played a full range of Polish and contemporary music until the fall of 1975, when Noreen married and left the state. It was then that the band took on a different form. Larry's wife, Jackie, played guitar or keyboard and Joan's husband, Dale, played electric bass, along with Larry and Joan. They became a foursome and recorded "Traveling the Roads" in 1979.
>
> Longtime musician and great friend of the family, Bobby Atkinson of Maple City, joined the band and provided a second accordion for a couple years until 1981. Noreen rejoined the band in 1983, after a seven-year absence, along with her husband, Tom, playing drums. The new foursome recorded "Family Style Polkas"[82] in 1985.
>
> During Larry's career, he shared the stage with such polka greats as Myron Floren, Jimmy Sturr, Eddie Blazoncyzk, and Marion Lush. "We played at hundreds of events in Leelanau County," said Larry.
>
> Larry and His Larks retired in the early '90s to spend more time with their families. However, they continued to play for family and community benefits; including the Cedar Polka Festival in 2019, with accordion player, Bobby Atkinson.

(Bobby was inducted into Michigan's Hall of Fame on July 5, 2002.)

* * *

---

82   Recorded at River City Studios, Grand Rapids, Michigan.

Other family bands:

Joanie and the Polka Tripps (Dale, Joan, and Bobby) established their band in 1982. Other musicians performing with them through the years were: Cheryl Dezelski playing piano. Rodney Beyer squeezing the concertina, Tommy Kulanda played a mean pair of bones, George Rosinski or John Gauthier played harmonica, and Todd Plamondon was a fiddle player.

Their band performed at many festivals, including in Boyne City, Cedar Springs, Frankenmuth, and Lake City, and at the Cedar Polka Fest and Posen Potato Festival. They retired around 2000, but continued to play for special occasions of family, friends, and the community.

Agnes and Her Polka Dotz was established in 1973. She played accordion, accompanied by her son Joe on bass guitar and Paul Courtade on drums. They recorded an album (we love those), *Dear Hearts and Polka People*, in 1993.[83] Besides the Cedar Polka Festival, Aunt Agnes performed in many festivals and places around the state, such as in Alpena, Gaylord, Lake City, Posen, Detroit, and Chicago, and at the Traverse City Cherry Festival. She learned songs in different languages such as Polish, German, Spanish, and Hawaiian. She retired in 1998, after playing what she guesses to be "about nine hundred gigs during her career."[84]

The tradition and love of music Dad and Mom shared with the family continues... as more generations have formed family bands, sing, dance, and/or play instruments.

In my own family, there are several grandchildren playing piano and/or string instruments, and one also plays the accordion. Music is a fun part of our family gatherings.

The Diddle Styx from Grand Rapids started playing in March 2000. The musicians are Julie and Ray's daughter and son-in-laws: Dawn, keyboard bass, saxophone, and clarinet; her husband, George, drums; and Dan Bizon, accordion. Dale Kivinen plays trumpet and accordion and Christopher Hedrich, trumpet and accordion.

---

83   Recorded at Soundwaves Studio in Traverse City.
84   Jen Murphy, "Amazing Accordionist," *Leelanau Enterprise*, July 7, 2018.

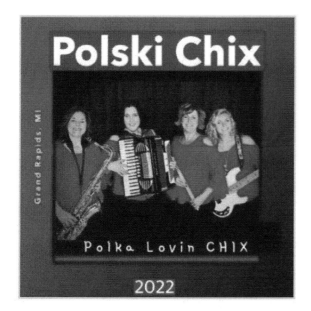

The Diddle Styx

The Polski Chix, formed in 2017, are also based out of Grand Rapids. They currently are the only all-girl polka band in America. The band's leader is Dawn. She plays the saxophone, clarinet, trumpet, drums, and keyboard bass line. Her sister, Debra, is the drummer, and Debra's daughter, Emily, plays bass guitar. Rhonda Lackowski plays the accordion. They released their first CD, *Polka Lovin' Chix*, on May 28, 2022, at the US Polka Association convention in Cleveland, Ohio. At this time, Dawn and Rhonda are regrouping the band.

Emily recorded her very own CD (along with an all-star cast of musicians) in 2014, entitled *Polkas on My Mind*. Her mother, Debra, was a huge part of the vocals.

* * *

Centennial Celebrations at Isadore

Holy Rosary Church at Cedar (formerly Isadore) celebrated its centennial in 1983. It was the only time Dad played his cherished violin in church since he was a young boy taking lessons from a nun. His sister, my Aunt Agnes, sat beside him playing accordion. They, and the music director, Cheryl Dezelski, playing piano, accompanied the choir singing liturgical music during mass, of which I was a member.

Holy Rosary School's centennial year was 1998, after providing one hundred years of education. Following the mass at church, outdoor festivities were held. Stories of "good old school days" were told by Dad and his former classmate Clem Mikowski (eighth-grade graduates in 1929). Family musicians Julie, Ray, and Aunt Agnes provided entertainment and accompanied my Aunt Theresa, who came from Detroit, and most of my siblings as we sang a medley of songs.

The following year, Holy Rosary School closed. The building remains useful and contains a concert hall, the Sala Koncertowa, Holy Rosary Books and Gifts, and faith formation classes, retreats, music, and guild classes.

The convent at Holy Rosary was used for other sources after the Felician nuns were replaced by lay teachers. During that time, the chapel was removed. In 2012, the chapel was rebuilt, blessed, and has provided perpetual adoration under the pastorate of Rev. Father Donald Libby. The former convent also contains the parish office and provides rooms for visiting clergy.

Aunt Theresa Rosinski (bottom left) joined family members singing at Holy Rosary School's centennial (1998).

40

Times for Rejoicing and Times of Sadness

Celebrating five generations. Back row (left): Janice, Ruth Ann's daughter, and Ruth Ann. Front row: Marie, Janice's daughter, Ed holding Kaitlyn, Marie's daughter, and Ed's great great-grandchild born on November 2, 1999.

Ruth Ann's story:

My husband, Keith, was a healthy, active man until he developed brain cancer (glioblastoma) in early December of 1999. His symptoms appeared while hammering a barn door and the hammer dropped from his hand to the ground. He came home telling me, "I was clumsy today." It was rapid. The next sign was when he dropped a glass of water to the floor. Two days later, we heard the "C" word in the emergency room at Munson Hospital. Surgery and treatment followed. He enjoyed a good recovery for nearly a year. He inspired my children. Some even called him "Pops" or "Dad." The grandchildren born during the six and a half years of our marriage had a special "Grandpa" Keith, who held them, took them to the garden, or the strawberry patch, or to pick cherries. He cherished his own children and grandchildren. He was helpful to me and everyone.

He participated in a Men's Breakfast Club at the Suttons Bay Congregational Church. Sadly, my beloved Keith died on May 9, 2001, at age seventy-four. His funeral was officiated by Rev. James Beadle, with burial at Keswick Maple Grove Cemetery.

Dad's cancer never returned after twenty-two years. With good humor, he attributed it to having a shot and a beer every day. However, he struggled with breathing issues, probably caused by working with asbestos and sawdust as a builder, and smoking cigarettes and cigars in earlier years. He needed oxygen at night and used a nebulizer machine a couple times during the day to clear his lungs. After giving himself a treatment, he enjoyed life to the fullest.

Ruth Ann's first photo taken of Keith after they walked the trail in Port Oneida (circa 1992).

He attended his usual meetings, called bingo, and worked as a volunteer. He went to senior lunches sponsored by the Leelanau County Commission on Aging. He enjoyed the outings. It was a chance to play cards with long-time friends in the community. Back in the days when Mom went with him, they both knew Fern Melichar, from Lake Leelanau. She was a widow. Dad and Fern started a friendship in 1998.

A couple years later, she was in Florida when he was hospitalized for a critical condition. As sick as he was, he was talking on the phone with me about marrying Fern. At the time, a priest was in the room. I tried to convince Dad to have the priest bless their relationship. I think the priest would have done that right then and there, but in Dad's mind, that wasn't the right thing to do. Instead, he honored the principles of his faith and the sacrament of marriage. His oxygen tank wasn't far from the altar when he and Fern Melichar married in February 2001, at St. Sebastian Catholic Church in Sebastian, Florida.

Upon returning north, Dad and Fern made their home at Birch Point, on Lake Leelanau, while he still maintained his Cedar home.

Eight months later, while Dad and Fern were attending a relative's wedding on October 20, his oxygen tank malfunctioned. News spread quickly to the family. The next day, weekend guests of a granddaughter, Jenna, and two of her friends accompanied me to visit Dad and Fern. Dad looked happy and healthy when he came outside to greet us, wearing a white, short-sleeved shirt and dark trousers, as if coming home from church.

Julie and Ray, Shirley, and her daughter Sarah also came over. We brought food, enjoyed a meal together, and helped with dishes. I suggested to Dad, "Why don't you rest?" He said, "I am rested." Then he wanted to play cards.

We played euchre. Dad partnered with Julie, and Ray and I were partners. Ray and I had a lucky streak and won every game. I turned to Dad and said, "You didn't win a single game!" He grinned and said, "I taught you too well!" Afterwards, it was just Dad and all of us girls sitting at the table talking girl talk. That was pretty neat!

As we left, I glanced at the front porch where Dad and Fern's suitcases were nearly packed for their trip to Florida that same week.

Later that evening, Joan phoned Dad to check up on him. She said, "Dad was in a good mood. We laughed so hard as I told him about my venture with Dale. I was knee deep in mud at the Tahquamenon Falls, in upper Michigan, where we celebrated our twenty-seventh wedding anniversary."

The next morning, on October 22, 2001, Dad overslept. Fern awakened him after Bernadette phoned inquiring about house cleaning, as she had been helping them out. Dad awoke, saying, "I'm so tired." He went to the living room and dropped to his knees as if to pray. He collapsed, and died peacefully. He was eighty-six years old. His life on Earth of helping and loving us was fulfilled, as was his desire to die here and not in Florida. Dad had told us time and again how thankful he was, "to get along with all of his children," since our mother's death, little over seven years ago.

When we gathered as a family, we prayed a rosary for Dad's eternal rest in heaven, his most faithful prayer.

Ed waving farewell (picture taken at Good Harbor Beach)

His funeral at Holy Rosary Church, officiated by Father Walter Anthony, was honored by the presence of his fellow fourth-degree Knights of Columbus Color Guard members. His life was celebrated with a polka mass played by Larry, Bobby, and Ray, and with multiple generations of the family singing the liturgy. At an appropriate time, the twelve of us sang "How Great Thou Art."

Dad's Christian burial was next to Mom's grave site, at Mt. Calvary Cemetery on the parish grounds of Holy Rosary Church. His granddaughter, Jenny (daughter of Mary Jane and Roger), played "Amazing Grace" on Dad's treasured violin that he played until the last of his days.

On April 28, 2002, in the presence of five Knights of Columbus fourth-degree members: Tony Zywicki, commander; Roger Hansen; Ed Drzewiecki; Jerry Jankowiak; and Russ Scholten, the Rev. Andrew Buvula from St. Kateri Tekakwitha Church in Peshawbestown presented a chalice (with Dad's name engraved on the bottom) to the family for the purpose of giving a new priest the precious chalice.[85]

Arrangements were made by a priest from Grand Rapids, Rev. Father Leonard Sudlick, and the chalice was sent to a remote chapel at a parish in Sagan, Haiti.

Left: Ed and Irene Fleis's children and their spouses at Ed's funeral at Holy Rosary Church, 2001. Right (from left): Randy, Jeanette, Chris, Ted, Mary Lou, and grandchildren Michael and Cassie prior to sending the chalice to Haiti (2003).

---

85   The Chalice Program is one of the most enduring programs that memorializes a deceased fourth degree knight and helps a priest acquire a precious chalice. https://www.kofc.org/en/members/for-patriotic-degree.

In 2016, the Ed and Irene Fleis family made individual contributions towards the restoration of a stained-glass window, "Finding Jesus in the Temple," at Holy Rosary Church.

After Notes:

Up until January 11, 2013, there were twelve of us. On that day in Haiti, our youngest sibling, Rita, and her husband, Jim (Cwengros), were serving the Lord on their mission to Seguin, Haiti. They were among four missionaries from Holy Spirit Catholic Church in Grand Rapids who were killed on the way to the small mountain village of Sequin. They were traveling on a curvy, mountainous road at Jacmel, when the brakes failed in their vehicle driven by a Haitian. Our whole family clung for support from each other and relied on faith to get through the deep sorrow (story in Rita's bio in Appendix A).

In my family, the oldest son, Steve, died on November 25, 2018, at the age of fifty-nine. He was a carpenter, a welder, and did outdoor maintenance at Lapeer Grand Valley Golf Course, Wisconsin. When hard times fell, he became a street vendor selling magazines in downtown Traverse City, which included a story or two of his own. A particular story tells of him as a boy scout and a fellow scout planting pine tree seedlings in Leelanau County.

Steve was a great storyteller and played the accordion and piano. His hard times were blessed with a renewal of his Catholic faith after receiving a miraculous medal of the Blessed Virgin Mary from a stranger, and a brown scapular from another. Unfortunately, smoking and drinking affected his health. Steve's funeral at Holy Rosary Church was officiated by Rev. Father Libby. His eternal rest at Mount Calvary Cemetery was between his brother John and infant sister Karen. Later, a memorial service was held at Central United Methodist Church in Traverse City.

Left: *Leelanau County Memories,* a coloring book for children, with a story told by Steve Thompson. Right: Nieces Jenny and Jeanette compiled a cookbook in 2003, which was updated in 2022 to *Our Family Recipes.*

My other children have endured much and remain strong and supportive. Janice, Donald, and Christine live in Leelanau County. Janice's expertise is quilting and crocheting. She's been employed at Cherry Republic. Donald is a walking encyclopedia of the great outdoors after years of hunting and fishing. He is self-employed in carpentry and masonry. Christine is the go-to person if you need help, and a long-time waitress and bartender. Victoria, of Benzie County, does home mechanical repairs. She owns a small business. Mary Lou, of Minnesota, enjoys sewing baby items for her online shop after she retired as an educational interpreter. Edward is the master chef and entrepreneur of a restaurant in Thailand.

Violin Story

Dad's cherished violin was up for grabs only minutes before gathering with my siblings to say a prayer. Each of us had time to review every possession he had. I was focused on a picture of "God Bless Our Home with the Sacred Heart," (the picture that hung in the remodeled living room in 1951).

Our names were written on golf balls and drawn from a hat. After twelve balls were drawn, the process was repeated. Julie's name was first. She took an item. My name was second. Ever so slowly, I walked towards the picture, turned around, and picked up the violin, saying, "Oh,

Lee Sloan (standing to the left of Ruth Ann) as they play violins at the Buckley Steam Engine Show.

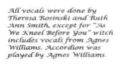

Immaculate Mary
Hail Holy Queen
As We Kneel Before You
On This Day Oh Beautiful Mother
Dear Lady Of Fatima
Sedezna Matko
Mary Full Of Grace
How Great The Art
O Sacred Heart
May The Good Lord Bless And Keep You

All vocals were done by
Theresa Rosinski and Ruth
Ann Smith, except for "As
We Kneel Before You" witch
includes vocals from Agnes
Williams. Accordion was
played by Agnes Williams.

Recorded on
August 3rd 2007

Prayers in song   **Ruth Ann's songbook**

the violin." Never in my life did I expect to have Dad's violin. As things turned out, I also got the picture I wanted the second time around.

The violin was in need of repair, which led me to meet Lee Sloan from Traverse City, an old fiddle player, as he came highly recommended and repaired the instrument. When I told him a little about my musical background, he encouraged me to learn to play the violin by ear, just as he had. He would say, "You have the music in you; all you have to do is bring it to the strings." That's what I did. He became my teacher, and together we played at several occasions in my home, and at jam sessions, including the Buckley Steam Engine Show.

It was a rare opportunity to sing with both Aunt Theresa and Aunt Agnes. From memory, we sang liturgical hymns honoring Mary (Mother of God) and recorded the songs on a cassette player. This resulted in producing a CD titled *Prayers in Song*.

When I decided to write a songbook, I wrote down every song I knew. This amounted to 147 songs, including spiritual, popular, children's songs, and Christmas carols. The songbook was titled *A Treasury of Family Songs* and dedicated to my parents, my husband, Keith, and my son, John, in 2004.

Whether joy or sorrow was in my life, there was always a song to soothe my soul.

41

Honoring Dad and Mom's Legacy

IN 2001, THE ED AND IRENE FLEIS EDUCATION FUND was established to honor the memory of both parents. It replaced the Irene D. Fleis Education Fund established by my brother, Ted, in 1994. A Spring Fling dinner/dance featuring music provided by family bands started the fundraiser. "Two hundred fifty people showed up and packed the house," Ted recollected, "and $8,500 was raised." Things started blossoming from there as he and Larry realized the fund would have a much greater impact if it were a nonprofit. By 2005, the fund's application to become a 501© (3) was approved with specific requirements.

The following year, scholarships were distributed to four students. As of 2023, more than four hundred students have received one or more scholarships. The recipients are high school or post high-school graduates. One requirement is the individual must be a current or former resident, or have a lineage connection, in Solon or Centerville townships in Leelanau County, Michigan. Beginning in 2015, the board voted to extend the scholarship opportunity to include all townships in Leelanau County, with the stipulation that the individual is a current or former resident, or has a lineal connection. That same year, the Jim and Rita Cwengros Humanitarian Award honoring the memory of our sister and brother-in-law was introduced.

We are fortunate to have recipients chosen by selection committees from either the Cedar Chamber of Commerce or the Cedar/Maple City Lions Club.

The fund's success is attributed to generous donors who have supported the dinner/dances, golf outings, and virtual auction fundraisers. The fund also has the strong leadership of a second generation, some of whom have taken charge of fundraising events or have held other positions.

Visit our website: **fleiseducationfund.org** for more information.

Founders of The Ed and Irene Fleis Education Fund, circa 2004. Outside circle (left to right): Bernadette, Edward, Ted, Julie, Ruth Ann, Mary Jane, Rita (center), Noreen, Larry, Jim, Joan, and Shirley.

Julie designated her daughter, Diane Pelak, to the board of directors in 2007. She retired in 2023.

Eric Cwengros represents his mother, Rita, as a board of directors member.

Ruth Ann's Parting Thoughts

While writing this book, I sought inspiration through prayer. A favorite motto I adapted from the Bible (Phillipians 4:13) was: "I can do all things through Christ, who strengthens me." Little did I realize my life was changing right along with the writing. It brought me self-healing and forgiveness, and I am now at peace.

For the past five years, my sister, Joanie, was my greatest support. She learned far more than me the process of getting this book published. We both extend our gratitude to Mission Point Press—in particular, Doug, Tanya, Sarah, and others. We couldn't have worked with a better team!

At the age of eight decades plus, an open-heart surgery on February 17, 2023, took me by surprise! I'm grateful for the support of my loving family and for my progression to a full recovery.

Lastly, I'd like to share a particular memory of an occasion in late October of 2001 (after 9/11), reminiscent of a Polish tradition.

While on a group tour in Rome, Italy, we joined a large audience at the Vatican. Excitedly, I watched Pope John Paul II (canonized as a saint on April 17, 2014) being assisted down the aisle and onto the stage. His first words of exclamation were: *"Niech Bedzie Pochwalony Jezus Chrystus."* My eyes filled up with tears as I immediately recalled the words of response and said loudly: *"Na wieki, wiekow. Amen!"* How endearing it was to hear the Polish phrase again after nearly forty years had passed since Grandpa Thomas Fleis spoke the blessing every time he visited our home.

This blessing originated in Poland, the homeland of the pope, and of our ancestor, great-grandfather Tomasz Fleis, who would have passed it onto his son. It left a lifelong impression on me.

I pass onto you the English translation of the greeting: "Praise be to Jesus Christ, forever and ever. Amen."

Just an idea on HOW TO INSPIRE MUSIC

If you want to instill sports in your children, you don't wait until they're older to get them excited and take an interest. You take them to sporting events and gift them with sports gear. You play catch, and throw the ball in the hoop; you give your child every opportunity to learn the game; cheer them on, even when they don't play well; you encourage them all the way. You are present.

It seems that whatever a parent loves, somehow it ultimately gets passed on to their children, even though the end result may just be all the memories and love you shared together.

That's how it was in the Fleis household. When it came to sports there were enough children for a good baseball game. In high school, some of the boys played basketball, and all eight girls were varsity cheerleaders in different years. As a family, we enjoyed sports ... but MUSIC was the love of our parents; so why wouldn't they naturally pass it on to us?

Appendix A

The Twelve of Us—

Where We Were and Are Now ...

Ruth Ann and family, circa 1997
Left to right: Edward, Mary Lou, Donald, Janice, Ruth Ann, Christine,
Victoria, and Steve

The author, Ruth Ann, was born in 1939. Her nine children are: Steve, Karen, Janice (Sean), John, Edward, Mary Lou (Todd), Victoria (Mike-deceased), Donald (Stephanie*) and Christine. Grandchildren are: Marie (Bob), Ryan, Jenna (Tyler), Hannah, Jacob, Skylah (Jordan), Savannah, Logan, Abigail, Jillian, Anastasia (Cory), Samantha, and Audrey. Great-grandchildren are: Kaitlyn,

Eli, Issy, Silas, Olivia, Owen, and two inherited, Sarah and Hayden, besides Keith's extended family. Sadly, Ruth's infant, Karen, died in 1960, at two months of age, and sons John in 1984 at age twenty-two, and Steve in 2018 at age fifty-nine.

Ruth Ann was a cashier at Mikowski's Market (Buntings) in Cedar from 1976 to 1979, and a social and activity director at Maple Valley Nursing Home in Maple City from 1979 to 1982. In 1983, she began her employment with Old Kent Bank (Fifth Third) in Suttons Bay, and continued to take many banking and community related classes. She retired as a certified teller from the Glen Arbor branch in 1994.

Ruth Ann married Keith Smith from Suttons Bay in 1994. He was a retired general manager of Frigid Foods, and a native third-generation cherry grower in Suttons Bay. He served the Army and Air Force as a sergeant in the 25th Communications Squadron in Wiesbaden, Germany. Keith died in 2001 from cancer at age seventy-four.

During retirement years, Ruth involved herself in journaling, writing classes at NMC, and with the first writing groups at Omena in Leelanau County and Zephyrhills, Florida.

Ruth's musical venture expanded to Florida starting in 2003. She led gospel singing and Christmas programs, and competed in talent shows, playing instruments and a song and dance routine. She also played accordion and fiddle at jam sessions, both in Zephyrhills, Florida, and with Lee Sloan in Traverse City.

There is no lack of music generated at her home. Whether she is there by herself or entertaining family and friends, it brings her so much joy to play a tune on her piano or bring out her accordion, and to see children dancing in her living room to Polish folk music.

Liturgical music followed her as a choir member at Holy Rosary Church in Cedar to St. Kateri Tekakwitha Church in Peshawbestown. As a member of St. Michael the Archangel Church in Suttons Bay, she serves the ministries of lectoring and rosary devotion.

She is a founding member and historian of The Ed and Irene Fleis Education Fund.

div.

Julie, Ray and family, circa 2019
Left to right: Douglas, Diane, Debra, Julie, Ray, Dawn, and Dale

Julie was born in 1940. She married Ray Watkoski in 1959. They had six children: Joseph (stillborn infant, 1960), Dale (Lynne), Diane (Tom), Debra (Dan),* Douglas (Carmen),* and Dawn (George). They have fifteen grandchildren: Daniel, Paul (Christina), Andrew (Elizabeth), Ryan (Michelle), Jennifer (Jeffrey), Scott (Kelli), Nathan, Lauren (Zachary), Kristie (Kyle) Parker, Blake, Emily, Matthew (Marissa), Kayla (Brian), Travis (Sandra), and eighteen great-grandchildren: McKenzie, Keegan, Lillian, Amelia, Mackenzie, Brady, Maylee, Claire, Levi, Sophia, Madison, Jack, Madelyn, Zoey, Grace, Everleigh, Harper, and Theo.

Ray and Julie have played in their polka band for over sixty years and were inducted into the Michigan Music Hall of Fame for Polka Music in 2002. For fifty years, they contributed their talents for Pulaski Days held on the first weekend of October in Grand Rapids, besides many benefits at Saint Anthony's, St. Isidore's, and Holy Spirit Parishes. For thirty-some years, they rented a bus at Christmastime and went caroling with other musicians to several nursing homes and homebound friends.

Albums they have produced are: *One to Remember*, *That Was Nice*, *Another One to Remember*, and *Celebrating 50 Years of Music* for the occasion of their fiftieth wedding anniversary in 2009.

Both entrepreneurs, Ray owned his own business since 1963, buying, selling, and transporting metalworking machinery. He sold the Morton Building in 2019 and semiretired, but remains available for customers' needs. He locates what they need or sometimes has to buy the machinery and sell it. Julie retired from her eighteen-year-old travel business in 2002. Having their own businesses allowed them to travel extensively and see every continent in the world.

They enjoy spending time with family and friends, playing music, and euchre. They are members of Holy Spirit Parish.

Julie was a founding member of The Ed and Irene Fleis Education Fund. Since 2007, her replacement is her daughter, Diane.

Edward, Barbara, and family
Left to right: Brian, Jeff, Edward, Barbara, Shelly, and Jerry

Edward (Ed) was born in 1941. He received a bachelor's of science degree in civil engineering from Michigan Tech in December 1963. He married Barbara Duperon in 1965. She became a licensed practical nurse through NMC. She worked in nursing at Munson Hospital in Traverse City and at Sunshine Hospital (Spectrum Health Special Care) in Grand Rapids after their marriage.

They had four children: Jeffrey (Kerry), Jerry (Christina), Michelle (Kyle), and Brian (Kristen). They also have eleven grandchildren: Brenna, Zachary, Katlyn, Matthew, Jessica, Scott (Becca), Lainey, Jack, Alex, Gabriel, and Beau.

Ed started his engineering career in January 1964 with Williams & Works, an engineering, planning, and surveying company located in Grand Rapids, Michigan. In 1975, they expanded their service area and in 1976, Ed, as regional manager, relocated his family to Sanford, North Carolina.

In April 1980, Ed moved the family to Orlando, Florida, when he joined the engineering and planning firm of Post, Buckley, Schuh, and Jernigan as a senior associate. One major project was the Aquarina Planned Unit Development, a 1,600-unit ocean-to-river condominium project. Ed then accepted the position of development director for the Aquarina PUD in Melbourne, Florida, in 1982.

In 1986, Ed started his own firm, EMF Development Services, eventually becoming Fleis

Engineering and Consulting, LLC. This company provided engineering design and construction administration services for site work related to oceanfront condominiums and residential land development projects. Barbara also worked with Ed until her retirement in 2004, overseeing the processing of regulatory permits and submittals. She became well known among members of the county staff and was very effective in following up with staff on regulatory permit submittals.

In 1990, Ed, with sons Jeff and Jerry, formed JERJEF Construction Co., Inc., which became a significant builder in the Melbourne, Florida, area, eventually employing a staff of thirty-five. JERJEF provided general contracting services for the build-out of a number of single-family, townhome, and multifamily residential developments, including all site work, as well as custom houses and commercial buildings. Four major residential projects were joint-ventured with a family from Scotland. When Edward retired from JERJEF in 2006, he turned the business over to Jeff and Jerry. Due to a significant recession that hit Florida from 2007 through 2009, they dissolved the company in 2009.

In May 2005, Ed, with his business partner from Scotland, acquired the Sugar Loaf Golf Course and other properties within the Sugar Loaf Resort Area near Cedar, Michigan.

In 2010, Ed, with son Brian, formed Monarch Homes of Brevard, LLC. This construction company has been primarily building out homes on residential projects designed and developed in-house, as well as custom homes on client-owned parcels.

Ed is a fourth-degree and lifetime member of the Knights of Columbus. He has been active in church and school and nonprofit organizations, as well as county committees. He is past chairman of the Melbourne Central Catholic High School board of directors, past chairman of the Brevard Alzheimer's Foundation, and treasurer of Helping Seniors of Brevard County.

Ed's hobbies include his work, golfing, boating, reading, and spending time with family and friends.

Ed and Barbara reside in Melbourne, Florida, in the planned-unit community of Capron Ridge, a project developed by his company. They have been members of the Holy Name of Jesus Church parish since 1982. They also have a summer home in the Sugar Loaf area.

Ed is a founding member of The Ed and Irene Fleis Education Fund and serves as vice president.

Mary Jane, Roger, and family, circa 2001
Standing from left: Natalie, Jenny, Roger, and Becky. Sitting: Roger Jr.,
Mary Jane, and Maureen.

Mary Jane was born in 1943. She married Roger Steup in 1966. They had five children: Rebecca (Marty), Jennifer (Jeff)*, Maureen (Jason), Roger Jr. (Electria)*, and Natalie (Timothy)*. Grandchildren and spouses are: Allison (Michael), Jacob, Tyler, Jeffrey, Haley (Alex), Riley, Todd (Kayla), Bradly, Jamie, Jesse, Tessa, Abigail, Madeline, and Joshua. Great-grandchildren: Jaxson, Nora, Ellis, Kinley, Logan, Aiden, Lincoln, Blakesley, and Maverick. A grandson, Riley, died in 2022.

Roger served on active duty in the army from 1958 to 1961. He was stationed in Japan for two years and four months, and honorably discharged with the rank of Sgt. E5.

In 2020, Mary Jane retired due to the COVID-19 pandemic from St. Joseph's Hospital, Fort Wayne, Indiana, where she had worked for the past thirty-five years. (She was an RN for a total of fifty-seven years.) She also had an RN license in Florida, and worked at hospitals in Sebring and Bradenton for several winters.

Roger retired in 1997 as vice president of mortgage services at Standard Federal Bank. Afterwards, he and two partners formed a company, Bridgewater Homes, a development of residential homes in Auburn, Indiana.

Mary Jane and Roger were highly involved during various years with church and community groups: Marriage Encounter (for married couples) and Engagement Encounter (for couples planning to marry), and Bible study/prayer groups. They served as eucharistic ministers and lectors at Immaculate Conception Church. Roger served on the finance committee for twenty-five years, and Mary Jane assisted teachers at Vacation Bible School while her young grandchildren were attending. They also assisted Catholic charities as RSVPs (retired seniors volunteer program) with the food bank and distribution of clothing to clients seasonally, involving family members, including grandchildren. Roger coached Little League, participated in Indian Guides, a father-son group, and was president of Talent Education, a Suzuki music education program where their children took violin and piano lessons and had community performances.

Roger and Mary Jane both have enjoyed playing their share of golf. However, most important are family gatherings. They spend many hours traveling north or south visiting family.

They reside in Fort Wayne, Indiana, and are members of St. Charles Borromeo Church.

Mary Jane is a founding member of The Ed and Irene Fleis Education Fund.

*div.

Ted, Mary Lou, and family, circa 2022
Left to right: Grandson Michael, son-in-law Randy, Jeanette, Mary Lou,
Ted, and Christopher

Theodore (Ted), born in 1945, served the US Marine Corps from 1963 to 1966. He married Mary Lou Fitzpatrick in 1967. They had two children, Jeanette (Randy) and Christopher. Jeanette and Randy had two children, Cassandra and Michael. Their granddaughter, Cassandra, died at age five in 2004.

Using his GI bill, Ted attended college half-time while holding down a job as a technician at Bell & Howell. He graduated from Grand Rapids Community College, and attended Aquinas College for two years. Ted progressed to regional sales manager at Bell & Howell, winning several sales achievement trips to exotic destinations, such as Tangiers, Portugal, Spain, and a cruise out of Puerto Rico, before parting ways after twenty-four years.

Ted has been the owner/president of Eagle Machine Tool Corporation since November 1993.

Ted said, "I'm proud to say I've won 'sales rep of the year' every year, but have to admit, I'm the only sales rep!" His wife, Mary Lou, worked for the company since its beginning, and currently works part-time in financial accounting while Ted assumes marketing. Their daughter, Jeanette, began working for the company in 1993, advancing to office manager and part-ownership.

Ted is a member of the Knights of Columbus and the Fraternal Order of Elks. He volunteered weekly at bingo at the Grand Rapids Veterans home for over twenty years. He and Mary Lou support many charities, including the Purple Pig, that raises money for the handicapped.

Ted's hobbies include his work, boating, golfing, Detroit Lions games, and spending time with his siblings and his grandson, Michael. He is known for singing the best rendition of the "Chicken Song" for over forty years.

Ted and Mary Lou reside in Allendale, Michigan, and are members of Holy Spirit Catholic Church.

Ted is a founding member of The Ed and Irene Fleis Education Fund and serves as president.

Jim, Doris, and family
Left to right: Travis, Doris, Melissa, Jim, and Jason

James (Jim) was born in 1947. He served in the US Army from 1966 to 1970. He received his associate's degree from NMC in 1976. He married Dorie (Milisavljevich) in 1976. She received a medical assistant degree from Ferris State University, and worked at Plainwell Hospital. She also worked as a dental assistant in Rogers City for thirteen years. They had three children: Jason (Christine)*, Melissa, and Travis, and three granddaughters, Juliana, Vanessa, and Alexandra.

In Rogers City, Jim is a life member and past grand knight of the Knights of Columbus, a life member of the VFW, past president of the Lions Club, and past president of the Chamber of Commerce.

Jim and Dorie owned the TNT Bar in Rogers City from 1976 to 1984, sold it, went through litigation, purchased it back, and resold it again in 1986. He started Fleis Excavation in 1984. In 1989, he started Fleis Construction. In 1990, Jim also operated a gravel pit for fifteen years. Through the years, Doris assisted him as a bookkeeper. He currently is exercising his options to keep himself busy during his retirement years.

Jim's hobbies are golfing, photography, travel, storytelling, and designing houses.

They reside in Rogers City and are working on relocating back to live in his hometown of Cedar, Michigan.

They are members of St. Ignatius Catholic Church.

Jim is a founding member of The Ed and Irene Fleis Education Fund.   *div.*

Bernadette and Ken, circa 2019

Keith, Jan, grandson Alex, and Toolie, the family dog

Bernadette, Ken, and Family

Bernadette was born in 1948 and married Kenneth Denoyer in 1966. They had three children: Keith (Jan), Scott, and Brian and one grandchild, Alexander. Sadly, Scott, at age five months, died in 1969, and Brian, at age five, died in 1976. Keith's wife, Jan, died from cancer in 2020.

Bernadette was the typing instructor at St. Mary's School in Lake Leelanau from 1975 to 1982, and then school secretary from 1982 to 1985. She owned and operated a retail shop, Basket Expressions, in Lake Leelanau, from 1987 to 2000. She also developed a food processing company, Northern Seasons, from 1990 until retiring in 2019. Her products were sold at local farm markets, community craft fairs and local grocery stores. Customers tasted products before buying as Bernadette prepared and served tasty samples.

Ken owned and operated KD Plumbing and Heating in Lake Leelanau for thirty-two years (1976–2008) until he retired.

Bernadette and Ken loved to garden, both flowers and vegetables. She cans and freezes home produce.

Since 1976, Bernadette and Ken, with three other couples from the Leelanau County area, celebrated their wedding anniversaries, which all fell during the month of October. Together, they picked a date in October each year and usually dined at a restaurant in Grand Traverse or Leelanau County.

From 2006 to 2021, they also met once a month with a group originating from their church for a "Potluck Dinner for Eight." They cherished sharing a meal at each other's homes and spending time with one another.

Since 1999, Bernadette has been an active member of a Thursday morning Bible study. She and Ken together had attended Leelanau Community Church, near their home in Lake Leelanau, Michigan.

Sadly, during Ken's last years, he was affected with dementia. He was called to the Lord at age seventy-seven, on May 30, 2023.

Bernadette is a founding member of The Ed and Irene Fleis Education Fund.

Larry, Jackie, and family, circa 2021
Left to right: Jodie, Jackie, Larry, Chelsea, and Ben

Larry was born in 1951. He graduated with a bachelor's degree in civil engineering from MSU in 1973 in five terms, with honors. He married Jacqueline Norconk in 1975. They had three children: Lawrence Ben (Kate), Chelsea (Wes), and Jodie (Kyle), and seven grandchildren: Jakob, Bruno, Isaiah, Elijah, Lincoln, Fiona, and Isabella.

Larry worked for Williams & Works from 1973 to 1993 and left the company as vice president. Larry is co-founder of Fleis & VandenBrink Engineering, F&V Construction, and F&V Operations and Resource Management. The company started with Larry and his partner, Steve, and their wives, and has grown to 250 staff with nine offices. Jackie worked for the company from its beginning, multitasking and eventually with the accounting group. The firm has received numerous national and state awards, including being recognized five times as a "Hot Firm," being one of the fastest growing engineering companies in the United States; as Western Michigan, Eastern Michigan, and National Best & Brightest Companies to Work For; and twice as Engineering Firm of the Year by the American Council of Engineering Companies of Michigan (ACEC). The firm has received numerous engineering and surveying excellence awards. Larry is semiretired and serves as chairman of the board of the parent company, F&V Companies, Inc. He plans to fully retire in the summer of 2023. Jackie retired at the end of 2020.

Larry was a board member and eventual president of the St. John Vianney school board, and later for the school board of St. Patrick, which is their current parish. He was a board member for the American Council of Engineering Companies (ACEC), chairman of the Rural Development Task Force and QBS (Qualifications-Based Selection) Coalition, board member and eventual chairman for the Engineering Advisory Board of the Engineering College of Michigan State University, and director for the Centennial Park Business Owners Association.

In 2019, Larry was honored with the Civil and Environmental Engineering Distinguished Alumni Award from Michigan State University. In 2020, he was given the Felix A. Anderson Image Award from the American Council of Engineering Companies of Michigan.

Larry has played the accordion since 1966. He formed the Larry and His Larks band in 1968 and played in the band for nearly twenty-five years. His induction into the Michigan Music Hall of Fame for Polka Music in 2010 was quite an honor. Larry and His Larks have continued to play for charity and family events.

His hobbies include attending all Michigan State home football games and tailgating with friends, family, or clients. He continues to hold years of season football tickets (since 1995). Jackie loves the MSU basketball games, for which Larry has held years of season tickets too—since 1999. He, along with family/friends, have traveled to many football bowl games and basketball playoffs. His favorite sport is golf, though you probably won't find "Larry the Golfer" on his tombstone.

In 2020, Larry became project manager and volunteers his time as the engineer of record for the planning of improvements of the Cedar River Waterway & Park Project, following his dad's footsteps thirty-seven years after the 1983 Cedar River Project.

Larry and Jackie have maintained a second home in the Cedar area. They travel back and forth from Grand Rapids frequently to enjoy the back-home country.

Larry is a founding member of The Ed and Irene Fleis Education Fund and serves as treasurer.

Shirley and family, circa 2018
Left to right: Sarah, Shaun, Douglas, Shirley, David, and Stephanie

Shirley was born in 1953. She graduated in August 1972 from Northwestern Beauty Academy in Traverse City as a licensed cosmetologist.

Her children are: Stephanie (Phillip), David, Douglas (Niki), Shaun (Sarah), and Sarah (Scott). Grandchildren are: Kara, Tyler (Lindsey), Adley, Kinley, Grant, Elisha, Alaythea, Isaiah, Azariah, Josiah, Aria, Noah, Kailey (John), Victoria, Emma, Grace, Mariah, Faith, Hannah, and Oksana. She has three great grandchildren: Braylon, Grayson, and Emilia. Sadly, an infant grandson, Hosea, died in 2013.

She has had a small beauty salon in the back of her home since 2000, called "Shirley's Salon." She serves the homebound with her porta-salon as well. She has held an elected position as Solon Township clerk from 2004 to present. She sold Home Interiors & Gifts, which she owned from 1998 to 2007, holding home parties and decorating homes.

Shirley's hobbies are eating, sleeping, working, and praying, and spending time with her family whenever possible.

She resides in downtown Cedar, and has been a parishioner at Holy Rosary Church most of her life. She attends mass daily, loves to attend devotions whenever possible, and is very active in the parish, belonging to several organizations and volunteering whenever she can. She, along with her sister, Joan, have co-chaired the Holy Rosary Church raffle since 2007.

Shirley is a founding member of The Ed and Irene Fleis Education Fund.

Joan, Dale, and family, circa 2010
Standing from left: Robert, Russell, and Dale Michael. Sitting: Dale and Joan.

Joan was born in 1956. She attended Davenport College of Business in Grand Rapids, and later NMC in Traverse City. She married Dale Gauthier in 1974. They had three sons: Robert (Deedz), Russell (Marissa), and Dale Michael. Their three grandchildren are Cabrini, Jack, and Henry.

Joan retired in 2018 from Munson Medical Center's Hearing Clinic, Traverse City, as office coordinator after nearly twenty-three years of service. She currently holds the position of treasurer for Solon Township, having served from 1988 to 1996, and 2003 to present. Dale retired in 2015 after working as a machinist at Cone Drive Gears in Traverse City for eighteen years, and as an "over-the-road" truck driver for over twenty years.

Joan actively served with the Traverse City Lions Club from 1996 to 2018, being a past president, and volunteered as a bell-ringer for the Salvation Army, for White Cane, and for road cleanup.

Joan was referred to as "The Wedding Drummer" (The Leelanau Enterprise, July 21, 2016, by Cala James), having been a drummer since the age of twelve and with Larry and His Larks until 1982, when a new band was formed: Joanie and the Polka Tripps, with husband Dale and friend Bobby Atkinson. "Music has been a passion … it's the thrill of making people happy and dancing to the music," she says.

During retirement, they are enjoying their grandchildren, spending fun times on their golf cart driving around their farm in Cedar, and spending special times on their happy place, the front porch, where all are invited. They love to travel for casino vacations, bus trips, and visiting warmer climates.

They are active members of Holy Rosary Church. Joan has been co-chair of the Holy Rosary Chicken Dinner raffle since 2007, with her sister, Shirley.

Joan is a founding member of The Ed and Irene Fleis Education Fund and serves as secretary.

Noreen, Tom, family, circa 2019
Left to right: Angela, Mark, Tom, Noreen, Ashley, Heather, and Jenna

Noreen was born in 1957 and married Tom Savage in 1975. They had five children: Angela (Dave), Heather (Chad), Jenna (Chris), Mark (Jacqueline)*, and Ashley. Their fourteen grandchildren are: Anna, Lydia, Sophia, Noah, Carter, Owen, Collin, Violet, Rose, Celeste, Layla, Mia, Penelope, and Charlotte.

Noreen graduated from Columbus Business University in 1976, while Tom received his associate's degree from the Ohio Institute of Technology in Columbus, Ohio, in 1977. After completing his schooling in Columbus, they moved to Grand Rapids, Michigan. Together they owned a retail gift shop, Gift Basket, from 1987 to 2004. Noreen has been an administrative assistant at Grand Valley State University from 2005 to present. Tom owns his own business, Savage Building & Remodeling, as a licensed building contractor from 1995 to present. He built their beautiful home where they reside in Walker, Michigan.

Noreen has been a member of Toastmasters International since 2006. She earned the Distinguished Toastmaster (DTM) award, the highest level of educational achievement in the organization. In August 2017, she competed at the Toastmasters International World Championship of Public Speaking in Vancouver, British Columbia, placing in the top twenty of over thirty thousand contestants with a speech dedicated to her mother, entitled "A Little Walk with Mom."

Noreen played piano and sang with Larry and His Larks polka band for twenty-five years, first with Larry and Joan as one of the original "larks," and then with husband Tom as drummer, and Larry's wife Jackie on the bass guitar.

Besides music, Noreen's interests include crocheting, a hobby she took up in 2016. She has since been on a quest to create a prayer blanket for each of her children and grandchildren. She calls them prayer blankets because she prays for the recipient of the blanket while she is crocheting it for them.

They have been members of the Parish of the Holy Spirit Catholic Church for more than forty years.

Noreen is a founding member of The Ed and Irene Fleis Education Fund.

*div.

Rita, Jim, and family, circa 2005
Left to right: Andy, Rita, Eric, Jim, and Laura

Rita was born in 1959 and married Jim Cwengros in 1979. They had three children: Eric (Roni), Andy (Bridget), and Laura, and nine grandchildren, five of them inherited through Eric's marriage: Randie, Jade (Austin), Jacie, Ryanne, Ralye, Jesse, and Esme, besides James, Nora, and Claire (children of Andy and Bridget). They also have three great-grandchildren: Damien, Charlotte, and Halston.

Rita and Jim were scoutmasters with the Boy Scouts of America long after their sons had finished. Rita had many community and school involvements in Grand Rapids, including West Catholic Band Boosters and football, Concerned Citizens from Covell to Collindale, and volunteering at the local medical clinics. Jim was involved with the Holy Spirit Church Ushers Club and the Five-Man Cigar Club.

Rita, a graduate of NMC, spent a number of years practicing as a registered nurse, and later was a regular volunteer at Health Intervention Services in Grand Rapids. Jim graduated with a bachelor's degree in pharmacy from Ferris State University, and later a doctor of pharmacy from the University of North Carolina. He originally started as a hospital pharmacist, and eventually became a clinical pharmacist involved as adjunct faculty with Ferris State, teaching for the pharmacy program. He then became a regional medical research specialist for Pfizer International.

Rita and Jim were very involved with their Catholic faith at Holy Spirit Church in Grand Rapids. It led them to a passion to serve with a medical mission team to assist yearly with Haiti's needs. Their lives were transformed as they talked about the people and how they hated to leave them behind. They adopted a Haitian family.

Sadly ...

Rita and Jim lost their lives together on January 11, 2013, serving the Lord on their mission to Seguin, Haiti. According to an article in the *Traverse City Record-Eagle*, they were traveling on a curvy, mountainous road, "when the brakes failed in their vehicle (driven by a Haitian driver who survived). Jim, 54, and Rita, 53, were among four missionaries from Holy Spirit Catholic Church in Grand Rapids killed on the way to the church's sister parish in the small mountain village of Sequin." They were making their fifth and third mission trips to Haiti, respectively, where they helped with dental and medical care, sanitation, and education.[86]

Rita's eleven siblings sang the "Song of Ruth" at their funeral on January 22, 2013, at Holy Spirit Catholic Church, Grand Rapids, that was previously sung at their wedding thirty-five years earlier.

"Wherever you go, I shall go; Wherever you live, so shall I live. Your people will be my people, and your God will be my God, too.

Wherever you die, I shall die; And there shall I be buried beside you. We will be together forever, and our love will be the gift of our lives." Ruth 1:16-17 (Their burial was at St. Philip's Cemetery, in Empire.)

Rita was a founding member of The Ed and Irene Fleis Education Fund. Her replacement is her son, Eric.

---

86   Marta Hepler Drahos, *Traverse City Record-Eagle*, January 18, 2013.

Appendix B

Mom's Siblings

Contribution from cousin Lucille:

Aunt Mabel was born in 1907. Mabel married Jacob (Jake) Rahe in 1934, at St. Mary's Church, Lake Leelanau. They had four children: Leonard (1936), Lucille (1940), Edward (1942), and Albert (1944).

Mabel loved to sew and made use of every scrap of fabric. She sewed quilts for her family and helped with quilting bees for the community and for St. Mary's Church in Kingsley. She also crocheted and played the organ, and sang many of the old songs. She loved going to parties and dancing.

Jake and Mabel both worked hard on their 140-acre family farm, milking cows and planting many crops to feed and sell. She canned all summer long to fill the shelves for the long winters.

Grandma Jennie and Grandpa Lugie moved in with them after Grandma had a stroke in June 1948. She could not walk or talk. It was in their home that Lugie suddenly died in December 1948. Mabel continued to take care of her mother until other family members took turns.

The Rahe farm, taken over by their grandson, is still in use. Uncle Jake died at ninety-two in 1987. Aunt Mabel died in 1993 at age eighty-six. Their son Leonard died in 2014 at the age of seventy-seven.[87]

Contributions from cousins, Luella and Alvin:

Uncle Clifford, "Cliff," born in 1910, received his lifetime teaching certificate from Western Michigan University in Kalamazoo. In 1933, Cliff married Theresa Gatzke at Holy Rosary Church. They had six children: Luella (1935), Eugene, "Gene" (1939), Cliff (1940), Alvin (1945), Sharone (1948), and James (1951).

---

87 *Lamie Book,* pp. 494-96.

Jacob Rahe family, circa 1984 (left to right): Albert, Lucille, Jacob, Mabel, Leonard, and Ed

Clifford Lamie family, circa 1981 (left to right): Alvin, Cliff, Luella, Jim with bride Sue, Theresa, Cliff, Sharone, and Gene

Benedict Lamie family, circa 1970 (left to right): Bobbie, Agnes, Ben, and Bonnie. Sitting: Jackie and Joyce.

Louis Lamie family, circa 1951 (left to right): Pauline holding Tom, Ed, Jerry, Don Desero, Louis holding Pat, Jude in front

Meda Lamie family, circa 1973 (left to right): Bob, Gertrude, Judy, Meda, Carol, and Larry

Joseph Harpe family, circa 1961. Standing (left to right): Eva, Jerry, Faye with husband Arnold, Gary, and Joseph. Sitting: Lucille, Ron, and Joseph.

Cliff taught at Martin School in Provemont (Lake Leelanau) for several years, and afterward, at a small school in Benzie County. His youngest sister, Lucille, born in 1922, was a student of Cliff's from fourth through seventh grade at Martin School.

It was quite a surprise when Alvin, their son, visited the Benzie County Museum and discovered a glass case with a tiny display featuring a graduation class photo that identified his dad, "L'ami," (misspelled) as the teacher.

During World War II, some of Cliff's relatives were working at the Willow Run Bomber Plant located east of Ypsilanti, Michigan. They contacted him and told him that they were "making money hand over fist. Come down and join us." So, Cliff wasted no time and moved his family down to Willow Run, where he worked there as a B-24 bomber inspector.

While working, he met a man from Marlette who owned a heating and refrigeration business and was ready for retirement. Cliff decided that was what he wanted to do. In 1939, he received a diploma from the Chicago Refrigeration and Air Conditioning Institute, and took a correspondence course learning how to install furnaces. In the spring of 1945, they moved to Marlette, Michigan.

Cliff's business started in his home, and after purchasing and renovating a bowling alley on Main Street, he named his store "Lamie Refrigeration and Heating." Theresa helped with the bookwork. His brother Med tended the store for a few years while he installed furnaces and made refrigeration service calls.

Marlette was surrounded by dairy farmers who stored milk in tall milk cans. When refrigeration would go out, they called Cliff to repair the problem. He also repaired refrigeration in grocery stores and beer taverns.

Cliff was tremendously busy and many times arrived home very late in the evening. Since he was the one who ran errands for the family, he told Theresa one day, "You need to learn how to drive a car!" So, she learned on his old-fashioned panel truck; then they bought her a car to drive.

When Cliff and Theresa were talking about retirement, he called the Teachers Association to apply for a teacher's pension. They told him if he worked two more years, he would get much more money on his pension. So, Cliff applied and got a teaching job in a one-room schoolhouse twenty-five miles from Marlette, where he taught grades one through eight. He then taught one more year in a school six miles west of Marlette.

"He was known as 'the last male country school teacher,'" said Alvin, their son.

In retirement, Cliff and Theresa enjoyed winters at Ocklawaha, Florida, and summers at Crystal Lake, Michigan, besides their main residence in Marlette.

Uncle Cliff died of a stroke in 1981 at the age of seventy-one. Aunt Theresa died in 1990 at the age of seventy-eight. Their son Cliff died in 2016. Luella died in 2021. [88]

Contributions from cousins, Joyce and Jackie, and Joyce's daughter, Shari Lynn:

Uncle Benedict, "Ben," was born in 1912. He played the clarinet and spoke articulately. He attended Ferris Institute in Big Rapids, where he earned his teaching certificate in 1932.

Ben married Agnes Nowak in 1935, at St. Mary's Church in Lake Leelanau. They had four daughters: Bonnie (1936), Barbara (1940), Joyce (1945), and Jacalyn (Jackie) (1948).

He taught two years at East Kasson School in Maple City, and then at the Solon School until 1942. When World War II was full-blown in 1942, Ben was exempt due to a back injury from falling from the barn's hayloft at his parents' farm; but that didn't stop him from working for the war effort at the Willow Run bomber plant, and then at a defense plant in Romulus from 1944 to 1945.

After the war, he and Agnes settled in Wayne, Michigan. Agnes was a stay-at-home mother who enjoyed embroidery, mending, and making alterations to clothing. Ben worked twenty years as a tool machine operator for Shadick Tool and Die in Dearborn, and later for Parker Hannifin in Plymouth.

"When he was forty years old, he threw his cigarettes out one day and quit smoking," his daughter, Jackie, said. "And did the same with alcohol. He was particularly proud of his association with Alcoholics Anonymous, which began in 1955 and lasted the rest of his lifetime of twenty years. He died at age sixty-two, just seven months before my parents' fortieth wedding anniversary in 1975."

"God's glory allowed sobriety to come about, along with the work, to get sober," said his granddaughter, Shari Lynn.

His daughter, Joyce, agreed. "His faith was very important," she added. "He prayed on his knees every morning and night and never missed mass. Without that faith, he may never have found sobriety."

"Ben would write, 'Gratitude is the highest form of praise,' at the end of letters he wrote when I lived in Florida," recalled Jackie, his daughter.

Ben also took his surname seriously. "Because the word 'Lamie' means a 'friend,'" Joyce remarked, "he wanted to honor that."

Aunt Agnes died in 2010 at ninety-seven.[89]

---

88 *Lamie Book,* minimal info, pp. 505–506.
89 *Lamie Book,* minimal info, pp. 517–18.

Contributions from cousins, Edward and Jude:

Uncle Louis, "Louie," born in 1914, left home in his late teens and joined the CCC (Civilian Conservation Corps) near Gaylord, Michigan. They had him doing forestry work and cutting timber all over the Upper Peninsula for two or three years.

In 1940, Louis married Pauline Harrand at St. Mary's Church in Hannah. They had five sons: Edward (1941), Jerry (1943), Jude (1945), Patrick (1949), and Thomas (1950). They also had a foster son, Don Desero.

For a few years, Louie and Pauline lived in Detroit, where he worked on the Willow Run B-24 Liberator assembly line in Ypsilanti, while Pauline worked there as a riveter ("Rosie the Riveter").

They returned to northern Michigan in 1944 and purchased his parents' (Lugie and Jennie Lamie's) farm on French Road. There, Louie raised potatoes, oats, wheat, and corn.

After selling the farm in 1967 to Rich Kohler from Suttons Bay, they moved to Traverse City, where both had jobs: Louie sold industrial brushes and Electrolux vacuum cleaners; Pauline worked as a nurse's aide at the Traverse City State Hospital after taking a nursing course.

Over time, the family suffered two tragic automobile accidents. The first resulted in the death of their son Patrick in 1968, when he was nineteen. Yet, like a couple of his brothers, Louie found sobriety in the AA program the year Patrick died. Tragically, just two years later, Uncle Louie died as the result of another car accident. He was fifty-six.

Pauline suffered serious injury in that accident. Yet, as hard as that was, her son Jude remembers her saying, "Losing your husband is nothing like losing a child."

Pauline remained a widow for a few years. "My mother was remarkably strong," Jude remarked. She married Reubin LaBonte from Traverse City in 1972. They were married for twenty-five years until he died in 2007. Another loss occurred when Don Desero, their foster son, died in 2015, preceding Aunt Pauline's death in 2017 at ninety-six.[90]

Contributions from cousins Bob and Carolyn:

Uncle Meda, "Med," was born in 1919. He married Gertrude Popa in 1941 in Detroit. Their four children are: Robert "Bob" (1942), Carolyn (1943), Lawrence (1944), and Judith (1945).

Med wore thick lenses all his life. When he registered for the draft during World War II, he was classified "4F" due to bad eyesight. When Med and Gertrude moved to Marlette, he worked a few years for Cliff, his brother, at Lamie Refrigeration and Heating.

---

90   *Lamie Book*, minimal info, pp. 521-22.

When he and Gertrude decided to go elsewhere, they moved to Traverse City.

Med worked for Parts Manufacturing in Traverse City and later "had the best job for the money," as he would say, "at Cone-Drive Gears [Textron]," a machine shop in Traverse City, where he worked until he retired. He also operated a refrigeration repair business on the side. Med was a member of the Knights of Columbus.

Gertrude worked some summers at Cherry Growers, Inc., in Traverse City, and was a volunteer with the Father Fred Foundation. She received a service award for her volunteerism from the Grand Traverse Medical Care Facility (now Grand Traverse Pavilions).

Their daughter, Carolyn, remarked that two great personal achievements Med accomplished were that "he quit smoking after a heart attack in his fifties, and living the life of sobriety the last twenty years." Like his brother Ben, Med was a faithful member of AA. She said, "The name Lamie means 'a friend.'" He wanted to honor that, as did his brother Ben.

Uncle Med died in 1991 at age seventy-two, and Aunt Gertrude at eighty-five in 2008. Their son, Larry, died in 2021.[91]

Contribution from cousin Faye:

Aunt Lucille, born in 1922, was taught by her brother Clifford in grades four through seven at Martin School. In 1941, Lucille married Joseph Harpe at St. Mary's Church in Lake Leelanau, Michigan. They had six children: Faye (1942), Gerald (1944), Gary (1946), Eva (1950), Joseph (1952), and Ronald (1959).

For many years, they lived in and around the Traverse City area. They started and operated several businesses, including: Green Acres Dairy, Harpe's Homemade Ice Cream, and Dollar Sanitation. Lucille also worked as a switchboard operator at the Traverse City State Bank, currently known as Fifth Third Bank.

In 1968, they suffered a tragedy when their son Joseph, age fifteen, died in a drowning accident in West Grand Traverse Bay. In 1990, they moved to St. Mary's, Kansas, where they became members of the Assumption Chapel Parish.

Uncle Joe died in 2001, at age eighty-four. Aunt Lucille died in 2010 at age eighty-eight. Their son, Gary, died in 2021. Another son, Gerald, died in 2022.[92]

---

91   *Lamie Book*, minimal info, pp. 556–557.
92   The Lamie family lineage is contained in the *Lamy/Lami/Lemay/Lamie Book*, authored by Eunice (Lamie) Novak and Lucia Novak in 1994.

Appendix C

Dad's Siblings

Leo and Betty Fleis, circa 1950s
(photo from Linda Schulte)

Susan Fleis, circa 1970s
(photo from Linda Schulte)

Roman and Virginia
Fleis, circa 1974

Roman and Virginia's children, circa 2005. (Left to right):
Sharon, Kasia, Sandy, and Roman Jr.

Albion Fleis family, circa 1979. Standing (left
to right): Ruth, George, Thelma, and Al. Sitting:
Phyllis and Albion

Thomas Fleis family, circa early 1970s.
Standing (left to right): Mary, Terry,
Patti, John, Tom Jr., Steve, Joe, Dorothy,
Daniel, and Rose. Sitting: Betty, Barbara,
Margie, Nancy, and Thomas

Sister Mary Therese,
circa mid 1960s

Clemence Fleis family, circa 1979. Standing (left to
right): Steven, Christine, Linda, DiAnne, Geraldine, and
Wayne. Sitting: RoseMarie, Margaret, and Clemence

Joseph Fleis family, circa 2005. Standing
(left to right): Camille, David, Karen, Dennis,
Donna, and Agnes. Front: Lucille and Joe

Boniface Rosinski family, circa 1981.
Standing (left to right): Jerry, Allen, Robert,
Maria, and Tommy. Sitting: Theresa and Bob

Ron Williams family, circa 2006. Standing (left to
right): Cindy, Agnes, Joe, Ron, Greg, and Susan.

Anthony Fleis family, circa 2002. Standing (left to right):
Patricia, Patrick, Angela, and Caroline. Sitting: Raymond,
Antoinette, and Tony. (photo from Linda Schulte)

Uncle Leo, born in 1913, married Betty Lamie in 1945. They resided in Traverse City throughout their lifetime.

Leo worked for Grand Traverse Metal Casket Company and Parsons Corporation. Aunt Betty worked for United Technology as a factory worker for seventeen years. He was a member of the Knights of Columbus—Council 1213, the VFW Cherryland Post 2780, and the Traverse City Senior Center.

Uncle Leo died from respiratory failure in 1994 at age eighty-one, and Aunt Betty in 2001 at seventy-five. They had no children.[93]

Contribution from Aunt Theresa (Fleis) Rosinski:

Aunt Susie, born in 1916, lived in Ann Arbor, beginning in 1950. She appreciated having the convenience of a Catholic church near her apartment. She drove little, and was employed as a factory worker. She crocheted and would sell some of her things. Aunt Theresa and Uncle Bob looked after her as she had serious health issues with asthma, emphysema, and spine issues that required shots.

In 1970, she returned to Traverse City. Aunt Susie died from respiratory failure in 1976 at the age of sixty. She never married.

Contributions from cousins Kasia and Sharon:

Uncle Roman, born in 1918, married Virginia Radomski in 1946. They made their home in Milwaukee, Wisconsin, and were parents of four children: Kasia (1947), Roman (1951), Sharon (1956), and Sandra (1966).

Beginning in 1946 and until 1974, Roman owned and operated Roman's Watch Hospital, which later was named Roman's Jewelers. He was the main horologist and jewelry salesman. Virgie was the internal accountant and managed all the finances and inventory. While maintaining the business, they purchased Rainbow Cottages near Cedar in 1972 on a trip back home to Michigan. Their oldest daughter, Kasia, managed the cottage business from 1972 to 1974.

In 1974, Roman and Virgie retired and moved to Cedar to manage Rainbow Cottages. He was a fourth-degree Knights of Columbus member with Council 1213, a past president of Cedar/

---

93   "Fleis Descendants," compiled by Linda (Fleis) Schulte.

Maple City Lions Club, and a member of the Cedar Chamber of Commerce. For five years, he drove the Glen Lake school bus.

When Uncle Roman passed away in 1981 from cancer at age sixty-three, Rainbow Cottages was sold, and Aunt Virgie moved back to Milwaukee, Wisconsin, where she lived until she passed away in 1985, at age sixty-one. Their son, Roman, died in 2020.

Contributions from Aunt Phyllis and her daughter, Ruth Ann:

Uncle Al, born in 1920, married Phyllis Richard in 1948. They made their home in Westland, Michigan, and were parents of four children: Albin (1949), Thelma (1951), George (1954), and Ruth Ann (1959), my godchild.

As a young man, Al earned a business degree in Traverse City. His first job was working as an accountant. He was employed as a desk clerk for thirty years at Penn Walt Chemical Factory, in Wyandotte, Michigan.

Phyllis enjoyed being a homemaker and a stay-at-home mom. She also worked as a volunteer with the Notre Dame Shamrocks, a group of women who worked tirelessly for Boysville of Michigan. She loves to crochet, and embroiders on pillowcases at age ninety-three.

Uncle Al died in 1980 from brain cancer at age sixty. Aunt Phyllis enjoys the caring and friendship of her children and all of her younger generations.

Contribution from cousin Dorothy:

Uncle Tom, born in 1922, married Betty Equitz in 1947. They had thirteen children: Nancy (1944), Barbara (1947), twins, Theresa and Thomas Jr. (1949), Steven (1951), John (1952), Dorothy (1953), Joseph (1954), Margaret (1955), Patricia (1956), Daniel (1958), Mary (1960), and Rosemary (1962).

In 1962, Tom moved his family to Traverse City after being a farmer at the O'Brien farm, which they had owned since 1948. For a short time he worked for my dad's construction business. He then worked as a carpenter for Tezak Construction and Grand Traverse Construction before forming his own business, Fleis Builders, which he operated for twenty years. Aunt Betty worked as a seamstress for Tru-Fit Trousers.

Tom, as a military veteran, was a member of VFW Cherryland Post 2780, and the American Military League. Betty's favorite pastime was playing bingo.

Uncle Tom died of cancer and cirrhosis in 1993 at seventy-one. Aunt Betty lived a long life and died in 2019 at age ninety-two. Their family suffered the losses of Thomas Jr. in 1972, John in 2003, Steven in 2017, Margaret in 2017, and Nancy in 2021.

Contribution from cousin Linda:

Uncle Clem, born in 1923, married RoseMarie Radomski in 1947. They lived in Milwaukee, Wisconsin, most of their lives. They had seven children: Linda (1949), Christine (1950), Wayne (1952), DiAnne (1955), Stephen (1957), Geraldine (1959), and Margaret (1961).

Beginning in 1953 and until 1983, Clem served two weeks each year in the US Army Reserves. He was discharged as a master sergeant E8. He was a life member and past adjutant of the American Veterans Post No. 60 and retired from the Army Reserves after thirty years as master sergeant of the 84th Regiment-84th Division.

While serving in the Army Reserves, he earned a watchmaker's license and worked for his brother Roman's watch shop full-time for twenty-two years. Due to family needs, he needed a better benefit package, and was then employed by PPG Industries as a store manager for thirteen years.

From 1967 to 1984, RoseMarie worked as a nurse's aide in the nursery at St. Francis Hospital. She then worked part-time as a temporary home-health aide for a few years.

Uncle Clem had pancreatic cancer. He died in 1985, at the age of sixty-one. Their son, Stephen, died at the age of thirty-seven, in 1994. Aunt RoseMarie died in 2018, at age ninety.

Aunt Irene "Sister Therese," born in 1925, entered the Felician Order of Nuns at Madonna Academy in Livonia in 1943. After her profession of vows, she served as a teacher and organist. In 1960, she received a master's of music degree from the University of Notre Dame.

She taught elementary grades at Catholic schools in Detroit, Plymouth, Hilliards, Parisville, Saginaw, Jackson, Hamtramck, Wyandotte, and Livonia. Her last teaching assignment was at St. Andrew's High School in Detroit. Sister Therese spent twenty-four years in religious life before a tragic car crash took her life in May 1967 at age forty-one.

(In a school article, a student said this about her: "Sister Therese taught us that there is good in the world, we just have to do our part to find it.")

Contributions from cousins Donna and Dennis:

Uncle Joe, born in 1927, married Lucille Zywicki in 1955. They were lifelong residents of Cedar, where they had six children: Agnes (1956), David (1957), Karen (1963), Donna (1966), Dennis (1968), and Camille (1974).

Joe got his start in construction and masonry, working for my dad's construction business. He and Dad worked side-by-side when building his ranch-style brick home. In 1958, Joe started working for Ben Hohnke Construction, which was bought out by Easling Construction in 1980, and worked until 1989. After retiring from Easling, he worked ten years for Bill Walters. His creative stonework can be seen in homes and businesses throughout Leelanau County. Lucille worked at the Sara Lee Bakery in Traverse City for over twenty-five years.

Joe was an avid sports fan; he loved the Detroit Tigers, Lions, and Pistons.

He was a member of the Knights of Columbus for forty years, and became a fourth-degree member with Council 1213. Lucille was a lifetime member of the Ladies' Rosary Society. In 1996, they endured the loss of their son David due to lymphoma. Aunt Lucille died in 2006 of the same cancer, at the age of seventy. Uncle Joe lived a long, fulfilled life until his death at age ninety-two in 2020.

Contribution from Aunt Theresa:

Aunt Theresa, born in 1930, married Boniface "Bob" Rosinski in 1950. Their first home in Detroit was the home of Bob's parents, Andrew and Eufrozyna (Zena) Rosinski, which they purchased in 1953, not quite two years after the death of Bob's father. His mother lived with them for another twenty-five years. They had five children: Allen (1951), Gerald (1952), Maria (1955), Robert (1958), and Thomas (1964).

Theresa worked for the Internal Revenue Service for sixteen years. Bob, as a successful salesman at First General Binding Corporation, won a trip in 1973 to Norway and Sweden, and Theresa went with him.

She began to have health problems on the flight over. When the plane ascended or descended, she lost her hearing. Otherwise, everything was fine. Soon, however, she couldn't taste anything except for smoked fish, so she went to a doctor. A myelogram revealed she had a brain tumor, called an acoustic neuroma, the size of a plum, which they had to surgically remove. Though she lost her hearing in her left ear, couldn't close her eyes for a long time, still had double vision and constant blinking in a very dry left eye, dealt with facial paralysis, lost her sense of taste for an extended time, and her weight receded to one hundred pounds, she considered it a miracle to survive such an ordeal.

After surgery, she discovered her taste buds again after someone brought in a large box of cookies, which seemed to be ten pounds, she said. "I ate them all in a week and gained some weight back."

One year, when she and Bob attended a class reunion, a classmate of his made kielbasa for the event. Theresa loved it. She had been used to eating good meat when she lived in Cedar and never liked any of the meats in Detroit. It took a while for the classmate's mother to part with the recipe, but Theresa has been making kielbasa ever since. "Every year I got better at it," she said. It's become a family tradition as more family members help, but she is still the boss and tells everyone what to do. In 2019, they prepared 160 pounds, which was all shared amongst the family. At age ninety-one, she still assisted with the seasonings.

Bob did co-partner in a business called Duplicating Sales, where he sold and repaired copy machines, before he retired.

"On August 4, 2005, [the dear heart of] my loving husband, my children's dad, [and] my grandchildren stopped beating at the age of seventy-seven," said Theresa. "He left emptiness, but left many wonderful memories. His favorite song was 'Let Me Call You Sweetheart,' which he sang many times to his grandchildren and to me."

Though Theresa's left eye still gives her problems, and she never regained hearing in her left ear and has a half smile, she still says, "Life is good." Aunt Theresa was ninety-two years of age in 2022.

Sadly, her son Thomas died in 2020 due to colon cancer.

Contribution from Uncle Ron:

Aunt Agnes, born in 1934, married (Carl) Ron Williams in 1956. He had recently returned from serving in the US Air Force during and following the Korean War. They made their home in Cedar. They had five children: Carolyn (born in 1957 with an open spine, she died at eight months), Susan (1958), Cynthia (1959), Gregory (1963), and Joseph (1965).

Agnes, who had started a band, Agnes and Her Polka Dotz, in 1973, retired in 1998. She had taught herself to play the accordion, guitar, banjo, harmonica, piano, and organ, and was a vocalist and cantor at St. Rita's Church in Maple City. Even after developing dementia in her eighties, her music continued at home, as did her practice of attending daily mass at Holy Rosary Church with her husband, where she was a lifetime member of the Ladies' Rosary Society.

Ron worked twenty-three years for Traverse City Iron Works, then established Williams Pumping in 1983. Agnes helped Ron with reception and scheduling duties. He sold the business to his son Joe in 1993. Joe in turn sold the business in 2017 to True North Environmental Corporation of Leelanau and Grand Traverse Counties. Ron served as Solon Township clerk, supervisor, and township assessor, and was a member of the Cedar Chamber of Commerce. He also was a Knights of Columbus member.

Uncle Ron died on February 17, 2022, at age eighty-nine, and Aunt Agnes three weeks later on March 11, at age eighty-seven.

Uncle Tony, born in 1936, married Patricia (Pat) Barczak, in 1962. They left Wisconsin sometime later after purchasing Grandpa's home near Centerville Township Hall in 1965. They had five children: Angela (1963), Antoinette (1965), Raymond (1966), Carolyn (1970), and Patrick (1973).

Tony was nicknamed "Stroh's" early on because of his favorite beer. He was a long-time member of the Cedar's Hilltoppers Snowmobile Club. He worked on projects and played cards. For a number of years, he worked for my dad's construction business. Later, he worked at Cone Drive Gear, a machine shop in Traverse City.

Pat was Leelanau County's Avon lady, selling products for forty years, besides working as a hostess at the Bluebird Restaurant in Leland and Applebee's in Traverse City.

They were long-time members of Holy Rosary Parish.

Uncle Tony died in 2003, at age sixty-seven, of renal failure due to diabetes. Aunt Pat died unexpectedly in 2012, at age sixty-nine.[94]

---

94   The full lineage of Fleis descendants has been compiled by Linda (Fleis) Schulte.

Appendix D

Mortgage Contract, Dated December 5, 1911

Thomas Flies Jr., and Agnes Flies, his wife

to: Tomas Flies Sr. and Josephine Flies, his wife

A declaration within the mortgage agreement stated provisions for their needs at the home place: "one large room and a bedroom, storage room in the cellar, storage room for wood in the woodshed and a passageway for getting water from the well and rainwater. First parties [Thomas and Agnes] are to keep the well and cistern in good repair, and second parties [Tomasz and Jozefina] are to have privilege of using said water from the well and cistern at all times, for as long as they shall live."

Then the remaining part of the mortgage contract took effect: [Thomas and Agnes] to furnish..."25 cords of sound and dry 18-inch body block wood each year, 30 bushels of good eating potatoes each year, one dressed hog to weigh at least 200 pounds each year, one hundred pounds of good beef each year, two barrels of good marketable apples each year, and privilege of early apples, cherries, plums and other fruits for their own use each year. Two pounds of good butter and two dozen fresh eggs each week, and one-bushel of good onions each year. A plot of ground of two acres for a garden to be selected by second parties on any of the lands above described and first parties are to prepare and manure the same each year and about one-quarter of an acre to be prepared by May 15, and the balance by June 1 of each year. One quart of good fresh milk each day. Four barrels of good wheat flour each year (one-third of this to be a gold Medal brand flour). One hundred pounds of granulated sugar each year, 25 pounds of 25 cent coffee each year and 15 pounds of 40 cent tea and five dollars' worth of good soup each year.

First parties [Thomas and Agnes] to pay for the repairs of a dwelling house in Traverse City, Mich at 446 Elmwood Ave. not to exceed the sum of $150.00 and $25.00 in cash each year or to the survivor of either of them. First parties to furnish on demand to the second parties [Tomasz and Jozefina] a horse and buggy or sleigh or two horses and wagons and sleighs to do any kind of work or drawing etc. ... and to pay expense[s] of a wedding for the daughter, Suzanna and to give her a good, milk cow at that time," etc.

Appendix E

Reflection on the Service of the Four Fleis Nuns

Daughters of Tomasz and Jozefina Fleis (left to right): Sr. Damascene (Agnes), Sr. Leontine (Josephine), Sr. Augustine (Elizabeth), and Sr. Faber Rose (Rose)

All four sisters entered the Felician community in Detroit from Holy Rosary Parish, Isadore. Each one of them had developed musical abilities which were inspired in their family circle.

Sister Mary Leontine, CSSF (Congregation of Sisters of St. Felix), was the first of the family to respond to Christ's invitation to a consecrated life. At the age of eighty-six, she had served sixty-eight years in religious life. She was a teacher for fifty-one years, and both a teacher and superior for ten years in twenty schools in the states of Michigan, Pennsylvania, Ohio, Minnesota, Wisconsin, and Illinois. When her health compelled her to retire from the active apostolate, she spent six years in our Lady of Good Counsel Infirmary—a woman of prayer. On January 2, 1973, the divine spouse called her to sing His praises with the angels and saints in heaven. Her body was laid to rest in St. Adalbert Cemetery in Niles, Illinois.[95]

Sister Mary Faber Rose, CSSF, was the youngest nun of the family. Her religious life of sixty-three years exemplified that the ordinary realities of everyday life, when assumed in the spirit of the gospel, can become powerful reflections of Christ's own harmony and joy. She served in the capacity of an organist and teacher in the Catholic schools of Illinois, Nebraska, Wisconsin, Missouri, Kansas, and Minnesota. She was also a superior and principal in St. Joseph, Missouri; St. Paul, Minnesota; Posen, Illinois; and Marinette, Wisconsin. During her last four years, before becoming seriously ill with cancer, Sister Faber Rose brought cheer and comfort to many patients at St. Mary's Hospital in Centralia, Illinois, as a pastoral associate. The serenity of her smile portrayed her internal peace and joy in God's service. She was eighty years of age when called to be with the Lord on October 7, 1978.

Sister Mary Damascene, CSSF, was a beloved member of the Felician Community of Sisters for seventy-three years. She entered a consecrated life after four years of education at St. Francis High School in Detroit, Michigan, graduating in 1907. The following year, she was appointed to the apostolate of teaching in the elementary schools of various dioceses, also as an organist or music teacher, and as a superior for eight years. These assignments took her to the states of Pennsylvania, Michigan, Illinois, Missouri, Texas, Wisconsin, and Nebraska. True concern for the youth characterized her encounters with the students. Consequently, she was not only a teacher of intellectual endeavor, but a moral influence on those she met. After sixty years of involvement in the active apostolate, and increasing pain-filled days caused by arthritis, diabetes, and kidney failure, Sister Damascene spent thirteen years in Our Lady of Good Counsel Infirmary, Chicago, Illinois. She was ninety years of age when she was called by the Lord for eternal rest, on September 10, 1981. Her burial was at St. Adalbert's Cemetery, Niles, Illinois.[96]

---

95   Sister Leontine kept up correspondence with her brother, John Fleis, in Poland and provided food and clothing for his family during the war.

96   Researched by Sister Mary Adolphine Kzioszk, CSSF archival associate, Mother of Good Counsel Providence, Chicago, Illinois, per Grace Marie Del Priore.

Sister Mary Augustine, CSSF, had ninety-one years of fruitful life. A pioneer sister of the Chicago Province, she was one of the first nuns who came to Chicago when the young province was formed in 1910. She had a varied apostolate, being a teacher from first through eighth grades; a principal; a superior; and an organist in Illinois and Wisconsin. She was a kind and motherly superior, never wanting to hurt any of the sisters in speech or action. She played the organ and sang in church. She also taught music to children, and helped them praise the Lord. She taught elementary grades from 1913 to 1968 in Wisconsin and Illinois, including at Sacred Heart, Holy Innocents, St. Helen, St. John of God, and St. Turibius in Chicago. In 1982, she went to the infirmary because of illness. Here too she was kind and always prayed the rosary. On June 6, 1984, Sister Mary Augustine joined her three sisters, who preceded her in death, to rest in God's joy and peace. (She was the nun who visited my parents in Florida when Dad had surgery in 1979.)

Appendix F

Memories of John Fleis Sr., Minikowo, Poland

John Fleis Sr. is the son of my great-grandparents, Tomasz and Jozefina. He migrated to Minikowo, Poland, at age eighteen (around 1898), so his Aunt Anna Fleis could come to Isadore. He eventually claimed the farm of ancestors [his grandparents], Thomas and Anna Fleis. He never returned to Isadore. John and his wife, Emma, had four children: Irena, Adele, John Jr., and Klemens.

German Invasion

Story from Krystyna, granddaughter of John Fleis, in September 1996:

John Sr. and Emma Fleis's granddaughters, Krystyna and Halina, were ages ten and fourteen, respectively, when Germany invaded Poland. The girls lived with their parents, Maximillian and Irena (Fleis) Babinski, in Plowce, a small village in north-central Poland.

As the German army advanced, the family retreated with the Polish army to the east, beyond Warsaw. When the Russians entered Poland from the east, the resistance ended. Krystyna's father (Maximillian) was arrested for his activity with the Partisans and taken to a German prison, and her mother, Irena, and the two girls returned to their abandoned home in the village of Plowce. There, the family was forced to board a German laborer, having to cook, clean his quarters, and wash for him.

Meanwhile, the Germans displaced her grandparents, John Sr. and Emma (Fleis), from their farm in Minikowo, which was well kept up in good condition, including a large remodeled house, stables for horses and cows, and a large wooden barn for grain, and replaced them with a German by name of Neibauer. They also arrested their oldest son John Jr., and sent him to a German prison for forced labor. A younger son, Klemens, was a teen, and allowed to stay with his parents in a small old home that had a small plot of land in the town of Lubrza.

When the Russians drove the Germans from the area, John Sr. and Emma returned to the farm in 1945, and began farming with nothing. They left not one cow, not one pig, and not one horse. Not even a chicken. They left the emaciated family dog that refused to go with the Germans.

As the battles raged between the Germans and Russians, Krystyna's parents' [Maximillian and Irena] home was destroyed by bombing, and the family was left with only the clothes on their backs, two pillows, and a salvaged white tablecloth.

Krystyna's Uncle Klemens came after them and brought the family to grandfather John Fleis Sr.'s farm in Minikowo. (The horse that her uncle came with was so emaciated that he could hardly stand up. He held the bridle so that the horse would not fall down. As they proceeded toward the farm, the Russians took the horse away from them. Later, Uncle Klemens bought the horse back for four cigarettes.)

In the evening, Krystyna's mother would wash the clothes, and they wore them the next day. This lasted for quite a while until one day, a nun came to the house from the convent in Wislawku, asking for some cloth to put on the altar in church, since they did not have any to put there for the Blessed Virgin Mary.

Her mother remembered that she had this tablecloth, and even though she wanted to make some shirts for her and her sister from the material, she gave it to the nun, and was not sorry, because she honored the Blessed Virgin Mary.

Her mother wrote to America, to Thomas Fleis (brother of John Fleis, Sr.), who was on the family farm (in Isadore, Michigan) and who distributed the letter to read, and it came to the attention of Sister Leontine, and she wrote back to them. The gift of the tablecloth to the convent turned into a repayment. Not long after, Sister Leontine sent them a big package of clothes and coats that were needed for the winter. Thus, for so little did the Blessed Mother Mary repay them. Other packages soon arrived and thus they were able to be clothed and fed.

It was because of this gesture that Krystyna attributes the survival and return of her father (Maximillian) and Uncle (John Jr.) from German prisons. John Jr. got a job as a forester. Thanks to the money he earned from this job , it was possible to buy some things. Later, Uncle Klemens, the youngest, was also imprisoned by the Russians for forbidden activity, and he also returned safely and worked on his father's farm.

Both John Jr. and Klemens died relatively young, at ages fifty-five and fifty-four, respectively, from their ordeals.

The grandparents, John and Emma Fleis, lived to celebrate their fiftieth wedding anniversary on the farm for which he suffered much. John Sr. died at age ninety-four and is buried alongside his beloved Emma.

John Fleis in Poland with a granddaughter (photo from Ray Brzezinski)

Krystyna's closing remarks:

"Thus, we lived with the good and bad. We all felt sorry for our grandfather, John Sr., who was homesick for America. From his stories, I could tell where he used to walk, where the woods were, where there were streams and where he crossed the bridges. He endured with love and was kind-hearted to his family and of goodwill to every person. Grandmother also had a big heart and was generous to all people, and was the greatest and best grandmother to us.

"In his stead, I was delighted and glad to see those relatives, Paul and Jean Brzezinski, from Traverse City, Michigan, that stood around the grave of Grandfather John Fleis, and placed a handful of soil brought from America, on which soil he was born,

"I thank everyone in memory of my grandfather, John Fleis; I am wishing the best to all the relatives in America," concludes Krystyna.

John Fleis Sr. and his wife and children kept up an occasional correspondence with his brothers, sisters, and cousins in America, until his death in 1972.

The brothers and sisters of John had worried about him as a brother who was living one crisis after another, including having to survive two world wars and occupations by Germans and Russians. The correspondence was very infrequent and censored.

Butch and Nancy Brzezinski and Janet Brzezinski, traveled with Paul and Jean Brzezinski in August 2000 to visit the homeland of our ancestors.

Acknowledgments

The idea of writing a family book was first presented to all of my siblings while sitting around a table after a board meeting of The Ed & Irene Fleis Education Fund. I wanted their support and their stories. Everyone agreed. My sister, Rita, was the first to submit her stories in the summer of 2012, only months prior to her tragic accident in Haiti.

I'm thankful for my sister, Joanie. She came on board to help me in the spring of 2018, after retiring from Munson Hospital's Hearing Clinic in Traverse City. Her encouraging words, "I will stay with you until the end," meant the world to me. Since then, "Life has thrown us curves," she said, "and in spite of having ups and downs with our health, we've succeeded until the end!" Joanie was a computer whiz! She showed me how to "cut and paste" among other techniques. She digitalized documents, critiqued, made phone calls, researched, read, and reread all of the stories. In 2019, we were excited when she became a grandmother for the first time, then a second time in 2020, and a third time in 2022. I expect she'll be telling many of these stories to her precious grandchildren, Cabrini, Jack, and Henry.

My sister Bernadette joined us next. She spent time reading and editing the manuscript. Another sister, Noreen, offered more suggestions. My dear friend, Sylvia Kievit-Milan, read and edited as well.

Initially, Gloria Lyon assisted with organization, followed by Peggy Byland, who created the idea of a book with several pages and photos. Later, Linda Alice Dewey, a professional editor, created chapters for the book.

My youngest brother, Larry, scanned all the photos, assisted by his daughter, Chelsea. His new scanner had the technology of restoring old photos. Chelsea, my daughter Mary Lou, and Tom Collins assisted with restoration and editing of some photos. Joanie was super involved again with the huge project of selecting them. Some photos came from my cousin, Linda Schulte.

Thank you, everyone (some of whom are deceased), for your contributions of a single story or more ... a biography, a military story, a community story, or another kind.

To Mom: Your short stories of family history in the *Lamy-Lami-Lemay-Lamie Book* were helpful in creating a larger story.

To Dad: The biography you wrote in a letter to me in January of 2000 was a total surprise! I believe your motivation to do so came after receiving the book *The Story of a Lifetime* from your granddaughter, Janice (my daughter). You accomplished what we started in the fall of 1999, when you only answered a few questions in your book.

To my son, Steve, for encouraging me to keep on writing when giving me the plaque: "Home is where your story begins."

To the unknown customer at Cedar Tavern in Leelanau County for telling her waitress, Christine (my daughter), "I have something for your mom," and handed her a *Leelanau Enterprise* article, "Love and War in the Homeland" (2000) about my Fleis great-grandparents.

I am grateful for the stories told at a Fleis family reunion in 2012 by Uncle Joe Fleis, Aunt Theresa (Fleis) Rosinski, and Aunt Agnes (Fleis) Williams, and for the ones we solicited from Aunt Phyllis Fleis and Uncle Ron Williams.

I am thankful for cousin Edward Lamie's research of Lamy (Lamie) great-grandparents, which added interesting elements to their story besides other documentation.

Thanks to cousin Don Pleva for stories he learned from his father, my Great Uncle Adam Pleva, and to cousin Ray Pleva for his interview and a scrapbook he loaned for the story of the 1983 Cedar River Project. (Ray and Don are my first cousins, once removed.)

I thank my sisters and brothers: Julie Watkoski, Edward Fleis, Mary Jane Steup, Ted Fleis, Jim Fleis, Bernadette Denoyer, Larry Fleis, Shirley Mikowski, Joan Gauthier, Noreen Savage, and Rita Cwengros. Thank you to my sisters and brothers-in-law: Barbara Fleis, Doris Fleis, Dale Gauthier, Ken Denoyer, Tom Savage, Roger Steup, and Ray Watkoski. And to my children: Steve Thompson, Janice Barr, Ed Thompson, Mary Lou Rachel, Victoria Nicholls, Donald Thompson, and Christine Thompson.

Thank you to nieces and nephews: Diane Pelak, Debra Bizon, Dawn Rosinski, Jeffrey Fleis, Jerry Fleis, Shelly Mackinnon, Brian Fleis, Becky Sordelet, Jenny Enrietto, Maureen Klotz, Roger Steup Jr., Natalie Pease, Jeanette Thurow, Christopher Fleis, Melissa Fleis, Stephanie Rice, David Mikowski, Douglas Mikowski, Shaun Mikowski, Sarah Herrington, Robert Gauthier, Dale M. Gauthier, Angela Helder, Heather Abram, Mark Savage, Jenna Grooms, Ashley Savage, and Eric, Andy, and Laura Cwengros.

Thank you to my Fleis and Lamie cousins: Al Fleis, Ruth Ann Strozeski, Linda Schulte, Sharon Gregor, Kasia Janka, Dorothy Grant, Dennis Fleis, Donna Gonder, Luella Elliott, Gene Lamie, Sharone Courter, Alvin Lamie, Lucille Zenner, Joyce Cook, Sheri Dewey, Jackie Brown, Jude Lamie, Bob Lamie, Carol Rose, and Faye Wurm.

And thank you to other contributors: Cecilia "Sally" Labonte, Theresa Walter, Dorothy

Chimoski, Pat Hobbins, Gordon Plowman, Roy Romanowski, Dave Taghon, Don Witkowski, Jim Lautner, Rose Ann (Fabiszak) Petsch, and Glen and Frances King. (All the others, please forgive me for not mentioning your name. Your name is credited in the body of this memoir and/or in the footnotes.)

A special thank you for monetary support from: Aunt Theresa Rosinski, Julie and Ray Watkoski, Edward and Barbara Fleis, Mary Jane and Roger Steup, Ted and Mary Lou Fleis, Jim and Dorie Fleis, Bernadette and Ken Denoyer, Larry and Jackie Fleis, Shirley Mikowski, Joan and Dale Gauthier, Noreen and Tom Savage, Diane and Tom Pelak, Eric and Roni Cwengros, Christine Thompson, and anonymous.

The *FLEIS SONG*

(My brother, Jim, composed this song so his children would
learn his siblings' names in age order.)

CHORUS:

THERE'S RUTH ANN AND JULIE....ED AND MARY JANE

THERE'S THEODORE AND JIM....ONE BY ONE, THEY CAME

THERE'S BERNADETTE AND LARRY.....SHIRLEY AND JOANIE

THERE'S NOREEN AND RITA...NOW THAT'S THE FLEIS FAMILY

1) ED MET IRENE ON THAT FATEFUL DAY.

AS THEY WALKED BY THE NARROWS, I COULD HEAR HER SAY,

DEAR ED, I LOVE YOU AND I'LL BE YOUR BRIDE,

IF YOU PROMISE TO STAY BY MY SIDE.

CHORUS:

2) ED WAS HIKING ON THE DAY THEY WED.

SEEMS AS THOUGH THEY LEFT HIM SLEEPING IN HIS BED.

AFTER THE SERVICE, ED WAS HEARD TO SAY,

TIME'S A WASTING, LET'S NOT WASTE THE DAY.

CHORUS:

3) IRENE LEFT US IN THE YEAR OF '94.

ANGELS MET HER AT HEAVEN'S DOOR.

THE CHILDREN WERE CRYING, BUT THE ANGELS SANG WITH GLEE

AS MOTHER MARY ROCKED HER ON HER KNEE.

CHORUS:

4) IN 2001, WHEN ED WAS 86,

GOD DECIDED ED'S LIFE HE WOULD TAKE.

HE WAS SO PEACEFUL WHEN HE CLOSED HIS EYES.

NOW HE'S PLAYING HIS FIDDLE IN THE SKY.

CHORUS:

LET'S NEVER FINISH THIS SONG WE SING TODAY.

LET'S NOT END IT...LET'S CONTINUE TO PLAY.

THE SONGS AND THE MUSIC, LET'S ALL SING ALOUD.

CARRY ON TRADITIONS THE FLEISES HANDED DOWN.

Made in the USA
Middletown, DE
13 August 2024

58652731R00221